THE DRACULA BOOK

by
Donald F. Glut

with Introductions by
Christopher Lee
and
William Marshall

The Scarecrow Press, Inc.
Metuchen, N. J.   1975

Cover illustration by Larry Byrd.

Library of Congress Cataloging in Publication Data

Glut, Donald F
The Dracula book.

Includes index.
1. Dracula. 2. Vampire films--History and
criticism. 3. Stoker, Bram, 1847-1912. Dracula.
I. Title.
GR830.V3G55   791.43'0909'351   75-4917
ISBN 0-8108-0804-8   791.435
                              G

To

CHRISTOPHER LEE

and

WILLIAM MARSHALL

ACKNOWLEDGMENTS

The author wishes to offer his sincerest thanks to the following contributors to The Dracula Book:

John Abbott; Dick Andersen, my co-editor of the fan publication Shazam; Edward Ansara; Barry Atwater; Tom Baker; the late Roy Barcroft; Calvin T. Beck, publisher and editor of Castle of Frankenstein; the late Otto O. Binder; Bill Blackbeard; Don Blyth; Carroll Borland; Jean-Pierre Bouyxou; Larry Brill of The Monster Times; Larry Byrd, my art director on Modern Monsters magazine; John Carradine; Bob Clampett; Frederick S. Clarke, publisher and editor of Cinefantastique; Chris Collier; Del Connell of Western Publishing Company; Gerry Conway; Ralph Costantino; Walter Daugherty; Maurine Dawson; the late Kenne Duncan; Mark Evanier; Victor Fabian; Mark Frank, editor and publisher of Photon; Luis Gasca; Lindagray Glut; Martin Goodman, Stan Lee and Roy Thomas of the Marvel Comics Group; Archie Goodwin; Brenda Gray; Bob Greenberg; Gene Gronemeyer; Peter Haining; Curtis Harrington; Ron Haydock; Eric Hoffman; Cortlandt B. Hull; Larry Ivie, publisher and editor of Monsters and Heroes; David Jones; Marvin Jones; Russ Jones; Paul Kalin; Allen G. Kracalik; Christopher Lee; Mark McGee; Raymond T. McNally and Radu Florescu, the world's foremost authorities on Vlad the Impaler, and authors of the books In Search of Dracula: A True History of Dracula and Vampire Legends and Dracula, A Biography of Vlad the Impaler; Laurence Merrick; Rick Mitchell; Doug Moench; Bret Morrison; Michael Nesmith; Norbert Novotny; William G. Obbagy, President of the American Bela Lugosi Fan Club and the leading authority on Lugosi; Gus Ocosta of Columbia Pictures; Robert Quarry; D. Scott Rogo; Mike Royer; Jesse Santos; Jim Shapiro; Erik Shiozaki; Adam Spektor; Ray Dennis Steckler; Barbara Steele; Jim Steranko; the late Glenn Strange; James Warren of the Warren Publishing Company; Jerry B. Wheeler; Alan White; Alan J Wilson of the Citadel Press; Bongo Wolf; Marv Wolfman; and Bill Ziegler.

Special thanks to Forrest J Ackerman, editor of Famous Monsters of Filmland, a former friend of Bela Lugosi and agent to this writer, for the complete use of his Dracula files, for the use of most of the photographs appearing in this book and for his perpetuating the Dracula image since the premiere of Universal's DRACULA in 1931; Jim Harmon, author of such books as The Great Radio Heroes and Jim Harmon's Nostalgia Catalogue and editor of Monsters of the Movies, for information concerning Dracula on the radio; and Bill Warren, who keeps as up-to-date on Dracula motion pictures as any film-going descendant of Abraham Van Helsing and has always promptly reported their titles to this author.

An outrageous thanks to the following compilers of Dracula movie titles and for their respective works, all of which were consulted repeatedly during the preparation of this book:

Ronald V. Borst, compiler of the "Vampire Film Checklist" in Photon, nos. 19 and 21 (1970 and 1971).

Walt Lee, author of the Reference Guide to Fantastic Films (1972-74).

And Donald G. Willis, author of Horror and Science Fiction Films: A Checklist (Scarecrow Press 1972).

To all of you, once again, thanks.

TABLE OF CONTENTS

7-187.

PREFACE

My first contact with Count Dracula, the cloaked King Vampire of Transylvania, was in 1956, just weeks before Bela Lugosi died.

I was a horror and science fiction movie fan back in those days of Howdy Doody, Davy Crockett and the birth of rock 'n' roll. But Count Dracula had been an alien name to me at the time. Perhaps it sounds illogical that an enthusiast of such motion pictures could have escaped any encounter with the bloodthirsty Count. But actually, in Chicago during the Fifties previous to the debut of SHOCK THEATRE in 1957, the Dracula movies never played on television. And the theatres that still ran them were either so run-down or far away that attending them was extremely impractical for a kid still a number of years away from a driver's license. My knowledge of such genre films was based solely upon memories and the product that was being made at the time.

At the time, I went to see virtually everything that might be termed horror or science fiction or that might have a monster lumbering through it, regardless of quality. It was not surprising, then, that one afternoon in 1956 I sat in a dank movie theatre watching two brand new science fiction atrocities entitled DAY THE WORLD ENDED and PHANTOM FROM 10,000 LEAGUES. The abominable double bill was playing first run at a tiny and shoddy theatre called the Crest, located on Chicago's Lincoln Avenue almost across the street from the Biograph where John Dillinger was shot. As I walked through the theatre lobby I noticed the posters for the next attraction, something called DRACULA. Though better than the two features, the preview trailers of DRACULA hardly excited me. I walked out of the theatre believing that

---

Opposite: Bela Lugosi in his first screen performance as Count Dracula

the man in tuxedo and cape who gestured hypnotically was some sort of nefarious Mandrake the Magician. Then I forgot about this Dracula character.

My next contact with Count Dracula was the day my mother read his obituary in our local newspaper, the Chicago Sun-Times. "Bela Lugosi died," she told me, knowing of my interest in horror films.

"Who's Bela Lugosi?"

"He played Dracula," she said.

"Who's Dracula?"

"Dracula was a vampire."

Well, I remembered what a vampire was ... sort of. I knew there were vampire bats that drank blood. And I remembered a story I'd read in an old issue of the comic book, Forbidden Worlds, in which a vampire was preying upon the survivors of a crashed airliner. But the vampire in this story was the pilot, who periodically transformed into a shaggy man-like monster with enormous bat wings. He was exposed at the end of the story by drinking water containing particles of silver.

I recalled another story I'd read in another old 1950s horror comic in which a man blundered into a town populated by vampires who had long grown weary of having to resort to the "frozen stuff."

Neither of these concepts seemed to have much, if any, correlation to the Dracula I had briefly viewed up on the screen that afternoon at the Crest Theatre.

Later in 1956 I saw a triple horror show of HOUSE OF FRANKENSTEIN, HOUSE OF DRACULA and THE MUMMY at a dilapidated old theatre called the Mode, and with Dracula's appearance in two of those films, I finally knew the meaning of the vampire (though he now looked more than ever like Mandrake). But I was confused at what I saw because the actor portraying the Count did not resemble the one I'd seen in the earlier trailer of DRACULA. Certainly, I thought, this actor in the black cloak had to be Bela Lugosi, because Lugosi was Count Dracula. I never considered the possibility that any other actor might have enacted the role and, consequently, never bothered to check the cast credits. What was important, though, was that I had instantly become a Dracula fan. How could any twelve-year-old monster buff not be fascinated by a character that so expertly transformed into a bat right on screen and then disintegrated neatly and completely beneath the rays of the sun?

Shortly afterwards I attended the screening of two of Lugosi's last motion pictures, THE BLACK SLEEP and the abysmal BRIDE OF THE MONSTER. The Lugosi that appeared in these two films was an old, wrinkled man. Yet I knew that even the years could not have distorted his features to this extent; he no longer resembled the "Lugosi" I thought I'd seen stalking the night in the two "HOUSE" movies.

Finally, in 1957 I began to attend theatres running the old Universal horror films. When I saw ABBOTT AND COS-TELLO MEET FRANKENSTEIN I was certain of one fact. The Dracula I had previously thought to be Bela Lugosi was another actor altogether. The next problem that faced me, since I was becoming interested enough in Dracula to care, was to learn the identity of the actor I had seen in HOUSE OF FRANKENSTEIN and HOUSE OF DRACULA.

My quest neared completion when I received in the mail a brochure from United World, a 16mm film rental company that had finally made available the Universal Dracula, Frankenstein, Wolf Man and Invisible Man series. The only actor's name other than Lon Chaney, Jr. (who, I knew, played the Wolf Man) to appear after the listings of both HOUSE OF FRANKENSTEIN and HOUSE OF DRACULA was John Carra-dine. It seemed likely that Carradine was, in fact, the actor who had twice played the Count. But I wasn't absolutely cer-tain until later that year when I saw a familiar face in FIVE CAME BACK, a movie run on television one night. The actor's lean features reminded me of the father of a friend of mine and I recalled that the actor in HOUSE OF FRANKEN-STEIN produced the same effect. Quickly turning to that treasured 16mm rental brochure, I noted the name of John Carradine, then asked my mother, who was also watching the movie, if that was the name of the actor on television. It was indeed John Carradine, and I felt mildly triumphant.

This book is the product of succeeding searches for information about the world's most famous vampire and, quite possibly, the world's most famous count. Originally, I had written a book entitled The Vampire Image, which compared the vampires of legend and tradition with their counterparts in the media. The final chapter of the book was titled

xi

"Dracula" and was a brief survey look at the Count in history, literature, theatre, films, radio and TV, comics, etc. When I later discovered that there was enough Dracula material for a separate book I removed the Count's chapter and expanded it to The Films of Count Dracula.

The Dracula Book brings the two books full circle, expanding the Dracula material even more and combining it with some of the material from The Vampire Image. The final marriage of the two books into this present volume originally resulted in well over 600 manuscript pages, with approximately 300 words per page. After much groaning from my editor, I heeded his request to cut the book down to its present length, a move which I finally realized was for the better.

Now, in the 1970s, there are more Dracula motion pictures, books and magazines than ever before. Perhaps the Transylvanians might follow the Chinese practice and dub these the "Years of the Bat." The Dracula Book is my contribution to the contemporary "Draculamania."

Donald F. Glut

April, 1974

INTRODUCTION I

In his book The Frankenstein Legend: A Tribute to Mary Shelley and Boris Karloff, author Don Glut showed not only an encyclopaedic knowledge of the cinematic presentations of this subject, but also a very real insight into the literary aspects of Mary Shelley's immortal work.

In The Dracula Book, he is performing the same service for countless devotees and in this case, perhaps, is tackling a somewhat harder task.

Although the cinematic history of this subject is well documented, there are probably many more books about the vampiric legend, as a result of Bram Stoker's renowned work, than there have been of Mary Shelley's Frankenstein. The latter story, as the world knows, deals with the concept of the creation of life and the possibility of prolonging it into immortality. It is common knowledge that this book was the result of a bet between Mary Shelley, Shelley, Byron and Dr. Polidori. No such authenticated reason attaches to the writing of Stoker's Dracula, although it is known that he was greatly interested in the subject of vampirism, and was fully acquainted with the historical aspects concerning the life of Vlad Tsepesh, Vlad Dracula, the Impaler. We do, of course, know that Stoker was brought up by his mother on a rich diet of Celtic folklore and legend, was bedridden to the age of eight and was deeply involved in the mysterious world of the supernatural. There is also the story that he wrote the book of Dracula after a restless night, brought on by a large lobster dinner....

The thread of immortality runs through the pages of the work. The concept of eternal life is also suggested by Mary Shelley, in a spiritual sense, though Man creating Man is the precise opposite of the doomed existence of the heroic figure of Dracula, destined to live forever against his will.

As I have some acquaintance with the presentation of the

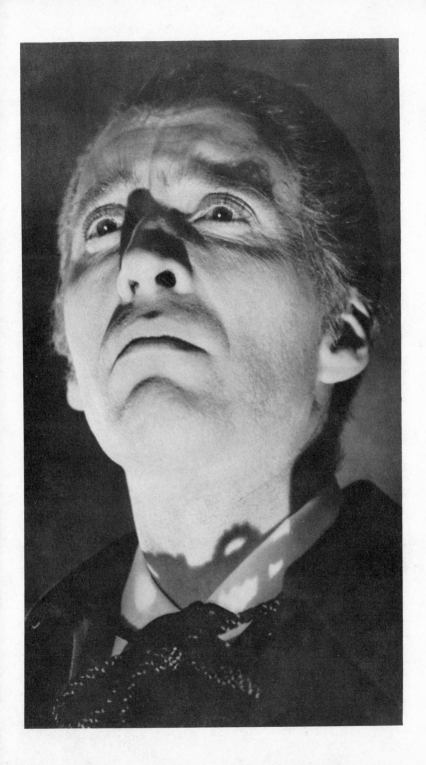

character of Dracula on the screen, a role I have shared with many eminent actors, I have noted with increasing dismay over the years the progressive deterioration of this essentially romantic and fascinating figure. It is my earnest hope that one day I, or some other actor, will be permitted the golden opportunity of presenting Dracula on screen exactly as Bram Stoker would have wished. There have been some attempts at doing this, but they have fallen by the wayside through a lack of adequate production.

It is my belief that as a researcher and anthologist in this particular field of the macabre, the fantastic and the weird, Don Glut has no peer. I am certain that The Dracula Book will be as fascinating and well documented as its predecessor, and there is always the possibility that the author may discover something which is new to us all.

Christopher Lee

London, England
July, 1974

INTRODUCTION II

I knew about the chill appeal of the Invisible Man and I'd been future-shocked by wars in outer space by the time I was invited to play Blacula, but Vampirism was still a closed book to me. My generation of movie-goers lined up for monster movies, I'm sure, but I was at the other theatre watching Westerns and rooting for what I used to think were the good guys, the trigger-happy paleface loners, who piously stole Indian land and kissed their horses instead of their girls before settling down to disrupt forever the balance of nature on which Indian life depended.

I have played Blacula not once but twice since then, so I had to learn fast, starting virtually from scratch. I began to read. I was conscripted into the Count Dracula Society. I asked myself and others why audiences are so responsive, decade after decade, to the Dracula story and variations on it. Most importantly, as an actor, I had to know about vampires from the vampire's point of view. And not just any vampire: how would an African prince in the early 19th century, at the height of the slave trade, feel about being taken captive in Transylvanian folklore and doomed to live out eternity hungering for human blood?

How Prince Mamuwalde felt about his fate is what I tried to contribute to the movie, first by insisting on collaborating in the revision of the screenplay and finally, of course, through the performance itself. The need for black input in making a movie meaningful to black audiences cannot be over-emphasized.

Within the last year I have won two coveted cinema awards: one, the first annual award of the Academy of

---

Opposite: William Marshall as Prince Mamuwalde in the second Blacula film, SCREAM BLACULA SCREAM

Horror and Science Fiction Films, shared with Kurt Vonnegut; the other, the 1973 Cinema Award of the Count Dracula Society. With these assurances that I've learned at least some of the essentials about the appeal of the Dracula story, I'll share some of my discoveries and speculations with you.

An effective vampire movie, I have discovered, must be flooded with urgent emotions of anguish, yearning, terror and, ultimately, relief. This holds true, I believe, if to a lesser extent, for all horror and science fiction movies. I began to see the need, within the structure of our world, which is experienced so often and by so many as monstrous, for other worlds in which to dwell, if only for an occasional hour or two at the movies.

For example, Americans didn't notice for a long time that the Vietnamese war was going on, but it's been impossible to shut it out or shut it off ever since. The destruction of fruitful land and fruitful people goes on and on, and no amount of turning the dial will blot the picture out. Or a fuel shortage suddenly disrupts millions of lives, whips the inflationary spiral higher, and subsides as suddenly as it began; in the catastrophic brief interval the profits of the oil companies rise more than 300%. Whales and sophisticated urban populations alike gasp for air. Blacks look for space in which to stand up straight at last. Israelis and Arabs insist fiercely on their national pride, while their resources and security are manipulated by other powers for other purposes. For the first time in history, doom is an immediate possibility in the minds of little children, and terrorist youth groups form to make guerrilla war on social inequity, sending tapes to announce their theory and tactics publicly.

The Center for Policy Research, an independent agency that studies social trends, reported in the spring that the proportion of the U. S. population now completely convinced that Satan exists has risen in nine years from 37% to 48%, with another 20% who now consider his existence probable. The figures were gathered a year ago, incidentally, before new interest in demonology was stimulated by THE EXORCIST.

The Center's senior research associate attributes the increased belief in the devil to a mood of "uncertainty and stress, when things seem to be falling apart and resources seem limited for coping with it." He says that in such circumstances, people trying to make sense of the world tend to "look for scapegoats" such as the devil. Americans recently witnessed an illustration of this trend at the highest government level, when a Presidential advisor invoked "sinister forces" to explain the wiping out of a crucial 18 minutes in a subpoenaed White House tape.

When events seem without reason or good purpose, as the researcher says, and the balance of good and evil seems to have "tipped in the direction of evil," it may be more refreshing than ever to step through the movie screen into other worlds--worlds in which the reality of terror and the sense of evil are present but are counterbalanced for an hour or two by fantasies of being able to understand, outwit, and overcome it.

This book by Don Glut is an expression of love for the labors of the writers, actors, directors, art directors, makeup artists and photographers who have helped to create these apparently needed and much appreciated other worlds, and who have helped put flesh on the monsters who, unlike the monsters regularly reported by the press and newscasters, can be controlled if not vanquished before it's time to leave the theater or switch off the tube.

Many factors help to account for the durability of the Dracula story and its variations as subject matter for movies. This book makes that clear. One unique factor in the story itself, however, deserves to be emphasized in closing this Introduction.

Late one night when we were shooting a street sequence for BLACULA in Hollywood, a very beautiful woman wearing a long black cape approached me as I stood waiting on the sidewalk to be called for the next shot. I had not seen her before in the small shifting crowd of observers.

"Are you the man?" she asked, looking at me intently.

"If I understand your question," I said, "yes, I am."

She smiled and confided eagerly, "I've always wanted to be a vampire."

It occurred to me that she might be inviting me to do something on the spot about her dream, but my camera call came. Turning to leave, I paused to ask, "Why?"

She answered without hesitation, her lovely face radiant, "Because vampires live forever! There's really no way to kill them. If you pull the stake out of their hearts, they revive. They can't really be hurt, no matter what happens."

William Marshall

Pacoima, California
June, 1974

Chapter 1

VLAD DRACULA, THE IMPALER

> Had you not answered me in this fashion, I would
> truly have impaled you on the spot.
> > --Vlad Dracula, September 1458

According to legend, the vampire is immortal, perpetuating his sanguinary career for generation upon generation
unless subjected to some prescribed form of destruction.
Count Dracula, the black-clothed un-dead lord of Transylvania,
is undoubtedly the most infamous vampire of them all. This
King of Vampires, as Bram Stoker crowned him in his classic novel Dracula in the latter nineteenth century, utilized
his stature to tower above other members of the fraternity
of the un-dead. For despite the innumerable destructions
he has suffered in the realm of dark fiction where he is king,
Dracula has somehow always managed to emerge from his
grave, apparently unscathed, to renew his eternal quest to
satisfy his thirst for human blood. At the risk of modifying
one superlative with another, Count Dracula is the most immortal of all the un-dead.

The name Dracula has virtually become a synonym
for "vampire," or a resuscitated, blood-sucking, "un-dead"
corpse. When the subject of vampirism or vampires in motion pictures or novels arises in contemporary circles, the
name of the Count who, with a bloody claw, ruled Transylvania, the "Land Beyond the Forest," a territory of Romania,
is usually soon to follow. I would feel confident in guessing
that the majority of people in the civilized world are familiar
with the name of the bloodthirsty Count. A smaller percentage

---

Opposite: Oil portrait of Vlad the Impaler, the historical
Dracula, hanging at Castle Ambras, near Innsbruck, Austria

1

of these, however, realize that the awesome, cloaked figure
who has haunted so many motion picture screens was not
merely a figment of author Bram Stoker's imagination. Dracula actually existed. He was, in fact, a fifteenth century
prince and one of the most bloodthirsty (though not in the
sense of supernatural vampires) monsters in the world's history, responsible for the gruesome deaths of at least 100,000
people, surpassing in cruelty even such despots as Caligula
and Ivan the Terrible. Because of the nature of his crimes,
the historical Dracula was also known, during his career, as
Vlad Tepes, or Vlad "The Impaler."

Hungary was a powerful nation in 1431. Her territori-
al powers extended to Wallachia, an area which is now Romania. During that year, King Sigismund, who later became
the Holy Roman Emperor, invested a certain voivode (warri-
or prince) named Vlad II with a particular reward for his battling the Turks. Sigismund had founded a cliquish society of
uniformed knights which he named the Order of the Dragon.
Upon the standard of the members of this organization was
the image of the great reptile. Vlad II was admitted to the
select group and carried the emblazoned standard with him
into battle. Since the Latin word for "dragon" is draco, Vlad
became known as Vlad Dracul. As Vlad was known for his
cruelties, superstitious peasants also interpreted the word
dracul for its other meaning, "devil." In some languages the
words "devil" and "vampire" are synonymous, a factor which
added to the mystique that surrounded Dracul. And, according to Ornella Volta in her book The Vampire, the word for
"vampire" in Moldavia is drakul. Among the peasantry mur-
murs arose that Vlad Dracul was actually in league with
Satan. The ruler's cruel acts were not kept secret and contributed to the peasants' fears.

But it was Dracul's son, also named Vlad, who became known as Dracula. Translated, Dracula literally means
"son of Dracul." In Venice, the son of Dracul became known
as Dragulia; in Germany he was famous as Trakle and Dracole; in Hungary he was referred to simply as Dracula. He
signed his name as Draculea (his favorite), Dragkwlya, Drag-
ulya, Drakulya, or Dragwyla; while history books have also
given him the more descriptive name of Vlad the Impaler.

Vlad Dracula was a striking figure, with a chalky complexion, long nose, large mouth and piercing green eyes. He
wore his hair long and sported a lengthy mustache. He is
represented, in an oil portrait made by an unknown artist, as

a handsome nobleman wearing a royal headdress and ermine cape. The portrait hangs to this day in Castle Ambras, near Innsbruck, Austria, and is but one in a collection of pictures illustrating human monsters and physically deformed characters of history.

Dracula was born about 1430 or 1431 in the Transylvanian town of Schassburg, into a family sworn to fight the Turks by the Order of the Dragon. In 1444, the youthful Dracula and his younger brother, Radu, accompanied their father Dracul across the Danube to meet the Turks. They were captured and Dracula remained a prisoner of the Turks until 1448, during which time he acquired a hardened cynicism, a low regard for human life and a crafty and brutal nature. When Dracul was assassinated for political reasons and an older son named Mircea was buried alive, soon after, by minions of the regent of Hungary, János Hunyadi, the twenty-year-old Dracula, fearing for his own life, fled to Moldavia where he remained until 1451. During these years, Hunyadi instructed Dracula in military tactics and strategy. The Dracula who would soon horrify the world was receiving an appropriate background.

In one respect, Voivode Dracula was a hero of Christianity. The wars he waged against the Turks to preserve his homeland have placed him in the history books as a valiant military genius. Dracula had been Prince of Wallachia in 1448 and also from 1456 to 1462. It was during this second reign in Wallachia that the Voivode crossed the Danube and, with his loyal cavalry, entered the Danubian city of Giurgiu. Dracula had been summoned, supposedly to engage the Turks in a peaceful meeting to settle the matter of disputed territories. Suspecting an ambush, Dracula took a Wallachian contingent, surrounded the appointed meeting place, and captured the Turks, who were then subjected to the Voivode's favorite method of torturous death--impalement on large wooden stakes. Afterwards, Dracula burned down the city of Giurgiu. His campaign against the Turks was officially underway. In the winter of 1462, the Turks invaded Wallachia and Dracula was forced to make a temporary retreat. The cunning Transylvanian then employed guerrilla techniques and, in a maneuver known as the "Night of Terror," led his army into the Turkish camp at night, slicing a bloody path through the slumbering enemy soldiers. Thousands of Turks were slaughtered, but before Dracula could get to the sultan himself, he was driven back by the enemy and forced to retreat. Sultan Mohammed II, realizing the bloodshed that

would result from further battling a fanatical leader like
Dracula, and also fearing the sudden appearance of plague,
withdrew his troops.

Castle Dracula was apparently an impregnable fortress.
Dracula himself, using the forced labor of his subjects, had
the castle built on the ruins of the Castle of the Arges in the
mountainous region at the source of the river Arges in southern Romania. In the construction of the castle, Dracula incorporated stones and bricks from a much older fortress, the
nearby Castle of Poenari. Recalling many aspects of Castle
Bran, the fortress of János Hunyadi, Dracula included in his
smaller fortress a secret passageway which led out of the
castle, through the mountain and to the banks of the river
Arges. This passageway would later save his life.

In 1462, the Turks threatened to besiege Castle Dracula. According to Romanian tradition, Dracula's first wife
committed suicide by hurling herself from a precipice and into the river rather than face the tortures of the Turks.
Dracula and a small group fled through the secret tunnel,
hoping to find refuge with King Matthias. The party that remained at Castle Dracula battled the Turks that night so that
the Voivode could escape unnoticed, but the Turks destroyed
much of the seemingly impregnable castle.

It was not so much his acts of heroism but rather his
almost inconceivable cruelties for which Vlad Tepes or Vlad
Dracula is best known. The sadist achieved his greatest
pleasure (and his nickname) from impaling his victims on
large stakes, which were especially rounded and oiled so that
the victims would writhe in agony for a while before succumb-
ing to the mercies of death.

In 1462, Dracula suddenly turned against his own countrymen, pillaging the Transylvanian city of Sibiu, torturing
and killing 10,000 of its residents and becoming more of a
blight than the Turks had ever been. Retaliating, the Ger-
mans of Sibiu forged the Voivode's name to three letters linking him with the Turks. As a result, Dracula was sentenced
to twelve years' imprisonment by King Matthias of Hungary,
son of the late János Hunyadi. While Dracula was confined
in the fortress of Visegrad in Hungary, the stories of his
tortures were already providing chills to eager readers and
listeners in many parts of Europe.

Germany was the first country to publish pamphlets

depicting and describing the grisly accounts of Dracula's cruelties. The first two accounts date from approximately 1462. In 1462 or 1463, German troubadour Michel Beheim took the stories of Dracula's acts of sadism and set them to verse in a work known as The Great Monster (which was published in a new edition in Berlin, 1968, under the title Die Gedichte des Michel Beheim). There were gasps in the courts of Emperor Friedrich of Austria and the kings of Hungary and Czechoslavakia when Beheim sang about "this greatest of all tyrants of whom I have ever heard on Earth."

After Dracula's death in 1476, more accounts of his atrocities were published and circulated. Among these, the earliest existing accounts are reprints from 1485 of news sheets published originally in the year of Dracula's death. The text had been reprinted by Bartholomeus Gothan in Lübeck, Germany, under the title, About a Wild Tyrant called Dracole Wayda who MCCCCLVI Years after the Birth of Our Lord Jesus Christ Carried out Many Terrible and Wondrous Deeds in Wallachia and in Hungary. Historie von Dracule Wajda, a recently discovered pamphlet about Dracula published in Leipzig, Germany, in 1493, presents Dracula as physically less handsome than the woodcut pictures shown in the other news sheets. The first Russian version of the Dracula story was Povesty o Mutyanskom Voyevode Drakule, written by a monk in the Byelo-Ozero monastery in the late fifteenth century, under the auspices of Ivan the Terrible (whose own gruesome deeds eventually earned him the nickname, "the Russian Dracula") who used it to condemn Catholicism and the Western world.

Other early versions of the Dracula story were published in Nuremberg in 1488, and in Bamberg, by Hans Spoerer, in 1491.

A pamphlet entitled About the Wild Bloodthirsty Berserker Dracula was published in 1499 by Ambrosius Huber in Nuremberg. The woodcut illustrates Dracula feasting in a forest of impaled victims, with the description: "Here begins a very cruel frightening story about a wild bloodthirsty man, Dracula the voevod. How he impaled people and roasted them and with their heads boiled them in a kettle, and how he skinned people and hacked them to pieces like a head of cabbage. He also roasted the children of mothers and they had to eat their children themselves. And many other horrible things are written in this tract and also in which land he ruled." A German pamphlet with a similar woodcut and with

the title, About the Wild Bloodthirsty Berserker, Dracula
Voevod, was published in 1500 by Matthias Hupfuff in Stras-
bourg.

The Romanian writer Mihai Sadovianu, in the sixteenth
century, produced an epic in three volumes entitled Voivoda
Dracula.   More pamphlets saw print in Nuremberg in 1515
and 1521.   Augsburg had its share of such news sheets in
1494, 1520 and 1530.   Slovo o Mutyanskom Voyevode Drakule
was another version circulating in Russia in the 1500s.   In
1554, Jan of Puchov translated Transylvanian, Hungarian and
Alemannic versions of the story and printed it in Prague in
the Czech language.   Antonio Bonfinius, the official court historian to King Matthias, wrote the most accurate version in
1543, while in 1584 Pope Pius II included Dracula in his published memoirs.

There are myriad German, Romanian and Russian versions of the Dracula story, with emphasis on his tortures.
Yet behind his perverse actions, in which he tortured both
countryman and Turk, Christian and pagan, was a strong
spirit of nationalism and an individualistic sense of justice.
Although he relished every scream of agony and every drop
of shed blood, Dracula's excruciations were also punishments
which he deemed befitting his victims.   Some were methods
for enacting revenge against his enemies, others were de-
vices by which he tested his wits against those of his intended
victims.   Impalement was the reward for those who failed to
match their cunning against Vlad Dracula.   In Dracula's case,
there was often method in his madness.   Some of these
stories follow.

Dracula noticed that one of his subjects wore a shirt
that was too short.   When he asked the man's wife the reason for her not altering his shirt, she replied that she was
too busy cooking and washing.   The Voivode had her impaled
on a long stake, then gave the man another wife, whom he
threatened with impalement unless she made him a long
enough shirt.

A group of ambassadors was sent to Dracula by Sultan
Mohammed II.   They had fezzes and wore them into Dracula's
palace.   When the Prince asked why their heads remained
covered, one of the Turks answered that it was the custom
of their homeland to leave on their hats.   Dracula remarked
that he would help to strengthen their customs and promptly

ordered his guards to nail the fezzes to the heads of the envoys.

Two clergymen were traveling through Dracula's land. One was a cunning Greek monk, the other a humble Romanian priest. The Greek spent much time belittling the Romanian. Dracula learned of the priests and summoned them to his palace, asking them what his people thought of their Voivode. The Greek monk fabricated a story, telling Dracula how he was deeply loved and respected by his subjects. Dracula, realizing the monk's deceit and attempted flattery, had him impaled. When asked the same question, the Romanian truthfully told how the ruler was the target of constant castigation by his subjects; he was allowed to leave Dracula's castle in peace.

Dracula had impaled a number of disobedient boyars and invited some other boyars to see what would happen to them if they were found in the master's disfavor. One of them remarked to Dracula that the Voivode should not be on the grounds, where the air was so foul, but should have remained in his palace. Dracula then had this boyar impaled on a stake higher than all the rest so that he would not be offended by the stench of rotting flesh.

A merchant from another land had considered the honesty of Dracula's subjects and left his cart in the street one night. In the morning, 160 gold ducats were missing from his treasure. The merchant appealed to Dracula who promised that the ducats would be returned that night. Dracula threatened to burn the town to the ground unless the gold was produced. Then he ordered that substitute ducats, plus one extra piece, be secreted on the cart. The merchant found the ducats and, fortunately, reported the additional gold piece to the Prince. Had he failed the test, Dracula told him, he would have been impaled.

Dracula had a golden cup placed at a fountain in the city of Târgoviste. The cup was there for all to use, and it was never stolen; anyone daring to steal the cup would have been impaled.

Dracula had a mistress to whom he was attracted physically and in no other way. She pleased him and, naturally, became concerned one day when he seemed quite melancholy. Hoping to bring him some cheer, she told him that she was pregnant with his child. Dracula denied the possibility of such a pregnancy. To prove his stand, he took his

sword and sliced her open to see for himself that she had
told him a lie.

When Vlad Dracula saw the vast numbers of beggars
and poor people, he recalled the old biblical passage about
earning one's bread by the sweat of the brow. He considered
the wretches worse than thieves, especially since many of
them were just lazy and preferred begging to working. One
day, Dracula summoned the beggars to him, each having been
outfitted with a new set of clothes by their Prince. They
were given a fabulous meal in an appointed house. The beggars stuffed themselves gluttonously and some of them fell
into a drunken stupor. While they were hardly able to move,
Dracula ordered the doors locked and the house set on fire.
After the beggars had been consumed by the flames, Dracula
said, "I bequeath to thee my kingdom without any beggars,
orphans or cripples, whom I have spared further suffering in
this world."

These were but some of Dracula's brutalities. He also buried men up to their necks and then shot at them. At
times, he would create a veritable forest of victims writhing
on tall wooden stakes. He impaled infants along with their
mothers, cooked men alive, and forced men into acts of cannibalism. Dracula was most bloodthirsty in matters of sex:
unfaithful wives were skinned alive, unchaste widows and single girls had their nipples cut off. Often he would thrust a
red-hot poker into the offender's vagina and force it through
until it burst from her mouth.

The German pamphlet of 1499 states: "And he led
away all those whom he had captured outside the city called
Kranstatt near the chapel of St. Jacob. And at that time
Dracula ... had the entire suburb burned. Also ... all those
whom he had taken captive, men and women, young and old,
children, he had impaled on the hill by the chapel and all
around the hill, and under them he proceeded to eat at table
and get his joy that way."

During his imprisonment, Dracula continued to live according to his spreading reputation. Now that he was unable
to secure human victims, he tortured small animals, often
by impaling them with sticks. The prison guards became
friendly with Dracula and catered to his bloodthirsty needs.
During his imprisonment, also, Dracula became romantically
involved with King Matthias's sister. Eventually, Dracula
would marry her, but as the King's sister was a Roman Cath-

olic, Dracula, who had come from a family with a long mem-
bership in the Greek Orthodox Church, had first to convert
to her faith.   This conversion placed him in disfavor in the
Orthodox world, especially since it was intimated that Dracula would be restored as Prince of Wallachia.

In 1474, Dracula was officially a contender for the
throne of Wallachia.   Two years later, he and Prince Steven
Bathory of Transylvania and an army composed of Transylvanians, Hungarians and Moldavians approached Wallachia.
On November 8, Dracula's forces invaded Bucharest, and
eight days later the battle had been won by the returning
Prince.   Dracula was restored as Voivode of Wallachia, but,
as a result of his religious conversion, found his remaining
forces reduced to a mere two hundred Moldavian soldiers.

Dracula died a violent death in 1476, at the age of
forty-five.   There are two versions of his death.   One--the
less heroic--has the Voivode assassinated by a band of personal and political enemies.   The other ascribes to Dracula
the death of a true hero, which, despite his torturing and
killing 100,000 people, is how he is regarded by Romanians
to this day.   Dracula and his Moldavians were battling the
Turks just outside of Bucharest.   Dracula, disguised as a
Turkish soldier, was spotted by his own men, who failed to
recognize their leader, and one of the Moldavians thrust a
spear into him.   Dracula killed five of his own men before
he fell to the ground, dead. Regardless of the precise method of his death, Dracula's head was severed (a method by
which vampires in the supernatural sense may be destroyed)
and sent to Constantinople, where the Sultan mounted it,
ironically, on a stake and displayed it for his subjects to
see.   Dracula's corpse was buried in an unmarked grave on
the island of Snagov.

The March 1968 issue of Fate, a magazine of psychic
phenomena, featured an interview of questionable authenticity
with Count Alexander Cepesi, a self-claimed descendant of
Vlad Dracula.   The interview, entitled "Meet the Real Count
Dracula," describes Cepesi as a Romanian expatriate, who
operates a blood bank, collecting plasma for hospitals in
Turkey and for Red Crescent agencies.   Having resided in
Istanbul since 1947, he sells blood for transfusion to those
persons preferring a private clinic to a public one.

Count Cepesi told writer Leo Heiman: "I have devoted
a lifetime of study to vampires and their history.   I had ac-

cess to old family chronicles, ancient manuscripts and hair-
raising tales heard from generation to generation. I grew
up in the very castle where the original Count Dracula committed his heinous crimes."

Dracula historians Raymond T. McNally and Radu
Florescu disavow that Vlad actually drank human blood, but
Alexander Cepesi has his own version of the Dracula story.
According to Cepesi, Dracula would chop the hands from his
impaled victims, collect the flowing blood in copper vats and
drink it down, either straight or blended with alcohol and
brewed with herbs of his liking. One year before his death,
Dracula, said Cepesi, killed numerous women by severing
their jugular veins with his teeth. When he rode out on his
black horse to fight the Turks, Dracula supposedly shouted,
"I am invincible, for I have drunk the blood of one thousand
Christians!" And within three years of his death, said
Cepesi, he was reported riding through the mountains of
Transylvania, showing his sharp white teeth and demanding
human blood.

According to McNally and Florescu, it was Bram
Stoker who linked the historical Dracula with the Romanian
folklore of the vampire. Still, the extant ruins of Castle
Dracula maintain their lingering legends. The ruins are a
haven for eagles, rodents, snakes, and those favorite animals
of Stoker's vampire Count, wolves and bats. The superstitious peasants, say McNally and Florescu, still believe that
Dracula never truly died, that his spirit yet haunts those
ruins, and that someday he will return from the grave as
some type of avenging messiah.

I have made reference to Raymond T. McNally and
Radu Florescu, the latter being descended directly from
Dracula's brother Radu III (known as "The Handsome"). In
1972 the New York Graphic Society (Greenwich, Connecticut)
published In Search of Dracula: A True History of Dracula
and Vampire Legends. This scholarly treatment of Vlad
Tepes is heartily recommended to anyone seeking a more detailed study of the Impaler; it is written in entertaining fashion and with an authoritative background in Romanian and
Hungarian history. The authors personally visited and in-
vestigated the sites important to the Dracula saga and studied
the ancient historical documents chronicling his life and crimes.
Particularly exciting is their passage on the search for Vlad
Dracula's tomb. When George Florescu, uncle of Radu, ex-
cavated the monastery at Snagov in 1931, under the authority

of Romania's Commission on Historic Monuments, all that he
disinterred in the traditional tomb of the Impaler were ox
bones and a few artifacts. Was this the result of a practical
joke perpetrated by the monks at Snagov upon the corpse and
spirit of one so perverse as this Wallachian prince? Or did
Dracula, as Stoker would have said, rise from his grave un-
dead? McNally and Florescu cite a second grave found in
the same church, hidden beneath the entrance, the contents
of which they describe as follows:

> ... it was found to contain a casket still partially
> covered by a purple shroud embroidered with gold.
> Both coffin and covering were mostly rotted away.
> Within the coffin lay a badly deteriorated skeleton;
> fragments of a faded red silk garment suitable for
> a person of at least boyar rank, with a ring sewn
> onto one sleeve; a golden crown ornamented with
> cloisonné and having claws clasping a jewel; and a
> necklace with the barely perceptible motif of a
> serpent. *

The authors speculate that this may be the authentic skeleton,
placed where the visitors to the grave would actually be stepping upon the remains, thereby expressing contempt rather
than veneration. The fact that this skeleton is not missing
a head presents more problems. The bones and objects found
in this hidden grave were placed in the History Museum of
Bucharest and later mysteriously disappeared.

To further add to the mystery concerning the existence
of Vlad's remains, the Weird Museum in Hollywood, California, in 1973, added to its exhibits (including the preserved
head of Landru "Bluebeard" and the traditional skull of the
Marquis de Sade) what it claims to be the authentic skeleton
of Vlad Dracula. The museum is operated by Dr. Donald
Blyth of the Ram Occult Center. A collector for over twenty-
five years of such items, Blyth asserts his belief that the
skeleton is genuine and is, in fact, the same one that vanished
from Bucharest. Blyth admitted to me that he is on a "suck-
er list," and that when anyone has something of this nature
for sale, he is the first potential buyer they call. He paid
$3,000 for the skeleton.

---

*McNally, Raymond T., and Florescu, Radu, In Search of
Dracula: A True History of Dracula and Vampire Legends
(Greenwich, Connecticut, 1972), p. 185.

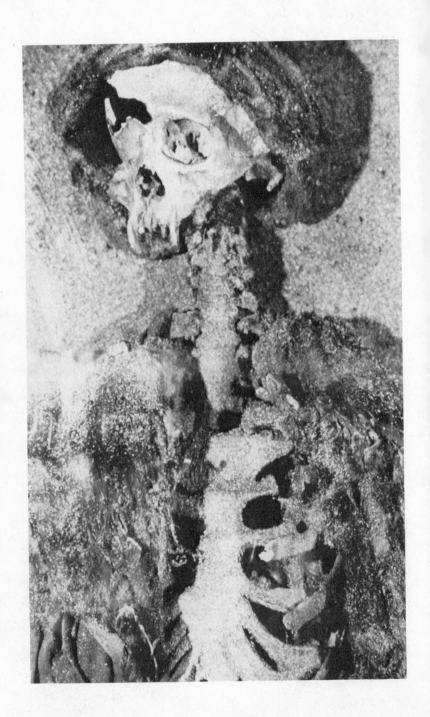

The alleged skeleton of Vlad is an impressive exhibit. The skeleton is black with age, wearing tattered clothing similar to that which Vlad has been pictured wearing. Blyth shows documents asserting the skeleton is five hundred years old based on carbon-14 tests. However, certain aspects of the skeleton seem too perfect. There is a depression in the left side of the rib cage as though something had been driven through the chest. And the canine teeth are unnaturally long and sharp, the absence of the lower jaw and most of the upper teeth making them appear all the more formidable.

"We rather think that this is some anomaly," Blyth told me in the presence of the skeleton, "some abnormality. Actually, historically there is no indication that there is any vampirism in the Dracula family at all. If Dracula were alive, the teeth in between the two canine teeth and the surrounding gum and lip tissue would serve to make those canines a lot less obtrusive than they are. They'd still be noticeable.... Eventually the head was returned by the monks at the monastery in Snagov. And if you'll notice carefully, the atlas vertebra is gone, and the one on the top is crushed. And the two little protuberances at the back of the skull have been cut off. So you can see that that head had been violently removed at one time. Also the lower jaw, as you'll notice, is missing. We don't know where it is. The lower jaw and the right hand. Other than that the skeleton is complete ... All except the ends and the back of the coffin is the original....

"We had intended to present Dracula as an historical figure, as a miliary figure, actually an early Christian who fought the Turks. We picked him up at the LA airport. And when we unpacked him my partner said, 'You're going to have a terrible time trying to convince people that Dracula was not a vampire.' I said, 'Why is that?' And he said, 'Look at him.' And we looked at those teeth and the general condition of the skeleton and I saw what he meant. Although we do tell people in here that there's no historical documentation of the vampirism, more people are inclined to believe that he was one than that he wasn't."

Blyth also offers two other opinions. The first, from Carl C. Francis, professor emeritus of anatomy at Case

Opposite: Skeleton exhibited as the authentic remains of Vlad Dracula at the Weird Museum in Hollywood. Photo by Erik Shiozaki

Western Reserve University in Cleveland, says, "I wish to
state that it is my opinion that ... the general appearance of
the remains would be commensurate with those of Vlad,
Prince Drakulya of Transylvania. " And George T. Gerber,
the medical examiner of Maricopa County, Arizona, says,
"After having completed my examination of the skeleton ...
I wish to state that it represents the remains of one Vlad
Dracula, an early Wallachian Prince. "

Whether or not the skeleton is indeed Vlad Dracula's
remains a mystery. However, there is an aura of magic
about looking into that coffin, standing up perpendicular, and
seeing that ancient skeleton in the eerie dim light.

Following the success of In Search of Dracula: A
True History of Dracula and Vampire Legends (the book made
the best seller list), the two authors prepared a follow-up
book entitled Dracula, an Historical Biography of Vlad the
Impaler, 1431-1476. It was published in 1973 by Hawthorn
Books under the abbreviated title, Dracula, A Biography of
Vlad the Impaler. Written on a more scholarly level than
the first book, it presents the complete history of Vlad with
many footnotes and extensive bibliographies.

Florescu and McNally (their names are interchanged
on the second book) also included new material pertaining to
Vlad's appearances on the stage and upon the printed page.
The Hungarian Adam Horvath published his Dracula play in
1787 and saw it performed on July 15, 1790 at Buda. In the
play, a revised version of which was published in 1792, Dracula
betrays Hunyadi to the Serbians as an act of vengeance for the
murders of his father and brother. Ion Catina, a Romanian,
wrote a two-act play entitled TEPES VODA in 1847, a drama that
never reached the stage because of political pressure. G. Mav-
rodullu's VLADU TZEPESHU DRAMA ISTORICA IN CINCI ACTE
("Vlad Tepes, Historical Drama in Five Acts") was performed
at Bucharest in 1856. In the late nineteenth century the Romanian Mihail Sorbul wrote PRAZNICUL CALICULOR ("The
Feast of Beggars"), a strange comedy based on Vlad's slaughter-
ing the sick and poor. Ludovic Daus saw his play IMPALER unsuccessfully performed in 1930 at Bucharest. Yet another
Dracula play was performed in Romania in 1969.

Dracula was portrayed as a villain in at least two
Hungarian songs, one by Matthias Nagybanki about 1560, the
other published in 1574 by Gaspar of Heltai in Cluj. Dracula
became the hero, called "The Noble, " in Tiganiada, an epic

song poem by Ion Budai-Deleanu which was published in 1875, half a century after Budai-Deleanu's death. Dracula leads an army of Gypsies against the evil boyars, Turks, the Devil himself and (ironically) female vampires, thereby achieving even greater heroic status. During the 1800s, Dimitrie Bolintineanu included Dracula the hero in his poem, "Battles of the Romanians," while Mihail Eminescu, in his poem "The Third Letter," brought the heroic Dracula back from the dead to kill the Romanian antipatriots. In 1940 George Calinescu, in his poem, "Life," considered Vlad a madman yet believed that the Voivode could save the Romanian race. Tudor Arghezi (real name, Ion N. Theodorescu), in his "Tepes Voda" ("The Impaler Prince"), brought Dracula down from his place of honor and dealt with his crimes. Yet another poem, "Dracula and His Wife," by Elizabeth Isanos, was published in Romania in 1968.

Dimitrie Bolintineanu, said Florescu and McNally, also wrote an historical novel about Dracula the hero in 1863; the same year, the Hungarian Miklós Jesiku wrote a derogatory novel in which he confused Dracula with his father Dracul. Another Dracula novel with the unobtrusive title, Love and Revenge, was written by Ion Lapedatu and published in Transylvania in 1877. A pamphlet titled Vlad Tepes "Vlad the Impaler," by G. Popescu, was published for children at Bucharest in 1964. Stramosii "The Ancestors," by Radu Theodoru (1967) and Vlad fiul Dracului "Vlad the Son of the Devil," by Georgina Viorica Rögöz (1970) were historical novels about the life of Dracula, each relying heavily upon fact. There was also a Turkish novel written about Dracula by Turhan Tan, with the title Akinda Ahina.

Florescu and McNally went on tour, lecturing about Dracula at colleges and speaking on radio and television shows to promote their books. McNally even appeared wearing a Dracula cape on the February 20, 1974 ABC-TV special, HORROR HALL OF FAME--A MONSTER SALUTE, which was part of the WIDE WORLD OF ENTERTAINMENT series. *

In 1972, Pan American Airlines, as a tie-in with the book In Search of Dracula, made available to travelers an

---

*The show starred Vincent Price who performed a brief scene as Dracula. Also featured were selected scenes from the films DRACULA HAS RISEN FROM THE GRAVE, BLACULA and Browning's MARK OF THE VAMPIRE.

eighteen-day tour with the alluring (or foreboding) title, "Spotlight on Dracula: An Adventure in Translyvania." The tour provided flight from New York to Dracula country in Hungary and Romania. There, tourists were not only treated to lectures and films about Vlad Dracula but were taken personally to the sites visited or occupied by the Impaler in the fifteenth century. A more economical (and less inclusive) version of the tour was called "A Taste of Dracula."

The Dracula Myth (originally announced as Exploding the Bloody Myths of Dracula and Vampires), by Gabriel Ronay (London: Gollancz, 1972), published in the U.S. as The Truth About Dracula (New York: Stein and Day), was another scholarly investigation of Dracula and the un-dead. Much space was devoted to the origins of vampire traditions and to Countess Elizabeth Báthory, whose deeds, according to Ronay, could have influenced Bram Stoker's literary creation of Count Dracula.

Other factual books about Vlad Dracula include Vlad Tepes si Naratiunile Germane si Rusesti Asupra Lui, by Ioan Bogdan (Bucharest, 1896); Michael Beheim's Gedicht uber den Woiwoden Wlad II Drakul mit historischen und kritischen Erlauterungen, by Grigore C. Conduratu (Leipzig-Bucharest, 1903); Viata si faptele lui Vlad Voda Tepes, by Petre Ispirescu (Cernauti, 1939); Egykorú Ujságlap Drakula Vajdárol, by Ilona Hubay (Budapest, 1947); and Povesti o Drakule, by Ya. S. Lurye (Moscow, 1964).

We shall see in a later chapter that the Impaler also figures into such novels as Kastgli Voyvoda, The Vampire Affair and The Dracula Archives.

In 1971, the British company, Border Films, made a twenty-seven minute travelogue entitled WINTER WITH DRACULA. The filmed tour of Romania made reference to Vlad the Impaler.

Vlad Dracula made a screen appearance in the person of Christopher Lee, who portrays Count Dracula in the British Hammer Films, in an hour-long motion picture, IN SEARCH OF DRACULA, made in color by Aspekt Films in Sweden. Based on the book In Search of Dracula and directed by Calvin Floyd, the picture employed McNally and Florescu as historical consultants. The film will probably be released directly to television. IN SEARCH OF DRACULA incorporates scenes from familiar Dracula movies but is primarily a documentary, shot in Romania, about the bloodthirsty Vlad. Lee appeared in four different roles, one being that of Vlad Tepes, in which he is made to resemble the portrait at Castle Ambras. Of the film, Lee told me:

"I went to Transylvania to do this documentary which is really about the vampire in fact (of course being the bat), in fiction (in part being the legend and superstition of the undead), and of course, the vampire in books, in the cinema, in theatre. So in this film I appear in four different, if you like, guises. One is myself as the narrator of the documentary, because although I narrate the film I still appear from time to time as myself. One is the Hammer Dracula. One is the Stoker Dracula. One is the historical Dracula, because I've dressed up as Vlad the Impaler and appeared as him in the castles of Transylvania and in this part of the world. I look exactly like him. That may sound a bit difficult to believe, but it is, in fact, true. The resemblance is extraordinary. We found some of the paintings of the Impaler in castles in Hungary and in the Tyrol and in the state museum in Budapest. And the resemblance is really ridiculous. It's almost the same face."

Late in 1973 a motion picture entitled DRACULA'S TRANSYLVANIA, to star Christopher Lee as Vlad in a film adaptation of the book In Search of Dracula, was announced. But this may be merely a new title for the above-cited film.

Earlier in 1973 a film company journeyed to the Dracula cities to obtain location scenes for a film about Vlad, while Russ Jones announced that he was writing the screenplay for a motion picture titled VLAD, THE IMPALER to be made by Avco-Embassy. And, as we shall see in a later chapter, Vlad was also incorporated in the MGM television adaptation of DRACULA, starring Jack Palance.

With the revival of interest in Vlad Dracula, a play based on his life was enacted nightly during the early 1970s at his Tirgoviste palace. Vlad was also depicted in the large black and white comic strips. Familiar stories of Vlad, "Dracula's Castle" and "Vlad the Impaler," written by Fred Ott and drawn by Auraleon, were published respectively in Eerie no. 10 (June 1973) and no. 6 (March 1973), issued by the Warren Publishing Company. Dracula Lives! (from the Marvel Comics Group) frequently referred to Count Dracula as the former Vlad the Impaler and, in the vol. 2, no. 1 issue (March 1974), published "The Boyhood of Dracula," writ-

ten by Tony Isabella and drawn by Val Mayerik. A wax figure of Vlad Dracula was brought to life by Satanic powers
and was defeated by a similar living effigy of Davy Crockett
in "Mystery in Wax," written by myself and drawn by Bill
Ziegler for the seventeenth issue of the color magazine, Mystery Comics Digest (March 1974), from Gold Key Comics.

In 1974, radio broadcasts and newspaper articles reported on new activities in Dracula country. The Romanian
government began a search to retrieve the missing remains
of Dracula, laying them to their proper rest (while also providing another attraction for the tourists).

Vlad Dracula did accomplish some positive things during his bloody career. He founded the city of Bucharest in
1459 and did, in fact, restore law and order and a feeling of
nationalism to a land rent by foreign invaders. Today, however, Dracula is most remembered as the fictional character
developed more than four centuries after Vlad's death by an
author named Bram Stoker.

Chapter 2

THE VAMPIRE IMAGE

> But first on earth, as Vampyre sent,
> Thy corpse shall from its tomb be rent;
> Then ghastly haunt thy native place,
> And suck the blood of all thy race ...
> --The Giaour (1813), by Lord Byron

Count Dracula is best known as a vampire, a creature so exploited in literature and motion pictures that even the youngest of his fans could jot down a list of his abilities and limitations and the methods by which to destroy him. The authors of fiction have often invented their own vampire lore for the purpose of storytelling. The vampire of tradition is not, in fact, entirely the same creature who haunts the printed page or the motion picture screen.

The vampire--the nosferatu, the un-dead--is not an intangible spectre or demon from Dante or Gustave Doré's visions of Hell, but rather a dreadful resuscitated corpse that haunts the world of the living, performing all manner of malevolent and atrocious acts. He is a dead man energized either by demoniac possession or by the very spirit that inhabited his body during life. Different cultures maintain their own theories as to what so energizes a corpse, but most accept the fact that the procedure involves the direct intervention of Satan.

The vampire of tradition and legend is a horror: emaciated, cadaverous, with the sallowness of a bloodless corpse (providing he has not yet feasted). Fiery red eyes stare from that dead white face and the full red lips barely cover the gleaming white teeth. The teeth are sharp, like those of an animal, with the canines especially elongated. The fingernails have grown into long hooked claws and hair grows from the monster's palms. His breath is foul with

19

the stench of decay. Although the vampire may have been
dead for centuries his physical appearance resembles that of
an incorrupt corpse with warm blood flowing through his veins
and (when he has recently supped) a ruddy tint to his white
cheeks. Unlike some of the film vampires, the traditional
species could hardly go about undetected. Even a disguised
vampire would drive most people away with his rancid breath.

The vrykolakas--the Greek species of vampire, known
also by a number of similar names including vroucolacas,
vourcolakas, vrukolaka and broukolakas--has, instead, a dark
complexion and a tough shriveled skin like the hide of a mummy. Hence the word vrykolakas translates from the Greek
as "drum-like." Some types of vrykolakas may be recognized
by a peculiar wine-colored skin pigmentation.

There are yet other varieties of vampire, some with
features which make them less distinguishable from human
beings. In some countries blue eyes or red hair are vampire attributes (which would suggest that there are hordes of
the un-dead prowling the busy streets of America alone).
Epilepsy and chorea are other identifying traits, while in
certain areas a man possessing a single nostril would undoubtedly be branded a vampire.

One common misconception is that the vampire's consumption of blood is a necessity and that, unless a prescribed
amount of the substance is taken during a set period of time,
the monster will perish. Actually, the traditional vampire's
drinking of blood is not particularly a matter of need (akin to
drug addiction or alcoholism) but of taste. The vampire enjoys sucking blood; he is governed by some demonic compul-
sion to so gorge himself.

The vampire satisfies his thirst for blood in various
ways. The un-dead might attack any number of places on the
human body, including the chest and feet, but usually (as
with Count Dracula) the jugular vein is where he plunges his
canine teeth and sucks out the blood. The vampire's victim
might afterwards have no recollection of the attack. But the
signs are apparant: twin puncture marks on the neck, loss
of coloration, apparent anemia and lethargy. Sometimes the
opening of a vampire's grave reveals fresh blood smeared or
caked upon his lips, while his body might be literally floating
in the scarlet liquid.

Blood drinking is actually but one of the traditional

vampire's practices.   As often as the monster will take the blood of his prey he will strangle, suffocate, perform other torments, or even have sexual intercourse.   The sexual implications of the un-dead are significant.   Blood in itself is sexually important, even arousing, perhaps because of its significance as symbolizing menstruation or the blood shed by a virgin during penetration.   (The canines of the vampire penetrate the flesh to release the blood.)   When a male vampire sinks his fangs into the neck of a female victim, she usually swoons, not from pain but from pleasure.   Freud studied the phenomenon of sexual arousal through sado-masochistic actions and so we can safely theorize that the vampire not only bites and sucks (which carries its own erotic implications) her blood but has also symbolically taken her to bed. Often, the vampires of fiction will attack only members of the opposite sex (unless the vampire is in bat form), to avoid any criticism from members of the audience who are aware of the sexual significance of the bite on the neck.

Vampires of tradition consume any type of food or drink, including (least appetizing of all) manure.   Frequently they have sat down to dinner with the families they had during life.   But blood remains their first gastronomic love.

A normal corpse, according to tradition, can become a vampire in a number of ways.   Romania, the home of Count Dracula, has its own proscriptions by which people are doomed to un-death.   A man will become a vampire within six months after his death if, during life, he sought material gain with more than average zeal.   A child who dies unbaptized shall return as a vampire after a seven-year waiting period.   If seven children of the same sex are born in a row to a single family the last will possess a tail and is congenitally destined to become a vampire.   The corpse of a man born with a caul shall become un-dead on his fortieth day of interment.   Pregnant women who do not eat salt carry a future vampire in their womb.   So does a woman at least six months pregnant who falls under a vampire's gaze, unless the process is checked by the Church.   In some Romanian countries every corpse is believed to be a vampire when the soul flees from its mouth.   (To prevent this the corpse is overturned so that the spirit will be confused and unable to regain entrance.)   A corpse will also become a vampire if a cat or man walks over it, or a human shadow falls upon it.

The Russians believe that a bird flying or a boy or cat jumping over a corpse can produce a vampire; in the

Ukraine the wind from the Steppe has the same unfortunate
effect. In certain other areas a person with "abnormal" interests, as in poetical expression, is considered to be a potential vampire. Greece also has its stipulations. Children
born on Christmas Day or between Christmas and Epiphany
are fated to become vampires because their parents had pre-
sumed to conceive simultaneously with the Immaculate Conception holy day of the Church. A man dying under ban of
excommunication or in a state of mortal sin, or found after
death without decay is a vrykolakas and must be exorcised or
destroyed. The Greek town of Elias adopted the belief that
anyone eating the flesh of a sheep killed by a wolf will become a vampire.

A man who has lived the existence of a werewolf will
become a vampire after death. A child born with teeth will
undoubtedly someday use those teeth as one of the un-dead.
A suicide will come back to pseudo-life as a vampire. (In
the Balkans and other countries, suicides were buried at the
crossroads so that they would be confused in their attempts
to reach town after their return from the grave.) But the
most common manner by which a person becomes un-dead is
to become the victim of a vampire. Usually the vampire's
victim does not die from a single bite but pines away from
repeated attacks. Then, having met death as a direct result
of the monster's bites, the victim himself becomes a vampire.

With these and so many other factors contributing to
the creation of vampires, it seems remarkable that the world
was not overrun by such fiends centuries ago.

THE VAMPIRE'S POWERS

Count Dracula has haunted the popular media, pitting
his vampiric abilities against his human adversaries. Among
all of his powers the ability to transform into a vampire bat
is the most widely known. It is therefore a vast surprise to
many people to discover that the traditional vampire cannot
and never has been able to change into a bat. The concept
of vampires assuming the shapes of bats was solely the fab-
rication of the writer--presumably Bram Stoker himself--who
invented this bit of "legend" for purely logical reasons.

In the late nineteenth century the authentic vampire

bats of South and Central Americas (not Transylvania) were
receiving much public attention. <u>Desmodus rufus</u> and <u>Diphylla</u>
are two species of vampire bat that have been known to drink
the blood of cattle and even men. Their attacks on livestock
were reported as far back as the 1700s. Vampire bats have
drained the blood from the combs of roosters, the color
changing to white, and inmates of Devil's Island were often
the shackled victims of vampire bats that flew about the prison. The animal removes a small section of the victim's
skin with its razor-sharp teeth, exposing the severed blood
vessels and allowing a steady flow of blood which is then
drunk (not sucked), passing through the tiny gullet and into
the bat's stomach. Hanging upside down, the vampire bat
rests while the newly consumed blood is digested.

Herein lies the similarity between the vampire bat and
the traditional vampire upon which the writer capitalized.
The vampire bat hunts by night and reposes by day, just like
the vampire of legend. The habits of both creatures so coincided that by the late nineteenth century the bat became
part of evolving vampire lore. There is in addition the fact
that bats are notorious carriers of rabies, while the human
vampire also occasionally brings with him the plague. If
legend did not associate the two creatures, it should have.

I have seen vampire bats in action. During the late
1950s a collection of living (so-called) "monsters" of the animal kingdom was exhibited at Riverview Park, the great
amusement park in Chicago. The exhibits proved not to be
the glamorously horrible monstrosities pictured on the posters but rather a group of lizards, piranha, a giant river rat,
a dying octopus ... and vampire bats. The showman announced, "Vampire bats! Not the legendary vampires like
Count Dracula, who rose from his coffin each night to drink
human blood, but real vampire bats! If you have a weak
stomach the exit door is to the left--because right before
your eyes these bats are going to drink human blood!"

The exhibitor brought out a jar of dark liquid which
he claimed was human blood acquired from a blood bank. He
poured the liquid into a small dish placed in a cage, then instructed the audience to look toward the upper corners. Con-
gestions of fur began to move in each corner, and wings
emerged from them. The vampire bats flopped to the bottom of the cage and walked upon wing-arms to their feeding
dish. The animals were small and hardly the formidable appearing monsters of the movies. But as they proceeded slop-

pily to splash about the dish of blood, discoloring their fur, and lapping up the liquid that had been tapped from the arms of anonymous human donors, they briefly conjured up an image of Count Dracula and his disciples enjoying the illicit pleasures of some dark orgy. Apparently satisfied, the gorged vampire bats then returned to the upper corners of the cage to await the return of their blood-thirst.

While the traditional vampire does not have the ability to transform into a bat, he can take on other shapes, including the form of a wolf. In folklore there is a distinct connection between the vampire and the werewolf, a creature which assumes the mannerisms and the partial or complete guise of a wolf. Often there is confusion between the two. The Slavik term vukodlak (also volkadlak and vulkodlak) is applicable to both the vampire and the werewolf. The Croatian-English dictionary identifies vukodlak--from "vuko," meaning "wolf," and "blaka," meaning "hair"--as synonymous for vampire or werewolf. Although there are additional Croatian words for vampire--vampir and krvopija, meaning "blood-sucker"--the word for werewolf remains vukodlak.

In Wallachia, a land once ruled by Vlad Dracula, tradition includes a creature called the murony, which seems to be a hybrid of vampire and werewolf. The murony can also assume the shape of a dog, cat, toad, and of all blood-sucking insects.

The Greek vrykolakas was believed by some people to be a living person (not un-dead) with a thirst for blood. This living vrykolakas is the same as the English werewolf. It is interesting to note the similarities in the words vrykolakas or vourkolakas and vukodlak. In Poland, the word vilkolak refers exclusively to the werewolf.

Since the traditional vampire does have the power to shift his shape to the form of a wolf, it often becomes difficult to differentiate between the vampires and werewolves of legend. The main criterion for the vampire is that he is a reanimated corpse. The werewolf, on the other hand, is not a walking dead man but a living person who enacts the role of a bloodthirsty wolf. Again, among many Slavik peoples, the werewolf in life is believed to be the vampire in death.

Besides the wolf, the vampire of tradition can metamorphose into other animals. In some legends, vampires and living, blood-drinking witches can assume the forms of

cats and hares. Among the Oraons, a primitive hill tribe of
Bengal, there is a legendary monster called the Chordewa, a
vampire witch capable of changing its soul into the image of
a black cat. This feline is the witch's familiar, and any
wounds inflicted upon it result in corresponding wounds on its
human form. The Japanese also have stories of vampire
cats. In Italy a belief existed in the Strega (also Strigia or
Strix), a vampire witch able to change into a crow that sucks
blood and breathes a fatal poison. The Lamia, the vampire
of ancient Greece, was depicted as a monster with a woman's
head and breasts and a snake's body.

The vampire can increase his size or shrink small
enough to pass through the cracks of doors and windows. He
can render himself intangible or become a floating mist, thereby transcending his physical properties. The Chinese Chiang
Shih was a hybrid of vampire and ghoul (a corpse-eating demon) that could possess a corpse and prevent its decomposition, or could appear as a mist. Chinese legend also includes the mist and haze of a swamp or mire that, vampire-
like, sucks away its victim's life and inflicts disease and
fever. A common legend is that a vampire's grave may be
discovered by several telltale holes, the circumference of a
man's finger, in the mound. Through these holes the monster, as a mist, enters and exits from his grave.

Among the un-dead's other supernatural abilities are
the controlling of his victims' will and power to control the
more disliked and destructive animals (such as rats, wolves
and locusts). He can also see in the dark with his red eyes,
and can perform great feats with his demonic physical
strength.

Still, with so many powers intended for evil use, the
vampire is sought after in some areas of the world to do
good. In Romania, live vampires (who never died) were
said to have the talent of extracting the best flavor from
foods. Others bring rain in times of drought and are actually hired by farmers to perform this task. With so many
powers listed in the vampire's favor, he would almost seem
invincible, yet he may be trapped and destroyed quite efficiently by those mortals who have memorized their vampire
lore.

DOOM OF THE VAMPIRE

Although the vampire is an extremely powerful creature of darkness, he is also extremely limited. And it is
because of his limitations that he is occasionally destroyed,
as Count Dracula said in the play by Hamilton Deane and the
film starring Bela Lugosi, by men who have not lived so
much as a single lifetime.

Count Dracula has usually been characterized in the
various media as a vampire who casts no reflection in a mirror. In Bram Stoker's Dracula the King Vampire also casts
no shadow. Such ideas are often of prime importance in a
vampire story, since the lack of mirror image or umbra
gives away the creature's true nature. Are such conceptions,
however, limitations which are found in tradition, or are they
the inventions of writers?

Bram Stoker researched the authentic vampire legends
at length. He did not, though, put all of his homework into
practice and realized that the concocting of so-called "myth"
could help to further his own story. In tradition and legend,
however, despite what mythology was born in Stoker's imagination, there is no mention of the vampire's not reflecting in
a glass. Stoker's reasoning on this matter was sound. If
the vampire is actually a creature without a soul of its own,
as many cultures attest, he might not cast a reflection since
that reflection might actually be one's spiritual self. For
Stoker (and for writers of vampire tales following Dracula)
the concept worked and has, like the creature's ability to
change into a bat, become a part of the "fictional mythology"
of the vampire.

The idea that the vampire throws no shadow is also
attributable to Stoker. Again his reasoning was based on
logic. If the vampire can become subtle and intangible, there
must be certain non-physical aspects about him. Something
that is not physical might not produce a shadow when obstruct-
ing the light. There is also a logical connection with the
equation, by some cultures, of the loss of a shadow with the
loss of a soul. Tales of men bargaining their souls to the
Devil often include the losing of the shadow. If a vampire
possessed a soul it could very well belong to Satan anyway.
But traditional vampires do possess shadows which throw off
sparks in the darkness--another of the seemingly countless
traits by which mortals can identify the fiends.

According to Montague Summers, the Devil intervenes in the creation of vampires. This makes the vampire anti-religious and compelled to cower from such articles of organized religion as ikons and the crucifix. The un-dead flees at the mere sight of the crucifix, a tar cross formed over a would-be victim's door, relics of the saints, a simple act of the Sign of the Cross, and above all, the Host of the Blessed Sacrament. As the Church has always dictated that Satan is at the root of all evil in the universe, it is not difficult to see why the vampire should exhibit trepidation in the face of Christianity.

In Greece the vampire's alienation from religion is especially strong. A vrykolakas resulting from excommunication can only be saved if the bishop lifts the ban that he imposed before the man's death. The lifting of the ban should bring immediate decomposition to the monster.

If no priest is available and there is no nearby store that sells religious articles, garlic, which can be purchased at the market or even grown in the backyard, will also throw fear into the traditional vampire. The odorous bulbs are most effective when hung about the home or strung around the neck. Unfortunately, such tactics tend to repel not only the vampire but the victim as well. In China and Malaya a child's brow is dampened with garlic to ward off vampires. Garlic is also used in the West Indies to prevent the attacks of demons and witches. The Sumatran Bataks or Battas use garlic to lure back the spirit of a person drawn away by a vampiric creature. After a vampire is destroyed, garlic may be stuffed into the monster's mouth and scattered about his coffin to keep him there.

Incense will force a vampire to flee, while the scattering of grain will compel him to pick it up piece by piece, a detainment which it is hoped will last until dawn. A rose laid upon his grave will keep him trapped within; buckthorn or whitethorn branches, symbolic of Christ's crown of thorns, are sometimes used as substitutes for a rose. Certain Chinese vampires cannot leave their graves if surrounded by scatterings of red peas, rice or iron. Count Dracula was further restricted, being unable to cross the threshold of a home unless first invited in by a member of the household. Though this was apparently a creation of Stoker's, the Greeks have a tradition that a man will die if he responds when a vrykolakas knocks at his door and calls his name.

Once a vampire has been discovered, there follows
the rather unpleasant task of his destruction. Since he is a
physical horror he must be destroyed accordingly (and often
messily). The Greek Orthodox Church regards any corpse
that has not decayed within forty days of its interment as a
vampire. If decomposition does not result from exorcism
there are more elaborate methods to insure that the vampire
can never use his body again.

The three most universally accepted practices by which
mortals (with strong stomachs) can destroy these blood-sucking monsters are to: 1) drive a stake through the vampire's
heart, 2) chop off the head, and 3) burn the corpse to ashes.
Any of these three methods should prove effective, but the
combination of all of them is the best way to insure that the
monster has been dispatched forever. Some traditions further stipulate that the stake be composed of iron or wood, or
of a particular kind of wood, like whitethorn or hawthown.
In Russia the stake is cut from maple or aspen, the latter
being associated with the wood of Jesus' cross.

Some traditions have facsimiles for the stake. Certain Mohammedans, who make their living as vampire exterminators, use a sharpened iron rod. A consecrated dagger
is equally effective in Albania and Dalmatia. And in certain
Indian traditions, a sword is permissible. Not only is the
material of the stake often important; so also is the manner
in which it is driven into the body. The stake must generally be pounded into the heart with but a single blow of the
mallet. According to certain legends, a vampire can return
to life if more than one blow is used. The heart is the usual target for the vengeful stake, but again there are variations. In Wallachia, for example, nails may be driven
through the navel, the temples, the eyes or through the entire skull.

Driving the stake through the heart is rather obviously
appropriate. The vampire gorges himself upon the blood of
the living. The heart is the organ which pumps the blood,
not to mention the widespread beliefs that the heart is the
center of the soul. It is therefore only logical that the stake
impale that organ, destroying the fiend's capability to circu-
late blood--either his own or that of his victims. But, most
important, again recalling that the vampire is physical, staking can be symbolic of "pinning down" the monster to his
grave or fastening him to the earth.

When the vampire is transfixed by a stake his body overflows with warm, fresh blood, while a hideous scream issues from his bloody mouth. The practice of staking vampires would seem to be quite effective, yet it is not always foolproof. In the village of Blow (or Blau), near the Bohemian town of Kadam, an allegedly authentic vampire only laughed and pulled the stake from his chest, thanking his would-be destroyer for leaving him a stick with which to fight off dogs.

A further precaution, to eliminate the possibility of having a vampire yank out his own stake, is to also decapitate him. The most common practice requires that the monster's head be severed with only one slice of a gravedigger's spade. Following the decapitation, garlic may be stuffed in the mouth, as mentioned earlier, for further insurance against the vampire's return.

As if impalement and decapitation were not grisly enough methods of vampire extermination, the most permanent (and universal) practice of insuring his destruction is cremation. The burning of the vampire's body is usually the next step taken in Greece if the removal of the ban of excommunication fails. Again there are variations according to the locale. Some traditions are content with mundane cremation. Others dictate that the body must first be hacked to bits. Often, these pieces must then be soaked in holy water or wine, or submerged in boiling oil. Frequently, the entire vampire corpse must be reduced to ashes. If any animals or insects are observed to crawl or fly from the smoldering pyre, they must likewise be burnt entirely, lest the vampire escape his fate while transformed into some other shape.

Staking, decapitation and cremation are the safest (and certainly the most pleasant) ways to destroy the un-dead. There are, however, other, less commonly practiced methods. The heart may be cut out, diced, and cooked in oil of vinegar. Sometimes, the splashing of scalding water on the monster's grave is sufficient. The most expensive and yet least effective technique is to fire a consecrated silver bullet at the approaching vampire, hoping that his appearance will not set your hand trembling so that you miss the intended target. Assuming that your shot was accurate, the vampire's remains must then be securely tucked away, for if exposed to the rays of the full moon after such an assault, he will surely walk again. In Bulgaria sorcerers pursue the vampire with an ikon, forcing him to flee into a bottle containing his favorite

food.   The sorcerer then corks the bottle (the cork containing a piece of the ikon) and throws the captured vampire into a blazing fire.

Those who are well acquainted with the Count Dracula
of motion pictures would also add that the vampire can meet
destruction by exposure to the rays of the sun.   It is shocking to most aficionados of the vampire of fiction that authentic legends make no mention of solar rays being fatal to the
un-dead.   Stoker created his own limitations for Count Dracula in regards to the sun, and the first vampire ever to dis-
integrate in the sunlight was in the film NOSFERATU.   Traditionally, the vampire is sometimes (not always) limited by
the time of day.   Most vampires of legend have been powerless to act during the daylight hours.   The vrykolakas is permitted to repose in his grave only on Saturday, a day with
religious significance to the Greek Orthodox Church.

It is not within the scope of this book to delve deeply
into the psychology behind the vampire legend and to discover
why this supernatural monster has persisted for centuries to
plague so many cultures separated by time and geography.
We may briefly speculate that vampires flourished during
times when religion dictated most of man's fears and that the
vampire condition of a corpse is actually attributable to pre-
mature burial.   A person allegedly dead but actually in a
state of catalepsy is buried unembalmed.   During his entombment he returns to animation and, in his attempt to claw his
way to freedom, breaks his own skin so that blood flows
about his own body and his coffin.   A corpse discovered in
such a condition--fresh, filled with blood, obviously having
moved--might readily be identified as a vampire.   There are
numerous explanations for the origins of vampire traditions,
with roots in cannibalism and rituals wherein blood is believed to possess certain magical properties.   Even in our
so-called modern world, human fiends make sensational newspaper headlines with their blood orgies.   Some psychopathic
vampires--in the human (and not supernatural) sense--have
climaxed their horrendous crimes with the drinking of human
blood.   And we shall presently discuss the most notorious
human vampire in all of history, Countess Elizabeth Báthory
of Transylvania, whose atrocities still make shocking reading.
For in-depth analyses of vampires, both human and traditional, with details concerning all aspects of the bloodthirsty
monsters, I suggest the following books:

Glut, Donald F.   True Vampires of History.   New York:

HC Publishers, Inc., 1971. A chronological collection
of documented vampire cases.

Hurwood, Bernhardt J. Monsters and Nightmares. New
York: Belmont Productions, 1967.

_____. Monsters Galore. New York: Fawcett Publications,
1965.

_____. Terror by Night. New York: Lancer Books, 1963.
Contains valuable insights as to the origins of vampire
legends.

_____. Vampires, Werewolves, and Ghouls. New York:
Ace Books, 1968.

Masters, Anthony. The Natural History of the Vampire.
New York: G. P. Putnam's Sons, 1972. One of the
finest studies of the vampire.

Summers, Montague. The Vampire: His Kith and Kin. London: Routledge and Kegan Paul, 1928. New Hyde Park:
University Books, 1960.

_____. The Vampire in Europe. London: Routledge and
Kegan Paul, 1929. New Hyde Park: University Books,
1962. These two books comprise the most thorough
scholarly works ever written on the subject of vampirism.
They have an additional interest in that Montague Summers believed entirely in the traditional vampire who
rises from his grave to seek human blood.

Volta, Ornella. The Vampire (published originally as Le
Vampire, la mort, le sang, la peur). Paris: Editions
Jean Jacques Pauvert, 1962. London: Tandem Books,
1965. Translated by Raymond Rudorff. Emphasizes the
sexual aspects of vampirism.

Wright, Dudley. Vampires and Vampirism. London: William Rider and Son, 1914.

THE BLOOD COUNTESS OF TRANSYLVANIA

In 1746 Vlad Dracula and an expedition led by Prince
Steven Báthory of Transylvania rode into Wallachia to claim
the former's throne. Approximately one century later the
Countess Elizabeth Báthory became the terror of Transylvania
and the most notorious vampiress in world history. Because
of recent associations linking Elizabeth with Dracula her story
is included here.

Countess Elizabeth Báthory was a lesbian who perpetrated incredible cruelties upon pretty servant and peasant
girls. Csejthe Castle, a massive mountaintop fortress over-

looking the village of Csejthe, was the site of Elizabeth's blood orgies and became known to the peasants as the castle of vampires and the hated "Blood Countess."

Born in Hungary in 1560, Elizabeth had family relatives including satyrs, lesbians and witches. At fourteen she gave birth to an illegitimate child fathered by a peasant boy and conceived at the chateau of her intended mother-in-law, Countess Ursula Nadasdy. Elizabeth and Count Ferencz Nadasdy had been betrothed since she was eleven years old. The marriage took place on May 8, 1575 when Elizabeth was fifteen. In those days, well before Women's Liberation, Elizabeth retained her own surname, while the Count changed his to Ferencz Báthory. The Count thrived on conflict and war, preferring the battlefield to domestic life at the castle, and earned a reputation as the "Black Hero of Hungary."

While Ferencz was away on one of his military campaigns, the Countess began to visit her lesbian aunt, Countess Klara Báthory, and began to participate in the woman's orgies. Elizabeth then realized her true ambitions, the inflicting of pain upon large-bosomed young girls. Not only was Elizabeth becoming infatuated with her specialized carnal pleasures, she also was developing an interest in Black Magic. Thorko, a servant in her castle, instructed her in the ways of witchcraft, at the same time encouraging her sadistic tendencies. "Thorko has taught me a lovely new one," Elizabeth wrote to Ferencz. "Catch a black hen and beat it to death with a white cane. Keep the blood and smear a little of it on your enemy. If you get no chance to smear it on his body, obtain one of his garments and smear it."

When the Countess became romantically involved with a black-clad stranger with pale complexion, dark eyes and abnormally sharp teeth, the villagers who believed in vampires had more reason to be wary of Csejthe Castle. Perhaps, to the imaginative, this stranger was Dracula himself, returned from the grave. The Countess returned alone from a sojourn with the stranger and some of the villagers stated that her mouth showed telltale signs of blood. When Count Nadasdy returned home he quickly forgave his wife's infidelity.

Now firmly rooted at her castle, Countess Elizabeth experimented in depravity with the help of Thorko, Ilona Joo (Elizabeth's former nurse), the witches Dorottya Szentes and Darvulia, and the dwarf major-domo Johannes Ujvary, who

would soon become chief torturer. With the aid of this crew
Elizabeth captured buxom servant girls at the castle, taking
them to an underground room known as "her Ladyship's torture chamber," and subjected them to the worst cruelties she
could devise. Under the pretext of punishing the girls for
failing to perform certain trivial tasks, Elizabeth used branding irons, molten wax and knives to shed their blood. She
tore the clothing from one girl, covered her with honey, and
left her to the hunger of the insects in the woods. Soon, the
Countess began attacking her bound victims with her teeth,
biting chunks of bloody flesh from their necks, cheeks and
shoulders. Blood became more of an obsession with Elizabeth as she continued her tortures with razors, torches and
her own custom-made silver pincers.

Elizabeth Báthory was a woman of exceptional beauty.
Her long raven hair contrasted with her milky complexion.
Her amber eyes were almost catlike, her figure voluptuous.
She was excessively vain and her narcissism drove her to
new depths of perversion.

As Elizabeth aged and her beauty began to wane, she
tried to conceal the decline through cosmetics and the most
expensive of clothes. But these would not cover the ever
spreading wrinkles. One fateful day a servant girl was attending to Elizabeth's hair and either pulled it or remarked
that something was wrong with her mistress' headdress. The
infuriated Countess slapped the girl so hard that blood spurted
from her nose. The blood splashed against Elizabeth's face.
Where the blood had touched her skin, the Countess observed
in a mirror, a miracle had seemingly transpired. In her
eyes, the skin had lost its lines of age. Elizabeth became
exhilarated in the knowledge that she could regain her lost
youth through vampirism.

Darvulia instructed the credulous Elizabeth how she
might again be young. The Countess believed the ancient cre-
do that the taking of another's blood could result in the as-
similation of that person's physical or spiritual qualities.
Following the witch's instructions, Elizabeth had her torturers
kidnap beautiful young virgins, slash them with knives and
collect their blood in a large vat. Then the Countess proceeded to bathe in the virgins' blood. When she emerged
from the blood she had seemingly regained her youth and ra-
diance. Elizabeth's minions procured more virgins from the
neighboring villages on the pretext of hiring them as servants.
When their bloodless corpses were discovered outside the

castle, rumors quickly spread that vampires inhabited the old fortress. Countess Elizabeth continued such practices after the death of her husband in 1604. (Count Nadasdy apparently died of poisoning although his death was also ascribed to witchcraft.)

When Darvulia died and Elizabeth found herself aging even more, another sorceress named Erzsi Majorova told her that the virginal victims must be of noble birth. But even though Elizabeth tortured young noblewomen and accompanied the blood baths with witchcraft rites, she could not retrieve her lost youth. For over a decade she perpetrated her acts of vampirism, mutilating and bleeding dry 650 maidens. Rumors spread that Elizabeth headed a terrible group of vampires that preyed upon the village maidens. Reverend Andras Berthoni, the Lutheran pastor of Csejthe, realized the truth when Elizabeth commanded him to bury secretly the bloodless corpses. He set down his suspicions regarding Elizabeth in a note before he died. The Countess was becoming so notorious that her crimes could no longer be concealed. Using the note written by Reverend Berthoni, Elizabeth's cousin, Count Thurzo, came to Csejthe Castle. On New Year's Eve of 1610, Count Thurzo, Reverend János Ponikenusz, who succeeded Berthoni and had found the note, and some of the castle personnel found Elizabeth's underground torture chamber and there discovered not only the unbelievably mutilated bodies of a number of girls, but also the bloody Countess herself.

For political reasons, Elizabeth never attended her trial. She remained confined in her castle while she and her sadistic accomplices were tried for their crimes. Elizabeth was tried purely on a criminal basis, while her cohorts were charged with vampirism, witchcraft and practicing pagan rituals. All of the torturers were beheaded, except for Ilona Joo and Dorottya Szentes, whose fingers were pulled off before their bodies were burned alive. The Countess was found to be criminally insane and was walled up within a room of Csejthe Castle. Her guards passed food to her through a small hatch. The trial documents were then hidden away in the castle of Count Thurzo and remained there, apparently "lost," for over a hundred years. Almost four years after her strange imprisonment, on August 14, 1614, a haggard looking Elizabeth Báthory, the Blood Countess of Transylvania, was dead.

Among the histories written about Countess Elizabeth

Báthory are Erzebet Báthory, by Lazzlo Turoczi (Budapest, 1744), recording the trial; Elisabeth Bathory (Die Blutgrafin). Ein Sitten-und Charakterbild mit einem Titelbilde, by R. von Elsberg (Breslau, 1904); Báthory Erzsébet, Nádasdy Ferencné, by Rexa Dezsö (Budapest, 1908); and Erzsebet Bathory, La Comtesse Sanglante, by Valentin Penrose (Paris, 1962). Discussed in the eleventh chapter of this book are the novels The Dracula Archives and The Witching of Dracula, both of which involve Elizabeth Báthory.

While the history of Elizabeth Báthory was rich enough to provide good (albeit gruesome) plot material for the motion pictures, it took until the 1970s, when violence and gore became film commodities, for her story to reach the screen. The Countess, now called "Marthory," appeared with such villains as Frankenstein's Monster, Montezuma, Attila, Satan and the Minotaur in NECROPOLIS, an Italian film of 1970, made in color by Cosmoseion/Q Productions and directed by Franco Borcani. The avant-garde film consisted of various episodes in which the main characters hedonistically seek self-fulfillment.

That same year Hammer Films in England filmed the Báthory story as a supernatural horror film under the misleading title, COUNTESS DRACULA, in an attempt to deceive the public into believing this to be another entry in their series of Dracula films. Posters for the film would inevitably carry such flagrantly misleading blurbs as, "The more she drinks, the prettier she gets," when there is no blood drinking in the picture, as well as no Countess Dracula.

In the role of Countess Elizabeth Báthory was the current sex symbol of motion picture vampires, Ingrid Pitt, who had already portrayed un-dead females in THE VAMPIRE LOVERS and THE HOUSE THAT DRIPPED BLOOD.

Countess Báthory is an aging widow who discovers that bathing in the blood of young girls restores her youth so that she appears to be in her twenties. Although these events follow reasonably closely those of history, the element of fantasy is employed and blood literally transforms her into a young woman. The Countess proceeds to order her daughter Ilona (Lesley-Anne Down) kidnapped and placed under guard while she masquerades as the young girl. When Elizabeth discovers that her regular blood baths no longer produce the desired effect, the scholar Fabio (Maurice Denham) reveals that only virgins' blood will continue the transformations, a

secret for which he is soon put to death.   The youthful-look-
ing Elizabeth is to be married to a military officer named
Imre Toth (Sandor Eles).   During the ceremony Elizabeth
predictably begins to lose her beauty, aging quickly until she
appears to be some monstrous hag.   In a last effort to regain her lost beauty and youth, the Countess lunges for her
daughter, who had been freed, but she inadvertently kills
Toth.   The final scene in the film shows Elizabeth chained
in a dungeon, awaiting her execution, as a woman bystander
curses, "Countess Dracula!" (the only such proclamation in
the picture).

COUNTESS DRACULA was, unfortunately, not only deceptive in its advertising; it is also a dreadful bore.   Peter
Sasdy's lacklustre direction of Jeremy Paul's often confusing
screenplay was further impaired by cheaply made sets
and a lead character who could not approximate the incom-
parable evil of the historical Elizabeth.   20th Century-Fox
added to the negative aspects of the film, which was not released in the United States until 1972.   In an attempt to
change the picture's R rating to a PG, the distributor excised
scenes depicting nudity or the actual nature of the Countess'
baths.   The result is an ambiguity that proves even more confusing to viewers not familiar with the historical account of
Elizabeth Báthory.

Countess Dracula, a novel based on the movie, was
written by Michel Parry and published in England by Beagle
Books in 1971.   A third motion picture, DAUGHTERS OF
DARKNESS, made in Belgium and directed by Harry Kumel,
was released in color by Gemini Releasing Corporation in
1971.   The film shows how Countess Elisabeth Báthory (Del-
phine Seyrig) survived into the Seventies as an un-dead vampire.   Countess Elisabeth and her pretty companion Ilona
Harczy (Andrea Rau) arrive at an almost deserted European
hotel.   One of the guests, Stefan Chiltern (John Karlen), is
a sadist who accidentally kills Ilona, while his girlfriend,
Valerie Tardieu (Daniele Ouimet), becomes a victim of the
Countess.   Elisabeth and Valerie then slash Stefan's wrists
and drink his blood.   The Countess perishes when she is
hurled through a car windshield, impaled on a stake and cremated as the vehicle bursts into flames.

Another Elizabeth Báthory film was announced in 1971
by Hungarian director Miklos Jancso.   Chapter 9 of this book
discusses two other Báthory films: NELLA STRETTA MORSA
DEL RAGNO and LA NOCHE DE WALPURGIS.   THE BLOODY

COUNTESS (1973) was made in Germany by Transcontinent
Films.   BLOOD CEREMONY, which went into production in
1973 with Film Ventures International, starred Ewa Aulin as
a Báthory-like bather in virgins' blood.

The eleventh issue of the comic book, Forbidden
Worlds (November 1952), published by the American Comics
Group, presented the Báthory story sans tortures and bloodbaths and portrayed Elizabeth as a bat-winged vampiress.
The first Nightmare Annual (Skywald Publishing Corporation),
issued in 1972, featured two illustrated stories based on
Countess Báthory.   "The Truth Behind the Myth of the Bride
of Dracula," written by Alan Hewetson and drawn by Xirinius,
told the famous Báthory story.   "Beauty Is Only Blood Deep,"
by Douglas Moench and artist Carrillo, was a Báthory-type
story in which a Countess bathes in and drinks the blood of
virgins, but dies because her last victim had previously been
fed rat poison.   The Marvel Comics Group depicted its own
version of the Báthory history in "This Blood Is Mine!" by
Gardner Fox and artist Dick Ayers, printed in Dracula Lives!
no. 4 (January 1974).   Count Dracula, regarding Elizabeth as
a competitor, distributes pamphlets revealing the horrors of
Castle Csejthe.   After the Countess is walled up, Dracula
drinks her blood, transforming her into a withered corpse.
An aged Voodoo houngan acquires Báthory's diary and attempts
to gain youth and immortality through similar blood sacrifices
in "End of a Legend!", a Brother Voodoo story by Moench
and illustrator Gene Colan in Marvel's Tales of the Zombie
no. 6 (July 1974).   And the old Báthory castle was the setting for two episodes in the future world Hunter series in
Warren Publishing Company's Eerie, issues 56 and 57 (April
and June 1974), by Bill Dubay and artist Paul Neary.   In
"Hunter: Blood Princess" and "Hunter: Demon-Killer," the
castle houses a nuclear bomb and the only existing member
of the Báthory family is the juvenile "Blood Princess."
"Blood Relation," by Manfred Oravec, published in Web Terror Stories, vol. 4, no. 6 (Nov. 1964), was influenced by the
film LA MASCHERA DEL DEMONIO. The sadistic tale, with
its many Dracula references, finds Elizabeth "Bartholy" entombed with a mask of spikes imbedded into her face.   Revived by a man's blood, her beauty tainted by the rotting
flesh of her torso, Elizabeth attacks her rescuer, making him
a vampire.   In 1973, Elizabeth Báthory was represented in
an exhibit at Hollywood's Weird Museum.

Chapter 3

THE ANCESTORS OF DRACULA

> With a plunge he seizes her neck in his fang-like
> teeth--a gush of blood, and a hideous sucking noise
> follows. The girl has swooned, and the vampyre
> is at his hideous repast!--Varney the Vampire
> (1847) by Thomas Preskett Prest

The nineteenth century was a productive period for
vampires in fiction. A quartet of literature's most enduring
vampires began their bloodthirsty careers during that hundred
years, and all of them had the distinction of influencing Bram
Stoker in his creation of Count Dracula. Like Count Dracula,
all four of these un-dead creatures bore impressive titles and
possessed the demeanor of nobility. They were Lord Ruthven,
Sir Francis Varney, Azzo, and Countess Mircalla Karnstein.

These celebrated vampires were the un-dead villains
of, respectively, "The Vampyre" (1819), by Dr. John Polidori; Varney the Vampire, or, The Feast of Blood (1847), by
Thomas Preskett Prest; "The Mysterious Stranger" (1860) and
"Carmilla" (1872), by Sheridan Le Fanu. Bram Stoker was
familiar with all four of these stories and there are traces
of all four un-dead creatures in his Count Dracula.

Lord Ruthven was the creation of Dr. John William
Polidori, the physician and personal secretary to Lord Byron,
whose scandalous adventures were the main gossip of the
Continent. Byron nicknamed Polidori "Polly-Dolly" and fre-
quently enjoyed sadistic humor at the doctor's expense. Lord
Ruthven would inevitably become the instrument through which
Polidori would seek revenge for Byron's ridicule.

"The Vampyre" was the result of an 1816 sojourn at
Lord Byron's summer house in Geneva, the Villa Diodati.
Among the friends present at the Villa were Polidori, Percy

Bysshe Shelley and Mary Godwin (the future wife of Shelley).
To pass the time, Byron suggested that they each invent a
ghost story.   Mary's contribution was the beginning of her
classic novel, Frankenstein; or, The Modern Prometheus.
Lord Byron provided the fragment of a proposed vampire
story.   The poet never completed his tale but the concept
was seized by Polidori who worked it up into "The Vampyre."

         What better way could there be for Polidori to ridicule
his occasional tormentor Lord Byron than to pattern his own
evil "vampyre" after the poet's image?   Byron had a reputation as a handsome philanderer whose effect upon beautiful
women was nearly fatal.   His single physical flaw was a
clubbed foot but the pale-faced Byron still managed to win
over virtually any woman he happened to desire.   Lord Ruthven, the "vampyre," shared the same title as his inspiration.
Like the poet, Ruthven was an exceedingly handsome character with a deathly pallor, whose mere presence was enough
to make women swoon with desire.   The Dracula image which
Bram Stoker presented to readers of his novel was that of a
creature of evil who yet remained attractive to females.
This image of a vampiric nobleman, with chalky face and a
dominating force over the opposite sex, definitely places Lord
Ruthven as an "ancestor" of Count Dracula and certainly as
a descendant of Byron who, at least symbolically, acted as a
vampire or human leech upon his hapless victim, John Polidori.   In this sense, two of fiction's most endurable horrors,
Count Dracula and Frankenstein's Monster, shared an origin
which germinated during that summer at Villa Diodati.   A
further association between Lords Byron and Ruthven was the
matter of a single physical deformity.   But while the poet's
masculine beauty was tarnished by a club foot, the vampire
possessed a "dead grey eye, which, fixing upon the object's
face, did not seem to penetrate, and at one glance to pierce
through the inward workings of the heart; but fell upon the
cheek with a leaden ray that weighed upon the skin it could
not pass. "

         The story was first published in the April 1, 1819 is-
sue of The New Monthly Magazine under the misleading title
"The Vampyre: a Tale by Lord Byron. " Byron's name was
associated with the story although he assured the public that
he was not the author.   When "The Vampyre" was finally
credited to its proper author, Byron dissolved all associations
with Polidori.   Many people continued, nonetheless, to link
the tale with Byron.

In "The Vampyre" Lord Ruthven becomes the sensation of an otherwise bored London society. A young man named Aubrey is fascinated by Ruthven and becomes his traveling companion, noticing that misery and misfortune follows in the nobleman's wake. In Greece Aubrey falls in love with Ianthe, a girl who instructs him in "vampyre" lore and is soon killed by such a monster. Bandits attack Aubrey and Lord Ruthven in the interior of Greece, shooting the latter in the shoulder. Dying, Ruthven makes Aubrey swear that for a full year and a day he will not reveal the facts of his crimes or that he has died, and that his corpse be placed on a nearby mountaintop and exposed to the first cold rays of the moon. Aubrey obeys, and later finds Ruthven's body missing from the pinnacle. Back in England, Aubrey learns that his sister is engaged to marry the revived Ruthven. The Lord casts Aubrey aside with his supernormal strength and the young man, still loyal to his oath, is unable to prevent Ruthven's marriage. "Lord Ruthven had disappeared, and Aubrey's sister had glutted the thirst of a Vampyre!" Ruthven is free to perpetrate crimes anew.

"The Vampyre," the Dracula of its day, was the first story of its type. In 1819 The Vampyre was issued as a volume in itself. The story became so popular that it was soon translated into many foreign languages. Cyprien Bérard wrote his own sequel to the tale in 1820, under the title, Lord Ruthwen ou les Vampires.

The first dramatization of Polidori's story LE VAMPIRE opened on June 13, 1820 at the Théâtre de la Porte-Saint-Martin in Paris. The melodrama was written by Charles Nodier and directed by M. M. Croznier and Merle. An actor known as Monsieur Philippe portrayed Lord "Rutwen." This version was set in Scotland with "Aubray" unaware that anything is amiss with his Lordship. The play continues with Rutwen about to sacrifice Malvina, "Miss Aubray" (Madame Dorval), at the nuptial altar. But the mystic hour of one o'clock ends Rutwen's power. LE VAMPIRE was ridiculed by the critics but was nevertheless a sensational success. The book of the play, Le Vampire, mélodrame en trois actes avec un prologue, went into immediate publication and enjoyed its own immense popularity. Alexander Dumas attended the 1823 revival of LE VAMPIRE and was so impressed that he praised the play in Mes Mémoires (1863), even comparing one of the characters in Le Comte de Monte Cristo (1844-45) to Lord Ruthven.

In 1851 Dumas wrote his own play of LE VAMPIRE which opened on December 20 at the Ambigu-Comique theatre. Lord "Ruthwen" was played by Monsieur Arnault. Dumas added a female Ghoul (Lucie Mabire) to his play and stated that the vampire must claim victims if he is to survive. A group of travelers stop at a notoriously haunted castle and begin to talk about vampires. Ruthwen makes his appearance and proceeds to attack members of the group. When young Gilbert de Tiffauges (M. Goujet) sees Ruthwen making an attack he stabs him with his sword. Dying, Ruthwen tricks the man into exposing him to the first rays of the new moon. The Ghoul then reveals to Gilbert how to destroy the revived vampire. The play ends with Gilbert Finding Ruthwen's grave in a deserted cemetery and impaling his heart with a sword rubbed with a mystic ointment and blessed by a priest.

After the phenomenal success of LE VAMPIRE, the Parisian theatre was swept by an epidemic of "vampire-mania." Vampire plays abounded, some of which were new versions of the Polidori tale. There was LE FILS VAMPIRE by Paul Féval. A comedy entitled LE VAMPIRE presented on June 15, 1820 at the Vaudeville in one act with seventeen scenes. Adolphe de Valberg (M. Isambert) arrives at a castle in Hungary, claiming to be the English Lord "Ruthwen," and terrifies the superstitious servants. Another comedy titled LE VAMPIRE, by Martin Joseph Mengals, played on March 1, 1826 at the Ghent theatre.

The Nodier version of the play was adapted by James Robinson Planché as THE VAMPIRE, OR, THE BRIDE OF THE ISLES, opening on August 9, 1820 at the English Opera House or Lyceum Theatre in London. T. P. (Thomas Potter) Cooke played Lord Ruthven. As the play was set in Scotland due to the preference of manager and proprietor Samuel James Arnold, Cooke wore a plaid kilt, a silver breast plate with steel buttons, a Scotch hat with feathers, leggings, and a sword and dagger. A special trapdoor called the "Vampire trap," through which Cooke could disappear, was invented for the production. This version of the play was also extremely successful.

DER VAMPYR was an opera presented on March 28, 1828 at Leipzig, Germany with the tale now set in Hungary. Planché then wrote his own version of the drama titled DER VAMPYR and booked it on August 25, 1829 into the Lyceum, where his earlier version had played. On September 21, 1828 another opera of the story played at Stuttgart and was adver-

tised as being based on Lord Byron's story. EIN VAMPYR,
by Ulrich Franks, was a farce based on LE VAMPIRE, by
Eugene Scribe and Mélesville, and played in Vienna in 1877.

THE VAMPIRE was a three-act version of the story
by Dion Boucicault, which opened on June 19, 1852 at the
Princess' Theatre in London.   Boucicault himself portrayed
the vampire and later revived the play as THE PHANTOM.
Alan Raby (new name for Ruthven), also known as The Phantom, was clothed entirely in black with a velvet cloak and
hat.   His head was partially bald, with long black hair swept
back behind his ears.   The face was "phosphoric livid" and
he had a black mustache and bushy eyebrows.   The first act
is set during the reign of Charles II in the ruins of the haunted Raby castle where Lucy Peveryl (Agnes Robertson) and her
fugitive cousin Roland are to rendevous.   But it is Alan Raby,
incognito as a puritan named Gervase Rookwood, who arrives.
A traitor and guilty of fratricide, Raby was once hurled from
a window but his body was never recovered.   When Raby is
discovered with a bloodless victim, he is shot but is revived
by the moon as the curtain falls.   The second act, set a century later, proceeded with "Rookwood," dressed in more modern black clothing, placing Ada Raby (again Agnes Robertson),
daughter of the castle's present owner, under his power.
But the vampire is finally discovered by Dr. Rees (Mr. Burnett), a student of the supernatural who shoots him with a
charmed bullet and casts his body into a deep chasm.

A burlesque entitled THE VAMPIRE, by R. Reece,
opened at the Royal Strand Theatre on August 18, 1872; it
was based on German legends, "Lord Byron's story" and
THE PHANTOM.   Edward Terry played vampire Allan Raby
as an errie figure who haunts Raby Castle, preying on the
minds and notes of two female novelists, vampirizing their
writings for his "penny dreadful" market and for his own
three-volume novel.

"The Vampyre" reached the motion picture screen--
or at least, almost reached the screen--in 1945, through the
courtesy of Republic Pictures.   THE VAMPIRE'S GHOST was
conceived as a screen adaptation of the Polidori story.   But
Republic, a studio primarily known for Westerns, movie
serials and other action films, had a penchant for tampering
with the properties they acquired.   Since "The Vampyre" was
in the public domain there was no one (save the purists who
would have preferred the film to remain true to Polidori) to
offend.   Thus Leigh Brackett was told to change her original

screen treatment which followed the Polidori tale and to alter
it to meet the demands of a typical Republic action picture.

The locale for THE VAMPIRE'S GHOST became Africa, with the natives somehow inheriting the vampire traditions of European peasants.   British actor John Abbott portrayed Webb Fallon, a vampire cursed since Elizabethan
times.   This was a vampire alien to horror movie fans accustomed to the Dracula films being made by Universal Pictures.   He did not sleep in a coffin but carried a miniature
casket containing some of his native soil.   The vampire
walked through the jungle during the brightest daylight, shielding his eyes with sunglasses.   Like Stoker's Count Dracula,
this vampire did not cast a reflection in a mirror.   Of this
scene, John Abbott informed the present writer: "They band-
aged my head and hands up in black and photographed me up
against a black background.   Then I held up a wine glass and
drank.   You could see the glass being held up by an invisible
hand.   There was no head.   Then I suppose they superimposed
the actual background on top of it.   You looked invisible except for the material things--coats and collars and wine
glasses."   Another effect shows the mirror shattering as the
vampire looks into the glass.

While leading an expedition to a lost temple in the
jungle, Webb Fallon is recognized by the natives as a vàm-
pire.   One of them hurls a spear into Fallon's chest.   Fallon
then instructs a member of the expedition to place his body,
à la Ruthven, beneath the rising moon, which restores him
to life (the only scene retained from Polidori).   While continuing his bloodthirsty attacks on the members of the expedition, the vampire finally comes to the temple and is there
eventually destroyed by fire.   THE VAMPIRE'S GHOST, which
presented no ghost, was directed by Lesley Selander.   A
legitimate motion picture based on the Polidori story, simply
entitled THE VAMPYRE, was announced in 1973.

For my own fiction writings, in tribute to Polidori's
story, I have invented the Ruthvenian, described as an extremely rare book with its title emblazoned on a copper cover
in blood-red gothic script.   The Ruthvenian is the ancient bible of the vampires, categorizing their traits and including
mystic spells applicable to the un-dead.

The first appearance of Lord Ruthven in comic strip
form was in an adaptation of "The Vampyre" in the first issue of Vampire Tales (1973), published by the Marvel Comics

Group. The story was written by Roy Thomas and drawn by
Winslow Mortimer and ends with Aubrey learning of his sister's engagement. Ruthven, Mircalla and Varney also appeared in "Dracula's Vampire Legion," in The Occult Files
of Dr. Spektor (see Chapter 12).

Successor to Lord Ruthven was Sir Francis Varney,
the un-dead antihero of Thomas Preskett Prest's mammoth
piece of fiction, Varney the Vampire, or, The Feast of Blood,
published in 1847. Prest was an unbelievably prolific writer
of lurid novels of mystery and horror, some of his other
titles being Sweeney Todd, the Demon Barber of Fleet Street;
The Skeleton Clutch, or, The Goblet of Gore; and Sawney
Bean, the Man-eater of Midlothian. Varney the Vampire was
Prest's masterpiece, if such a word may be attributed to the
"penny dreadful" market for which he wrote. The book consisted of 220 chapters and 868 pages, certainly the longest
vampire epic ever written. Varney the Vampire provided a
staggering amount of horrors and thrills for anyone patient
enough to stay with it to the end.

Sir Francis Varney was originally known as Marma-
duke Bannesworth who had committed suicide, for which heinous act he was condemned to live the dark existence of a
vampire. He was described as a tall, cadaverous man, "cold
and clammy like a corpse" and with "eyes like polished tin."
A century later, in the 1730s, Varney haunts Ratford Abbey
and engages in a long chain of adventures. Unlike most vampires, Varney is not totally corrupt. Unable to curb his unearthly thirst, Varney attacks young maidens, attracting them
with the suavity and force of a Lord Ruthven or Count Dracula. As Prest was paid by the word, he heaped a tonnage of
adjectives and figures of speech upon the reader. Varney is
supposedly killed by almost every method imaginable (stakings,
bullets, and hangings, to name a few), only to be repeatedly
resurrected, like Ruthven, by the rays of the moon. Varney
finally tires of his loathsome existence and decides to commit a permanent suicide that even the moonbeams cannot rec-
tify: he climaxes his vampiric career by leaping into the
active crater of Mount Vesuvius.

Like Bram Stoker, Prest researched the vampire
legends before writing Varney the Vampire, or, The Feast of
Blood, increasing its value to scholars of the occult. The
original edition of the book (and its reprint in "penny parts"
in 1853) is extremely scarce and those modern day readers
who wanted to read the entire 868 pages had to wait for a re-

print in 1971.   Varney, as Lord Ruthven, also extended his career to the theatre.

While Count Dracula owes much of his image to Lord Ruthven and Sir Francis Varney, the similarity of his story to another vampire tale is too close for it to be sheer coincidence.   Bram Stoker had probably read "The Mysterious Stranger," a German vampire story published about 1860 in a volume entitled Odds and Ends.   The story chronicled an adventure with a knight named Azzo, who proved to be as horrendous a vampire as Ruthven or Varney.   Azzo's story seems to have been a prototype for the plot of Dracula.   Like his predecessors, Azzo, his repulsive nature notwithstanding, is somehow considered attractive by his female victims.

"The Mysterious Stranger," like Dracula, was set in the Carpathian Mountains where a small group of people, including a young woman named Franziska, come to the ruins of the reputedly haunted Castle Klatka.   There, they are beset by wolves when a man dressed like a soldier of some former time appears from the shadows and scares off the beasts with a gesture (as Dracula would in Stoker's novel).   The group returns to the castle at a later date to find the coffin of one "Ezzelinus de Klatka, Eques."   Again Franziska encounters the mysterious stranger--a thin, pale man with grey eyes, short black hair and a black beard.   Identifying himself as Azzo, he refuses to drink wine.   Azzo begins to visit Franziska, growing healthier in appearance as she shows signs of anemia, complains of dreams about a nocturnal visitor and exhibits wounds on her neck.   It is Woislaw, a giant knight with a metal spring-operated hand to compensate for one lost in battle, who learns the true nature of Azzo.   When Woislaw grasps Azzo with his artificial hand, the vampire mistakes him for another creature possessing supernatural strength.   Woislaw takes Franziska to the ancient coffin of Ezzelinus de Klata, finding the corpse of Azzo.   To be well again, Franziska performs the ritual prescribed by Woislaw-- driving three long nails through the coffin lid and letting the escaping blood touch the wounds on her neck.

Lord Ruthven, Varney and Azzo were the male ancestors of Dracula.   But the King of Vampires also relied upon a female of the species for his own existence in literature. The vampiress was named Countess Mircalla Karnstein.   She was the villainess of the short novel "Carmilla," written by Dublin author Sheridan Le Fanu and first published in a collection of his stories entitled In a Glass Darkly (1872).   Fol-

lowing his wife's untimely death, Le Fanu became a recluse
and devoted his time to writing. In the years before he died
his writings usually focused upon the supernatural, his best
being the gothic tale, "Carmilla." Le Fanu, like Stoker and
her predecessors, researched vampire lore for his story and
applied his findings especially to the condition of the vampire's body and the methods employed in her destruction.

"Carmilla" opens with the lovely heroine, Laura, recalling a childhood dream about a strange woman appearing
at her bedside in a castle in Styria and inflicting puncture
marks upon her neck. Twelve years later Laura meets a
beautiful young victim of a wagon wreck and takes her in as
a house guest. The visitor says her name is Carmilla.
Laura insists that she was the woman in her dream and Carmilla states that she had dreamed of the young Laura twelve
years earlier. To Laura's amazement, Carmilla looks identical to a 1698 portrait of Countess Mircalla Karnstein, even
to the long brown hair and the mole on her neck. A close
relationship steeped in lesbian implications develops between
Carmilla and Laura, the former suffering inexplicable visita-
tions by a monstrous cat and a female phantom which leave
her weak and drained of energy. When a general visits the
schloss with a similar story about a vampire named Millarca
who destroyed his daughter, Carmilla is deduced to be Millarca and Mircalla, Countess Karnstein. Carmilla is discovered in a blood-filled coffin in the ruins of the Karnstein
Castle and is promptly staked, beheaded and cremated.

Bram Stoker first read "Carmilla" when he was not
yet twenty-four years old. The tale retained an important
niche in his imagination and was perhaps his greatest inspiration to write his own vampire novel more than a decade later.
He would even pay tribute to Le Fanu in his posthumously
published story, "Dracula's Guest," acknowledging a story
which had been, previous to Dracula, the greatest vampire
tale ever written.

Mircalla, Countess Karnstein, returned to her blood-
and woman-lusting existence in the century following her de-
struction--on the motion picture screen, in comic strips, on
television and even phonograph records. VAMPYR (known in
England as THE STRANGE ADVENTURE OF DAVID GRAY),*

---

*In 1943 General Foreign Sales Corporation released VAMPYR
in the United States as THE VAMPIRE. The film was also
given the American title CASTLE OF DOOM. In 1943 scenes

made independently by Carl Dreyer in 1932, was loosely based
on "Carmilla. " David Gray (Julian West, actually Baron
Nicolas de Gunzburg, who helped finance the production) arrives at a village inn where a mysterious old man (played by
Maurice Schutz) gives him a package to be opened if the latter dies. Following the shadow of a one-legged gamekeeper,
Gray comes during a witch's Sabbath upon a house where the
village doctor gives an old woman (played by Henriette Ge-
rard) a flask of poison and the gamekeeper builds a coffin.
Again following the gamekeeper's shadow, Gray comes upon
the chateau of the old man, who dies of a bullet wound and
leaves two daughters. The older daughter Leone (Sybille
Schmitz) is fading away from an unknown malady. Gray opens
the package and finds a book, Strange Tales of the Vampires.
He gives Leone a transfusion upon the doctor's request.
While his blood is being drained from him, Gray envisions
himself locked in a coffin, with a vampire (the old woman)
peering at him through the lid's transom. Gray regains consciousness in a graveyard where he discovers the grave of
the real vampire--the old woman. A servant from the chateau rams an iron pole through her heart. After the vampire decomposes to dust, the doctor, gamekeeper and other
accomplices are driven to their deaths by the ghosts of the
monster's victims and Leone returns to normal.

VAMPYR is regarded by critics as one of the true
masterpieces of the horror film, a picture of atmosphere and
subtlety. Dreyer had cinematographer Rudolph Maté shoot his
scenes through gauze to impart an eerie dreamlike quality to
the film. David Gray's graveyard journey became even more
terrifying with the camera replacing him in the casket. VAM-
PYR was a mood piece, and it disappointed audiences expect-
ing to see a more traditional Dracula-type film. It was thus
quite unsuccessful.

More in accord with public tastes was the second
"Carmilla" film, ET MOURIR DE PLAISIR ("And Die of Pleasure"), which was made in color by E. G. E. Films and Italian
Documento in 1960. Roger Vadim directed and his wife, the
beautiful blonde actress Annette Vadim, portrayed Carmilla
von Karnstein. Carmilla is possessed by the spirit of a long-
entombed vampire. The lesbian elements in the Le Fanu

from VAMPYR were incorporated into the National Roadshow
film, DR. TERROR'S HOUSE OF HORRORS. More recently,
scenes from the Dreyer film were seen in Pedro Portabella's
documentary, VAMPIR.

novelette were more blatant in this French/Italian film, one
scene showing Carmilla tenderly kissing a drop of blood from
the lips of beautiful Georgia Monteverdi (Elsa Martinelli)
while the camera held on their frozen embrace. In another
sequence Carmilla dreams that she is the victim in some
bizarre operation, and in yet another she beholds her reflection in a mirror and sees herself covered with blood. According to the lore of ET MOURIR DE PLAISER the vampire
must return to its grave once each night. While hurrying to
the tomb of the vampire's corpse, Carmilla stumbles upon a
wooden shaft that pierces her breast. A censored American
version of the film was released the following year by Paramount, with the title BLOOD AND ROSES. A paperback
novel of Blood and Roses, by Robin Carlisle, was published
by Hillman in 1960.

   A rather faithful adaptation of "Carmilla" was LA
MALDICION DE LOS KARNSTEINS ("The Curse of the Karnsteins"), made by Hispaner Films in Spain and Mec Cinematografica of Italy in 1963 and released in the United States
by American-International as TERROR IN THE CRYPT. *
Christopher Lee** portrayed Count Ludwig Karnstein. Using
the mystic pentagram, Ludwig's housekeeper summons the
spirit of a vampiress, executed centuries ago, to take revenge upon the Karnsteins. During the film's climax, Laura
is led through the woods by the blonde stranger who had appeared at the castle. But when the vampire corpse is staked
in her crypt, the stranger dies and vanishes. The film is
often dull in its direction by Camillo Mastrocinque (also
known as Thomas Miller), but is beautifully atmospheric,
photographed in black and white by Julio Ortas. In the late
1960s Carmilla's daughter was featured in a short film,
VAMPIRE (see Chapter 9).

   "Carmilla" became the basis for a series of color motion pictures in the 1970s, with Hammer Films in England
discovering that Le Fanu's vampire could even rival their

---

*The film was released in England with the title CRYPT OF
HORROR, in France as LY CRYPTE DU VAMPIRE, and in
Italy as LA CRIPTA E L'INCUBO ("The Crypt of the Incubus").
The film is also known as THE KARNSTEIN CURSE, KARN-
STEIN, CATHARSIS and simply CARMILLA.
   **In an Italian fumetti magazine adapted from LA
MALDICION DE LOS KARNSTEINS, Christopher Lee was de-
picted on the cover as a fanged vampire, to capitalize on his
Dracula reputation.

seemingly indefatigable Count Dracula.   THE VAMPIRE LOV-
ERS (1970) was made in association with American-International Pictures and was directed by Roy Ward Baker.   The
film explored the lesbian possibilities of the theme and received an "R" rating in the United States.   THE VAMPIRE
LOVERS retained Le Fanu's vampire image: Carmilla can
transform into a cat, vanish and reappear somewhere else,
and her victims simply die from her attacks.

A single vampire escapes when a vengeful baron destroys the un-dead of the Karnstein castle.   Years later a
beautiful woman named Marcilla (voluptuous Ingrid Pitt in her
first vampire role) is introduced to the social world by a
countess (Dawn Addams).   Marcilla lures Laura (Pippa Steele)
away from her fiancé and satisfies her bloodlust by biting the
girl's left breast, causing her to die.   Emma Morton (Made-
leine Smith) is the next victim of the vampire, now called
Carmilla.   A doctor (Ferdy Mayne) deduces that a vampire
is sapping away Emma's blood.   Finally, vampire killer
Baron Hartog (Douglas Wilmer), the General (Peter Cushing)
and Carl (John Finch), Laura's father and fiancé respectively,
go to the grave of the Karnstein vampiress, taking her body
to a chapel where it is staked and beheaded. *   A paperback
book of The Vampire Lovers, including "Carmilla" and other
Le Fanu stories, was published in 1970 by Fontana Books.

LUST FOR A VAMPIRE (filmed as TO LOVE A VAM-
PIRE) was the first sequel to THE VAMPIRE LOVERS.   The
film was directed by Jimmy Sangster and released in 1971 by
American Continental Films.   Portraying Mircalla Karnstein
was blonde Yutte Stensgaard, a Danish beauty as fetching as
Ms. Pitt in her scoop neck and diaphanous gowns.   As Count
Karnstein, Mike Raven, attired in black with a long scarlet-
lined cloak, and with hair cut into a widow's peak, resembled
Christopher Lee.   The resemblance was hardly accidental,
since the close-ups of Count Karnstein's eyes were actually
stock shots of Lee from one of his Dracula films.

Mircalla is revived by the Count and his wife, by the
blood of a young woman, and is enrolled in a girl's school
near the castle.   The villagers grumble when the vampiric
attacks resume.   Giles Barton (Ralph Bates), a student of the
supernatural who is secretly in love with Mircalla, sees her

---

*Scenes from THE VAMPIRE LOVERS appeared on a tele-
vision screen, watched by another vampire, in THE RETURN
OF COUNT YORGA.

kill one of her roommates during a midnight swim.   After
hiding the corpse, he too is killed by the vampire.   Richard
Lestrange, an author of horror stories, next falls in love with
Mircalla but discovers her secret through Barton's notes.
Mircalla attempts to save her parents when the villagers set
the Karnstein castle on fire.   Lestrange then attempts to save
the woman he loves from the fire but is instead attacked by
her.   Impaled through the chest by a burning rafter, Mircalla
becomes a rotting corpse.   A novel of the movie, Lust for a
Vampire, by William Hughes, was published that year in England by Sphere Books and in New York by Beagle Books.

Hammer's third entry in the series was TWINS OF
EVIL (originally announced as THE GEMINI TWINS and then
VIRGIN VAMPIRES), directed by John Hough and released in
1972.   Maria and Frieda Gelhourn (Madelaine and Mary Col-
linson), identical twins, come to the village of Karnstein to
reside with their Uncle Gustav Weil (Peter Cushing), leader
of a witch-hunting group called the Brotherhood.   When a
vampire preys upon the populace (with the wicked doomed to
become un-dead), suspicion falls upon the newest Count Karnstein (Damien Thomas) who is not a vampire.   In trying to
summon Satan, the jaded Count sacrifices a young girl, whose
blood enters Mircalla's coffin and revives the vampiress.   Attacked by Mircalla, the Count becomes a vampire and soon
makes Frieda a sanguinary creature like himself.   The Count
switches the twins, leaving the innocent Maria in danger of
being burned as a witch at Weil's stake.   Frieda attempts to
save her sister but is decapitated by the leader of the Brotherhood.   Capturing Maria, the Count murders Weil with an
axe but is soon destroyed by a lance thrust through his heart.

The same studio took a side-excursion on the Carmilla
theme in 1972 with the film CAPTAIN KRONOS: VAMPIRE
HUNTER (originally titled simply KRONOS), written and directed by Brian Clemens and released in color by Paramount
the following year.   Captain Kronos (Horst Janson) is a nineteenth century swashbuckler who specializes in destroying the
Un-Dead.   The vampires in this film proved to be a unique
species, draining away their victims' youth.   Toward the end
of the film, the vampiress Lady Durward (Wanda Ventham)
admits to having been born a Karnstein (or "Karstein").
Kronos defeats her vampiric husband in a sword fight, after
which Lady Durward joins him in aging to a withered corpse.
Another sequel was announced by Hammer in 1974.

LA FILLE DE DRACULA ("The Daughter of Dracula")

was actually another "Carmilla" movie. Jesus Franco directed
this 1972 color French/Spanish/Portuguese co-production released by Le Comptoir Français du Film. Britt Nichols portrayed the vampiress in this modern day tale, while Howard
Vernon, who had played Dracula in an earlier Franco film,
appeared as Count Karnstein. LA NOVIA ENSANGRENTADA
("The Bloody Fiancée" or "The Bloody Bride") was yet another "Carmilla" film made that year. The Spanish picture
was directed by Carlos Duran and starred Alexandra Bastedo
as Mircalla. A new CARMILLA was announced in 1974.

"Carmilla" was adapted to British television's MYS-
TERY AND IMAGINATION series in the late sixties; to a
comic strip by Robert Jenney in Creepy, no. 19 (March 1968);
and as a record album, Carmilla, A Vampire Tale (Vanguard,
1972), by the Etc Company of La Mamma, New York, directed by Wilford Leach and John Braswell. In 1970 Dover
Publications published two Le Fanu stories under the over-
all title, Carmilla & The Haunted Barnet.

Lord Ruthven, Sir Francis Varney, Azzo, and Mircalla, Countess Karnstein had all come before the notice of
Bram Stoker. Within his own imagination was the germ of
a story of vampirism and gothic horror. And while Ruthven
and the others slumbered in their graves, the King of all the
Un-Dead would soon rise from his own castle crypt and make
his eternal impression upon the world.

Chapter 4

BRAM STOKER'S CLASSIC

> ... There seemed a strange stillness over every-
> thing; but as I listened I heard as if from down
> below in the valley the howling of many wolves.
> The Count's eyes gleamed, and he said--
>   'Listen to them--the children of the night.
> What music they make!'--Dracula, by Bram Stoker

The author of the novel Dracula was born in November 1847 in Dublin, Ireland. Bram Stoker was a sickly child
born to Abraham and Charlotte Stoker. The doctor who delivered the boy feared that Bram would not survive. It was
only the care of his parents and young Bram's own determina-
tion to survive that kept him alive. Anyone looking at the
outspoken adult Bram Stoker, with his large and sturdy frame
and full beard, would find it difficult to believe that he had
been a frail child whose legs would not permit him to walk
until he was eight years old. During the eight years in
which Bram was bed-ridden he had developed a shyness which
led him to find his friends within the pages of his father's
collection of books. At the age of sixteen, Bram's interest
in literature had grown into a desire to write. He also developed a deep love for the theatre and for publications about
the stage.

Bram Stoker entered Trinity College, Dublin in November of 1864. During his years at Trinity, the husky
Irishman attended an event which would be one of the incidents that would lead to his writing the world's greatest vampire novel, Dracula. The nineteen-year-old Stoker had attended the Theatre Royal to see a performance of THE RI-
VALS. Featured in the production was an actor named Henry

Opposite: Portrait of Bram Stoker taken six years after the
publication of Dracula

Irving whose performance affected Bram's spirit permanently.
Bram would never forget his elation over Irving's powerful
performance. Someday the lean face which dominated the
theatre stage that night would find a strange immortality in
the pale visage of the King of Vampires.

In 1870, Bram Stoker graduated from Trinity College.
When Irving returned to Dublin with the play TWO ROSES
and the local newspapers failed even to mention the actor's
name or evaluate his performance, the infuriated Stoker
stormed into the editorial offices of the Dublin Mail. Having
thoroughly convinced the editor of the newspaper that the publication needed a drama critic, Stoker himself acquired the
position but worked without payment. His first column appeared in the Dublin Mail in November 1871.

The following year, Bram Stoker discovered "Carmilla," the great vampire story written by another Dublin author,
Sheridan Le Fanu. But although the story of Countess Karnstein aroused in him ideas for his own vampire tale, his
position with the Dublin Mail left him no time to devote to
such a task.

Stoker's writing career began to show more promise
when he took over continuation of a serial entitled The Chain
of Destiny which was being run in a periodical called Sham-
rock. The story was rich in phantoms and curses and romance. Bram then began to write a novel based on the terrible stories his mother had related to him about the cholera
plague that struck Sligo, Ireland in 1832.

All the while Bram Stoker continued to write praises
for the acting of Henry Irving. Flattered by the honors repeatedly showered upon him by Stoker, Irving wanted to meet
the young Irishman. Irving was already a star of the Shakespearean stage when he met Bram Stoker for the first time
in 1876. The respect and admiration the two had for each
other was deep. From that moment Bram Stoker and Henry
Irving enjoyed a friendship and partnership which would endure until the actor's death on October 13, 1905. While on
tour in Glasgow, Irving sent a telegram to Stoker, requesting
his presence. When Stoker arrived Irving informed him that
he had taken over the management of the Lyceum Theatre in
London and required the services of an acting-manager.
Bram immediately resigned from previous commitments, married Florence (whom he had not planned to wed until the following year) and promptly assumed the position at the Lyceum.

While fulfilling his duties at the Lyceum Theatre, Stoker continued to apply his creative talents to writing. He continued functioning as drama critic, newspaper editor and author of fiction. He developed his ability to convey horror through dramatic prose, always remembering his mother's narrative of the cholera epidemic and "Carmilla."

An introduction significant to the creation of Dracula occurred in 1890 when Bram Stoker made the acquaintance of Professor Arminius Vambery from the University of Budapest. Vambery, whose title was Professor of Oriental Languages, was a scholar and traveler, and his tales of other lands were absorbed by the fascinated Stoker. Among Vambery's stories were accounts and legends of vampires--bloodsucking creatures neither dead nor alive but un-dead--which were believed to have existed in such remote areas of the world as the mountains of Transylvania. The tales of vampires augmented Stoker's interest in Le Fanu's "Carmilla."

Vambery's descriptions of Transylvania further prompted Stoker's imagination. Transylvania, a province which then belonged to Hungary, certainly seemed to possess an aura of romance and mystery. Its mountains, castles and superstitious peasants provided the necessary background for a supernatural story and its very geographical remoteness from nineteenth century London would perhaps lend credibility to the hideous creatures of legend.

His imagination whetted by Vambery's stories and by the lingering images of "Carmilla," Bram Stoker one night had a nightmare (which he later jovially attributed to indigestion resulting from a dinner of crab meat) about a dreadful and powerful vampire. This was no mundane living corpse who attacked slumbering maidens in diaphanous nightgowns, but rather a King Vampire who reigned with demonic supremacy over all the un-dead.

Thus inspired, Bram Stoker set upon writing the ultimate vampire story. He began to haunt the British Museum Library. There, he studied every published account of vampirism that he could find, until he had become a veritable authority on vampire traditions. He also studied maps and books about Transylvania so that his own novel would be both geographically and historically accurate.

During his extensive research at the British Museum, Stoker uncovered writings pertaining to Vlad the Impaler,

widely known as Dracula. Vlad's preference for impaling his
victims (a method of destroying vampires) and the Voivode's
bloodthirsty nature further inflamed Stoker's imagination.
The name Vlad, or Dracula, could still frighten the peasant
children of Transylvania. Whether or not this historical
Dracula ever really drank blood was not important. Stoker
was a writer and his mind associated the sanguinary practices of the legendary vampire with the bloodthirsty character
of Vlad. Stoker also combined these two elements with the
real-life vampire bat whose habits were so similar to the
legendary un-dead. Retaining the powerful sounding name ascribed to Vlad Tepes, Stoker amalgamated the fruits of his
research. The resulting character was a powerful figure who
loomed above his bloodsucking kin, a black-garbed monarch
of all the evil un-dead who issue from their graves at night,
hungering for warm blood. This was the King Vampire:
Count Dracula.

DRACULA

Dracula, Bram Stoker's masterpiece, was published
in a small and unimpressive looking hard-bound volume with
a brown cover by Constable, a London company, in May,
1897.

Stoker had utilized the knowledge gained from his days
as a newspaper editor. He employed a series of intricately
woven first-hand accounts--journals, diaries, newspaper
clippings, letters, phonograph records and so forth--to give
the novel immediacy and authenticity. The style also was
indebted to Wilkie Collins, whom he admired. Stoker, however, found himself writing in various styles and from a number of different viewpoints. He was also hampered by the
feminine attitudes of those unliberated years. Despite such
obstacles, Stoker managed successfully to interconnect his
myriad accounts into a lengthy and complex novel.

Dracula beings with the journal of Jonathan Harker, a
real estate agent from London, sent by his employer, Peter
Hawkins, to transact a sale of property with a certain Count
Dracula who resides in an ancient castle in the Carpathian
Mountains of Transylvania. On the opening page of his journal Harker reveals that his knowledge of that wild area came
from the source Stoker himself visited--the British Museum.

Jonathan Harker finds Transylvania a rugged frontier, with jagged mountain peaks and hazardous mountain roads. The peasants in the area exhibit a strange apprehension when he reveals that his destination is Castle Dracula. They cross themselves and implore him not to journey to that mysterious place. But when Harker makes it plain that he must fulfill his mission, the wife of the landlord of the hotel at Bistritz gives him a small rosary to wear, "For your mother's sake."

Securing passage by stagecoach, Harker rides through the splendid mountains and woods of Transylvania, noting the natural splendor of his surroundings. The sky has already grown dark as the coach reaches the Borgo Pass, where Count Dracula's own coach is to meet them. Harker's fellow passengers begin to cross themselves as a calèche drawn by four black horses rushes beside the coach. The driver is a tall man with a long brown beard and wearing a large black hat. Harker notices that the strange driver's eyes are bright and red, that his lips are a dark crimson and his teeth resemble sharpened ivory. When the driver helps Harker down from the coach Harker is impressed by his apparently titanic strength. As the man in black takes Harker along the Borgo Pass, the calèche is suddenly surrounded by a pack of hungry, snarling wolves. Then the driver performs an incredible act: he simply raises his hands and utters a forceful command, and the wolves obediently disperse. (The driver is, of course, actually the Count in disguise.) The remainder of the journey to Castle Dracula is uneventful.

At the time- and battle-worn Castle Dracula, Harker is greeted by an old man clad totally in black, carrying an antique silver lamp in his hand. "Welcome to my house!" He beckons invitingly, "Enter freely and of your own will!"

Harker inquires if the man in black is his host, and he replies, "I am Dracula; and I bid you welcome, Mr. Harker, to my house. Come in; the night air is chill, and you must need to eat and rest."

The image of the Count with which Bram Stoker presented readers of Dracula was a composite from several sources. The legends he had researched at the British Museum provided the basic description of the traditional vampire image. "The Vampyre" by Polidori and Varney the Vampire, or, The Feast of Blood by Prest presented the then popular conception of a vampire as a nobleman with great power and attraction for the female sex. In researching the

historical Dracula, Vlad the Impaler, Stoker may also have
come upon a picture of that Prince whose egregious crimes
rivaled the fictional atrocities of the King of Vampires. But
the final contributing factor to Stoker's depiction of Count
Dracula was the man the author worshiped, Henry Irving.
Just as Dr. Polidori had patterned his Lord Ruthven after
Lord Byron, Stoker drew upon the lean strong face of Irving
for his conception of Count Dracula.

In the May 5 entry to his journal, Harker records his
own observance of Count Dracula.

> His face was a strong--a very strong--aqui-
> line, with high bridge of the thin nose and particu-
> larly arched nostrils; with lofty domed forehead,
> and hair growing scantily around the temples but
> profusely elsewhere. His eyebrows were very mas-
> sive, almost meeting over the nose, and with bushy
> hair that seemed to curl in its own profusion. The
> mouth, so far as I could see it under the heavy
> mustache, was fixed rather cruel-looking, with pe-
> culiarly sharp white teeth; those protruded over the
> lips, whose remarkable ruddiness showed astonish-
> ing vitality in a man of his years. For the rest,
> his ears were pale, and at the tops extremely
> pointed; the chin was broad and strong, and the
> cheeks firm though thin. The general effect was
> one of extreme pallor.
> Hitherto I had noticed the backs of his hands
> as they lay on his knees in the firelight, and they
> had seemed rather white and fine; but seeing them
> now close to me, I could not but notice that they
> were rather coarse--broad with squat fingers.
> Strange to say, there were hairs in the centre of
> the palm. The nails were long and fine, and cut
> to a sharp point. As the Count leaned over me and
> his hands touched me, I could not repress a shudder.
> It may have been that his breath was rank, but a
> horrible feeling of nausea came over me, which, do
> what I would, I could not conceal.

The tradition of the gothic novel had become one of
mystery and romance, with the apparently supernatural phenomenon inevitably revealed through purely natural (albeit unlikely) explanations. Readers of gothic fiction had come to
expect that the spectral monk or headless ghost haunting the
ruins of the chateau would be revealed as a villain who,

through ingenious trickery, is attempting to frighten the innocent heroine out of her inheritance or some other desirable
prize. But Dracula centered upon horrors which were, within the context of the story, real.

Jonathan Harker becomes aware of the authentic terrors of Castle Dracula in the opening chapters of the novel.
To his perplexity, Harker notices that his titled host is always absent during the daylight hours.

The estate called Carfax, which Dracula is purchasing
in London through Harker's employer, Peter Hawkins, dates
back to medieval times and is nearly as gloomy and forboding
as Castle Dracula itself. In one scene Harker shaves himself before a small mirror. (There are no other mirrors in
the entire castle.) Dracula approaches him from behind and
Harker notices that the Count casts no reflection in the mirror. Harker cuts his finger on the razor and when the Count
beholds the blood he is seized by a demonic rage and grabs
at the man's throat. But when Dracula encounters the rosary
and cross strung around Harker's neck "for his mother's
sake," he recoils from them in horror.

After sunrise, Harker learns the truth of his predicament.

> ... The castle is on the very edge of a terrific
> precipice. A stone falling from the window would
> fall a thousand feet without touching anything! As
> far as the eye can reach is a sea of green tree
> tops, with occasionally a deep rift where there is
> a chasm. Here and there are silver threads where
> the rivers wind in deep gorges through the forests.
> But I am not in heart to describe beauty,
> for when I had seen the view I explored further;
> doors, doors, doors everywhere, and all locked and
> bolted. In no place save from the windows in the
> castle walls is there an available exit.
> The castle is a veritable prison, and I am
> a prisoner!

Harker decides it is best not to arouse the Count's
suspicions about what he is only beginning to comprehend.
The following midnight the two of them chat, with Dracula in-
forming the Englishman of his family's past history. He
claims to be a descendant of Attila the Hun. Again Stoker
utilizes the fruits of his British Museum research through the

dialogue of one of his characters. When Count Dracula speaks
of a certain "ancestor" he not only is recounting his own existence before returning from the dead as a vampire; he also
spouts the history of Vlad the Impaler as re-edited by Stoker.

> ... Who was it but one of my own race who as
> Voivode crossed the Danube and beat the Turk on
> his own ground? This was a Dracula indeed! Woe
> was it that his own unworthy brother, when he had
> fallen, sold his people to the Turk and brought the
> shame of slavery on them! Was it not this Dracu-
> la, indeed, who inspired that other of his race who
> in a later age again and again brought his forces
> over the great river into Turkey-land; who, when
> he was beaten back, came again, and again, and
> again, though he had to come alone from the bloody
> field where his troops were being slaughtered,
> since he knew that he alone could ultimately tri-
> umph! They said that he thought only of himself.
> Bah! what good are peasants without a leader?
> Where ends the war without a brain and heart to
> conduct it? Again, when, after the battle of Mo-
> hacs, we threw off the Hungarian yoke, we of the
> Dracula blood were amongst their leaders, for our
> spirit would not brook that we were not free. Ah,
> young sir, the Szekelys--and the Dracula as their
> heart's blood, their brains, and their swords--can
> boast a record that mushroom growths like the
> Hapsburgs and the Romanoffs can never reach. The
> warlike days are over. Blood is too precious a
> thing in these days of dishonourable peace; and the
> glories of the great races are as a tale that is
> told.

The horrors of Castle Dracula increase for Jonathan
Harker. He beholds the Count "slowly emerge from the window and begin to crawl down the castle wall over that dreadful abyss, face down with his cloak spreading around him like
great wings*... with considerable speed, just as a lizard
moves along a wall. "

On another night Harker enters a room forbidden him

---

*This is Stoker's first mention of Dracula's wearing a cloak.
The present-day image of the Count cloaked in a floor-length
black cape was actually the creation of Hamilton Deane for
his DRACULA stage play in 1924.

by the Count and dozes off, awakening to find three beautiful
young women standing in the moonbeams. None of them casts
a shadow and all three, like the Count, have sharp white
teeth and voluptuous lips. Two of them were undoubtedly the
sisters of Dracula, with dark hair and high aquiline noses.
The third, however, was probably a former mistress of the
Count, for she was fair and with "great wavy masses of gold-
en hair and eyes like pale sapphires." The three strange
women move seductively toward the reclining Harker. The
blonde woman proceeds to place her mouth at his throat when
suddenly Count Dracula himself bursts into the room and
tosses her aside, forbidding any of them to touch the Englishman until he is "done with him." To appease their hideous
desire, the Count tosses them a small bundle which Harker
knows to contain a live baby. Taking with them the terrible
bundle, the women "fade into the rays of the moonlight and
pass out through the window." Harker faints from the horror
and later revives with the knowledge that the castle is inhabited by bloodsuckers.

Days later, Johathan Harker, realizing that soon his
blood will be surrendered to Dracula and the three women,
climbs out his window, makes his precarious way along the
wall, and slides through the very window of the Count's room
--the same window from which Dracula had emerged so many
times like a human fly. Opening a heavy door at one end of
the room, Harker finds that it leads through a stone passageway, down a flight of stone steps, through a tunnel and eventually to the ruins of a chapel. There Harker discovers
what remains of an ancient burial ground, with fragments of
old coffins and fifty coffin-like wooden boxes filled with earth
dug from this graveyard. In one of the boxes Harker makes
a ghastly discovery: there, reposing before him, either dead
or asleep, is Count Dracula.

When Harker later demands to be allowed to leave the
castle, Dracula politely escorts him to the door. But as the
Count opens the door, the Englishman sees that snarling
wolves are waiting for him to leave the building. Harker
realizes more than ever that Dracula is not about to let him
go.

In the morning, Harker again surreptitiously enters
the burial chamber, searching for a key to freedom. What
he beholds in the Count's coffin-like box exhibits some of the
vampire lore invented by Stoker--in this case the concept that
a vampire grows younger with his intake of stolen blood.

... and then I saw something which filled my very soul with horror. There lay the Count, but looking as if his youth had been half renewed, for the white hair and mustache were changed to dark iron-grey; the cheeks were fuller, and the white skin seemed ruby-red underneath; the mouth was redder than ever, for on the lips were gouts of fresh blood, which trickled from the corners of the mouth and ran over the chin and neck. Even the deep, burning eyes seemed set amongst the swollen flesh, for the lids and pouches underneath were bloated. It seemed as if the whole awful creature were simply gorged with blood. He lay like a filthy leech, exhausted with his repletion. I shuddered as I bent over to touch him, and every sense in me revolted at the contact; but I had to search, or I was lost. The coming night might see my own body a banquet in a similar way to those horrid three.

Jonathan Harker then realizes the nature of Count Dracula's master plan: "This was the being I was helping to transfer to London, where, perhaps, for centuries to come he might, amongst its teeming millions, satiate his lust for blood." Enraged, Harker grabs a shovel and sends it crashing down upon the Count's head just as it turns toward him, inflicting a deep gash above the forehead. Harker flees from the horror. The Szgany and Slovaks whom the Count had hired drive him and his fifty boxes of earth from the castle. Still a prisoner in Castle Dracula, Harker resolves to scale the towering walls even though it cause his death. His final thoughts, of his fiancée Mina Murray, thus end for the present, the writings in his journal.

Most of Bram Stoker's enthusiasm for creating a mood of terror seems to have been concentrated in these early chapters of Dracula. The Transylvanian setting is so starkly realistic that the reader often finds difficulty in believing that the author had never, in fact, visited that rugged land. The scenes which Stoker set within the gloomy Castle Dracula, with its broken battlements and mood of lurking evil, have rarely been equaled in horror fiction.

We must remember that readers discovering Dracula in its initial edition experienced more horror than today's readers, jaded as we are through countless Dracula stories and motion pictures which have not only over-familiarized us with the character but have more often than not presented a diluted or even humorous image of the vampire Count. The first readers of Stoker's Dracula discovered, along with Jonathan Harker, the true horror of his predicament at Castle Dracula and the sanguinary and un-dead nature of the Count.

Stoker next introduces us to Mina Murray and her close friend, Lucy Westenra. Lucy has a trio of suitors -- a Texan named Quincey Morris, the affluent Arthur Holmwood, and the director of a sanitarium, Dr. John Seward. All three of these characters have shared adventures in different parts of the world. Of the three, all of whom have proposed to her, Luch favors Holmwood.

The most prominent patient at Dr. Seward's sanitarium is the zoophagous R. M. Renfield who craves and devours flies and spiders. Renfield then develops an appetite for birds and small mammals, and Seward deduces that the maniac is attempting to absorb their lives by devouring them.

At Whitby Harbour (a place which Stoker and Irving had visited together) a Russian ship called the Demeter, after enduring a terrible storm at sea, is run ashore. The only person on board the ship is the dead captain, who had tied himself to the wheel as a final act. The ship's cargo is the fifty boxes of earth. The captain's log tells of a horrible monster who had destroyed the entire crew. The only living thing aboard the Demeter is a huge, untamed dog. Count Dracula has arrived in London.

Lucy becomes the Count's first victim in London. She begins to grow weak as though some inexplicable force were draining away her energy. Mina discovers that Lucy has been sleepwalking and finds her draped across the tombstone of a suicide near Whitby. Briefly she also glimpses a dark-clad form with a chalky face and red eyes crouched over Lucy. In the nights that follow, Lucy grows steadily weaker and paler. About this time Mina learns that her Jonathan is convalescing in a Budapest hospital and will soon come home.

Dr. Seward, meanwhile, notes that Renfield acknowledges servitude to some unknown "Master." When Lucy's condition worsens, Seward sends for the famous Dutch physician of "obscure diseases," Professor Abraham Van Helsing of Amsterdam.

Van Helsing was also one of Bram Stoker's composites. The name "Abraham" was a tribute to his own father Abraham

Stoker. The character was essentially Arminius Vambery and, throughout Dracula, would exhibit the latter's knowledge on the subject of vampirism. Stoker paid additional tribute to the man who instructed him in the lore of the vampire when he had Van Helsing refer to his "friend Arminius, of Buda-Pesth University."

Despite the efforts of Dr. Seward and Professor Van Helsing, Lucy's condition worsens. Blood transfusions have no effect on her and so the Professor begins to take strange measures. He places garlic about the windows of Lucy's bedroom and around her neck. When her mother, ignorant to Van Helsing's motives, removes the foul-smelling plants, she beholds a large gray wolf at the window and suffers a fatal heart attack.

Finally, Lucy lies upon her deathbed, emaciated and nearly pure white from lack of blood. Before she dies she takes on a strange beauty and voluptuousness.

Meanwhile, Jonathan and his bride Mina are attending the funeral of Peter Hawkins, Harker's employer. Later that day (vampires being permitted to walk about during the daylight hours according to Stoker's lore) Harker sees "a tall, thin man, with a beaky nose and black mustache and pointed beard" who is staring at a pretty girl. When the girl's carriage drives off, the man hails a hansom cab and follows her. Jonathan, horrified, reveals that this was Count Dracula, but grown young.

After Lucy's entombment a mysterious Lady in Black, a "Bloofer Lady," begins to prey upon the children at Hampstead Heath, enticing them with candy, then biting their necks. Van Helsing is now certain that Lucy is a vampire, one of the "Un-Dead." Accompanied by Holmwood (who is now called Lord Godalming), Seward and Morris, Van Helsing goes to Lucy's tomb. The vampire Lucy is seen returning to her coffin, clutching a child to her breast. Her mouth is smeared with blood, her teeth are sharp. When Van Helsing brandishes a crucifix before her livid face, Lucy cowers from it. The following night the foursome returns to Lucy's Tomb. The Professor reads from a prayer book as Godalming, as instructed by Van Helsing, drives a wooden stake, the point of which has been hardened by tar, through Lucy's heart. The thing that was Lucy shrieks as the blood spurts from her chest. Van Helsing completes the gruesome task by sawing off the exposed part of the stake, cutting off the head and

stuffing the mouth with garlic, and finally sealing shut the
coffin.

Van Helsing finally tells the people who had been close
to Lucy of the lore of the vampire, speaking in his curious
dialect.

> ... The nosferatu do not die like the bee when he
> sting once. His is only stronger; and being strong-
> er, have yet more power to work evil. This vam-
> pire which is amongst us is of himself so strong
> in person as twenty men; he is of cunning more
> than mortal, for his cunning be the growth of ages;
> he still have the aids of necromancy, which is, as
> his etymology imply, the divination of the dead, and
> all the dead that he can come nigh to are for him
> to command; he is brute, and more than brute; he
> is devil in callous, and the heart of him is not; he
> can, within limitations, appear at will when, and
> where, and in any of the forms that are to him; he
> can, within his range, direct the elements; the
> storm, the fog; the thunder; he can command all
> the meaner things: the rat, and the owl, and the
> bat--the moth, and the fox, and the wolf; he can
> grow and become small; and he can at times vanish
> and become unknown.

It is now obvious that the Count Dracula who menaced
Jonathan Harker is the vampire responsible for Lucy's fate
and that he is the "Master" to whom Renfield frequently al-
ludes. The house at Carfax is known to be the place where
Dracula's boxes of earth, each a facsimile grave, have been
delivered. Van Helsing organizes the Harkers, Seward, Morris and Godalming to go to Carfax and destroy the boxes and
Count Dracula. But first he continues his informal lecture.

> ... The vampire live on, and cannot die by mere
> passing of the time; he can flourish when that he
> can fatten on the blood of the living. Even more,
> we have seen amongst us that he can even grow
> younger; that his vital faculties grow strenuous, and
> seem as though they refresh themselves when his
> special pablum is plenty. But he cannot flourish
> without his diet; he eat not as others. Even friend
> Jonathan, who lived with him for weeks, did never
> see him to eat, never! He throws no shadow; he
> make in the mirror no reflect, as again Jonathan

observe.   He has the strength of many of his hand
--witness again Jonathan when he shut the door
against the wolfs, and when he help him from the
diligence too.   He can transform himself to wolf,
as we gather from the ship arrival in Whitby, when
he tear open the dog; he can be as bat, as Madam
Mina saw him on the window at Whitby, and as
friend John saw him fly from this so near house,
and as my friend Quincey saw him at the window
of Miss Lucy.   He can come in mist which he
create--that noble ship's captain proved him of this;
but, from what we know, the distance he can make
this mist is limited, and it can only be round himself.   He can come on moonlight rays as elemental
dust--as again Jonathan saw those sisters in the
castle of Dracula.   He become so small--we our-
selves saw Miss Lucy, ere she was at peace, slip
through a hairbreath space at the tomb door.   He
can, when once he find his way, come out from
anything or into anything, no matter how close it
be bound or even fused up with fire--solder you call
it.   He can see in the dark--no small power this,
in a world which is one half shut from the light.

But Van Helsing then points out that, despite his seeming omnipotence, the vampire is not unlimited.

... He may not enter anywhere at the first, unless
there be one of the household who bid him to come;
though afterwards he can come as he please.   His
power ceases, as does that of all evil things, at
the coming of the day.   Only at certain times can
he have limited freedom.   If he be not at the place
whither he is bound, he can only change himself at
noon or at exact sunrise or sunset.   These things
we are told, and in this record of ours we have
proof by inference.   Thus, whereas he can do as
he will within his limit, when he have his earth-
home, his coffin-home, his hell-home, the place
unhallowed, as we saw when he went to the grave
of the suicide at Whitby; still at other times he can
only change when the time come.   It is said, too,
that he can only pass running water at the slack or
the flood of the tide.   Then there are things which
so afflict him that he has no power, as the garlic
that we know of; and as for things sacred, as this
symbol, my crucifix, that was amongst us even now

when we resolve, to them he is nothing, but in
their presence he take place far off and silent with
respect.   There are others, too, which I shall tell
you of, lest in our seeking we may need them.   The
branch of the wild rose on his coffin keep him that
he move not from it; a sacred bullet fired into the
coffin kill him so that he is true dead; and as for
the stake through him, we know already of its
peace; or the cut-off head that giveth rest.   We
have seen it with our eyes.

Van Helsing concludes his speech by linking the Count's
vampiric state to a possibly demonic origin:

> ... He must, indeed, have been that Voivode Drac-
> ula who won his name against the Turk, over the
> great river on the very frontier of Turkey-land.
> If it be so, then was he no common man; for in
> that time, and for centuries after, he was spoken
> of as the cleverest and the most cunning, as well
> as the bravest of the sons of the "land beyond the
> forest. "   That mighty brain and that iron resolution
> went with him to his grave, and are even now ar-
> rayed against us.   The Draculas were, says Armin-
> ius, a great and noble race, though now and again
> were scions who were held by their coevals to have
> had dealings with the Evil One.   They learned his
> secrets in the Scholomance, amongst the mountains
> over Lake Hermanstadt, where the devil claims the
> tenth scholar as his due.   In the records are such
> words as "stregoica"--witch, "ordog, " and "pokol"
> --Satan and hell; and in one manuscript this very
> Dracula is spoken of as "wampyr, " which we all
> understand too well.

Morris then notices a large black bat observing the
group through a window.   The Texan fires his gun at the
creature but it flies off into the night.

Mina Harker subsequently becomes a victim, like Lucy.
Renfield makes feeble attempts to warn the group of Mina's
danger, and he is eventually found dying, his back, neck and
skull broken.   Before he dies, Renfield reveals that he had
worshiped the Count, who promised him all manners of lives
to devour.   Then he confesses that he brought Dracula into
the sanitarium to attack Mina.   But when the Count failed to
deliver as much as a single fly, Renfield retaliated and for
that was punished.

The group rush to Mina's room and find Dracula himself, just as Harker described him, right to the forehead scar, forcing her to drink blood from a burst vein in his chest, a type of blood baptism to initiate her into the rites of vampirism. Holding an envelope containing the Sacred Wafer, Van Helsing drives him back and watches the Count transform into a mist and pass under the door.

Van Helsing and his band of vampire hunters begin their frantic pursuit of Dracula. First they visit Carfax and purify the earth-filled boxes with pieces of the Sacred Wafer; then they proceed to trace the Count's other hiding places and the search concludes in an empty house at Piccadilly. Of the nine remaining boxes, only eight are in the house. Suddenly, the Count enters the room. Since it is daytime, he possesses only the strength and power of an ordinary mortal and he barely escapes Harker's slashing Kukri knife and Van Helsing's Sacred Wafer. Dracula leaps through a window, shattering the glass. Before departing the Count gloats that he still has one box of native soil and that he shall yet have his vengeance.

Dracula enacts a type of telepathic control over Mina and it is through this power that the group inevitably destroys the fiend. The lulls in Stoker's novel following the scenes set at Castle Dracula are compensated for by the tremendous excitement of the chase as Van Helsing and his partners set out to pursue Dracula to his final destruction. The Count desperately attempts to return to the protection of his mountaintop fortress. But Mina, her mind linked with his through the bond of blood, is able to reveal, via Van Helsing's hypnosis, the route Dracula is taking. Financed by the wealthy Lord Godalming, the group frantically pursues Dracula to his native land.

Van Helsing arrives with Mina outside Castle Dracula. He draws a protective circle around her in the dirt and sanctifies it with the Sacred Wafer. Mists swirl in the descending snow and assume the forms of the three vampire women seen earlier by Harker. When the vampires attempt to lure Mina out of the circle, the Professor scares them off with more of the Sacred Wafer. In the afternoon Van Helsing explores the castle and finds a huge, nobly proportioned tomb with the inscription ... DRACULA. After placing a Sacred Wafer in Dracula's tomb, he locates the coffins of the three

vampire women, driving stakes through their hearts and
severing the heads, after which the bodies decompose to dust.

As the sun begins to set, the Count's body, sleeping
in its box of earth, is being sped by horse-drawn wagon to
Castle Dracula by a band of Gypsies.   Morris and Seward
ride their mounts hard from the south toward the Gypsy
horsemen and wagon, while Lord Godalming and Harker ride
from the north.   Van Helsing and Mina also prepare for a
battle, drawing pistols.   But Dracula not only has Gypsies
loyal to him; there are howling wolves in the vicinity which
begin to move toward their helpless master.   The Gypsy car-
avan halts as Harker and Morris call out to them and raise
their rifles.   Seeing that the sun is dipping lower, Harker
and Morris dash for the box, despite the Gypsies guarding it.
Jonathan heaves the great box off the wagon, while Morris is
wounded by a Gypsy's knife.

Mina reports the destruction of Count Dracula in her
journal.

> ... The sun was almost down on the mountain tops,
> and the shadows of the whole group fell upon the
> snow.   I saw the Count lying within the box upon
> the earth, some of which the rude falling from the
> cart had scattered over him.   He was deathly pale,
> just like a waxen image, and the red eyes glared with
> the horrible vindictive look which I knew so well.
> As I looked, the eyes saw the sinking sun,
> and the look of hate in them turned to triumph.
> But, on the instant, came the sweep and
> flash of Jonathan's great knife.   I shrieked as I
> saw it sheer through the throat; whilst at the same
> moment Mr. Morris' bowie knife plunged into the
> heart.
> It was like a miracle; but before our very
> eyes, and almost in the drawing of a breath, the
> whole body crumbled into dust and passed from sight.
> I shall be glad as long as I live that even
> in that moment of final dissolution, there was in
> the face a look of peace, such as I never could
> have imagined might have rested there.

Contrary to popular misconception, Dracula is not
destroyed by a wooden stake through the heart, but by equally

effective weapons of metal. In his destruction, we see that
perhaps the creature known as Count Dracula was not totally
corrupt and that even so evil a monster as the King of Vampires might find contentment in ending his existence of horror.

Thinking that the outlanders possess supernatural abilities for their miraculous destruction of the man in the coffin-
like box, the Gypsies flee, leaving the ancient Castle Dracula
standing starkly against a blood red sky.

The reviews of Dracula were generally favorable.
Some of them follow:

Pall Mall Gazette: "It is horrid and creepy to the
last degree. It is also excellent, and one of the best things
in the supernatural line that we have been lucky enough to
hit upon."

The Lady: "Its fascination is so great that it is impossible to lay it aside...."

The Bookman: "Since Wilkie Collins left us we have
had no tale of mystery so liberal on manner and so closely
woven. But with the intricate plot, and the methods of the
narrative, the resemblance to the stories of the author of
'The Woman in White' ceases; for the audacity and horror of
'Dracula' are Mr. Stoker's own.... A summary of the book
would shock and disgust; but we must own that, though here
and there in the course of the tale we hurried over things
with repulsion, we read nearly the whole with rapt attention.
It is something of a triumph for the writer that neither the
improbability, nor the necessary number of hideous incidents
recounted of the man-vampire are long foremost in the reader's mind, but that the interest of the danger, of the complications, of the pursuit of the villain, of human skill and
courage pitted against inhuman wrong and superhuman strength,
rises always to the top."

Daily Mail: "In seeking a parallel to this weird, pow-
erful and horrible story, our minds revert to such tales as
'The Mysteries of Udolpho,' 'Frankenstein,' 'Wuthering
Heights,' 'The Fall of the House of Usher,' and 'Marjery of
Quelher.' But 'Dracula' is even more appalling in its gloomy
fascination than any of these."

Not all the reviews were favorable, however:

Punch: "The story is told in diaries and journals, a rather tantalising and somewhat wearisome form of narration, whereof Wilkie Collins was a past-master ... This weird tale is about vampires, not a single, quiet, creeping vampire, but a whole band of them, governed by a vampire monarch who is apparently a first cousin to Mephistopheles. It is a pity that Mr. Bram Stoker was not content to employ such supernatural anti-vampire receipts as his wildest imagination might have invented without venturing on a domain where angels fear to tread. But for this we could have reservedly recommended so ingenius a romance to all those who enjoy the weirdest of weird tales. "

Finally, the Athenaeum: "'Dracula' is highly sensational, but it is wanting in the constructive art as well as in the higher literary sense. It reads at times like a mere series of grotesquely incredible events; but there are better moments that show more power, though even these are never productive of the tremor such subjects evoke under the hand of a master. At times Mr. Stoker almost succeeds in creating the sense of possibility in impossibility; at others he merely commands an array of crude statements of incredible actions.... Still, Mr. Stoker has got together a number of horrid details, and his object, assuming it is to be ghastliness, is fairly well fulfilled. "

Bram Stoker's Dracula is not only the finest vampire story ever published, it is also one of the best examples of supernatural horror literature. The scenes involving Jonathan Harker at Castle Dracula are unequaled for sheer atmosphere and terror. Unfortunately, that mood is disrupted in much of the wordage that follows, with too much text devoted to the often frivolous interactions between some of the characters instead of to sustaining the eeriness and horror of those early scenes. Dracula himself rarely appears after his actions at the castle and the bulk of the novel illustrates the effect his presence has on others.

Dracula is Bram Stoker's masterpiece. Perhaps the greatness of Dracula is best demonstrated by the book's durability. Like Mary Shelley's Frankenstein, the Stoker novel has been reprinted in countless editions, both in hard cover and paperback, and in myriad languages. Any publisher today who publishes his own edition of Dracula has a sure selling item. In 1972, Doubleday and Company capitalized on both the Shelley and Stoker classics by publishing them together as a single hard cover volume entitled Dracula and

DRACULA

BY BRAM STOKER

Frankenstein. The wrap-around dust jacket featured a beautiful painting of both Count Dracula and Frankenstein's Monster by artist Frank Frazetta.

Almost a century after its first publication, Dracula remains the definitive vampire novel. To many aficionados and critics, the present writer included, it is also the definitive horror story. The book established the pattern for most of the vampire stories that would follow. But while there would be countless imitations, Bram Stoker's Dracula would, like the Count himself over the other un-dead, reign supreme. (In Italy Dracula was known as Dracula Il Vampiro and in Japan as Devil Man Dorakyura.)

AFTER DRACULA

Following the success of Dracula, Bram Stoker continued to pursue his literary career. He wrote a number of books and short stories, many of which delved into the realms of horror and the supernatural, but none ever captured the reading public reached by his novel about the Transylvanian vampire Count. In 1900, Stoker took Dracula and edited the text drastically so that it could be reprinted (the original version already being in its sixth printing) in a small paperback version. That same year he also began to write another novel of the supernatural entitled The Mystery of the Sea, involving a witch and psychic phenomena. Three years later Stoker saw the publication of the novel The Jewel of the Seven Stars, concerning an Egyptian mummy and ancient powers.

But Stoker's audience had expected him some day to produce another novel of the calibre of the horrifying Dracula. Again utilizing the format of an assembly of interconnected journals and similar first-hand writings, the Dublin author wrote The Lady of the Shroud, which was published by Rider and Company in 1909. The "Lady of the Shroud" is the Voivodin Teuta Vissarion, a beautiful woman, clad only in burial cerements, who reposes during the daylight hours in a glass-topped coffin. Rupert St. Leger, the hero of the story, assumes that the young woman is a vampire. Complications arise when Rupert falls in love with the mysterious woman of darkness. Stoker then fell victim to the trappings of the

Opposite: Cover of paperback edition published in 1965 (copyright Dell Publishing Co.) depicts the Count as Stoker described him. Painting by Paul Davis.

typical gothic romance (which he had avoided in Dracula) by
exposing the Voivodin's "Un-Dead" condition as being a hoax
for political reasons. Rupert finally comes to the aid of her
people, his inheritance providing the required military might.
Unlike Dracula, Bram Stoker's Lady of the Shroud is little
known today.

Bram Stoker's last novel was The Lair of the White
Worm, a horror tale about monstrous antedeluvian worms,
one of which took on the shape of a lovely woman. The story
was written during a period in which Bram suffered from
Bright's disease (a condition which resulted from his gout).
At sixty-four years of age, in April 1912, Bram Stoker, ill
and weary from an active life, closed his eyes for the last
time. The doctor said that he had succumbed to exhaustion.

Surprisingly, another Dracula story by Bram Stoker
was published posthumously by his widow, Florence. The
first chapter written for Dracula was never included in the
final manuscript. The novel was almost four hundred pages
without it, and Bram found it best to excise it.

The chapter was an early adventure of Jonathan Harker's
en route to Castle Dracula. While staying in a Munich hotel
on the dreaded "Walpurgisnacht," when the dead leave their
graves and walk the earth, Jonathan Harker goes on a coach
ride. When the coach driver stops at a certain road and refuses to take him any further, Harker continues his excursion on foot, coming upon a village deserted long ago because of the un-dead. During a terrible snowstorm Harker
takes refuge in an ancient tomb, the roof of which is pierced
by a tremendous iron stake. The tomb bears the curious inscription:

COUNTESS DOLINGEN OF GRATZ

IN STYRIA

SOUGHT AND FOUND DEATH

1801

And in the back, in large Russian letters:

"The dead travel fast. "

Looking within the tomb, Harker discovers the body of

a "beautiful woman, with rounded cheeks and red lips, seemingly sleeping on a bier." When a bolt of lightning dislodges the stake, the woman returns to animation, giving out a chilling scream. Harker hears a pack of howling wolves approaching as he falls victim to the snowstorm. When Harker revives, he finds a large wolf with fiery eyes pressing its warm furry body against him. The wolf seems to be guarding and warming Harker; then its yelps signal the uniformed soldiers who have been instructed by telegram by Count Dracula to see to the safety of the Englishman. The wolf flees as the soldiers fire their guns. Harker's final words are:

> I was certainly under some form of mysterious protection. From a distant country had come, in the very nick of time, a message that took me out of the danger of the snow-sleep and the jaws of a wolf.

The story, in which a female vampire transforms into a wolf, was written by Stoker as an acknowledgment to Sheridan Le Fanu's "Carmilla," which had impressed him as a young man. The vampiress of "Carmilla" was also a Countess and a suicide who haunted Styria.

The deletion of the chapter in no way affected the plot of Dracula. And so this excellent piece of writing remained among Stoker's papers, virtually forgotten. Not until 1941 was the chapter given the title "Dracula's Guest" and published by Florence Stoker as part of an anthology of her husband's short stories. The collection, Dracula's Guest, not only featured the title story, but also "The Judge's House," "The Squaw," "The Secret of the Growing Gold," "The Gipsy Prophecy," "The Coming of Abel Behenna," "The Burial of the Rats," "A Dream of Red Hands" and "Crooked Sands." "Dracula's Guest" was written with all the mood and gusto of the opening scenes of Dracula and remains an excellent short story complete in itself. *

A Biography of Dracula: The Life of Bram Stoker, by Harry Ludlam, was published in 1962 for the Fireside Press by W. Foulsham and Co., London. The book presented the complete story of Bram Stoker, with emphasis on his career

---

*"Dracula's Guest" was titled "Dracula's Daughter" for The Ghouls, a collection of stories that were the basis of motion pictures. The anthology was edited by Peter Haining for Stein and Day in 1971.

at the Lyceum and his relationship with Henry Irving.   For
anyone desiring a thorough biography of Stoker, A Biography
of Dracula is recommended by this writer.

In 1973, Hammer Films digressed from producing
Dracula motion pictures and announced a biography about the
Count's creator, Bram Stoker.   VICTIM OF HIS IMAGINA-
TION was to be produced by Howard Brandy, who also produced
Hammer's BLOOD FROM THE MUMMY'S TOMB (1971).   The
latter film was based on The Jewel of the Seven Stars, the
first non-Dracula Bram Stoker tale to be adapted to film.

Count Dracula, as Bram Stoker had envisioned him,
had tried to infect the world with the taint of vampirism in
the novel of 1897.   His ignominious ambitions were, however,
disrupted by the interference of a small group of intrepid
mortals who heroically forced upon him what appeared to be
a permanent destruction.   But Count Dracula would not remain truly dead.   He would prowl again, among other places,
upon the stage, as a highly successful dramatic property.

Chapter 5

DRACULA DRAMATIZED

> You Fools! You think with your wafers, your
> wolf's-bane, you can destroy me, me, the king
> of my kind? You shall see. --DRACULA, by
> Hamilton Deane and John L. Balderston

The very first theatre adaptation of Dracula was presented by the author of the novel, Bram Stoker. The play
was performed on Tuesday, May 18, 1897, within days of
the novel's first publication.

The drama was entitled DRACULA OR THE UN-DEAD.
Stoker really had no intention of presenting a great dramatic
piece that night at the Royal Lyceum Theatre, where his now
famous characters first came to life on the stage. He was
more inclined to protect his property than to impress his
audience or even his close friend Henry Irving. The performance of DRACULA OR THE UN-DEAD actually served to
copyright his original story.

The Royal Lyceum Theatre group furnished the fifteen
actors and the stage, with Count Dracula portrayed for the
first time anywhere by an actor listed in the program simply
as "Mr. Jones." A "Mr. Passmore" played Jonathan Harker,
"Mr. Reynolds" was Professor Van Helsing, and Edith Craig,
daughter of Lyceum leading lady Ellen Terry, was Mina.

DRACULA OR THE UN-DEAD was written for the
stage by Bram Stoker himself. Apparently the author had
realized the impracticability of adapting some of the novel's
more ambitious scenes to the dramatic medium and made
some alterations in the plot. The play consisted of forty-
seven scenes, a score of which differed from the novel. He
did, himself, in effect, what most authors abhor when their
works are adapted to other media by different writers: he
changed his own original story.

The play, with a prologue and five acts, ran a staggering four hours.   It demonstrated little dramatic creativity, either on the part of the actors or of Stoker himself.   It was hardly more than a dramatic reading of the book.   Henry Irving, when Stoker sought his opinion of the performance, summed up his feelings quite simply: "Dreadful. "

It wasn't until the turn of the century, after the release of two Dracula motion pictures (DRAKULA and NOS-FERATU, EINE SYMPHONIE DES GRAUENS), that another Count Dracula emerged from the grave of the printed page and made his dramatic appearance on the stage.

The novel Dracula had frightened away prospective writers who had considered adapting it to the theatre.   Its length, the numerous locations and characters, its format of many first-hand accounts, the grand scope, all presented hectic problems that left potential adaptors shaking their heads. For five years, a young Irish actor named Hamilton Deane approached various writers with the challenging project and always the results were negative.   It seemed that Dracula would never again be dramatized on the stage.

Hamilton Deane, a former bank clerk in London, made his acting debut in 1899 with the Henry Irving Vacation Company.   Deane became acquainted with Bram Stoker and it was inevitable that he would acquire and read a copy of Stoker's masterpiece.   He was a man of vitality and ambition and, seeing the stage possibilities of the story of the King Vampire, he determined that he would not allow Count Dracula to remain truly dead.

In 1923, Deane was enjoying the peak of his success. He now had his own theatre group, the Hamilton Deane Company, and was relishing stardom and the adulation of his fans. This was also the year in which Deane approached a writer, for the last of many times, to adapt Dracula, only to receive the customary "No. " Dora May Patrick, his leading lady and future wife, asked why he didn't adapt the story himself. Deane had ability as a writer and here, indeed, was the logical solution to his long-lasting problem.

A fateful illness was more than indirectly responsible

Opposite: Hamilton Deane, who adapted Dracula to the stage in 1924 and created the image of the Count, later to be established by Bela Lugosi.

for the completion of his play DRACULA. Deane said:
"Fortunately, I then developed a severe cold, for it put me
to bed and, idly at first, I began to write a draft of the play.
I then became so immersed in it that on obtaining Mrs. Bram
Stoker's permission, I went ahead with the script and did not
stop until I had completed it four weeks later."

Hamilton Deane's adaptation solved the problems that
had frightened off other writers. The play retained the basic
theme of the novel but had a simplified plot that worked on
the stage. Jonathan Harker's nightmare visit to Castle Dracula in Transylvania--the very best section of Stoker's novel--
was eliminated. The story now took place entirely in London.
The play was done in three acts: "The Study of Jonathan
Harker's House on Hampstead Heath (Evening)," "Mrs. Harker's Boudoir (Night)," and "The Study of Jonathan Harker's
House (Afternoon)," plus the epilogue, "The Coach House at
Carfax (6 p.m.). This may have infuriated readers of the
novel who expected to see recreated the grandeur of Transylvania with its majestic mountains and weather-eroded castles,
but the concise story did retain the novel's basic outline.

Deane saw great visual impact in the black cloak of
Count Dracula which, although now so familiar, was only
casually mentioned by Stoker. He also decided that the Vampire King should always appear in full evening dress, while
Stoker's Count was always clad entirely in forboding black.
This image of Dracula, with white tie and tails and the long
bat-like cloak, soon became the one the public identified with
the character. Today, no self-respecting Dracula would consider going anywhere without his formal attire, which makes
him rather conspicuous, especially in the more uncomfortable situations, such as walking through a mist-enveloped
graveyard at night or entering the home of casually dressed
residents.

Deane's Dracula image was basically patterned after
his own physical characteristics. He was two inches over
six feet in height and had a lean face with piercing, almost
sinister eyes. He also saw the King Vampire as a man of
about fifty, with a conspicuously green face, deep voice, and
suave continental mannerisms. Deane insisted that the portrayal be witty and melodramatic, but never over-acted so
as to become ludicrous. Although Deane had aspirations to
play the Count himself, he was forced to drape his black
cape around actor Edmund Blake, whose gold front tooth
made him even more striking in appearance. Deane took,

instead, the part of Dr. Abraham van Helsing (the "van" having lost its capital) since there was no other actor readily available to portray that more difficult role. G. Malcolm Russell portrayed Dracula's slave Renfield, and Dora May Patrick became Mina.

The curtain rose on DRACULA at the Grand Theatre in Derby, England, in June of 1924. Deane was delighted at this "sneak preview" of the play, for it gave him an opportunity to see that his condensation of the original story worked. The play was immediately successful and offers to purchase it came even from producers in the United States. By 1926, the play had become Deane's main interest--and his main source of income.

Raymond Huntley became one of the most famous Count Draculas of the 1920s.

On February 14, 1927, DRACULA opened at the Little
Theatre in London. The actors performed according to the
script despite the jeers of the more snobbish drama critics
and playhouse managers.   There were some changes in casting by this time.   Raymond Huntley, only twenty-two years
old, accepted the role of the centuries-old vampire Count.
Bernard Jukes assumed the role of insectivorous Renfield,
eventually playing the part more than four thousand times.

The reviews of Deane's DRACULA were both favorable
and unfavorable--but mostly the latter. Some critics called
it a terrible "hack" piece, or complained about Huntley's unconvincing mask (he was not wearing any), but DRACULA
proved its durability and would not, as the Count himself
would not, return to a permanent grave.   The play would not
be transfixed by the stake-like pens of harsh critics.   According to the Evening News, "... while glittering productions
costing thousands of pounds have wilted and died after a week
or so in the West End, 'Dracula' has gone on drinking blood
nightly.... "

DRACULA continued at the Little Theatre, then moved
to the Duke of York's and the Prince of Wales Theatre,
amassing an impressive three hundred ninety-one performances.   The drama, immune to the severe attacks by the
press, had become a smash success.

Hamilton Deane began to think like P. T. Barnum,
becoming more of a showman during succeeding performances
of DRACULA.   For example, he hired a nurse to be on duty
in the theatre lobby to attend to those hapless patrons who
might be so unfortunate as to faint from the ghastly visage of
Count Dracula.   (Such tactics would become commonplace in
motion picture promotion in the years to come.)

In 1927, DRACULA was purchased by American producer Horace Liveright.   He suggested that the play be revised to make it more modern.   Agreeing to make such alterations, Deane collaborated with writer John L. Balderston in
drafting a new version of DRACULA (also known as DRACU-
LA, THE VAMPIRE).   Among the changes in the play were
exchanging the characters of Lucy and Mina and simplifying
the settings.   The three acts were now set in the library of
Dr. Seward's sanatorium at Purley London, in Lucy's boudoir,
and, for the final act, in Seward's library and a secret vault.

This version, set in then contemporary England, opens

with Jonathan Harker and Dr. Seward (now about fifty-five
years old) discussing the strange malady that has left Lucy
Seward, Harker's fianceé and (in Deane's version) the doctor's daughter, pale and anemic. Among the patients in the
sanatorium is Renfield, a mad, repulsive youth, who has a
sickening habit of eating flies and spiders and who occasionally emerges from his apparent madness into moments of acute
sanity. Seward has sent for Abraham Van Helsing (the capital "V" being restored) to cure his daughter.

Count Dracula is a new neighbor of Dr. Seward.
When the nobleman from Transylvania visits Dr. Seward,
Lucy exhibits both repulsion and fascination for him.

> SEWARD: Count Dracula, Professor Van Helsing.
> (The two MEN bow.)
>
> DRACULA (Crosses down a few steps; bows to VAN
> HELSING): A most distinguished scientist, whose
> name we know even in the wilds of Transylvania.
> (To SEWARD) But I interrupt a consultation.
>
> SEWARD: Not at all, Count. It's good of you to
> come, and we appreciate your motives.
>
> HARKER: Dr. Seward has just told me of your
> offer, and I can't thank you enough.
>
> DRACULA: It is nothing. I should be grateful to
> be permitted to help Miss Lucy in any way.
>
> LUCY: But you do, Count. I look forward to your
> visits. They seem to make me better.
>
> VAN HELSING (Crosses to MAID up L.; whispers
> to her): And so I arrive to find a rival in the field.
>
> DRACULA (Crosses to LUCY): You encourage me,
> Miss Seward, to make them more frequent, as I
> should like to.
>
> LUCY (Looking at him fixedly): I am always glad
> to see you.

Dracula, who has already killed Mina with his bite,
continues to make his attacks on Lucy. He places Seward's
maid under his hypnotic spell. Dracula having been left alone

with Lucy, she sees his face appear through a tapestry (a
trick done with lighting) and receives a telepathic message
from her master. Obediently, the maid removes the crucifix
and wolf's-bane (which Deane substituted for Stoker's less romantic garlic) left there by Van Helsing. As the dogs begin
to bark and wolves howl, Dracula enters Lucy's room, stalking toward her with his hands outstretched and cape hanging
on his arms like bat wings. As the vampire kisses her,
then opens his mouth and bites her throat, the curtain falls
on the second act.

     Van Helsing learns that Count Dracula is the vampire
(or Werewolf, as Deane inaccurately also referred to him
through his characters), and that he has brought his proxy
grave to England by airplane. Van Helsing learns that Renfield is a type of apprentice vampire, promised eternal life
through un-death by his evil master. When Renfield is left
alone in Seward's library, Dracula enters, accusing Renfield
of betraying him by warning the others of his plans to take
Lucy as his un-dead bride. The Count approaches his mad
servant menacingly, while Renfield pleads that he not be
killed with so many innocent lives on his soul. Suddenly,
Van Helsing, Harker and Seward burst into the room. Harker
and Seward brandish crucifixes, while Van Helsing holds the
Sacred Host. Dracula dashes about the room, trapped from
all sides by the symbols of Goodness.

     VAN HELSING (Looks at watch): Four minutes un-
til sunrise.

     DRACULA (Crossing to below sofa, looking at wrist
watch): Your watch is correct, Professor. (Facing down R.)

     VAN HELSING (Step C.): Your life in death has
reached its end.

     SEWARD (Step toward C.): By God's mercy.

     DRACULA (HARKER steps toward DRACULA.
DRACULA, turning to them, suavely): Its end?
Not yet, Professor. I still have more than three
minutes to add to my five hundred years.

     Dracula warns them that, though they have already
destroyed five of his boxes of native soil, they have not yet
found the sixth, where he plans to hide for a hundred years.

Furthermore, the Count threatens that Lucy will die by night, which will guarantee her joining him as a vampiress (Deane's innovation), to be set up above all his other un-dead wives in Transylvania a century later.

Anxious to destroy him, Seward and Harker each grab the vampire's cloak, while Van Helsing approaches with stake and hammer. The sun is almost up when Dracula calls upon the last of his demonic powers before the daylight renders him helpless, and vanishes, leaving them holding an empty cloak (accomplished with the aid of a trap door).

It is Renfield whose actions betray the whereabouts of Count Dracula. In an effort to avoid being destroyed by Van Helsing and Seward, the maniac reveals that Seward's book-case is actually the entrance to a secret passageway. Van Helsing, Seward and Harker follow him through the passage-way, finding themselves in a vault which the doctor did not know existed. There they discover Dracula's last coffin and open it. Harker efficiently dispatches the vampire with his wooden stake, thus saving his fiancée.

As the audience began to leave the theatre after the play appeared to have ended, Van Helsing, still in character, would casually address them: "Just a moment, Ladies and Gentlemen! Just a word before you go. We hope the memories of Dracula and Renfield won't give you bad dreams, so just a word of reassurance. When you go home tonight and the lights have been turned out and you are afraid to look behind the curtains and you dread to see a face appear at the window--why, just pull yourself together and remember that after all there are such things."

DRACULA opened at New York's Fulton Theatre in October of 1927, starring a newcomer to American theatre named Bela Lugosi as the Count and also featuring Jukes as Renfield.

At the 250th performance of DRACULA at the Prince of Wales Theatre, the patrons were treated to a special gift. Everyone attending the anniversary performance was given a sealed envelope, to be opened after the play had ended. The surprise proved to be Dracula's Guest, Stoker's posthumously issued anthology of short stories, complete with an artificial bat that flew into the air when released by an elastic band.

There was no stopping DRACULA now.   The play was
booked solid for a full year in advance and the demands were
exceeding the play-dates.   There was no other solution than
to form additional companies, each with its own production of
the play.   Percy Broadshaw, the lean W. E. Holloway and
Courtney White continued in the Dracula role, appearing and
vanishing on stages in clouds of theatrical smoke.   Deane
eventually attempted to curb the DRACULA performances by
presenting a dramatic version of FRANKENSTEIN, written by
Peggy Webling, with himself playing the infamous Monster.
But FRANKENSTEIN was also successful, and the result was
that Deane had to present the two plays on alternate nights.

The motion picture version of DRACULA made in 1931
had already made a star of Bela Lugosi and he concentrated
on film rather than stage performances.   Deane hoped that
the adaptation to the film medium would allow him to take a
vacation from the vampire play.   He was wrong, however;
the movie version thrust the play into even greater demand,
and Deane presented the play another forty times.

In 1939, Hamilton Deane finally took over the role for
which he had longed since its inception and which he had actually written for himself.   From the very beginning, Deane's
conception of the Count more resembled himself than Stoker's
character.   His clean-shaven, strangely handsome interpretation was the one Lugosi and his followers brought to the
screen.

In a London theatre in March of that year, Hamilton
Deane, in blue and green stage make-up, with crepe hair af-
fixed to his forehead, and with darkened lips, debuted before
his waiting audience as Count Dracula.   Behind him were the
spirits of twelve stage Draculas.   Now the characterization
he had developed was truly his own.

That same year, Hamilton Deane finally brought the
play to the very stage once managed by Dracula's creator,
Bram Stoker.   Deane's DRACULA was presented with pride
at the Lyceum Theatre.   The play was followed by a short
run of HAMLET.   The once prosperous theatre, the adopted
home of Henry Irving and Bram Stoker (and in a sense,
Dracula himself), then closed forever.

Opposite: The Hungarian actor Bela Lugosi assumed the
starring role in the 1927 stage play, DRACULA, and eventually became identified with the role of the vampire Count.

The Lyceum performance of DRACULA was indeed memorable, for it presented an on-stage confrontation between Hamilton Deane and the film star whose fame as the vampire Count began in that same play. Two Draculas greeted each other as Bela Lugosi rushed onto the stage and embraced the man in greasepaint and wing-like cloak.

Hamilton Deane's final portrayal of Count Dracula was at St. Helen's in Lancashire, England, in 1941. Seventeen years later the tall actor-author-producer who had dramatized DRACULA was dead.

The DRACULA play did not perish with its author. Many actors have played the role right on up through the present. In Cheshire, England, about 1933, John Abbott starred as Count Dracula without having seen the Lugosi stage or movie versions. Uninfluenced by previous interpretations, Abbott was able to create his own characterization of Dracula. About his performance, Abbott told me:

> I made myself some sharp ears out of nose putty.
> I put red inside the rims of my eyes and green out-
> side. And on each eyelid I stuck a sparkling spang-
> ly thing. Oh, and I made myself somehow a pair
> of tusks which fit on the upper eye teeth. I had a
> very greenish color and painted up the hollows in
> my cheeks. The companies that presented this play
> usually rented a special kind of coffin which had a
> double bottom in it. When they pretended to drive
> the stake through your heart, there was a brief
> blackout. The actor sank down through the false
> bottom into the real bottom and the false bottom
> closed up like a pair of doors, and it looked as
> though he vanished. They were going to have a bat,
> cut out of a piece of cardboard, and shine it like
> a silhouette on the curtains. But since that was
> representing me, I was more fussy and I made my
> own bat. I made a beautiful little bat with a furry
> body and ears and two eyes which I linked up to a
> battery inside the body. I made some kind of
> frame inside so that I could hinge the wings onto
> it. I made the wings out of wire coat hangers and
> covered them with rubber. They flapped up and
> down. And the way I got them to flap was to have

Opposite: Edward Van Sloan as van Helsing confronts Bela Lugosi as the Count in the 1927 stage production.

the body suspended from a straight thread like a
fishing line.   I had a fishing pole so you could lift
the thing up and down like a dead fish.   Suspended
from the top of the fishing rod to either wing was
a long thin black elastic.   That caused the wings
to flap when I moved the fishing rod.   I worked
the bat myself and just before, when I heard the
cue coming, I linked up the battery with the wires
that made the eyes shine red, and there I was in
my incarnation into 'batdom. '   As Dracula, I wore
a cloak with a red lining, a tuxedo and a top hat.

I always got the giggles on stage in those
days.   I found it awfully difficult to control hysterical laughter if anything struck me as being absurd.
My first entrance, a man comes to Van Helsing
and announces that there is a Count Dracula arriving.   And this terrible creature, with these spar-
kling eyes, long ears, green face and tusks arrives
and says, 'I am Dracula. '   And he just came up to
me and said, 'Oh, how do you do, ' as though I
were his brother-in-law or something.   That caused
me to exercise some control not to giggle.

I scared a woman in the street, the day after
she'd apparently been to the theatre.   I was walking
through the streets, either going over the words or
going to lunch or something.   She came around the
corner and we faced each other.   And she had a
child with her and she stopped dead in her tracks.
She wouldn't speak to me.

Some of the many other actors who have starred as
the Vampire Count in Deane's DRACULA are Jack Reitzan,
John Gregory, Robert Ballinger, Louis Hayward and, in 1972,
Hurd Hatfield (best remembered for his performance in the
film THE PICTURE OF DORIAN GRAY) and Edward Ansara
(with a remarkable resemblance to Lugosi).   Hatfield attempted his own interpretation of the role until audience reaction demanded that he enact an imitation of Lugosi's voice
and accent.

DRACULA is still being presented, both professionally
and in amateur productions at high schools and colleges.
There have been attempts to play the somewhat dated melodrama for laughs, with every actor playing tongue-in-cheek.
But there still exists a certain reverence for the creaky old
play, so that even for our more sophisticated modern culture
DRACULA is usually presented as written, with straight faces
on serious actors.

Bela Lugosi exhibits his best bedside manner in a 1952 stage revival of DRACULA.

        John Carradine, who played Dracula for the first of many times in the 1944 film HOUSE OF FRANKENSTEIN, ignored the Deane/Lugosi characterization for his interpretation of the role when he starred in DRACULA in the 1950s.   Carradine did his own make-up, referring to the pages of Bram Stoker's Dracula.   The tall, thin actor appeared with an aquiline nose and white hair and a long white mustache.   But during a performance in Detroit where everything, including the prop vampire bat, seemed to misfunction, and the audience began to snicker at melodramatic lines said in earnest, Carradine realized that he needed something to recapture the audience before the final curtain.   After the stake had seemingly been driven through his heart, Carradine would emerge from the coffin to take his final bow.   In all seriousness, he addressed the audience with a line of his own that topped Van Helsing's final warning:

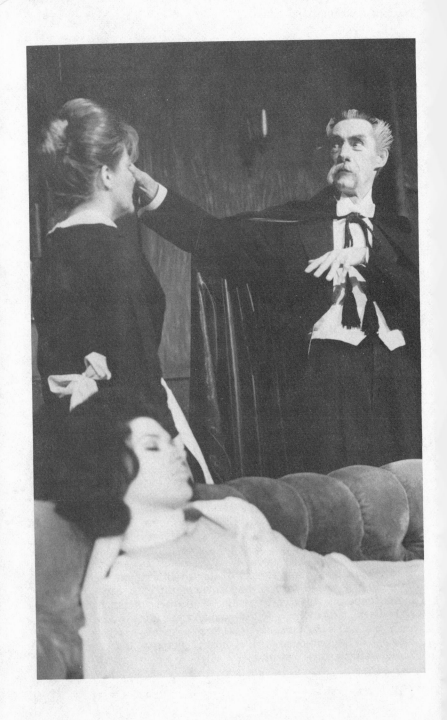

"If I'm alive, what am I doing here? On the other hand, if I'm dead, why do I have to wee-wee?"

The line received a big laugh (although groans were probably heard issuing from the graves of both Bram Stoker and Hamilton Deane) and Carradine has included it in his performances in DRACULA ever since.

In 1973 Deane's DRACULA opened the summer theatre productions of the Nantucket Stage Company on Nantucket Island, Massachusetts. Edward Gorey designed the play in a two-dimensional, black and white illustrator's style, complete with a backdrop painting showing a bat-winged Count Dracula. Gorey's design, Dennis Rosa's direction and the sobriety of the actors are said to have resulted in a quite frightening play.

DRACULA MAKES A COMEBACK

While Hamilton Deane's DRACULA play is usually played absolutely straight, there have been other versions of essentially the same production, revised and played, however, for laughs. DRACULA, THE COMEDY OF THE VAMPIRE, produced in Europe in the 1930s, was presumably a satire of the Deane play.

Recently, a take-off on DRACULA was presented by Theatre Three, Inc., entitled COUNT DRACULA: OR, A MUSICAL MANIA FROM TRANSYLVANIA. The production was written by Laurence O'Dwyer and directed by Norma Young. Songs, including such numbers as "The Transylvania Polka," "Renfield's Plea: Insanity," and "Sunset Lullaby," were by Jac Alder. Charles Roberts portrayed Count Voivode Dracula, Bob Floyd was Van Helsing, Richard Michaels was Renfield, Gene Ross was Dr. Seward, James Burton was John Harker, and Ronda Berkman played Lucy.

There were other Dracula comedies which were not based on Deane's work. I WAS A TEENAGE DRACULA, a mystery in three acts by Gene Donovan, was presented on the stage at Roosevelt Junior High School in Coos, Oregon

---

Opposite: During the 1950s, John Carradine starred in a presentation of DRACULA, patterning his make-up after the description of the Count in Stoker's book. Photo by David Mobley.

(1958). In the play, a superstitious maid believed that young Steve Dracula (certainly a suspicious sounding name), played by Jay Neuville, was actually a descendant of the blood-hungry Count. THE REVENGE OF DRACULA, a high school play written by Charles Jackson in the early 1960s, pitted Van Helsing against the sinister Count Bremen (the name inspired by the town in the film NOSFERATU).

DEAREST DRACULA (which was originally to be titled POOR MISS LUCY) opened September 27, 1965, at the Olympia Theatre in Dublin, Ireland. This play, written by Margaret Hill, Charlotte Moor and Jack Murdock for the Dublin Theatre Festival, had a more or less original plot. Songs with such titles as "Balkan Blues," "Love Beyond the Grave," "Dracula," and "Poor Miss Lucy" give some indication of the flavor of the play. Jonathan Harker (Robert Hornery) is at Castle Dracula in Transylvania, suffering from some mysterious disease. When his friends from England--including Dr. Seward (David Holliday), Sir Arthur Holmwood (David Morton) and Dr. Van Helsing (Pitt Wilkinson)--journey to the castle to investigate the matter, they discover him almost bloodless and eating flies. Count Dracula (John Gower) and three beautiful vampire women attack their guests and open up in song. Executives from Hammer Films were offered the screen rights to DEAREST DRACULA, but upon seeing the play declined. DEAREST DRACULA was poorly received on all counts.

A spoof of the Stoker novel, simply titled DRACULA, was presented in August, 1965 by the Open State Company in Hartford, Connecticut. Lucy "Fairchild" (Eileen Filocco) suffers from some unknown sickness after Jonathan Harker (Gibbs Murray) locates an old abbey for his client Count Dracula (Donald Maack). Dr. Seward (Peter Bailey) summons his friend Van Helsing (Richard Kline) and again the Professor gets busy hunting down the vampire Count.

A musical spoof based on the original novel, again entitled DRACULA, played on weekends from May 13 through June 4, 1966 at the Muse Theater in Ravenna, Ohio. Dracula, with both upper and lower fangs, hypnotizes a maid to remove some wolfbane while singing "Hear and Obey" to her. As he prepares to bite Mina he sings "Mina Is Mine," while his "Black Sunrise" precedes his destruction by wooden stake. Other songs included in the play were "Bad Dreams" and "Ballet for the Wives of Dracula."

The Count was on the stage again in the 1969 production, DRACULA, BABY! The musical comedy by Bruce Ronald premiered on April 25th at the Town Hall Theatre in Centerville, Ohio. DRACULA SUCKS, which played the Horseshoe Theatre in Hollywood the same year, spoofed the 1931 Lugosi film and also included additional dialogue from the Stoker novel. Jerry B. Wheeler produced and directed DRACULA SUCKS, with Murray Langston as a bisexual Dracula who liked to attack both male and female victims. Wheeler had been advised to change the names of his characters since the play followed the plot of the copyrighted movie. Therefore, David Manzy portrayed Ratfield, Bob Lossier was Dr. Sewer, Chris Bailey played Jonathan Hooker and Lee Corrigan played Van Hesling. For a while the play was scheduled to move off-Broadway and was being considered for filming by American-International Pictures. As evidenced by these titles, the Dracula plays following Hamilton Deane's dramas have tended to be comedies. More of the same cropped up in the Seventies; the first, with the incredible title, JOHNNY APPLESEED AND DRACULA, opened in Hollywood in 1970.

One of the latest of the modern Dracula spoofs was I'M SORRY, THE BRIDGE IS OUT, YOU"LL HAVE TO SPEND THE NIGHT, a musical comedy by Sheldon Allman (of the record album Sing Along with Drac) and Bob Pickett (former Lugosi imitator on rock 'n' roll records of the 1960s), and directed by Maurine Dawson (who made the Dracula film, TALES OF BLOOD AND TERROR). The spoof opened on April 28, 1970, at the Coronet Theatre in Los Angeles. Not only was Count Dracula featured, but also Dr. Victor Frankenstein and his Monster, hunchbacked Igor, the Mummy, and Renfield (Tony Lane; later Chuck Cypers), who waited for his master to make him un-dead while singing a number called "Flies."

Count Ladislav Dracula was played in Lugosi style by Peter Virgo, Jr., and later by the show's original Frankenstein Monster, John Ian Jacobs. The Count, his black-attired wife Natasha Dracula (Gloria Dell) and a horde of vampire girls (who chorus a song called "The Brides of Dracula"), inhabit the castle of Dr. Frankenstein. When pretty Mary Helen Herriman and her fiancé John David Wellgood take refuge in the castle after a storm washes out the bridge, Dracula decides to take her blood and make her his own. Countess Dracula, on the other hand, focuses her gaze on Wellgood, while the other monsters in the castle all want the

couple for their own degenerate reasons. I'M SORRY, THE
BRIDGE IS OUT, YOU'LL HAVE TO SPEND THE NIGHT,
was written with great affection for the genre it spoofed.
Dracula speaks such lines as "Ah, to be truly dead ... that
must be glorious," taken directly from the 1931 DRACULA
film. The comedy managed to be both funny and respectful.

With all of this Dracula insanity becoming a tradition
on the modern stage, it is remarkable that a serious play on
the subject of the vampire Count opened in 1970 at the Judson
Poets' Theater in New York. DRACULA: SABBAT, written
by Leon Katz and directed by Lawrence Kornfeld, was a totally new concept in dramatizing the sanguinary escapades of
the infamous vampire. Dracula (Duane Tucker) is not only
un-dead, but the bare-chested and masked embodiment of
Satan, who cavorts with demons in a nightmare world of horror and profanity. Nudity and eroticism were prevalent in
DRACULA: SABBAT, with the King of Vampires transforming Victorian virgin Lucy (Crystal Field) into a depraved
creature while vampire women and witches dance and collide
to the vibrant strains of organ music. Dracula offers Lucy
in a Black Mass. Later, her fiancé Arthur chops off Lucy's
head.

A rock musical version of DRACULA, adapted from
Stoker's novel by Larry Ferguson and David Davidson and directed by Ferguson, was presented in May, 1973 at UCLA's
Macgowan Hall. In his review of the play for the Los Angeles Times, theatre critic Dan Sullivan remarked, "The plot
is vaguely Bram Stoker but the costumes and playing style
are a melange of Story Theater, 'Hair,' 'Godspell' and camp
melodrama. Dracula wonders if there were any phone calls.
Renfield--the fellow who likes to eat flies--tells you that he
'coulda been a contender'." During the play the vampire Lucy
(Cheri Susan Bard) seduces a young boy on the streets and
Dracula tempts Renfield (John Peterson) with a bowl of flies.
Finally, Van Helsing (James Bohlin) slits Renfield's throat to
learn the whereabouts of the Count. Then a group of mortals,
including Mina (Joyce DeWitt) and Seward (David Jorns), catch
Dracula (James Cady) and rip him to pieces.

A new version of DRACULA, written by Stanley Evel-
ing, Alan Jackson, David Mowat, Robert Nye, Bill Watson,
Clarisse Eriksson and John Downing, played to favorable

Opposite: Lugosi spoofed the role that had given him fame
in his 1954 stage show, THE BELA LUGOSI REVIEW.

reviews in London in 1972, while yet another new DRACULA, written and directed by Crane Johnson and featuring the Count in a modicum of appearances, opened at New York's Royal Playhouse in 1974. COUNT DRACULA (1974), a play by Ted Miller, was a modernization of the story, based both on the Stoker novel and Deane play. Eric Tavaris played the Count.

Count Dracula was spoofed by Bela Lugosi in an early 1930s Vaudeville act which also featured Ed Sullivan and Arthur Treacher; and in the 1948 stage show that accompanied the first-run booking of the film ABBOTT AND COSTELLO MEET FRANKENSTEIN. Lugosi starred in his own Las Vegas stage show in 1954, THE BELA LUGOSI REVIEW, and, as Dracula, menaced pretty Joan White.

Around the turn of the century, a circus performer called Dracula, the Aerial Contortionist, astounded the patrons of such amusement centers as Luna Park in Coney Island. Brief appearances by Count Dracula were made in LENNY, a 1971 play about Lenny Bruce, in the French puppet show LES POUPÉES DE PARIS (as a marionette), in the 1972 ICE FOLLIES and in Sid and Marty Krofft's H. R. PUFF 'N' STUFF* live show (1972), with three vampiric girls called The Dracula Trio singing "A Fright at the Opera." In 1972 there was also a satire of the Dracula theme entitled NIGHT OF THE BITE, presented by the Originals Only company at the Crossroads Theatre. A pretty vampire girl bites a teenage boy, and this starts a chain reaction that vampirizes his entire family. Zankor, the bushy-haired Dracula-type father of the vampiress, is infuriated over the abundance of un-dead and returns them to normal using a mystic spell.

From the 1930s and up through the early seventies, live horror shows played theatres in the United States. The shows had titles like Dr. Neff's MADHOUSE OF MYSTERY (with "Dracula's Daughter"), Dr. Satan's SHRIEKS IN THE NIGHT SHOW, Dr. Sin's HOUSE OF THE LIVING DEAD and TERRORS OF THE UNKNOWN.

The best of these shows was the ASYLUM OF HORRORS, hosted by a professional magician called Dr. Silkini, whose posters usually advertised: "See DRACULA change

---

*Scenes from this show were incorporated into the WORLD OF SID AND MARTY KROFFT AT HOLLYWOOD BOWL, a special televised by Los Angeles station KTTV on August 14, 1974.

into a BAT and FLY into the AUDIENCE among YOU!" The
actual performance of this feat was disappointing. After
about an hour of magic tricks and ghostly routines involving
intrepid members of the audience, Dr. Silkini would bring
Dracula and the other monsters onto the stage, while lightning flashed upon the motion picture screen and the strains
of eerie music nearly shook the walls of the theatre. "Dracula" would appear in a rather unconvincing costume and make-
up and start for the audience, raising his cape as the lights
dimmed to black. Whether or not Dracula ever made it into
the audience is doubtful, particularly with teenage boys trying
to prove their courage to their screaming girlfriends by
throwing anything that happened to come to hand. If Dracula
was smart, he ducked backstage, allowing the glowing bat to
be manipulated by a man with a long pole. Dr. Silkini
switched, in 1973, after approximately forty years of these
shows, to his HAPPENINGS OF HORROR, a more spectacular stage presentation than ever, in which both Count Dracula
and the Frankenstein Monster (in elaborate costumes and Don
Post masks) seemingly captured a boy from the audience,
dragged him to an operating table, and before everyone's
eyes cut off his bleeding head. The effect was quite startling.

Count Dracula had become popular on the stage, but
already by the 1920s, the growing art of motion pictures began to show his pale face in terrifying close-up. On film,
the King of Vampires would achieve infamy anew.

Max Schreck as Count Orlock in the 1922 silent film NOS-
FERATU, EINE SYMPHONIE DES GRAUENS.

Chapter 6

DRACULA ON THE SILENT SCREEN

> Ist dies Ihre Frau? Welch schoner Hals!
> (Is this your wife? What a beautiful neck!)
> --Title card for Count Orlock, NOSFERATU

Three years before Hamilton Deane brought Bram Stoker's novel to the theatre, the first Dracula film was made during the silent era of motion pictures. While the screams of Dracula's victims were never heard in the films of the 1920s, movie theatres resounded with the shrieks of terrified audiences.

DRAKULA was a Hungarian production directed by Karoly Lajthay in 1921. It is not known whether DRAKULA was a horror film based on Stoker's work or was actually an historical film depicting the infamous career of Vlad the Impaler. Other film versions of Dracula are reported to have been made about this time--one being Russian--but there is no real verification to substantiate these claims.

The first film of which we have definite knowledge as being adapted from Dracula is NOSFERATU, EINE SYMPHONIE DES GRAUENS (NOSFERATU, A SYMPHONY OF TERROR), made by Prana, a German film company, in 1922. NOSFERATU was directed by F. (Friederich) W. Murnau, a young director of the German school of expressionism. In 1920, Murnau had delved into classic horror literature for source material for films and made DER JANUSKOPF, a version of Robert Louis Stevenson's The Strange Case of Dr. Jekyll and Mr. Hyde. DER JANUSKOPF starred Conrad Veidt in the dual role and featured a young Bela Lugosi. In 1926 Murnau would direct his classic FAUST. German expressionists continually brought supernatural horrors into their films of this era and it seemed appropriate that Count Dracula would soon be hunting victims on European motion picture screens.

Murnau, however, did not take the most ethical (or legal) route in adapting the Stoker novel to the film medium. Dracula was still in copyright in 1921 when the film went into production.   Unlike Hamilton Deane, who had acquired the rights to adapt the play from Stoker's widow, Murnau simply proceeded to make his film, although he took some precautions in making his bootlegged version, in case he should encounter any legal difficulties.   Inevitably, he would.

First, Murnau changed the title of his project to NOSFERATU. *   The word nosferatu--or more correctly nosferat, the Romanian term for a special breed of vampire that causes husbands to become impotent--did appear in Dr. Van Helsing's dialogue in the original Dracula novel.   The word certainly has an ominous sound to it and made a suitable title for the film.

Among other changes the location of the story was switched from Transylvania to Germany, and Bremen was substituted for London.   And while the novel was set in the late nineteenth century, the movie was sent back in time to 1838 to coincide with Bremen's great plague.

Although the characters remained relatively consistent with those in the book, the names in NOSFERATU were

*Eventually NOSFERATU was shown in various forms with no pretext of being anything but a version of Dracula.   In the early 1960s, NOSFERATU was shown on SILENTS PLEASE, a half-hour television series that programmed condensations of silent films.   NOSFERATU, edited to eliminate all references to the Renfield and Van Helsing characters, was simply titled DRACULA.   The Count and other characters were given back the names ascribed to them by Stoker.   Shortly after this version was shown on television, Entertainment Films Company made an 8mm home movie version available under the title TERROR OF DRACULA (probably to capitalize on the success of Hammer's HORROR OF DRACULA), slightly shorter than the SILENTS PLEASE version, the main omissions being the scenes shot in the negative.   In 1972, Blackhawk Films made the feature available to movie collectors as NOSFERATU, THE VAMPIRE and simultaneously released the SILENTS PLEASE abridgement as simply DRACULA.   In 1945, scenes from NOSFERATU appeared in a semidocumentary on vampires made in France, entitled LE VAMPIRE, directed by Jean Painleve.   Scenes from NOSFERATU were also seen in the VAMPIR and CASUAL RELATIONS.

changed (in this case to protect the obviously guilty Murnau).
Thus, Jonathan Harker became Waldemar Hutter (played by
Gustav von Wangenheim), Van Helsing became Professor Bulwer (John Gottow), Lucy became Annie Harding (Ruth Lands-
hoff), Mina became Ellen (Greta Schröder) and Renfield was
changed to Knock (Alexander Granach), now the head of the
real estate company that sends Hutter to the vampire's castle.
(Eventually, the wild-haired Knock, mad with his craving for
small creatures, leads the police on a wild rooftop chase before he is killed.)

Bulwer has little to do in NOSFERATU. He does not
launch the usual crusade to find and destroy the vampire, as
he did in the novel, and does in the plays and later film versions. Bulwer's function was mostly to introduce the audience to the fact that vampiric creatures do exist in nature,
in both the animal and vegetable kingdoms. His most memorable scene in the picture was a demonstration of the car-
nivorous appetite of the venus fly-trap, accompanied with
close-ups showing the hungry plant in action.

The most irreverent name change in the film was that
of Count Dracula himself, to Count Orlock (or in various versions to Orlac and Orloc). Not only did Murnau change the
name of the King Vampire; he also provided him with an image different enough, he apparently hoped, to further deceive
the copyright owner of the original property. Murnau patterned his Count Orlock more after the vampire of legend
and tradition. Those who have read some of the vampire accounts of the past may well imagine the figure of Count Orlock and note his resemblance to the variety that still terrifies the peoples of various primitive societies.

Count Orlock, the Nosferatu, was portrayed superbly
by Max Schreck (an actor who appropriately took his name
from the German word for fear). While Stoker's (and
Deane's) Dracula was an impressive, strangely handsome and
undeniably noble character, Schreck's Orlock was a bald, human rodent, resuscitated from some foul smelling grave,
moving stiffly as if impaired by the restrictions of rigor
mortis. He wore no tuxedo or cloak, but a simple, contemporary suit, the long coat buttoned up the front.

Schreck's Orlock remains as possibly the most hideous
vampire ever to prowl the screen. His orbs seemed to burn
from the blackened eye sockets, which contrasted starkly with
the pale face. The ears were pointed, as if belonging to

some hellish demon rather than a being that was once a living man. The incisor teeth were elongated and sharp, and protruded from the front of the mouth. (Vampires have traditionally been described with the canines longer than the other teeth. The placement of Schreck's fangs in the front of his mouth suggested the teeth of some bizarre, human rabbit.) Schreck's hands had been made-up with great, animal-like claws, which he extended like the talons of some monstrous vulture when advancing toward his victims. Schreck's Count Orlock was the perfect screen portrayal of a vampire.

After Murnau changed the Count's name and physical appearance, he modified some of the powers and limitations listed by Stoker (and Van Helsing) in Dracula. But Stoker himself had invented some of his vampire lore and so perhaps Murnau was justified in his rewriting of tradition. Unlike Count Dracula, Orlock did make shadows, some of which, as photographed by Fritz Arno Wagner, were incredibly effective, substituting for Schreck himself like some dark living creature. He also had a mirror image, which showed prominently when the vampire knelt between the reflective glass and his final victim. Orlock was powerless to transform himself into a bat, although numerous bats fluttered about the tower of his castle. His victims perished from his taking their blood, and they did not emerge from the grave as un-dead creatures themselves. Thus Murnau simplified the plot by eliminating a few vampiric characters as well as characteristics.

The story, adapted to the screen by Henrik Galeen, remained quite faithful to the novel--more so, in fact, than the later versions made by Universal Pictures and Hammer Films.

Some of the scenes in NOSFERATU have never been equaled in effectiveness. When Hutter discovers Count Orlock sleeping corpse-like in his crypt, the quick cut to the fanged monster is frightening even today, when audiences have been conditioned to shock cuts to body-hacking psychos and screeching creatures leaping at them from the shadows in vivid, bloody color. The scenes aboard the ship are especially terrifying. Close-ups of scuttling rats are shown in the boxes of earth that Count Orlock is bringing to Bremen. In one shot, the ship's mate investigates the cargo hold of the vessel in order to learn the truth behind the thing that has been killing off the members of the crew. The vampire then rises from his coffin with hellish ease, propped up like some ghastly seesaw. After the terrified mate leaps overboard to a more desirable death, Count Orlock boldly stalks across the deck of the ship, fingers extended, eyes wide with anticipation (with Murnau's camera at a low angle to emphasize the vampire's sheer power in this final act at sea) of his final victim--the captain (Max Nemetz), who had determined to see the voyage to its fateful climax by binding himself to the ship's wheel.

NOSFERATU was virtually a location piece. Except for some rather obvious studio interior sets, the film was made in some Central European locations which are breathtaking, particularly the mountains and forests, a nearby town with narrow streets and looming buildings closely spaced to one another (which reinforced Orlock's tall and rigid appearance), and an authentic castle that could not be duplicated on any studio lot. Making the film on location was uncharacteristic of the German expressionists, who usually preferred to build their own cities and create totally their own macabre settings. The locations in NOSFERATU may have displeased some of Murnau's peers but they gave the film an authenticity lacking in most studio-shot vampire movies. Murnau was making a silent film and it was relatively simple to move a production crew into a castle, without the cumbersome burden of modern sound equipment, and take advantage of the numerous corridors and archways. The effect is staggering. There is no doubting the reality of the vampire's domain with its barren walls and atmosphere of sterility and death.

Murnau filmed the scene in which Hutter is taken by the coach and its weird driver (actually Orlock himself) in the negative to give the forest, dominated by white trees, a feeling of unreality. By today's standards, there is nothing spectacular about the scene; but in 1922 it was quite revolutionary. In various other scenes, such as the stagecoach moving through the ghostly woods and Orlock himself loading a wagon with his coveted boxes of native soil, Murnau undercranked his camera so that the vampire appeared to move with superhuman speed. This was a mostly unsuccessful attempt to illustrate the line from Dracula, "the dead travel fast." Seen today, the speeded-up scenes are, unfortunately, ludicrous.

Unlike the ending provided by Stoker in his novel, Count Orlock is not destroyed after a long pursuit back to his ancestral castle. With the arrival of the vampire in Bremen,

a terrible plague strikes the town.   He has directed his fear-
some appetite toward Hutter's wife, Ellen.   After having observed the solemn procession of coffins of plague victims
being carried through the street by pallbearers in black suits
and stovepipe hats, Ellen realizes that the only way to save
her husband is to offer herself to the monster and keep him
occupied until sunrise.

Here Murnau created more of his own mythology, which
would inadvertantly become accepted by the public as authentic vampire lore.   Murnau's reasoning that sunlight would destroy a vampire was sensible.   The vampire is a creature of
the night which can be symbolically equated with Evil.   He is
always defeated by some force of Good--or light.   Sunlight
was an ideal deus ex machina to enter and wipe out the fiend
when his lust for blood became so great that he dared tempt
the passing of his own element, the night.

Ellen willingly offers herself to Count Orlock, who
leers at her through the window.   Hutter has already gone
off to seek the help of Professor Bulwer.   With his awesome
shadow moving like a living entity, Orlock creeps through
Ellen's house and into her bedroom.   After satisfying his unnatural craving on Ellen's blood, Count Orlock hears the
crowing of a rooster, which signals his approaching doom.
Rising from Ellen's prostrate form, the Count faces the window as the sky grows light.   Struck by the rays of the sun,
Orlock dissolves to a rising wisp of vapor.   The evil of nosferatu has ended.   But Ellen, who had wilfully spent the night
with the un-dead, perishes in Hutter's arms.

This ending contradicts other scenes in the film which
clearly show Count Orlock cavorting and using his vampiric
powers in broad daylight.   He drives Hutter in his coach to
the castle, stalks across his self-made ghost ship, then, carrying his coffin, vanishes through a closed door, all with the
sun blazing down upon him.   These appear to be outrageous
errors on the part of Murnau, especially in view of destruction of the vampire by the sudden appearance of sunlight at
the climax of the film.   The only possible explanation for
these apparent mistakes is that we no longer screen the original prints of NOSFERATU.   Often, silent film-makers conveyed the illusion of night by tinting a daylight scene blue.
This was a primitive technique predating day-for-night shooting, which is accomplished through the use of special filters
that darken exterior scenes taken during the day.   We might
credit Murnau's intelligence by assuming that such was the
case in NOSFERATU.

Variety reviewed the film in its December 25, 1929 issue:

> Murnau proved his directorial artistry in 'Sunrise'
> for Fox about three years ago, but in this picture
> he's a master artisan demonstrating not only a
> knowledge of the subtler side of directing but in
> photography.
>
> One shot of the sun cracking at dawn is an
> eye filler. Among others of extremely imaginative
> beauty is one which takes in a schooner sailing in
> a rippling stream photographed in such a manner
> that it has the illusion of color and an enigmatic
> weirdness that's more perplexing than the ghost ac-
> tion of the players.
>
> His funeral scene in the deserted town street
> where the bodies of the plague victims are carried
> in coffins held aloft by straggling pallbearers is un-
> usual to say the least. Empty shattering buildings
> photographed to suggest the desperate desolation
> brought on by the vampire is extremely effective
> symbolism.
>
> Max Schreck as the vampire is an able pan-
> tomimist and works clocklike, his makeup suggest-
> ing everything that's goose pimply. He did his
> worst on every occasion--which was good.

NOSFERATU was never given wide distribution. The
plot of the film was so faithful to Stoker's book that charges
of copyright infringement forced it out of circulation. Florence Stoker legally compelled Murnau to withdraw his picture
in July, 1925. Despite the court order to destroy all nega-
tives and prints, NOSFERATU survived and was screened for
a limited engagement in London three years afterward. In
the United States the film was released in 1929 under the title NOSFERATU THE VAMPIRE; this was the version which
Variety reviewed. The American release was intended to
capitalize on Murnau's popularity as a Hollywood director, but
the film, already dated by Hollywood standards, was, in general, poorly received.

Dracula is now in the public domain and there is no
problem with showing NOSFERATU legally or making new
versions of Stoker's original story. Unlike many films made
during the soundless era of motion pictures, NOSFERATU
holds up remarkably well despite its age. It is almost always interesting and at times both exciting and terrifying.
Christopher Lee, who became the Count Dracula of the movies

in the 1960s and 1970s, has stated that NOSFERATU remains
"the greatest vampire film ever made, I think. "*   Barring
the obvious weathering by time, perhaps it is.

A curiosity made in 1921 by the German company
Deutsche Film-Produktion is DIE ZWOLFTE STUNDE ("The
Twelfth Hour"), directed by Dr. Waldemar Ronger.   The film
is described as a "record of the making of NOSFERATU."**

A modern day "remake" of NOSFERATU is the Italian
color movie of 1971, HANNO CAMBIATO FACCIA ("They've
Changed Faces"), made by Garigliano Films and directed by
Corrado Farina.   The film tells the same story as NOS-
FERATU but with gangsters substituted for vampires.   Adolfo
Celi played the gangster boss in the role which replaced that
of Count Orlock.   When the hero of the film thinks he has
killed "Nosferatu," the criminal does not die.

DRAKULA and NOSFERATU, EINE SYMPHONIE DES
GRAUENS would soon be virtually forgotten by the general
movie-going public.   The sound era had already dawned (symbolically bringing destruction to the silent Draculas just as
Count Orlock was destroyed by the rising sun) when NOS-
FERATU was first released in the United States.   Two years
later the most famous Count Dracula of all would raise his
black cloak on American screens.

---

*"Interview With Christopher Lee," The Monster Times, May
10, 1972, p. 15.
     **DIE ZWOLFTE STUNDE is also known by the title
EINE NACHT DES GRAUENS ("A Night of Terror").

Chapter 7

DRACULA HAUNTS UNIVERSAL

> I never drink ... wine.
>   --Bela Lugosi in DRACULA (1931)

During the height of popularity of Hamilton Deane's DRACULA play, Universal Pictures announced its plans to make an authorized movie version of the story. The film DRACULA was to be directed by Tod Browning, who had directed silent film star Lon Chaney, the famed "Man of a Thousand Faces," in numerous pictures including the vampiric LONDON AFTER MIDNIGHT for Metro-Goldwyn-Mayer in 1927. LONDON AFTER MIDNIGHT was based on The Hypnotist, a novel written by Browning.

Chaney was the undisputed master of make-up and pantomime in silent pictures. In LONDON AFTER MIDNIGHT he portrayed an alleged vampire with distended eyes, scraggy hair and a mouth filled with upper and lower uniformly sharp fangs. The make-up was excruciatingly uncomfortable, including wires that distended the eyes, but Chaney was accustomed to undergoing such torture in order to perfect his bizarre characterizations. A black outfit with a cape cut in the form of bat's wings and a tall black beaver hat completed the awesome guise. But actually this vampire was revealed to be a police detective who had assumed a double identity to trap a murderer. *

Tod Browning, born in Louisville, Kentucky, on July 12, 1882, began his professional career as a circus clown

---

*Grosset & Dunlap published a novelization of London After Midnight (New York 1928), by Marie Coolidge-Rask. This was a "Photoplay" edition with stills from the movie.

and at the age of thirty-two turned to acting in such films as
SCENTING A TERRIBLE CRIME. In 1917 he began to work
as a director, some of his films including THE JURY OF
FATE (1917) and THE LEGION OF DEATH (1918). Browning
is best known for the horror films he directed. His final
directorial job was for a 1939 film entitled MIRACLES FOR
SALE. The eighty-year-old Browning died in Hollywood on
October 6, 1962.

Browning had always been satisfied by Lon Chaney's
performances and his role in LONDON AFTER MIDNIGHT
made him a likely choice for the part of the King Vampire
in the film DRACULA. Chaney was approached by Browning
and considered accepting the role in the first talkie version
of Stoker's story, but never gave Browning a final answer.
He died in 1930, the same year that DRACULA went into production, after expressing an interest in doing the part. We
can only speculate as to how the make-up of Count Dracula
would have appeared as created and worn by Lon Chaney.

Four other actors came to the minds of Universal's
studio executives for the starring role of Count Dracula.
They were Conrad Veidt, who has starred in numerous silent
horror films including Murnau's version of the Jekyll and
Hyde story entitled DER JANUSKOPF; Paul Muni, who the
following year would star in the gangster classic SCARFACE;
William Courtney; and Ian Keith, who would in 1946 play a
cloaked, wide-eyed vampiric role in Republic Pictures' VAL-
LEY OF THE ZOMBIES. All of these actors had the proper
facial characteristics to portray the vampire Count, but none
was chosen for the part. It seemed more appropriate to select an actor born near Dracula's own homeland.

Bela Lugosi had been chilling audiences as the Transylvanian Count in the stage production during the period
when Browning was trying to reach a final decision about
casting the main role in DRACULA. The actor had already
appeared in a Browning film, THE THIRTEENTH CHAIR
(1929). Browning saw the Hungarian performer's background
as ideal for an impersonator of the Count (and this would
later prove invaluable in the film's publicity). The actor was
born in Lugos, Hungary, on October 29, 1882 as Bela Blasko.
(Briefly he would be known on the European silent screen as
Arisztid Olt.) He eventually took his permanent stage name
from the town of his birth, but for all practical purposes,
Lugosi seemed to have been born in the wilds of Transylvania.

'I am ... Dracula," says the Count (Bela Lugosi) to Renfield (Dwight Frye) in Universal's DRACULA (1931).

On March 27, 1931, after DRACULA's release to theatres, Bela Lugosi said in a radio broadcast: "Although DRACULA is a fanciful tale of a fictional character, it is actually a story which has many elements of truth. I was born and reared in almost the exact same location of the story, and I came to know that what is looked upon merely as a superstition of ignorant people, is really based on facts which are literally hair-raising in their strangeness--but which are <u>true</u>."

Bela Lugosi had acted upon the stages of Europe from the time when he graduated from elementary school in Lugos. He studied drama at Budapest's famous Academy of Theatrical Arts and later received the recognition of his countrymen as one of the nation's greatest actors. At the time, Lugosi

was not known as a bogeyman. He was starring in productions such as ROMEO AND JULIET.

In 1914, Lugosi received his first film role, in a silent movie made in Hungary. A number of German silent
films followed. But although Lugosi, when he accepted the
part of Count Dracula, was already a notable star in Europe,
as far as American movie audiences were concerned he was
only the star of the DRACULA play and an unknown on the
motion picture screen.

He was, nevertheless, Browning's obvious choice after
the death of Chaney. Lugosi's background and the aura of
mystery surrounding an "unknown" who was also a suave foreigner with a far-off look in his eyes, were to his credit,
and he had already gained notoriety doing the stage presentation.

Two of the film's principal actors had appeared with
Lugosi in the stage version. Dwight Frye recreated his wonderful role as Renfield, the usually insane, insectivorous
slave of Dracula. Frye, who would play many such roles
with the same leering enthusiasm, including the sadistic hunchback Fritz in FRANKENSTEIN (1931), enacted the part of Renfield with staring, popping eyes and a wide, toothy grin. He
relished in monologues that would allow him to exclaim about
"Rats! Rats! Rats!" and descriptions of his master's powers at work. His performance remains one of the true high-
lights of the film. *

_____
*Dwight Frye virtually repeated his Renfield portrayal in two
motion pictures following DRACULA. In 1933 Frye played
Herman Gleib in the Majestic film THE VAMPIRE BAT, directed by Frank Strayer. Herman is a lunatic who keeps pet
bats. A mysterious cloaked figure prowls the night, claiming
human victims and leaving them bloodless. Naturally, the
villagers suspect that the bat-keeper is a vampire. After a
chase through the hills, the townspeople trap him in a cave
and kill him. Actually the vampire scare is a hoax perpetrated by mad scientist Otto Von Niemann (Lionel Atwill) who
has created life in the form of a pulsating blob that requires
blood to survive. Using telepathic control, Von Niemann
sends his servant Emil Borst (Robert Fraser), wearing a
flowing cloak, out at night to seek the required victims.
Frye's other Renfield type role was Zolaar in DEAD MEN
WALK (PRC 1943), directed by Sam Newfeld. George Zucco
portrayed a vampire and his living identical twin while Zolaar
(cont. on p. 113)

Edward Van Sloane, who performed with Lugosi in the 1927 Fulton Theatre presentation of DRACULA, was again cast as Professor Van Helsing. Made-up to look considerably older than he was off-screen, Van Sloane spoke to the audience as Deane had on the stage, telling viewers that the un-dead did exist. This epilogue has, unfortunately, been snipped from currently circulating prints of the film. Van Sloane would, like Lugosi and Frye, virtually recreate his DRACULA role in other Universal entries like FRANKENSTEIN and, the following year, THE MUMMY.*

Jonathan Harker was portrayed by David Manners, who typified the bland movie heroes of the 1930s. Mina was played by Helen Chandler and Dr. Seward by Herbert Bunstun. The film was photographed by the great German cinematographer Karl Freund, who achieved some effects and utilized techniques that were quite astounding for the time. His camera concentrated on such non-union performers as armadillos and spiders that crept from coffins otherwise occupied only by skeletons and moved about the castle of Dracula. In some close-ups Freund focused lights on Lugosi's already piercing eyes to emphasize their hypnotic power.

DRACULA was not, unfortunately, a strict adaptation of Stoker's novel. Rather, it was based on the Hamilton Deane stage play, with the addition of opening scenes of Dracula in his Transylvanian castle and with Renfield replaced by the novel's Jonathan Harker in those early scenes. Therein lies the picture's greatest fault. The bulk of the film is virtually a photographed stage play, with the camera occupying the place of a theatre patron seated front row center. The scenes are static and often uninteresting or boring,

(cont. on p. 116)

was the blood-drinker's hunchbacked servant. This was PRC's only vampire film. Perhaps after seeing the results, the studio decided against making more.

*To an extent, THE MUMMY, directed by Karl Freund and starring Boris Karloff in the title role, was a "remake" of DRACULA. Karloff portrayed Im-ho-tep, an Egyptian buried alive and revived in the twentieth century. Masquerading as Ardoth Bey, the living mummy seeks to reclaim his reincarnated lover. Edward Van Sloane played an archaeologist with a Van Helsing-type knowledge of the supernatural and a fervent desire to destroy Ardoth Bey before he can transform the reincarnated princess into a creature like himself. The battle of wits between Ardoth Bey and his opponent are similar to those between Count Dracula and Van Helsing.

Scenes from the first sound version of DRACULA. Above, the insectivorous Renfield (Dwight Frye) dies for his betrayal in the powerful grip of his master. Opposite: top, Count Dracula (Lugosi) places the vampire's bite upon the sleeping Mina (Helen Chandler); bottom, Van Helsing (Edward Van Sloan) wards off the vampiric Count with a potent weapon.

despite some of the atmospheric sets, with their trails of
ghostly mist settling among the time-eroded Castle Dracula
and Carfax Abbey, created by the Universal craftsmen.
Deane himself visited the set of DRACULA occasionally and
must have been pleased to see director Tod Browning so
faithfully capturing the atmosphere of his play.

The opening scenes of DRACULA, which were not tak-
en from the play, are as great today as when first projected
on theatre screens in 1931. Renfield is warned to stay away
from Castle Dracula by the typically Transylvanian peasants,
then told that if he must go there, he should wear the crucifix they give him "for your mother's sake." The scenes in
which Renfield is taken in the coach, actually driven by a
disguised Dracula, through the majestic yet forboding Carpathian Mountains is reminiscent of Murnau's seeming authenticity of locale in NOSFERATU. When Renfield looks out of
the coach window to ask his driver to slow down, he sees
only a bat flapping above the fear-crazed horses, but does
not yet fully realize the implications of that winged creature.

Renfield finds Castle Dracula the remnant of some
other age. After a short wait, the Count himself appears.
"I am ... Dracula," he says, appearing at the top of the
worn stone staircase, dressed formally with his long black
cape hanging like bat's wings, and holding a candle. There
is a peculiar, never fading smile on the Count's face which
has a disturbing effect on the young man.

Renfield should have heeded the warnings of the peasants that Dracula was a bloodthirsty vampire. On the stairs,
Dracula had walked through an enormous spider's web. When
the Count offers his guest a bottle of the finest wine, he himself declines Renfield's offer to join him with the suspicious
revelation, "I never drink ... wine." And when Renfield cuts
his finger, Count Dracula's brow wrinkles, his eyes stare
like twin points of fire, his hand raises like a clutching claw,
and he stalks toward the bleeding wound. Only the sight of
Renfield's recently acquired crucifix saves him from the
Count's thirst--at least for the present.

Left alone in the room, or so he believes, Renfield
encounters Dracula's three vampire sisters. They are clad
in white and stalk wraith-like through the swirling, moonlit
mists, until the Count himself appears in the shape of a large
vampire bat and causes his victim to fall unconscious. Then,
once more in human form, Dracula feasts on the blood of
Renfield, thereby placing him under his spell.

Dracula then sails to London, his coffin protected while aboard ship by Renfield, who is now a raving fly-eating lunatic. When the death ship drifts into port, a weird laughter is heard coming from the hold. The hold is opened and Renfield, dark-encircled eyes open wide, dark-lipped mouth frozen open in a terrible grin, gapes up at them. Renfield is given residence in Dr. Seward's sanitarium, where he continues to pursue his insectivorous habits.

DRACULA proceeds with elements of plot taken both from the book and from the play. At first he destroys Lucy, transforming her into the mysterious "woman in white" who preys upon children. Then he sets out to transform Mina into a creature like himself, with the opposition of Van Helsing.

Today, DRACULA is a disappointment to many modern viewers, especially those seeing it for the first time. The pacing is slow and the staging extremely theatrical. Despite the beautifully atmospheric moments at Castle Dracula and the scenes in which Count Dracula summons Mina (with the aid of lights focused just on his eyes by Freund to give them a sense of hypnotic force) and leads her away to Carfax Abbey, the film drags. There is no music, save for a scene wherein Dracula attends a concert and for the title music from Swan Lake (which served in this capacity for a number of early sound horror films). Much of the action, which could have been quite exciting, is never on screen but is related by other characters: Jonathan Harker gazes out a window and states that he just saw a large wolf run across the lawn; Renfield describes how the Count appeared to him in a swirling red mist and then commanded his army of obedient rats.

The climax of the film is hardly thrilling. Van Helsing and Harker pursue Dracula to Carfax Abbey just as the morning sun begins to rise. Within the ancient structure they discover two coffin-like boxes. The Professor opens the first to discover the comatose figure of the King Vampire. He proceeds to partially open the second box, then looks up to Harker, assuming that Mina lies inside in the vampire condition. But as Harker goes off in search of a rock with which Van Helsing can drive the wooden stakes through their hearts, the Professor learns that Mina is not within the box, implying that she has escaped the fate of becoming a vampire. Harker finds Mina and the camera is on the reunited lovers as Van Helsing, off screen, destroys Dracula with the wooden stake. The audience sees none of the Count's destruction nor,

as in the novel, any decomposition. There is only a scene
of Mina clutching her breast as if she feels the stake being
hammered home, and Van Helsing's announcement that "Dracula is dead forever. "

Special effects for Dracula's transformation into a bat
are likewise disappointing. The Dracula vampire bat was
actually a simple prop, made larger than its real-life counterpart (like all movie vampire bats), and suspended from
an "invisible" wire. As the wire was gently moved up and
down, the very balance of the prop would cause the wings to
flap. The bat was a fairly convincing effect in 1931 but still
left much to be desired.

Unfortunately, the Universal technicians neglected to
show an actual on-screen metamorphosis from Dracula to bat
(or vice versa). One wonders why in view of the special effects wizardry in such pre-DRACULA silent films as THE
LOST WORLD (1925), in which prehistoric monsters were
brought to life through various methods including model animation, superimposition, rear projection and matte work--
and which John Fulton would later develop for Universal in
the 1933 classic THE INVISIBLE MAN. Instead of showing
a transformation, Freund photographed the bat flapping its
wings in Mina's window. Then there would be a cutaway to
his slumbering victim. Next we would see Dracula, his bat-
like cloak draped over his shoulders, raising his hands and
approaching the bed. In later Dracula films made by Universal, the transformation from man to bat would develop into
an art.

Modern audiences sometimes snicker at the performance of Bela Lugosi, calling it hammy and artificial. We
must remember that Lugosi was primarily a stage actor with
a very poor command of the English language. He was accustomed to playing to the back rows of packed theatres.
His style of acting was the result of many years upon the
European stage. In the film DRACULA, Lugosi was essentially recreating his stage role. Motion pictures were still
developing their newly acquired voice and many performers
and directors had difficulty distinguishing between stage and
film acting. Lugosi once commented on his transition from
stage to screen and his performance in DRACULA:

> In playing in the picture I found that there
> was a great deal that I had to unlearn. In the
> theater I was playing not only to the spectators in

the front rows but also to those in the last row of
the gallery, and some exaggeration in everything I
did, not only in the tonal pitch of my voice but in
the changes of facial expression which accompanied
various lines or situations was necessary.   I 'took
it big,' as the saying is.

But for the screen, in which the actor's distance from every member of the audience is equal
only to his distance from the lens of the camera,
I have found that a great deal of the repression was
an absolute necessity.   Tod Browning has continually had to 'hold me down.' In my other screen roles
I did not seem to have this difficulty but I have
played Dracula a thousand times on the stage and in
this one role I find that I have become thoroughly
settled in the technique of the stage and not of the
screen.   But thanks to director Browning I am un-
learning fast.

Perhaps Lugosi fell victim to this problem to a greater degree than most actors.   But even if he seems hammy by
today's standards, he did play the role with sincerity and dignity, and in a language that was not his own.   That was one
reason why the audience of the time loved both him and the
picture.

We should not, then, judge DRACULA too harshly.
Movie audiences were not as sophisticated in 1931 as they are
today.   They had not been accustomed to over thirty years of
shockers, humorous monsters like television's Herman Munster, the Japanese Godzilla epics with huge prehistoric creatures destroying cities, lives and each other.   In 1931,
DRACULA scared audiences.   And while the supernatural elements in most American films up to that time were usually
explained away as hoaxes, DRACULA established the fact the
vampires could be portrayed on the screen as real.   In that
sense DRACULA began the first cycle of authentic horror
films in the United States.

Irene Thirer's review of DRACULA in the February
13, 1931 edition of the New York Daily News said:

It is superbly photographed, and presented
to audible screen audiences at the capable movie
direction of Tod Browning--megaphoner of so many
mysteries that he knows every trick of the type.
Carl Laemmle, Jr. counts 'Dracula' among his

productions for the season, and the boy's done well
again. He chose director, cast, and story wisely.
... Bela Lugosi's performance as Count
Dracula is a repetition of his stage role. He's
simply grand.

Bela Lugosi, utilizing the image of Count Dracula pop-
ularized by Hamilton Deane, established the film vampire that
would endure for decades. Although audiences knew he drank
human blood, they were shown neither blood nor fangs. The
true repulsiveness of the traditional vampire, including hairy
palms and a breath that reeked of decay and the grave, were
eliminated in favor of a Dracula who was immaculate, well-
mannered and desirable to women. He was more the mysterious and romantic continental rather than a reanimated
corpse--a Rudolph Valentino of sorts, with a cape and a coffin to sleep in during the day. Most subsequent vampire
films featuring un-dead noblemen would imitate Lugosi's
Count Dracula.

DRACULA had made Bela Lugosi an American motion
picture star. It had placed him in great demand, primarily
for horror films. But DRACULA also doomed him. Lugosi's
stylized method of acting hurt his career. As motion pictures began to evolve away from the conventions of the 1930s,
Lugosi's acting hardly changed. In the minds of the motion
picture executives he was eternally the Count Dracula of 1931,
and he was condemned to continue enacting virtually the same
performance in numerous films that were to follow. Lugosi
found himself foisted into such atrocities as THE INVISIBLE
GHOST (1941) and RETURN OF THE APE MAN (1944), both
of which were made by the "Poverty Row" studio, Monogram
Pictures. He did an occasional class feature such as Universal's SON OF FRANKENSTEIN (1939), wherein he played
one of his only roles that did not seem to be a variation of
his Dracula--that of the broken-necked Ygor, which made
him almost unrecognizable under the heavy make-up of Jack
Pierce.

The actor made perhaps the greatest mistake of his
life when he turned down the role of the Monster in FRANK-
ENSTEIN. It was a role without dialogue and that did not
appeal to his star ego. Boris Karloff, a veteran screen actor who was still relatively unknown to movie-goers, accepted
the part. An Englishman and a far better actor than Lugosi,
Karloff became the top star in horror films, nosing the Hungarian performer into second place status. Having become a

star on the basis of one picture, Lugosi was shoved aside by
the superior merits of a second picture by the same studio
only a year later.

By accepting parts in low-budget horror films made
by companies like Monogram and PRC, Lugosi maintained his
star image. He was, unfortunately for his career, however,
starring in totally indistinguished productions while Karloff
went on to perform in higher-budgeted films, some of which
had nothing to do with monsters or horror. Lugosi had become the perennial and usually mad bogeyman, hopelessly
typecast and usually photographed in some pose reminiscent
of Count Dracula.

After DRACULA, Lugosi's health went progressively
downhill. Increasing body pains which he developed in the
early 1930s forced the actor into taking morphine, and he became tragically addicted to the drug. Shortly after a volun-
tary stay in a hospital to treat his addiction, Lugosi returned
briefly to the screen and, on August 18, 1956, passed away.
His final request, that he be buried wearing the black cape
of Count Dracula, was honored.

Several years after the actor's death, William G. Obbagy founded the American Bela Lugosi Fan Club, which sends
out such items as The Bela Lugosi Journal and other fan club
paraphernalia to members. At this writing, Obbagy is nego-
tiating for publication of his definitive biography on Bela Lugosi entitled Dracula Without His Cape. Another biography,
The Count: The Life and Films of Bela "Dracula" Lugosi,
by Arthur Lenning, was published by Putnam in 1974.

DRACULA, still a popular movie despite its age, certainly established the form of the vampire film. Most Dracula and other vampire films that would follow owed something
to the 1931 classic. DRACULA is frequently shown on television and was re-released to theatres in 1968 with crisp,
brand new 35mm prints on a double bill with Karloff's
FRANKENSTEIN. When the two films were "premiered" in
Hollywood, Universal provided a party with television news
coverage for privileged members of Donald A. Reed's Count
Dracula Society, a group "Devoted to the Serious Study of
Horror Films and Gothic Literature," some of whom came
dressed in garb imitative of the King of Vampires.

Not many people are aware that an alternate version
of DRACULA was also filmed by Universal in 1931. Sound-

Carlos Villarías as "Conde" Dracula looms menacingly over Mina in the Spanish version of DRACULA made by Universal in 1931.

dubbing techniques had not yet been satisfactorily developed and the studio did not want to lose its Spanish-speaking audience.   Thus, a second version of DRACULA was filmed using the same sets but a different cast, including Carlos Villarías as "Conde" Dracula, Lupita Tobar, Barry Norton, Alvarez Rubio and Carmen Guerreo.   George Melford directed.

Count Dracula had been impaled by Van Helsing's wooden stake.   Van Helsing believed it unlikely that the King Vampire would ever emerge again from his coffin.   Yet the doctor had not suspected that old Dracula had other interests than drinking blood and might have even been a family man. There were still members of the Dracula household anxious to prowl the night in their ebony mantles. *

---

*Scenes from the Bela Lugosi DRACULA appeared in GAMES
(cont. on p. 123)

THE FAMILY OF DRACULA

Count Dracula's impaled corpse lay at rest for several years within the stark walls of Carfax Abbey. But these were years as reckoned in the real world, not in the twilight world pictured on the screen. DRACULA'S DAUGHTER, the sequel to DRACULA, was started just after the completion of the original film and was issued by Universal Pictures in 1936. Count Dracula himself did not appear in DRACULA'S DAUGH-TER except for a few scenes in which he was "portrayed" by a convincing wax dummy in the likeness of Bela Lugosi.

DRACULA'S DAUGHTER proved that the old Count did more in his Transylvanian abode than Tod Browning had re-vealed. The question of who was Dracula's wife might have given the more sophisticated viewers of the day some pruri-ent thoughts, as the only women shown in the castle in the first film were the Count's three sisters. However, there

---

(1968), a horror mystery film made by Universal and direc-ted by Curtis Harrington, and in THE INNERVIEW (1973), an experimental film by Richard Beymer. In 1932 the image of Lugosi's Dracula appeared in the "coming attractions" trailer for MURDERS IN THE RUE MORGUE, a Universal film star-ring the Hungarian actor.

Both Lugosi and Boris Karloff, referring to one an-other by the names they made famous, were filmed playing chess on the set of yet another Universal horror film THE BLACK CAT (1934), their dialogue being:

    KARLOFF: Ready for the test, Dracula?

    LUGOSI: I'm ready ... Frankenstein.

    KARLOFF: Then ... let us begin. (LAUGHTER)
           You understand, Bela, don't you, that the one
           who wins this little game of chess is to lead
           the parade at the Film Stars Frolic.

    LUGOSI: Okay, Boris. Your move.

    KARLOFF: Right.

This film clip was included in "Monsters We've Known and Loved" on the January 6, 1964 episode of the Wolper tele-vision documentary series HOLLYWOOD AND THE STARS (NBC). Scenes from NOSFERATU and Lugosi's RETURN OF THE VAMPIRE were also included.

Footage from DRACULA and its Universal sequels were also incorporated into various television documentaries such as "Wayne and Shuster Take an Affectionate Look at the Mon-sters" (Canadian, 1966) and "I Never Drink ... Wine" (NET, 1970).

were numerous peasant girls romping about the Carpathian Mountains who could have been taken as his bride.

London-born Gloria Holden starred in the film as Countess Dracula, alias Countess Marya Zaleska, the ill-fated daughter of Dracula. She was a beautiful actress with dark brown hair and a classic face. As Countess Zaleska, Ms. Holden was perfect, wearing a lengthy black gown with plunging neckline and with a pallid face that rarely altered expression. Her marble-like features and restrained performance conveyed her torment over her un-dead existence and suggested that she was not the wantonly evil creature her father had become.

After reading the script by Garrett Fort, Gloria Holden remarked: "Why, this author has made me a ruthless vampire, a beast in human form. I don't believe any woman has ever been asked to play such a poisonous role before. He's made me an insatiable fiend. I would just like to meet the man who wrote such an inhuman role for me. He must be a monstrous, horrible person."

More vampiric in appearance than Countess Zaleska was her surprisingly human servant Sandor, played by future motion picture director Irving Pichel. Sandor's face was chalk white (due to the make-up artistry of Jack P. Pierce, who created all of the Universal monsters and fiends), with lush dark lips and deep set eyes. His straight black hair was parted down the middle. For some unexplained reason even Sandor shrank from the sight of the crucifix. He resembled a walking corpse and made Countess Zaleska look like a sun-bather by comparison.

Edward Van Sloan returned in DRACULA'S DAUGHTER as Dr. Van Helsing, the role for which he would be best remembered. Playing the practical-minded Dr. Jeffrey Garth was Otto Kruger, doing his best to prove that vampires did not exist.

DRACULA'S DAUGHTER was reputedly based on Bram Stoker's story "Dracula's Guest." But other than that it was

Opposite: Scenes from DRACULA'S DAUGHTER, Universal's 1936 sequel to the original Lugosi film. Top, Countess Marya Zaleska (Gloria Holden) burns the staked remains of her un-dead father. Bottom, Sandor (Irving Pichel) looks more like a vampire than the Countess herself.

about a vampire countess, the film's story was completely
original. The motion picture opens on the Carfax Abbey set
left over from DRACULA. Dr. Van Helsing is found in Carfax by the police with the corpses of Renfield and Count
Dracula. Van Helsing attempts to explain to the constables
that he has destroyed a menace by driving a stake through
the heart of the man in tuxedo and cape. But the policemen,
seeing only a gentleman in a coffin with a stake lodged
through the chest, arrest the elderly doctor on a charge of
murder. Unlike Stoker's Count Dracula, this vampire did
not decompose when the stake impaled his heart. He sports
no animal-like fangs and appears to be no more than a normal human being with a pale face. Van Helsing is clearly
in an embarrassing predicament, stuck with an explanation
which most sensible men would not believe. The doctor sends
for his former pupil, Dr. Jeffrey Garth, whose views on the
subject of vampirism coincide with those of the police.

At night a mysterious woman clothed entirely in black
enters the morgue where Dracula's corpse has been placed.
Utilizing a mysterious ring that emits hypnotic light, she
puts the two constables guarding the corpse into a trance and
then steals the body. She then sets about cremating the body
of Dracula on a funeral pyre in a secluded wooden glen. By
now viewers were aware that this could only be the "Dracula's
daughter" of the title. In the most effective and atmospheric
sequence in the film, she proceeds, holding a crucifix over
the corpse but forced to turn away her head. Then she says:

> Unto Adoni and Aseroth, into the keeping of
> the lords of the flame and lower pits, I consign this
> body, to be for ever more consumed in this purging
> fire. Let all baleful spirits that threaten the souls
> of men be banished by the sprinkling of this salt.
> Be thou exorcized, O Dracula, and thy body long
> un-dead, find destruction throughout eternity in the
> name of thy dark, unholy master. In the name of
> the all holiest, and through this cross, be the evil
> spirit cast out until the end of time.

It was remarkable that the vampiress could even grasp the
cross. Nevertheless, the darkly clad figure uses it during
her exorcism, then proceeds to burn the corpse of Count
Dracula.

Countess Dracula, using the name of Marya Zaleska,
has intentions which are contrary to those of her late father.

While the Count enjoyed his un-dead condition, his daughter regards herself as a wretched creature and desires a cure. That might have given her more of a complex had she considered the matter a bit more deeply. She was a vampire. And vampires are living corpses. If she did find a cure, would she resume life as a normal, living human being? Or would she fall back in her grave as a cold and lifeless corpse? The matter apparently did not concern her.

Meeting Dr. Garth at a party, Countess Zaleska is immediately attracted to him and begins to relate her problems. Garth advises that she must confront her mysterious problem head-on before she can overcome it. Back at her apartment, Zaleska sends out her servant Sandor to bring back a subject on the pretext of painting her on canvas. Sandor goes out and prevents a girl named Lili (Nan Grey) from committing suicide, then brings her back to the Countess. Believing the young English Dr. Garth to be a threat to the eternal life promised him by the Countess, Sandor hopes that the Countess will not be able to control her blood-lust. Countess Zaleska tells Lili that she wants to do a study of her head and shoulders and requests that the girl drop her shoulder straps. Zaleska watches her curiously, eyes staring wide. After the pretty girl exposes her shoulders and innocently tries to cover herself, the vampire woman is enflamed by temptation. As Countess Zaleska approaches the girl to perform her unholy action the camera pans to a leering mask on the wall. We hear Lili scream and are left to imagine what really happened.

The lesbian aspect of a female vampire aroused by the beauty of a female victim dates back to Le Fanu's "Carmilla." But Universal had always been a studio of taste, even in its horror pictures. Count Dracula was never shown with fangs; nor was blood ever shown smearing the vampire's mouth or spewing from his impaled heart. Atmosphere substituted for gore. It was understandable that so delicate a scene as the one in DRACULA'S DAUGHTER should be handled in such a way, leaving the true perversity to the imagination of the audience.

Sandor's wish had been fulfilled. His mistress could not combat her dark cravings. His loyalty to the Countess was based on her promise to make him un-dead and therefore immortal. He already looked like a vampire, so, he must have thought, why not become one? It was not explained why the Countess did not simply bite him on the neck and thus

convert him into one of the un-dead, instead of just constant-
ly promising to give him eternal life.

Finally, events happen which convince Dr. Garth that
vampires do exist. He notices that the Countess casts no
reflection in a mirror. He also examines the still living
Lili. Under hypnosis, she reveals that she was attacked by
something hideous; then she dies. Van Helsing makes Jeff
Garth believe that Countess Zaleska is actually the daughter
of Dracula.

Realizing that she cannot be cured, Zaleska asks
Garth to return with her to Transylvania to "share eternal
life." When Jeff refuses, the Countess commands Sandor to
abduct his fiancée, Janet Blake (played by Marguerite Church-
ill). Garth and Van Helsing, now cleared of his murder
charge, pursue the fleeing vampire, Sandor and their captive
to Transylvania. Back in the ancestral castle of the Draculas,
the Countess rises from her coffin and resumes her former
role as an evil vampire. As Garth approaches Castle Dracula, Sandor fires arrows from above. Jeff enters the grim
structure to find Janet in a trance-like state. The Countess
appears and tells him that Janet will die unless he remains
in the castle with her. Dr. Garth can only comply. The
Countess' powerful gaze meets his but as she moves toward
his throat with her mouth, the jealous Sandor acts. Watching from above the act which would forever rob him of his
eternal life, Sandor releases an arrow. But as the Countess
sees imminent death in store for the man she loves, she
steps in the shaft's path, receiving the arrow through the
heart. The police, led by Van Helsing, arrive in time to
shoot Sandor. On the misty balcony of her castle, Countess
Zaleska dies. Van Helsing replies to a policeman's com-
ment on her beauty, "Yes ... as beautiful as she was when
she died ... over 500 years ago."

DRACULA'S DAUGHTER was directed by Lambert
Hillyer, whose film achievements were sometimes inconsistent.
In 1943 he would direct the somewhat ludicrous movie serial,
BATMAN (a comic book character who took on the guise of a
human bat but without first becoming a vampire), made by
Columbia Pictures. Unlike most sequel films, DRACULA'S
DAUGHTER proved that a second film in a series could be
better than the original. The camera now moved and the act-
ing was more restrained, especially in the title role. The
Dracula film had come a long way in five years.

Weekly Variety for May 2, 1936 reviewed DRACULA'S
DAUGHTER:

> This is a chiller with plenty of ice; a surefire
> waker-upper in the theatre and a stay-awake influ-
> ence in the bedroom later on. Rates tops among
> recent horror pictures and, as such, figures to
> deliver nice grosses.
>
> Entire E. M. Asher production rates bows,
> from the scenario groundwork up through the act-
> ing, direction and photography.
>
> For a change, this is a picture that is quite
> entertaining along with its shocks. It's light in
> spots, thanks to the good dialog and the acting of
> Otto Kruger, Marguerite Churchill and Billy Bevan,
> while the heavy portions are more than adequately
> handled by Gloria Holden, portraying Dracula's vam-
> pire daughter, and Irving Pichel, her jealous serv-
> ant. Edward Van Sloan, who played the scientist
> in the original Dracula film, is ditto in this, and
> just as convincing....

If Count Dracula had a daughter whom Stoker knew
nothing about, it was also conceivable that he had a son. Although Lon Chaney, Sr. never played the role of Dracula, his
son, Lon Chaney, Jr., enacted the titled role in Universal's
SON OF DRACULA (1943). Chaney, Jr. was a popular star
during the early Forties, his most masterful horror role being that of the sympathetic werewolf in THE WOLF MAN
(Universal 1941). In 1943 Chaney was ripe to play Dracula's
son, but he was, unfortunately, miscast.

Chaney's roles could be both sympathetic and brutal.
He abandoned his ability to convey pathos, however, in his
portrayal of the son of Dracula. In his attempt to act the
part of a suave foreign nobleman Chaney seemed to be a
brutal American who looked out of place in the well-groomed
mustache and formal wear and seemed uncomfortable delivering the often stilted dialogue. His acting in SON OF DRAC-
ULA was adequate but the role was simply not suited to his
personality. Nevertheless the film gained popularity at least
in part because of Chaney's presence.

The script for SON OF DRACULA was written by Eric
Taylor, who based the story on an original idea by Curt
Siodmak. Some of the things Taylor did with vampire lore
upset many viewers but actually did not contradict tradition.

In DRACULA and DRACULA'S DAUGHTER great stress was placed on the vampire's lacking a mirror image. An equal amount of effort went into showing his reflection in this third film in the series. Viewers in the audience who were familiar only with the vampire lore invented by Bram Stoker cringed with disappointment over the lack of continuity with the other films, unaware that this vampire interpretation was actually closer to the "real" thing.

For the first time in a Dracula movie the vampire was shown to transform into a bat, right before the startled eyes of the audience. A mechanical bat (the best yet to ever appear in a movie) was constructed by the Universal Pictures prop department. The creature could perform a number of realistic movements and flew on "invisible" piano wires, which guided it through a number of believable actions.

The studio's optical effects wizard, John P. Fulton, was given the problem of making this transformation from man to bat (or the opposite) on screen. He was a master of such visual effects and his ultimate work for Universal was in the 1933 motion picture, THE INVISIBLE MAN. Fulton made expert use of the traveling matte, a process by which two separate pictures may be combined by providing each with reciprocal masks and then double-exposing the film. Fulton used shots of the mechanical bat and the human Chaney and photographed both from the same camera set-up. Using the matte process Fulton then showed the transformation stages in animation. The effect was startling, with the wings of the bat smoothly enlarging and reshaping into the cloak of the son of Dracula.

The male offspring of Count Dracula went under the name of Count Alucard, cleverly spelling the family name backwards. (This was the first use of the name "Alucard." In later years the overuse of the backwards spelling would become laughable.)

Count Alucard, a nobleman from Transylvania, is to be the house guest at Dark Oaks, a great plantation in the southern United States. Beautiful Katherine Caldwell (Louise Albritton) had met the Count while sojourning in Europe and had invited him to the mansion in which she lives. But when

Opposite: Lon Chaney, Jr. as Count Alucard, another blood-thirsty offspring of the King of Vampires, in Universal's 1943 entry, SON OF DRACULA.

Frank Stanley (Robert Paige), the man who loves Kay, and
Dr. Harry Brewster (Frank Craven) go to meet his train,
Count Alucard is not there. All that arrives is a coffin-like
trunk bearing the name ALUCARD and several boxes of earth.

Kay is a morbid-minded person and so, when Count
Alucard fails to appear at the gala party she has prepared
for him at the mansion, she goes to consult the old Hungarian queen Zimba (Adeline Reynolds) in her hut in the swamp.
The hag warns Kay that she will be married to a corpse and
live in a grave. Suddenly, a large bat flies into the hut and
plucks at her eyes. The old crone dies of fright.

A mysterious cloaked figure arrives at Dark Oaks
after the party has ended. Raising his cape, he transforms
into a bat and flies through the upstairs window. Again at-
taining human form, the figure attacks Kay's father (played
by George Irving), then starts a fire.

Shortly after, the cloaked figure stands at the door to
the Dark Oaks mansion, announcing himself: "I am Count
Alucard." He is told that the master of the house is dead.
The following night, Count Alucard lures Kay to the swamp,
where she sees his trunk rise to the surface of the dark
waters. Mist, seemingly alive, issues from the sides of the
trunk and reshapes into the solid figure of Count Alucard.
This was another depiction of authentic vampire legend. And
just as the traditional vampire was forbidden to cross running
water, Count Alucard (probably more for effect than in an attempt to remain faithful to legend) stands atop the trunk as it
floats to shore. Count Alucard and the mesmerized Kay proceed to a justice of the peace. As they are married, lightning flashes outside, as if to protest the unholy bond.

Learning of the loss of Kay, Frank hurries to Dark
Oaks and confronts Alucard at gunpoint. Kay steps behind
Alucard as Frank fires, the bullets mysteriously passing
through the unharmed nobleman and killing Kay. His mind
unhinged, Frank runs from the house, passing through the
graveyard as Alucard pursues him in bat form. Only the
moonlight illuminating a cross at a grave forces Alucard to
resume human shape and flee. (This scene makes one wonder how so many movie vampires panic at the sight of the
cross, yet find no difficulty parading through cross-filled
ceneteries.) When Frank confesses to Dr. Brewster that he
has killed Kay, the physician goes to visit the newlyweds,
finding the entranced Kay alive. Alucard warns Brewster that

they have decided not to receive visitors any more and that his work will force them to sleep during the daylight hours. Later, Kay's body is found in a casket in the family crypt and Frank is incarcerated for murder.

As DRACULA had its Van Helsing, SON OF DRACULA had its gray-haired Professor Lazlo (J. Edwards Bromberg), a professor of the occult, who cleverly deduces that "Alucard" is "Dracula" spelled backwards and that they are dealing with a vampire. "I am convinced," says Lazlo, "that he is either a victim of or a direct descendant of the original Dracula."

In more recent years there has been some controversy as to the proper identity of Count Alucard. A number of publications devoted to films and monsters have somehow "proven" that Alucard is no son of Dracula at all, but the original Count himself. This misconception seems to arise from a line of dialogue later made by the vampiric Kay, "He's Count Dracula." In considering this suspect conclusion, first, we must remember that Dracula is not a complete name, only a surname. In this respect, Countess Zaleska from DRACULA'S DAUGHTER has as much right to say "I am Dracula" as her father or any brother or sister. Secondly, one must examine the continuity between the various Universal Dracula films. In DRACULA'S DAUGHTER the impaled corpse of Count Dracula is burned on a pyre. In the Dracula film following SON OF DRACULA the Count's first appearance is in the form of a staked skeleton which has been taken from Castle Dracula in the Carpathians. Purists might rationalize that the fire had merely burned the skin off Dracula's corpse and that Countess Zaleska took her father's bones back with her to Transylvania. The continuity (admittedly stretched a bit) works between the second and forth Dracula films. The third picture is obviously a film set apart from the others, with Alucard's appearance and final destruction in no way contingent on the preceding or following movies. Lastly, there is the title of the film itself--SON OF DRACULA-- which, to me, hardly seems deceptive.

As Professor Lazlo instructs his friend Dr. Brewster in the lore of the un-dead, a mist seeps under the door and forms into the tall, powerful figure of Count Alucard. The vampire gloats that he has left his dry homeland for the blood-rich New World. But as he prepares to attack Dr. Brewster, Lazlo wards him off with a crucifix, forcing him to change into a mist and slip out of the room under the door.

As Frank waits in jail, mist issues from Kay's coffin and takes on bat form. The bat enters Frank's cell, and when Frank awakens he finds the woman he thought killed standing before him. Kay reveals that she has willingly become a vampire to attain eternal life. She still loves Frank and has married Alucard solely for immortality. Wanting Frank to destroy Alucard and join her so that they can be together eternally, she reveals the location of Alucard's coffin. A short time later Frank escapes jail.

Frank locates Alucard's coffin in an old drainage tunnel and proceeds to burn it so that the vampire will have no place to return to before sunrise. From outside the tunnel, a vampire bat assumes the shape of Alucard, who reacts with rage upon seeing his casket in flames. Alucard shields himself from the fire, then tries to force Frank to extinguish the fire. When Alucard realizes that his coffin is beyond salvage he tries to enact a final vengeance upon his adversary. The vampire seizes Frank's throat in his super-strong grip and squeezes, but suddenly, a look of horror contorts the hate-filled expression on Alucard's face as he perceives the ominous light of dawn. Count Alucard releases Frank and falls into the foul water of the tunnel. A close-up reveals his hand dissolving to that of a skeleton--the first of many such scenes that would appear in future Dracula films. Following the destruction of Count Alucard, Frank burns the coffin and corpse of Kay, thereby saving her soul from the evil of the vampire.

SON OF DRACULA was directed by Robert Siodmak, the brother of writer Curt Siodmak. The film is not generally accepted as a classic Dracula film and many snobbish film aficionados dismiss it as ludicrous. I contend, though, that SON OF DRACULA is the slickest and most entertaining of the trilogy. The special effects are the best of any entry to Universal's Dracula series. Although Chaney had none of the suavity or menace of Lugosi, he did embody the physical strength of the un-dead better than his predecessors and presented a different interpretation of the vampire. SON OF DRACULA was made during a time when the old monsters had more difficulty actually scaring audiences and so turned to thrilling them instead. Siodmak's direction placed less emphasis on the terror of the vampire as shown in DRACULA and DRACULA'S DAUGHTER and relied more upon action and visual effects. SON OF DRACULA was a perfect example of the horror film trends of the 1940s.

One review of SON OF DRACULA appeared in the Los
Angeles <u>Times</u> for November 19, 1943:

> Who should ever expect Old Man Dracula, the Vam-
> pire Kid, to have a son? Well, he did, according
> to Universal Studio writers, and the said offspring,
> a chip off the old block, bobs up in 'Son of Dracu-
> la, ' which opened yesterday at the Hawaii Theater
> in company with another chiller-diller, 'The Mad
> Ghoul. '
>   The son of Dracula inherits his dad's love
> of fresh human blood, especially that of young girls.
> So he hops over to America and grabs off Louise
> Albritton, and who could blame him? But he is
> foiled at last by the girl's sweetheart, who camps
> right on his trail through thick and thin until he
> hunts out the vampire and destroys him.
>   This is in accordance with the legend that
> only when he is kept from his daily beauty sleep,
> with his coffin bed destroyed, can the vampire be
> killed. But we bet writers will find some way to
> bring him back to life!
>   Really eerie touch is the manner in which
> Dracula changes, before your eyes, into a huge bat.
>   Lon Chaney is fast catching up with his
> father in ability to project a horrific atmosphere.
> Robert Paige is especially to be praised for his
> fine work. He is a fine emotional actor and should
> be given opportunity in a larger sphere.

The other members of Count Dracula's family were
doomed to permanent deaths. There was nothing for Universal's writers to do (unless there were some grandchildren of
Dracula lurking in Transylvania) but turn again to the original
Count. He had been cremated, but perhaps enough of the
Count's staked bones were extant to star him in another movie. And so the studio reintroduced the original Count Dracula.

DRACULA AND THE MONSTERS

Universal Pictures began to realize that the audience
for horror films in the Forties was generally younger than
that of the Thirties. Consequently, the Dracula movies of
the mid-1940s placed even more emphasis on action. The
studio still had faith in its stock company of creatures,

Dr. Niemann (Boris Karloff) removes the wooden stake and
revives Count Dracula (John Carradine) in Universal's multi-
monster epic, HOUSE OF FRANKENSTEIN (1944).

especially Count Dracula and the Frankenstein Monster, but
individually these classic horrors were no longer the frightful
creatures they had been when beheld by virgin audiences in
1931.   Universal may have felt that they had exhausted the
potentialities of both characters or may have believed that the
new, younger audience would not pay at the box office to see
either the Count or the Monster alone.   In 1943 the studio
had tried an experiment, pitting two of its most profitable
monsters against each other in a single film.   The result, an
action thriller entitled FRANKENSTEIN MEETS THE WOLF
MAN, was an enormous success.   The film reaped impressive profits, but it also presented the studio's writers with
another problem.   How does one top a film starring such
heavyweights as Frankenstein's Monster and the Wolf Man?

The answer was simple and inevitable: two monsters were
no longer enough.

Count Dracula's name still had power at the box office. Thus the unskinable King of Vampires was added to the
roster of horrors in the studio's proposed film THE DEVIL'S
BROOD. Universal announced that the film would have a
staggering total of "not one, not two, not even three ... but
five monsters." The film eventually went into production in
1944 under the more commercial title, HOUSE OF FRANKEN-
STEIN, with its cast of five monsters, "All Together! The
Screen's Titans of Terror!" Three of these were the obvious
Frankenstein Monster, Count Dracula and Wolf Man. The
validity of calling the last two "monsters" is questionable
(they were a mad doctor and a hunchback). However, the
billing of "five monsters" made for some highly potent advertising.

Although the original Dracula was to return in HOUSE
OF FRANKENSTEIN, the original star, Bela Lugosi, was not.
Two reasons have been given for Lugosi's not appearing in
the multi-monster film. The first is that the Hungarian actor was under contract to other studios at the time. The
second, given me by the actor who would portray Dracula in
HOUSE OF FRANKENSTEIN, is that he had finally grown
weary of the role and its identification. That same year,
though, Lugosi had accepted the Dracula-type lead in Columbia's RETURN OF THE VAMPIRE. The former explanation,
therefore, sounds more reasonable.

An ideal choice for the part in HOUSE OF FRANKEN-
STEIN was the gaunt Shakespearean actor, John Carradine,
who was freelancing at the time. He was born Richmond Reed
Carradine on February 5, 1906 in New York (not England, as
is commonly thought). As his father was an artist (also an
attorney, poet and newspaper correspondent) the young John
Carradine originally planned to take up sculpture as a pro-
fession. But after seeing the great Shakespearean actor
Robert Mantell in a performance of A MERCHANT OF VEN-
ICE, Carradine decided upon a thespian career. He moved
to Hollywood in 1929 and secured parts in various plays, preferring to do Shakespeare. The following year he played
Zeke in his first motion picture TOL'ABLE DAVID.

The motion pictures in which Carradine appeared
varied greatly in quality. His powerful performances included some very important roles in some of America's

finest films, including THE PRISONER OF SHARK ISLAND (1936), STAGECOACH (1939) and THE GRAPES OF WRATH (1939). In the latter, Carradine played his favorite movie role, that of a drunk minister. He also starred in such "poverty row" abominations as REVENGE OF THE ZOMBIES (1943), RETURN OF THE APE MAN and VOODOO MAN (both 1944), which are only worth watching on television for the unintentional humor and for Carradine's performances. Carradine had the ability to lend a touch of class to some of Hollywood's worst horror films. While HOUSE OF FRANKENSTEIN was certainly above the "poverty row" productions, it was still a "B" film. John Carradine gave it "A" film acting.

Carradine was perfect for the role of Count Dracula. Physically, he more resembled Bram Stoker's description of the Count than did Lugosi, one reason being that Carradine went to the original Dracula novel rather than to the Hamilton Deane play for his interpretation of the role. In an interview with Carradine, conducted by film historian Richard Andersen and myself, the actor said: "When they asked me to do it I said, 'Well, I'll do it if you let me make him up something like how he is described in the novel--with the mustache and the hawk nose.' And they let me do it to a certain extent. But I certainly didn't want to do it with the same black pompadour that Bela had. At that time I hadn't done the play. I've done the play since. "

Carradine as Count Dracula, with his gray-streaked hair and small mustache, conveyed a sense of death that permeated all of his scenes in HOUSE OF FRANKENSTEIN. Although the actor has been known to overact in some roles which had obviously been accepted solely for the salary, his performance as Dracula was beautifully restrained. There was more of a feeling of the supernatural in his portrayal than in Lugosi's mysterious foreigner. In effect Carradine had taken the very basic Lugosi/Dracula image and reshaped it to suit his own abilities. The result was a more modern and believable character than the Dracula image as presented by Lugosi.

HOUSE OF FRANKENSTEIN was directed by Erle C. Kenton and boasted an all-star cast familiar to horror film fans. Boris Karloff portrayed mad scientist Dr. Gustav Niemann, Lon Chaney recreated his role of Lawrence Talbot (alias the Wolf Man), J. Carrol Naish was Daniel the murderous hunchback, and Glenn Strange portrayed Frankenstein's

Monster.   Other notables in the cast were Lionel Atwill as
the perennial police inspector, George Zucco, Frank Reicher
and Michael Mark.

Basically there were two parts to HOUSE OF FRANK-
ENSTEIN.   The first involved Dr. Neimann and Daniel with
Count Dracula. *   The second part involved the same two
characters with the Wolf Man and the Frankenstein Monster.
Both parts were connected through the actions of the mad
Niemann and his hunchbacked friend.

Dr. Niemann and Daniel escape prison during a thunder
storm.   Niemann had been sentenced to jail for emulating the
experiments of Frankenstein by robbing graves and attempting
to give a dog a man's brain.   Once free, the mad doctor
hopes not only to prove his eccentric theories but also to enjoy revenge on the men whose testimony sent him to prison.
Niemann promises to give Daniel a new body and the hunchback becomes his homicidal servant in return.

The Dracula section of HOUSE OF FRANKENSTEIN
was shorter than the Frankenstein/Wolf Man section and considerably unrelated to the remainder of the film.   It was obvious that writer Curt Siodmak and scripter Edward T. Lowe
needed an excuse to involve Dracula in the action.   The
writers' problems included giving Niemann a logical reason
to encounter three of filmdom's most infamous monsters, all
of them originally isolated geographically: Count Dracula
hailed from Transylvania, Frankenstein's Monster should be
somewhere in Germany and the Wolf Man originated from
England.   Niemann's meeting with the Count was sheerly co-
incidental.

As Dr. Niemann and Daniel flee from the prison, they
are saved from the downpour by a pair of circus wagons
painted to identify them as Professor Bruno Lampini's traveling Chamber of Horrors.   Included in the show's exhibits is
the supposedly authentic skeleton of the original Count Dracula.   Lampini (George Zucco) explains to his new passengers
that he had "borrowed" the staked skeleton from its castle in
Transylvania and had spread a layer of soil in the bottom of
the coffin to simulate a grave; but if the stake were removed

---

*A condensed version of the Dracula part of HOUSE OF
FRANKENSTEIN has been made available for home use by
Castle Films, under the title DOOM OF DRACULA.

the bloodthirsty vampire would again rise from his grave to take to the night sky in the shape of a large bat.

When Lampini refuses to take his unidentified passengers to Reigelberg, a town in which Niemann wants to begin his campaign of revenge, the mad doctor orders Daniel to kill him and the driver. Then the two fugitives assume the identities of Professor Lampini and his assistant. Their first stop is Reigelberg where Herr Hussman (the very German actor Sig Ruman) is now burgomaster.

Setting up his Chamber of Horrors, the disguised Dr. Neimann calls an audience around him and opens the coffin of Count Dracula, revealing a skeleton with a wooden stake protruding from between its ribs. "Dare I but remove this stake from where his heart once beat," he says, "and he would rise from the grave! Ladies and gentlemen, the actual skeleton of Count Dracula, the vampire!"

Among those in the audience is Herr Hussman, who not only denounces the authenticity of the skeleton but also almost recognizes Niemann. After the audience leaves, Niemann yanks the wooden stake from the skeleton. Again John P. Fulton showed the power of the vampire. A network of veins, then muscles, begins to form over the skeleton until finally the formally attired Dracula lies within the casket. The Count takes in a deep breath of air, then gazes at the mortal who still holds the deadly stake precariously near his chest. Dracula attempts to use his mesmeric power to force Niemann to drop the stake. But the doctor's will is also strong and he manages to fight off the hypnotic gaze. Threatening to ram the stake back into Dracula's heart (which would have been difficult for even a younger man without a hammer), Niemann makes the vampire an offer. Niemann says he will protect Dracula's coffin providing Dracula does as he wishes. The vampire agrees and is thus involved in Niemann's bizarre scheme of vengeance.

Giving his name as "Baron Latos of Transylvania," Dracula offers his coach to the departing Hussman, his grandson Carl (Peter Coe) and the latter's pretty wife Rita (Anne Gwynne). Herr Hussman returns the favor by inviting Latos to his home for some wine. Apparently Dracula's habits had changed since the 1931 movie with Lugosi. For he accepts and drinks the wine that Lugosi would have refused. Dracula is attracted to Rita and gives her his ring (the same one worn by Lugosi). It shrinks to fit her finger and imparts to her strange visions of a world where people are dead yet alive.

Later, Dracula enters Hussman's room, forcing him into an unconscious state by the hypnotic control of his eyes. Then, transforming into a bat through Fulton's wizardry, he drains the burgomaster's blood.   Carl discovers his grandfather's corpse with the marks of the vampire on his neck and telephones police inspector Arnz (Lionel Atwill).   But as Carl hangs up the phone he sees that Dracula has lured Rita, entranced by the ring, to his coach.   Before Carl can stop him, Dracula drives off with his wife.   Arnz and his mounted gendarmes arrive and a chase follows that ranks with the best action scenes of the high-budgeted Westerns.   Sweeping pan and exciting trucking shots show Dracula driving his black horses hard, pursued by the relentless posse.   Also involved in the chase are Niemann and Daniel, who fear apprehension by the police.

The sun begins to grow light with the first rays of dawn.   Dracula frantically tries to get to the circus wagons and the protection of his coffin before daybreak.   In an attempt to divert the attention of the police, Daniel casts Dracula's coffin from the wagon.   To complicate matters, Dracula's horses break free of the carriage.   The Count leaps to the ground as his carriage overturns.   Then he struggles to reach his coffin which is resting on the ground.   But as the vampire attempts to reach the coffin bearing the Dracula crest, he is trapped by the rays of the rising sun.   Trying in vain to shield himself from the solar rays, Dracula drops to the earth, then crawls to his casket.   There is a close-up of his white gloved hand becoming transparent and dissolving to bones.   Carl and the police arrive to see Dracula's ring fall from Rita's finger, his evil influence over her eradicated.   Presumably Count Dracula was destroyed forever since even Universal's writers had no escape for a vampire defeated by sunlight.

The rest of HOUSE OF FRANKENSTEIN takes Dr. Niemann and Daniel to the ruins of Dr. Frankenstein's castle, where they discover the bodies of the Monster and the Wolf Man frozen in ice.   Freeing both monsters, Niemann proposes to have his revenge on his last two enemies by a series of brain transplants.   The Wolf Man is eventually shot with a silver bullet (also apparently killed for the last time); the Frankenstein Monster is revived by electricity and kills Daniel, who had turned on Niemann when he failed to provide the hunchback with the promised perfect body.   The film ends with the torch-carrying villagers pursuing the Monster, who is carrying the wounded Niemann, into the swamp.   Both the Frankenstein Monster and the mad scientist are swallowed up in a pool of quicksand.

HOUSE OF FRANKENSTEIN shows the downward trend in the Universal horror films. The three primary horrors (Frankenstein Monster, Dracula and Wolf Man) have little to do in the picture. The story is really that of the mad doctor and the hunchback. Nevertheless, HOUSE OF FRANKENSTEIN was a good action film, still with much of the old Universal atmosphere. The cast was first-rate, as were the direction, set design, make-ups by Jack Pierce and special effects by John Fulton. The picture was so well made, in fact, that the coincidences employed to bring together the three most monstrous creatures in Universal's horror mythology could easily be overlooked.

Hollywood Reporter for December 15, 1944, reviewed HOUSE OF FRANKENSTEIN as follows:

> 'House of Frankenstein' comes very close to being the horror picture to end all horror pictures. At least it sets quite a mark to shoot at. Likewise, so far as Universal's array of chill-thrill characters of established fame is concerned, it poses quite a problem for a follow-up, since all of them are killed very dead in this one, with only a couple of very small loopholes left for bringing them back to life.
>
> For this one, Paul Malvern shot the works and staged a complete roundup, using practically all the horror characters so far known in a Universal series. So here we have Dracula, the Wolf Man, the Monster, Boris Karloff once more in the role of a soulless scientist and J. Carrol Naish as an unlovely hunchback. About the only one missing is that Egyptian mummy which has been emerging from the 'U' lot with considerable regularity, and it seems only fitting that someone should ask Mr. Malvern why the mummy was slighted to the point of exclusion.
>
> Universal also shot the works on the picture in the matter of lavish staging and gross expenditure, assembling a lengthy and, for the most part, high priced cast. The result is one which should please the most avid horror fan and the company has no cause to worry about the financial intake.

Universal had apparently been thinking of HOUSE OF FRANKENSTEIN as the last film of the series. The above reviewer, however, like most fans of these films, probably

knew that, despite the seemingly inescapable deaths of all
three monsters, they would someday and somehow lurk again.
HOUSE OF FRANKENSTEIN was a profitable picture and the
studio heads began to realize that it may have been wrong in
giving it's bread winners so untimely a death. Somehow
there had to be at least one last sequel. HOUSE OF DRAC-
ULA* was inevitable. But reviving such "permanently" destroyed characters as Dracula and the Wolf Man presented
problems. The decision was finally made not to bother with
explanations. HOUSE OF DRACULA would have to stand on
its own merits and risk the criticisms of frustrating purists
who demanded rigid continuity.

HOUSE OF DRACULA (1945), directed by Erle C.
Kenton, was the last serious entry in Universal's Dracula
series. It was also the shortest, totaling only sixty-seven
minutes (two minutes shorter than DRACULA'S DAUGHTER).
Like its predecessor, HOUSE OF DRACULA featured five
"monsters": Count Dracula (Carradine),** the Wolf Man
(Chaney), Frankenstein's Monster (Strange), another mad scientist (played by Onslow Stevens) and a new hunchback, a very
non-monstrous nurse named Nina (Jane Adams).

Universal must have known that this would end its
Dracula/Frankenstein/Wolf Man series of films. The motives
and fates of some of the creatures in HOUSE OF DRACULA
intimated the culmination of their careers even more decided-
ly than in HOUSE OF FRANKENSTEIN. The film opens with
a giant vampire bat flapping outside the castle of Dr. Franz
Edelmann, who would not become the advertised mad doctor
until later. The bat transforms into the lean figure of Count
Dracula, now with snow white hair. The Count enters the
castle. (The title of the motion picture was misleading, as
this was really the house of Dr. Edelmann and not that of
Count Dracula.)

Count Dracula's character was somewhat changed in
that he was tired of his life as an evil vampire and wanted
Edelmann to cure his condition. Again, the fate of a cured
vampire (as in DRACULA'S DAUGHTER) was not considered
by Dracula, the doctor or script-writer Edward T. Lowe.
Dracula meets Dr. Edelmann, announcing himself again as

*HOUSE OF DRACULA was released in Italy as LA CASA
DEGLI ORRORI ("The House of Horror").
**Carradine's stand-in for HOUSE OF DRACULA was
Arthur W. Stern.

Baron Latos. When "Latos" takes Edelmann into the basement of the castle and reveals his coffin, he admits to being Count Dracula, a supernatural creature begging release from his cursed existence. Dr. Edelmann denies the reality of supernatural vampires. But when he cannot arrive at an explanation as to how the mysterious visitor brought a coffin into a castle in which all doors are locked, he agrees to try to find a cure.

Edelmann's lovely assistant Miliza (Martha O'Driscoll) has met Baron Latos on an earlier occasion. As they reminisce, Edelmann calls the vampire into his laboratory and begins his tests, aided by the hunchbacked nurse whom the doctor has promised also to cure some day. Edelmann takes a sample of Dracula's blood. He learns that certain parasites

The Count (John Carradine) reveals his earth-filled coffin to Dr. Edelmann (Onslow Stevens) in Universal's HOUSE OF DRACULA (1945).

in the Count's blood have caused him to exist as a vampire
and that the cure lies in finding an antibody to combat these
parasites.   Thus writer Lowe had devised a new scientific
explanation for vampirism.

As if two "monsters" requiring cures were not enough,
Dr. Edelmann is next visited by Lawrence Talbot.   When
Edelmann is too busy to talk to him, Talbot leaves and sur-
renders himself to the jail in the town of Visaria.   Inspector
Holtz (Lionel Atwill) later calls Edelmann to see the obviously mad prisoner, and Edelmann and Miliza watch as the tor-
mented Talbot is changed into a werewolf by the moonbeams
entering the jail cell window.

Now there is also Talbot awaiting a cure in the castle.
Again science tries to debunk the supernatural.   Edelmann
deduces that Talbot's lycanthropic condition is attributable to
a certain pressure on his brain and self-hypnosis induced by
the full moon.   Edelmann has been growing a certain type of
mold which he believes will allow him to soften Talbot's
cranium, relieve the pressure and, consequently, cure him.
But since there is not yet enough mold to cure Talbot, the
young man tries to commit suicide by leaping into the sea.

Edelmann is later lowered by a harness, off the cliffside to the water, and comes upon a cave, where he is attacked by the Wolf Man who regains human form before he
can kill the doctor.   Miraculously, the cave happens to offer
the best conditions to grow the mold which will cure Talbot.
It also contains the barely living body of Frankenstein's Monster and the skeleton of Dr. Niemann, still where they had
been deposited with the quicksand from the last movie.

Meanwhile, Dracula renews his past interest in Miliza
and apparently reconsiders his desire to be cured, deciding
to return with her to Transylvania.   He places her under his
control.   Nina notices that when he and Miliza leave the castle, only the woman casts a reflection in the mirror.   Edelmann later tells her that Latos is really Count Dracula and
that emergency measures must be taken.   When the doctor
later tries to give Dracula another transfusion, the vampire
puts him in an hypnotic trance (the picture becoming hazy)
and instead gives the doctor a transfusion of his own polluted
blood.

Reviving, the weakened Edelmann hurries to save Miliza.   The vampire bat enters the bedroom of the mesmerized

Miliza and transforms into human shape. But Edelmann
saves her, driving the Count away with a crucifix as Talbot
enters the room. (This was the first on-screen confrontation between Dracula and Talbot.) As dawn begins to break,
Edelmann hurries to the basement where Dracula has already
retired to his coffin. Dragging the casket under the rays of
the sun, Edelmann throws open the lid. Bathed in the solar
rays, the sleeping body of Dracula dissolves to bones with
yet half the film remaining.

This destruction-of-Dracula scene was most erroneous.
In most instances where vampires are destroyed, their graves
are open during the day when the un-dead are helpless to act;
it is then that the stake is driven into the heart. Script-
writer Lowe apparently did not realize that his destroying the
vampire by merely opening his coffin lid obviated the use of
a stake. It must be remembered that most vampires who
perished by the stake were not wealthy noblemen like Dracula and could not afford the luxury of shadowy crypts that kept
out all sunlight. For most of them a regular grave in the
ground had to suffice.

This being technically a Dracula film, Edelmann was
not yet finished with the character despite his destruction by
the sun. To his horror, Edelmann learns that his blood has
been contaminated by the blood of Dracula. Now the scientist
becomes a type of Dr. Edelmann and Mr. Hyde, a living
vampire with a pale face and dark set eyes and a mad desire
to kill and attack people's jugular veins. (The publicity might
have better advertised a "Mr. Hyde" instead of another "Mad
Doctor.") In one impressive scene, as the blood of Dracula
overcomes him, Edelmann gazes into a mirror. And as he
transforms into his monstrous alter ego he observes his reflection vanish in the glass. In his delirium Edelmann is
haunted by the images of Dracula, of Nina, and of himself
commanding the Frankenstein Monster.

In his normal state Edelmann realizes that he must
use the mold to cure his nurse while there is yet time. But
she convinces him that Talbot's operation is more urgent.
After the operation, Talbot faces the full moon's rays and
remains a human being, apparently never again to be resurrected by Universal's script-writers. But before Talbot can
thank his savior, Edelmann, now again possessed by Dracula's
blood, is outside and thirsty for a victim. He sees his hired
man Siegfried (Ludwig Stossel) driving his horse-pulled wagon
toward the village. Jumping into the wagon, Edelmann

(actually stuntman Carey Loftin) kills him like a human vampire. The resulting death brings the villagers in pursuit of the madman, with some excellent photography by George Robinson showing Edelmann's giant shadow upon the buildings of Visaria. The mysterious killer is pursued back to Dr. Edelmann's castle. Since Siegfried was apparently killed by the teeth of a wild animal, Inspector Holtz naturally suspects the murderer to be Talbot. As the police and the villagers storm the castle with their torches, Edelmann confesses all to Talbot, who understands how a man can be forced to kill. Talbot agrees to hold back the mob until Edelmann has time to operate on Nina.

In the laboratory, however, Edelmann once again becomes transformed by Dracula's blood. Instead of proceeding with the operation, Edelmann begins to revive the Frankenstein Monster with his electrical apparatus. When Nina tries to stop him, the doctor strangles her, cackling insanely (and with more eerie shadow work on the laboratory wall). Summoned by Nina's screams, Talbot, Miliza and Holtz rush to the laboratory, where they see the mad Edelmann and the obedient Frankenstein Monster. The Monster kills Holtz. Immediately afterward Talbot grabs the policeman's luger and when Edelmann begins to stalk toward Talbot, the former werewolf is forced to shoot the man who cured him. The doctor's face transforms into the visage of the kindly Edelmann and he dies a human being. Seeing his master killed, the Frankenstein Monster lashes out at Talbot, who retaliates by knocking over some racks of chemicals. A fire starts and Talbot, Miliza and the mob flee from the burning building, leaving the Monster to face his doom.

Despite the good performances of Carradine, Chaney, Strange, Atwill, and especially Onslow Stevens as the schizoid Dr. Edelmann, plus the impeccable make-ups by Jack Pierce and the exciting special effects of John Fulton, HOUSE OF DRACULA was a poor attempt to capitalize on the success of HOUSE OF FRANKENSTEIN. Most of the action took place within the walls of Edelmann's castle, and the burning demise of the Monster was lifted from an earlier film, THE GHOST OF FRANKENSTEIN. It seemed hardly credible that a creature as knowledgeable as Dracula could inhabit the same house as the Wolf Man and Frankenstein's Monster without even being aware of their existence. The single most outstanding feature of the movie was the performance of Stevens, who emerged as a quite capable horror actor (though his roles in the genre were few).

Despite its flaws, HOUSE OF DRACULA was well received. The Hollywood Reporter for November 29, 1945 reviewed the film:

> Universal holds another congress of its whole array of indestructible monsters in the Paul Malvern production called 'House of Dracula. ' It is a mighty good show they put up, the realms of pseudo-science interestingly invaded, and the squeamish proceedings given steady pace under the knowing direction of Erle C. Kenton. Box office expectancies should match, possibly even better, the hit grosses of the studio's previous release 'House of Frankenstein. '
>   Dracula has grown taller and thinner since joining Universal's stock company and is here played by John Carradine. The literal minded in his audiences may still be disturbed by one point, however. Who does his laundry? His shirt front remains immaculately white after those many hours spent lying in coffins-ful of his native soil. Obviously it is laundered. But how?
>   ... the greatest burden of acting is asked of Onslow Stevens as Dr. Edelmann. He performs his chores to excellent effects.

Count Dracula had come to his final end at Universal Pictures. At least, that was what pessimistic studio executives thought at the time HOUSE OF DRACULA was made. Yet there was still some supernatural life in the old Dracula bones--life that might at least be good enough for a laugh or two.

ABBOTT AND COSTELLO MEET DRACULA

Serious students of the horror film cringed when Universal Pictures became Universal-International and announced plans in 1946 to make a movie entitled THE BRAIN OF FRANKENSTEIN. The title seemed ordinary enough and the scheduled agenda of stock monsters--Frankenstein's Monster, Count Dracula, the Wolf Man, and even Kharis the Mummy and Count Alucard from SON OF DRACULA--seemed likely enough. But, horror upon horrors, the film was also to star Bud Abbott and Lou Costello, the studio's number one comedy team. Before Robert Lees, Frederic Rinaldo and

John Grant finished the script of THE BRAIN OF FRANKEN-
STEIN, they eliminated two characters.   Purists hoped that
the two missing characters would be Abbott and Costello but
it was the Mummy and Alucard that went back into limbo,
apparently because Chaney might have had to play both roles
in addition to the Wolf Man, and because five legitimate monsters might be too much for even Universal's writers to
handle.   After the script of THE BRAIN OF FRANKENSTEIN
had been completed, it eventually underwent a title change to
the less graphic and more explanatory ABBOTT AND COS-
TELLO MEET FRANKENSTEIN. *   The motion picture was
made in 1947 and released in 1948.

As in the past two Frankenstein/Dracula films the
Monster was portrayed by Glenn Strange and the Wolf Man by
Chaney.   But for the portrayal of Count Dracula, fans of the
original 1931 movie were due for a pleasant surprise.   John
Carradine had abandoned the role for other pursuits.   Returning to the part of the Count for the first time since
DRACULA was Bela Lugosi.   The Hungarian actor had learned
much about American film technique since 1931.   Thus his
performance in ABBOTT AND COSTELLO MEET FRANKEN-
STEIN was more subdued, more suited to the motion picture
medium.   Lugosi had aged and his face bore the lines to
prove it.   But the new Universal-International make-up maes-
tro, Bud Westmore (who had replaced Jack Pierce when the
studio changed ownership), managed to restore his lost youth.
Westmore gave Lugosi a chalk-white face, dark lips, jet
black (dyed) hair and Satanic eyebrows.   Gone was the mustache as worn by Carradine.   Added to his cloak were slits
like the sinister eyes of a cat.   In this slightly altered image
Lugosi enacted his best screen portrayal of Dracula.

This new Count Dracula had apparently learned much
since the sun reduced him to bones in HOUSE OF DRACULA.
Unlike his counterpart in Stoker's novel, he could fly in bat
form over running water.   Like his son Count Alucard, he
also cast a reflection and director Charles Lamont went out
of his way to show Dracula's mirror image.   This must have

---

*In England the film was known under the titles MEET THE
GHOSTS and ABBOTT AND COSTELLO MEET THE GHOSTS;
in France, ABBOTT ET COSTELLO CONTRE FRANKEN-
STEIN and also DEUX NIGAUDS CONTRE FRANKENSTEIN
("Two Simpletons Against Frankenstein"); in Belgium, AB-
BOTT ET COSTELLO ET LES MONSTRES ("Abbott and Cos-
tello and the Monsters").

Dracula (Bela Lugosi) mesmerizes the bumbling Wilbur Brown
(Lou Costello) in Universal-International's ABBOTT AND
COSTELLO MEET FRANKENSTEIN (1948).

aided Dracula greatly in slicking back his hair or dusting off
the native soil from his tuxedo.   It is surprising that Lugosi,
who had played Dracula so many times on the stage in addition to his role in the 1931 movie, did not mention this lack
of consistency to the director.   Perhaps Lugosi, tired and
addicted to drugs, no longer cared; or he may have mentioned the inconsistency and no one listened.   Since ABBOTT
AND COSTELLO MEET FRANKENSTEIN was not really a
sequel to HOUSE OF DRACULA the people who made such
decisions might not have deemed a change in the script necessary.

        Two crates, supposedly containing the dead body of
the Frankenstein Monster and skeleton of Count Dracula, are

delivered to McDougal's House of Horrors by shipping clerks Chick Young (Abbott) and Wilbur Brown (Costello). Once in this museum of horror, Dracula emerges from his coffin and revives the Monster with a miniature electrical device. Wilbur is put in an hypnotic trance by Dracula but witnesses the escape of the two monsters. When McDougal (Frank Ferguson) finds his exhibits missing, Chick and Wilbur are held responsible. The more practical minded Chick refuses to believe Wilbur's story that the two figures are alive. The only person who believes Wilbur's wild story is Lawrence Talbot, who arrives from Europe after long attempting to locate Dracula and the Monster.

Dracula's plan is to find a new brain for the weakened Frankenstein Monster (the brain of the original title), but one that is simple and pliable and easy to command. The vampire's assistant, Sandra Mornay (Lenore Aubert), has feigned a romantic interest in Wilbur and she assures the Count that the Monster will soon have that new brain. She and Wilbur are to attend a masquerade ball on the following evening.

In order to get his exhibits back, McDougal hires an insurance investigator, blonde Joan Raymond (Jane Randolph), who also pretends to be interested in Wilbur. Wilbur promptly also makes a date with the unknown investigator and goes along with Chick and Joan, to meet Sandra, who resides in a gothic castle hidden in the swamp. There Wilbur meets Count Dracula, who identifies himself as "Dr. Lahos" (almost the same as Carradine's Baton Latos) and gleams at the thought of acquiring the fat man's brain. While Wilbur and Chick are waiting to leave for the ball, Joan discovers the Frankenstein records in Sandra's possession. Sandra tells Dracula that it is too dangerous for her to perform the brain transplant. To insure her cooperation, Dracula bites her neck and makes her a vampire.

At the masquerade party, Talbot tries to warn everyone that the man dressed as Count Dracula is not wearing a costume. Wilbur, dressed in a vampire outfit, goes for a moonlight stroll through the woods with the vampiric Sandra. Alone with the chubby shipping clerk, Sandra tries to hypnotize him (with bats seen flapping in her staring eyes) and bite his neck. Talbot transforms into a werewolf and nearly kills McDougal. Dracula changes into a bat and flies after Wilbur.

Dracula's ability to metamorphose into a bat had not improved since HOUSE OF DRACULA. The quick Fulton

transformations, usually shown from behind, were convincing.
But Fulton, like Pierce, was not retained when Universal
went International. Now Dracula's changes, created by David
S. Horsley and Jerome H. Ash, were accomplished through
extremely cartoon-like animation that folled no one. In many
scenes a cartoon vampire bat was substituted for the more
realistic prop bat that flew about on unseen wires.

In bat form, Dracula pursues the shrieking Wilbur to
a waiting speedboat and takes him back to the castle. Chick,
Talbot and Dr. Stevens (Charles Bradstreet), a scientist
working for "Dr. Lahos" but unaware of the nature of the
upcoming experiment, set out to rescue Wilbur. Sandra is
about to remove Wilbur's brain when Chick and Talbot burst
into the laboratory. Chick attempts to slam Dracula with a
chair but inadvertently knocks out Sandra instead. But when
Talbot begins to release the strapped-down Wilbur from the
operating table, he transforms into the Wolf Man. Using his
foot to launch the table across the room, Wilbur finds his
platform intercepted by Dracula. Suddenly the Wolf Man is
on the other end of the operating table. Then Count Dracula
rushes out of the room with the Wolf Man in snarling pursuit,
leaving Wilbur to the mercies of the Frankenstein Monster,
who is bursting his bonds.

The rest of ABBOTT AND COSTELLO MEET FRANK-
ENSTEIN is sheer and wonderful pandemonium. Chick and
Wilbur run from room to room, encountering either the
Frankenstein Monster or Dracula and the Wolf Man, who continue their battle. Finally, Dracula hurls a vase at the Wolf
Man and finds himself on a balcony overlooking the sea. The
King of Vampires changes into a bat as the Wolf Man leaps,
catching the winged mammal in its claws. Both monsters
plunge off the balcony and into the sea below. (Anyone up on
his vampire lore knows that running water can trap a vampire forever.) With Dracula and the Wolf Man out of the
way, Chick and Wilbur now need only contend with the Frankenstein Monster. The two zanies jump into a rowboat as the
Monster hurls barrels at them from the pier. Dr. Stevens
then sets fire to the pier, engulfing the Monster of Frankenstein in flames. Chick and Wilbur, believing they have seen
the last of the monsters, suddenly hear the mocking voice of
the Invisible Man (Vincent Price).

Despite its castigation by serious horror critics, AB-
BOTT AND COSTELLO MEET FRANKENSTEIN is a good
film on every level. The picture is certainly the best spoof

of the horror genre ever made, with top production values
and good performances throughout. Lugosi, Chaney and
Strange played their roles with dignity and rarely stepped out
of character. The picture was surely one of the best Abbott
and Costello films and technically, one of the best of the
Frankenstein/Dracula/Wolf Man movies. The three monsters
were played by professionals who did not violate the "sanctity"
of their performances in previous films. Remove the two
comics and a basic horror film plot remains. *

Reviewers who accepted ABBOTT AND COSTELLO
MEET FRANKENSTEIN for what it was gave it favorable cri-
tiques. The following review is from the Hollywood Reporter
for June 28, 1948.

The idea of teaming Abbott and Costello with the
stable of monsters that cavort at U-I is one of those
brainstorms that could be nothing less than hilarious
in its completion. Happily 'Abbott and Costello
Meet Frankenstein' is just that--a crazy, giddy show
that combines chills and laughs in one zany sequence
after the other. There is something called a story
involved but it isn't important when Messrs A & C
begin clowning with the Wolf Man, Dracula, and
Frankenstein's monster. Robert Arthur's production
spells out showmanship right down the line, and
Charles T. Barton's direction keeps things moving
at a lively, vigorous pace. Arthur and Barton both
know Abbott and Costello fans and their handling of
the comedy is geared to the best slapstick traditions.
This can be tabbed as a substantial boxoffice entry
in its bracket.

... Abbott and Costello do their usual good
job of building gags and keeping the laughs running
consistently through the action. Their encounters
with the monsters get the biggest giggles, naturally.
Lon Chaney, as the wolfman, and Bela Lugosi, playing his old role of Count Dracula, make excellent
foils, as does Glenn Strange in the spot of the monster ...

Charles Van Engers' camera work helps

---

*Scenes of Dracula from ABBOTT AND COSTELLO MEET
FRANKENSTEIN were used in THE WORLD OF ABBOTT AND
COSTELLO (1965), a documentary film compiling sequences
from the comedy team's funniest mcvies, and in IL VICINO
DI CASA.

establish the eerie mood, and the art direction of
Bernard Herzburn and Hilyard Brown is excellent.
Frank Skinner supplies a good musical score, and
editing is a credit to Frank Gross.

Bud and Lou continued to meet the monsters.   In AB-
BOTT AND COSTELLO MEET DR. JEKYLL AND MR. HYDE
(Universal-International 1953), directed by Charles Lamont,
the figure of a mustachioed and bearded Count Dracula (played
by an unidentified actor) haunted a wax museum. *   MUNSTER,
GO HOME! (Universal 1966) brought a comedic Dracula to the
screen (see Chapter 10).   Universal released CHAPPAQUA in
1967, a psychedelic film made in color the previous year by
Regional, produced, written and directed by Conrad Brooks.
Dracula has a brief cameo in which he delivers a pint of
blood to a doctor.

Count Dracula had gone through many films at Universal.   The King of Vampires had become popular on his own
merits, then through the efforts of his offspring, then shar-
ing the billing with other monsters, and inevitably, as a
straight man for Lou Costello.   But while the image of the
Count scared audiences in the Thirties it would take a new
breed of Dracula to shock the fans of the late Fifties and continue to shock them through the Sixties and Seventies.   For
the revamped Dracula the cameras would roll in England, and
a new star in black cloak and with crimson-soaked fangs
would emerge.

_____

*In France the film became DEUX NIGAUDS CONTRE EL DR.
JEKYLL ET MR. HYDE ("Two Simpletons Against Dr. Jekyll
and Mr. Hyde").

Chapter 8

THE HAMMER HORRORS OF DRACULA

> You would play your brains against mine ...
> against me who has commanded nations.
> --Christopher Lee, in DRACULA A.D. 1972

Hammer Films in England assumed the ebony mantle of Count Dracula in the late 1950s, adopting its own series of films based on Stoker's creation and filling the vacancy left by Universal. The first gothic horror film lensed by Hammer was THE CURSE OF FRANKENSTEIN (1957). What Universal had concealed in atmospheric shadows or in characters reacting to off-screen happenings, Hammer displayed graphically, often in lingering close-ups and in vivid color, with especially generous helpings of red. Hammer's top executive, James Carreras, enjoyed the profits of the new Frankenstein film and realized that Count Dracula would probably draw equally impressive profits.

Carreras commissioned Jimmy Sangster, the writer of THE CURSE OF FRANKENSTEIN, to script a new version of Stoker's Dracula. Sangster's script was simply entitled DRACULA and the film was released as such in England. In the United States DRACULA was released by Universal-International under its more famous title, HORROR OF DRACULA (as we shall refer to it in this text to avoid confusion with other adaptations titled DRACULA).* HORROR OF DRACULA

---

*In Spain the film was released as DRACULA IL VAMPIRO ("Dracula the Vampire"); in France, as LE CHAUCHEMAR DE DRACULA ("The Nightmare of Dracula").

Photographs from HORROR OF DRACULA were seen in BLOOD FIEND (Hemisphere 1966), a film, starring Christopher Lee, about a living vampire killer plaguing Paris. The film is also known as FEMALE FIEND and was released to American television under the British title, THE THEATRE OF DEATH.

was replete with trappings that would soon become an established part of the Hammer image. These trappings may well be grouped into two general categories: sex and gore. Hammer's casting office endeavored to stock these films with well-stacked actresses who looked even more endowed in low-cut gowns and push-up bras, while the prop department began to manufacture what seemed like gallons of artificial blood.

Both Sangster and executive producer Michael Carreras realized that the old Lugosi image of Count Dracula, who never dared to show his fangs or the blood that he took from his victims, no longer frightened audiences. Lugosi's vampire image belonged to another era. Audiences were no longer terrified by the screen appearance of an impeccably attired nobleman who stared hypnotically from beneath a wrinkled brow and spoke in slow, drawn-out sentences. Masterful as Lugosi's performance was in its day, audiences of 1958 demanded to actually see the vampire in all his monstrous majesty, doing the monstrous things that vampires do. A new type of actor was required to don the familiar black cloak, an actor who could portray the Count as both a supernatural and a brutally physical creature. In short, the vampire needed to be revamped.

A British actor named Christopher Lee had enacted the role of the Creature in THE CURSE OF FRANKENSTEIN, his name freshly added to the roster of horror film stars. Lee was tall (six feet four inches) and thin, fitting the physical requirements set down by Bram Stoker. He was also a fine actor whose career, before the Frankenstein film, was going nowhere. Christopher Frank Carandini Lee had the royal background suitable for portraying the nefarious Count Dracula. He was born in London on May 27, 1922, a descendant of the infamous Borgias on his mother's side. It was a Count (though not Count Dracula) who aroused Lee's interest in acting. In 1947, Count Niccolò, an Italian ambassador to England, introduced his cousin Christopher Lee to a Two Cities Films executive. Within three weeks Lee was featured in the Two Cities production, CORRIDOR OF MIRRORS, which was followed by THROTTLE TRUE (1948), PRELUDE TO FAME (1949) and CAPTAIN HORATIO HORNBLOWER (1950). But it was not until THE CURSE OF FRANKENSTEIN that the public took notice of Lee. Since the actor's

---

Opposite: Christopher Lee, red eyes glaring and fangs dripping with blood, portrayed Count Dracula as a dynamic, feral creature of darkness in Hammer Films' HORROR OF DRACULA (1958).

features were buried under layers of make-up in CURSE, a curious audience of horror movie aficionados was eager, when advertising posters boasted the name of Christopher Lee as the Count in HORROR OF DRACULA, to discover what this "unknown" actor looked like in the flesh.

Unlike the established Lugosi/Universal conception, Lee portrayed the Count with more of the physical aspects of the traditional (and Stoker's) vampire. Hammer make-up artist Phil Leakey outfitted the actor with a wig of thick, gray-streaked hair, combed straight back in such a way as to give the illusion of pointed ears, and commencing with a pronounced widow's peak. Leakey also designed a set of elongated canine teeth (a characteristic of the vampire never shown in any of the Universal films) that snapped on over the actor's own teeth, and a pair of red contact lenses which he wore with considerable discomfort. "Oh, it's terrible," Lee told me, "very painful, very uncomfortable. I can't see properly. Everything goes blurred. And it makes me cry. I get acute discomfort, particularly when I'm leaping about, charging around and doing things. You can't see where you're going." Asked whether or not the fangs proved an encumbrance, the actor replied, "No, you can even talk with them in your mouth and nobody knows you've got them in. They don't show. No, that's not a problem." Lee was clothed entirely in black (not the white tie and tails established by Hamilton Deane) and a solid black cloak completed his image of Count Dracula.

Cloaked in the mantle of Dracula, Christopher Lee began to mold Stoker's character to fit his own abilities and personality. Lee's Dracula was a dynamic figure, leaping across rooms like some human animal, fangs bared and dripping blood, red eyes flaring with Satanic fire. He would toss his victims about like the truly supernaturally strong character that Stoker had described. His manner of speech coincided with this dynamic image. Thus Lee's Dracula spoke his words rapidly and with supreme cunning and self-assurance, thus removing the self-consciousness and unintentional humor from such overly familiar lines as "I am ... Dracula," which Lugosi stretched out to almost five seconds. A younger and more energetic man than Lugosi, in addition to being a finer screen actor, Lee created a Dracula that established the modern image of the King Vampire. Lee's performance in HORROR OF DRACULA is the finest interpretation of the role yet.

"I tried to remain true to the book," Lee told me.
"But otherwise it was entirely personal. What came onto the
screen was a combination of my having read the book and trying to invest the character with his dignity and nobility, ferocity and sadness; also, my own personal interpretation of
the character as I saw it from the script I was given."
Christopher Lee did not see the Lugosi DRACULA until years
after the filming of HORROR OF DRACULA.

Posters advertising HORROR OF DRACULA boldly
stated: "The terrifying lover who died yet lived!" Lee took
the sexual implications of the vampire myth and made them
obvious. His female victims would await his arrival with
burning desire, their large Hammer-required breasts rising
and falling in anticipation. At first, Dracula would tease his
beautiful prey, nudging them with his lips but never surren-
dering his kiss. Then he would sink his fangs into their
necks, at which moment they would lapse into ecstasy. Sex
was now an integral part of the Dracula legend, which was
stripped of the subtleties of previous Dracula films or the
symbolism of the Stoker novel.

HORROR OF DRACULA was directed by Terence Fisher, the director of THE CURSE OF FRANKENSTEIN. Fisher
chose his cast well for the new Dracula film. Carol Marsh
portrayed Lucy, Melissa Stribling played Mina, John Van
Eyssen was Jonathan Harker, and Michael Gough, who would
be featured as a second-string horror star (à la Universal's
Lionel Atwill) in numerous fright films, played Arthur Holmwood. In the role of Dracula's vampire mistress was voluptuous, raven-haired Valerie Gaunt. Peter Cushing, the excellent British actor who portrayed Baron Frankenstein in
THE CURSE OF FRANKENSTEIN, portrayed Dr. Van Helsing
with dedication and dignity.

Writer Jimmy Sangster was required to alter Stoker's
plotline to allow for Hammer's budget. For although the
Hammer horror films would give the illusion of "A" productions, with their lavishly decorated sets and particular attention paid to eighteenth century period detail, they were in
fact low-budget productions. Costs had to be cut wherever
possible.

Sangster began his streamlining of Dracula by setting
the entire story in the same area of Central Europe. (The
location was never identified as Transylvania.) Count Dracula never journeys to England, thus obviating any need for

modes of transportation other than horse and buggy. The character of Renfield was eliminated altogether. The relationships existing between some of the characters were changed and a new and spectacular ending was devised for the film.

HORROR OF DRACULA opens, as per Stoker's novel, with Jonathan Harker arriving at Castle Dracula. Harker goes to the castle on the pretext of indexing the Count's journals and books, but in actuality, he has been sent to the gothic structure by Van Helsing to investigate the mysterious Dracula in connection with a recent epidemic of vampirism. After dining on the meal provided by his yet unseen host, Harker is approached by a beautiful woman with long black hair and wearing a diaphanous white gown. She insists that she is Dracula's prisoner and begs Harker to release her. Suddenly she reacts with terror to the dark figure of the Count, standing at the top of the staircase. The woman flees down a hallway as the cloaked man descends the stairs, immediately announcing himself: "I am Dracula."

Count Dracula shows Harker his room and explains his duties as librarian. Before the nobleman leaves, he notices the picture of Harker's fiancée, Lucy Holmwood. (In the Stoker novel Harker was engaged to Mina Murray and Lucy Westenra was the fiancée of Arthur Holmwood. But despite these changes, Sangster managed to produce a logical storyline.) After Dracula leaves, Harker deduces that he is a vampire and resolves to destroy him.

Later, in the library, Harker again encounters the beautiful woman in white. This time, as she places her head against his shoulder, she opens her mouth to reveal the sharp fangs of a vampire. The woman attacks, biting his throat and drawing blood. But Harker has not yet encountered the full horror of the castle.

Suddenly the motion picture screen is filled with the hate-filled visage of Count Dracula, eyes blazing red, blood-smeared mouth open in a snarl, fangs caked with crimson gore. The scene, shown in close-up and backed by the blaring music of James Bernard, is frightening, even today, and remains one of the truly classic images in the history of the horror film.

Dracula springs across the room like a wild beast and attacks the vampire woman with his fangs. Overcome with horror, Jonathan Harker faints. When Harker awakens during the afternoon in his room, he sees the wounds on his neck, inflicted by the vampire. Vowing to destroy the Count, Harker discovers the crypt in which Dracula and the vampiress are sleeping. Harker proceeds to destroy the woman with a wooden stake through the heart and watches her shrivel into a toothless old woman. (Instead of making-up Ms. Gaunt to appear ancient, an aged woman was hired to do this one scene.) Harker should have destroyed the Count first, for the sun has already begun to set. Harker finds Dracula's coffin empty, then beholds the King Vampire standing at the doorway. Harker's fate is inevitable.

Eventually, Van Helsing comes to Castle Dracula in search of Harker, and as he arrives he sees a black hearse pulled by two white stallions and bearing a white casket, speeding away from the ancient fortress. Van Helsing finds the slumbering Harker in the vampire state and drives a stake into his chest.

A scene was filmed showing the impaled Harker in the early stages of decomposition. But the scene was removed by the British censor when the film was released in English-speaking countries. This is surprising, since the brief scene was not nearly as gruesome as some of those which were left in the film.

From this point on, the plot of HORROR OF DRACU-LA follows the storyline of Dracula reasonably closely, with Lucy falling prey to the Count's attacks. But Dracula's motivations had changed from the original story and he demands Lucy as a replacement for his staked mistress. Van Helsing, meanwhile, states (into his recording machine) what he knows about vampires, explaining that such abilities as transforming into bats and wolves are attributable only to myth. (This was Sangster's attempt to make the vampire a more physical and, hence, more believable character. Also, a studio attempting realistic bats and transformations, without the talents of a John Fulton, would be likely to produce ludicrous effects.)

As in Stoker's classic, Lucy dies from Dracula's attacks and returns from her tomb as a child-lusting vampire. Van Helsing touches a crucifix to Lucy's forehead, burning the shape of a cross into her flesh. Then Van Helsing and Arthur Holmwood destroy her with a stake.

Mina is Dracula's next target of attack.   To Van
Helsing's horror, he discovers the white coffin of Dracula hidden in the Holmwood cellar, which explains how he entered
the house without the ability to change form.   The doctor,
after tossing a cross into the dirt-filled casket, is joined by
Arthur Holmwood.   Dracula flees with the entranced Mina to
his castle, with Van Helsing and Holmwood in pursuit.   Dawn
is almost upon them when Van Helsing and Holmwood arrive
at Castle Dracula, just in time to stop the Count from burying Mina in an empty grave.   Holmwood attends to Mina as
the doctor pursues the fleeing vampire into his castle.

The climax of HORROR OF DRACULA remains one of
the most breath-taking sequences in the genre.   Van Helsing
and his un-dead opponent battle physically, with Dracula
grasping the doctor's throat in a superhuman grip.   Apparently unconscious, Van Helsing relaxes as the Count grins, exposing his animal-like fangs, and leisurely lowers his head
for the bite that will make the scientist a creature such as
himself.   But Van Helsing revives, kicking back the vampire.
Then, with a superhuman effort, the doctor nearly flies
across a long table and leaps, Batman-style, upon the thick
red draperies, ripping them down to let in the morning sunlight that bathes the vampire's foot.

Dracula screams hideously, his foot reduced to ashes
in the burning sunlight.   Despite the excruciating pain, the
vampire tries to pull himself from the deadly rays, but before the Count can move, Van Helsing fashions a makeshift
cross from two silver candlesticks and brandishes them in the
vampire's face, forcing him back into the searing rays.   Van
Helsing seems ill as he watches the once powerful Count
Dracula turn gray, then begin to decay until he crumbles to
dust which is blown away by the breeze of morning.

The scene of Dracula's destruction was also attacked
by the British censor.   What appear in the prints shown in
English-speaking countries are the shots of Dracula's foot col-
lapsing, his face gray, his rotting hand pulling the crumbling
flesh from his face, and a shot of his final dissolution to dust.
The scenes showing various stages of decomposition were left
intact, however, in certain foreign releases of HORROR OF
DRACULA.   "Those two sequences, the one of John Van

Opposite: In a graphic scene from HORROR OF DRACULA,
the Count (Christopher Lee) decomposes beneath the deadly
rays of the sun.

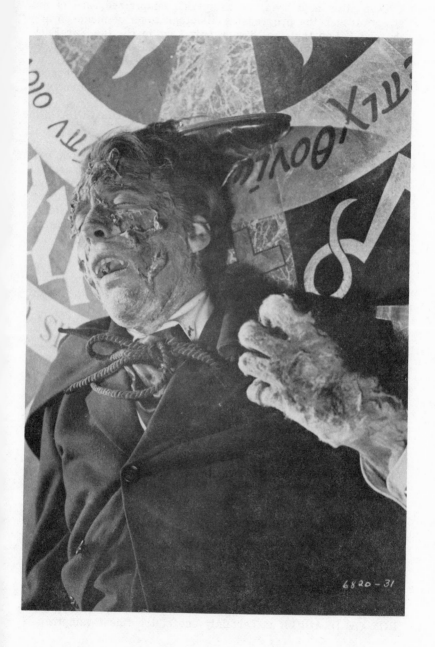

6820-31

Eyssen after he'd been, so to speak, vampirized, and of me going through the progressive disintegrations of make-up at the end," Lee told me, "were only kept in for the Far East and various other parts of the world because, perhaps, they considered them too gruesome in those days. I did have at least two or three make-ups for the disintegration sequence, which goes very fast in the version that you see nowadays."

Weekly _Variety_ reviewed HORROR OF DRACULA in the May 7, 1958 issue:

> There's gore aplenty in this import turned out by Michael Carreras' Hammer Films Productions. Specializing in raw heads and bloody bones product, Hammer also has to its credit last year's 'Curse of Frankenstein,' which mopped up at the wicket. As was 'Curse,' 'Dracula' too is in color--a factor that tends to heighten the exploitation values inherent in the film.
>
> For those familiar with the original 'Dracula' thriller, the Jimmy Sangster screenplay has ably preserved the sanguinary aspects of the Bram Stoker novel ...
>
> Both director Terence Fisher as well as the cast have taken a serious approach to the macabre theme that adds up to lotsa tension and suspense. Peter Cushing is impressive as the painstaking scientist-doctor who solves the mystery, Christopher Lee is thoroughly gruesome as Dracula, and Michael Gough is suitably skeptical as a bereaved relative who ultimately is pursuaded to assist Cushing.

Christopher Lee said of the film: "It's the only one that I've done that's ever been any good, in my opinion. It's the only one that remotely resembles the original book."

HORROR OF DRACULA achieved a type of legendary quality within a few years after its original release. Horror film buffs who had, until that time, been familiar only with the well-mannered Dracula of Universal either loathed the film for its explicit gore or loved it. Some fans immediately labeled HORROR OF DRACULA as the greatest horror movie ever made, a reputation that, despite its failings, continues to linger. Though not the greatest of all horror films, HORROR OF DRACULA is certainly one of the finest vampire

movies ever made and gave a much needed boost to the centuries-old and dusty Count. *

HORROR OF DRACULA established Christopher Lee
as a bona fide star of horror films. Unlike some actors,
who attempt to abnegate an association with such motion pictures in order to further a more "legitimate" acting career,
Lee, like Karloff, realized that he could benefit from being
type-cast.   Since Lee was a first rate actor and not merely
someone to animate the monster costumes, he found the horror films to be a lucrative home, while occasionally spreading his talents to other types of motion picture. Following
HORROR OF DRACULA, Christopher Lee went on to star in
such films as THE MUMMY, THE HOUND OF THE BASKER-
VILLES and THE MAN WHO COULD CHEAT DEATH, all
made by Hammer and released in 1959.

HORROR OF DRACULA was such a financial success
that Hammer made a sequel, BRIDES OF DRACULA, which
was released by Universal in 1960.   The title was misleading, especially since the posters publicizing the film depicted
virtually the same artwork of the Count as for HORROR, although Count Dracula himself did not even appear in BRIDES
OF DRACULA.   Apparently, writer Jimmy Sangster and director Terence Fisher thought the original Count to be beyond
revivification, his dust having been blown away by the wind.
Thus a narration at the opening of BRIDES OF DRACULA explains that, although the evil Count has met his demise, he
has many disciples who continue his evil practices.

The vampiric nobleman who assumed Dracula's role in
BRIDES OF DRACULA was the sinister Baron Meinster,
played by David Peel.   This portrayal of the vampire was a
digression from the image created by Lee.   Unlike Count
Dracula, Baron Meinster was handsome in a pretty sort of
way, with wavy blond hair, almost feminine features, and
wore a light blue cloak.   As Dracula's disciple, the Baron
apparently learned more about the vampire business than even
his mentor had known.   For, despite what Van Helsing had
emphatically denied in the previous film, this vampire could,
in fact, transform into a giant bat--a creature which bore
his own facial features.   This physical contrast with the

---

*Scenes from HORROR OF DRACULA were later used in the
Hammer film DRACULA, PRINCE OF DARKNESS (1965).

Dracula-type vampire was apparently an attempt by Hammer to individuate the Baron from the original Count.

The opening of BRIDES OF DRACULA follows school teacher Marianne Danielle (played by beautiful Yvonne Monlaur) across the Transylvanian countryside on her way to take up a position at the Badstein Girls' Academy. En route, she is persuaded to rest at the chateau of a recluse named Baroness Meinster (Martita Hunt). At night Marianne observes a handsome young man walking in the garden. The Baroness later explains that the man is her son and is suffering from a mental disorder. Marianne discovers that the handsome Baron is kept prisoner, secured by a long chain. Sympathizing with the Baron, she frees him. When the house servant, Greta (Freda Jackson), later reveals to Marianne the blood-drained corpse of the Baroness and an empty coffin, she reveals the fact that Marianne has inadvertently freed a vampire. (The element of symbolic incest, with the new sexual connotation attributed to vampiric attacks through the Hammer productions, was mildly daring for 1960.) Inevitably the old Baroness becomes a vampire herself, self-conscious of her newly sprouted fangs.

Marianne flees to the woods, where a funeral for another of the Baron's victims is under way. Meinster traps the girl but is forced to retreat with the coming of dawn, and the unconscious Marianne is rescued by the ultimate crusader against vampires, Dr. Van Helsing (again played by Peter Cushing), who is continuing his war upon the un-dead. Van Helsing takes Marianne to the school, then proceeds to drive stakes through the hearts of the victims of Baron Meinster.

Van Helsing, heading for the Meinster chateau, is attacked by an enormous bat. Only the crucifix which falls from his doctor's bag saves him. Proceeding to the chateau, Van Helsing encounters the un-dead Baroness and her son, now in human form. After a battle with Van Helsing, the Baron escapes, leaving his mother to submit voluntarily to the scientist's wooden stake. Later, the Baron boldly visits the girls' academy, seeking to make both Marianne and a student named Gina (Andrée Melly)* his victims. Gina dies

*Andrée Melly was cast as the vampiric Natalia, a role obviously imitating her part in BRIDES OF DRACULA, in THE HORROR OF IT ALL. This comedy film, directed by Terence Fisher, was made by Associated Producers and released by 20th Century-Fox in 1964.

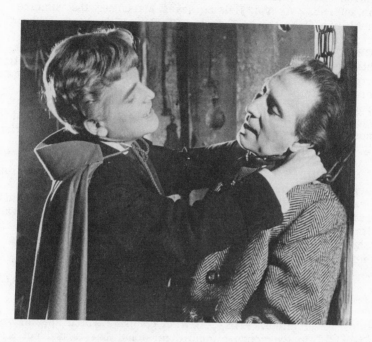

Although Count Dracula did not appear in Hammer's BRIDES OF DRACULA (1960), his disciple, Baron Meinster (David Peel), nearly destroys the crusading Dr. Van Helsing (Peter Cushing).

from the vampire's bite and is temporarily laid to rest in the school stable, where she returns to pseudo-life as one of the brides of Baron Meinster. But the Baron also wants to add Marianne to his un-dead harem.

The climax of BRIDES OF DRACULA is staged in a deserted windmill. Van Helsing enters the mill and is attacked by Gina and Meinster's other vampiric bride. The Baron himself bites the doctor, tainting his flesh with the mark of the vampire, then goes off to the academy to abduct Marianne. Meanwhile, Van Helsing uses a hot metal bar and holy water to burn the vampire's marks from his flesh. When Meinster returns to the mill with Marianne, Van Helsing splashes holy water in his handsome face, which now burns as though it had been seared by acid. Fighting the pain, the

Baron kicks over a hot brazier and the old windmill becomes
an inferno. As Van Helsing saves Marianne, the vampire
nobleman flees the holocaust. Displaying the same athletic
prowess that had trapped Dracula himself in HORROR OF
DRACULA, Van Helsing leaps upon a vane of the windmill,
his weight causing the sails to move and simulate a gigantic
cross against the full moon. Trapped by the shadow of the
cross, Baron Meinster screams as he perishes, never to
rise again. (Apparently to give the scene a more unreal
quality, Fisher showed only the shadow of the "cross" and
not that of the windmill itself, as though the latter had briefly ceased to exist.)

BRIDES OF DRACULA was a well-made Hammer film,
yet it lacked the dynamic quality of HORROR OF DRACULA.
And David Peel's foppish characterization of the Baron could
hardly compete with Christopher Lee's powerful Count. While
its predecessor would come to be regarded as a modern
classic, BRIDES OF DRACULA would be documented as no
more than a competently made sequel film.*

Variety of May 17, 1960 reviewed BRIDES OF DRACU-
LA:

> Hammer Films, British company which specializes
> in the goose-pimple diversions, has turned out a
> technically well-made film embellished with color.
> However, if the true aficionado of the horror cult
> is seeking a real eerie experience, he'll be disap-
> pointed.
> Dracula's modern counterpart, as depicted
> by David Peel, hardly achieves the same degree of
> terror. Moreover, color--although considered an
> advance--detracts rather than adds to the horror
> aspect. It would have been considerably more
> scary if it had been filmed in old-fashioned black
> and white.

BRIDES OF DRACULA was successful enough for Hammer's executives to realize that substantial profits could be
made if the Dracula theme were expanded to a series. But
audiences wanted to see the original Count Dracula cavort
upon the screen, not some blond-haired disciple. Dracula
had seemingly been destroyed beyond any possible hope of

---

*Scenes from BRIDES OF DRACULA appeared in the 1973
British film THE PUBLIC EYE.

resuscitation in the first film of the series. Yet Dracula had, somehow, to be logically revived in the person of the actor whom audiences wanted to see in the role, Christopher Lee.

For a while Hammer had been considering making a third Dracula film, again scripted by Jimmy Sangster, with the title DISCIPLE OF DRACULA. The film went into production in 1965 under the shooting title, DRACULA III (and possibly also under the name REVENGE OF DRACULA), with Fisher again directing. But so much of Sangster's original story had been changed that he removed his name from the film's credit and replaced it with the ficticious "John Sansom." The following year the finished product was released by 20th Century-Fox under the impressive title DRACULA, PRINCE OF DARKNESS. *

Christopher Lee had become a high-priced star since his debut as Count Dracula in 1958. Since his salary was computed on a daily basis, Hammer realized that to afford the actor in this and any subsequent Dracula films his scenes would have to be reduced to a minimum. In DRACULA, PRINCE OF DARKNESS, Lee's scenes were not only brief, he also had no dialogue. This seemed to be an attempt to make the King of Vampires a more spectral character, bearing in mind his apparently final demise in HORROR OF DRACULA. Lee's lines in DRACULA, PRINCE OF DARKNESS were replaced by a catlike hissing, which often elicited snickers from audiences who would otherwise have shuddered at the actor's magnificent deep voice.

DRACULA, PRINCE OF DARKNESS opened with footage from the climax of HORROR OF DRACULA, showing the Count's ignominious defeat by Van Helsing and the morning sun. The plot of PRINCE was rather pedestrian and hinged upon the tired gothic story device of the group of hapless mortals who stop to rest in a haunted house or castle. Four English travelers, Charles Kent (Francis Matthews), his wife Diana (Suzan Farmer), his brother Alan (Charles Tingwell) and Alan's nagging wife, Helen (Barbara Shelley) stop at a local inn in the Carpathian Mountains. There, a monk named Father Shandor (Andrew Keir) admonishes them against visiting the castle of Dracula in nearby Carlsbad. Naturally the travelers proceed to the castle, but find that their coachman will not transport them all the way. The group appears

---

*DRACULA, PRINCE OF DARKNESS was released in the Far East as THE BLOODY SCREAM OF DRACULA.

stranded until a horse-drawn carriage with no driver stops
before them. By now they should have reconsidered the
priest's warning, but instead, they enter the carriage, which
promptly dispatches them to Castle Dracula.

Dinner has already been laid out for the foursome at
the castle. A strange butler named Klove (Philip Latham),
dressed in black, announces himself as the manservant of the
former and now deceased master of the castle. (Klove must
have been on vacation in Hammer's first Dracula movie.)
The four guests retire to bed after dinner. Later, when the
curious Alan investigates a noise in the cellar, he is killed
by the butler.

Since Count Dracula had been reduced to dust in HOR-
ROR OF DRACULA, a certain ingenuity was required to bring
him back. Hammer was a studio where graphic gore was an
art and thus the King of Vampires would return in one of the
most majestic bloodbaths the screen had ever witnessed.
Klove, the butler, places the dust that had been his master
(and which he must have spent immeasurable time gathering
from the blowing wind) into the bottom of an open coffin.
Then he hoists the bleeding corpse of Alan over the coffin,
permitting the blood to splatter atop Dracula's ashes. Revitalized by the human blood, the vampire slowly begins to
re-form amid rising smoke, until the familiar figure of the
Count is once again upon the screen. Although special optical effects are rare in Hammer Films, the superb scene in
which Dracula is revived is the highlight of the film. The
scene is more realistic than the revivification scenes of the
old Universal films, especially since Dracula regained his
form au naturel and did not miraculously (and ludicrously) appear fully and meticulously clothed.

The puritanical Helen becomes Dracula's first victim
and is thereby transformed into a seductive vampiress. Next
on Dracula's agenda is Diana. Appearing in her room (in a
scene taken from Stoker's Dracula) he opens a vein in his
chest and entices her to drink his blood, thereby joining his
ranks in a baptism of blood. Charles rescues Diana from
the Count, then flees with her to the nearby monastery, where
Father Shandor instructs them in vampire lore. Among the
facts related by the priest is the vampire's inability to cross
running water (a traditional element, foreign until this time
to the motion picture screen). Helen enters Diana's bedroom
at the monastery and attacks her, but Father Shandor manages
to stake the she-vampire through the heart.

Dracula has a servant at the monastery, a mysterious fellow named Ludwig (Thorley Walters), who leads Diana to the Count, now waiting in Father Shandor's own study. Dracula then escapes with his prize in a wagon driven by Klove. A chase follows, with Charles and the priest after the vampire's coach. Charles shoots Klove and the coach overturns tossing the Count onto the ice-covered moat of his own castle. As Dracula and Charles grapple on the frozen moat, the monk repeatedly fires his gun at the ice. Charles escapes as the ice cracks and traps Count Dracula beneath the chilled waters, where he would conveniently remain until Hammer decided to make another film in the series.

DRACULA, PRINCE OF DARKNESS marked the beginning of advertising gimmicks with Hammer's Dracula movies. Free Dracula fangs were given out to theatre patrons, along with zombie masks that publicized the motion picture cofeatured with PRINCE, Hammer's first movie devoted to the walking dead, PLAGUE OF THE ZOMBIES.

According to Weekly Variety, January 19, 1966:

This simple yarn is played reasonably straight and

A helpless Count Dracula (Christopher Lee) drowns in the icy waters outside his castle in Hammer's 1966 entry to the series, DRACULA, PRINCE OF DARKNESS.

the main snag is that the thrills are mainly dropped
in and do not arise sufficiently smooth out of atmosphere.   After a slowish start some climate of eeriness is evoked but more shadows, suspense and
suggestion would have helped.   Christopher Lee, an
old hand at the horror business, makes a latish appearance but dominates the film enough without dialogue.   Barbara Shelley, a beautiful and much un-
derrated actress, who appears to be trapped in the
horror business, makes a spirited vampire and
Andrew Keir, Francis Matthews, Charles Tingwell,
Suzan Farmer and others provide useful aid.   This
film has apparently cost more than its predecessors
and its color, sound and lensing are invariably okay.
Pity that more care has not been given to cutwork
values.   The castle in the background is always the
same back projected view.   Typical British foliage
has to make do also in Carpathia, and so on.   But
when Dracula is on the prowl at night (it's never
quite nocturnal enough) the less pernickety audiences
will not worry overmuch about such blemishes.

DRACULA, PRINCE OF DARKNESS established Christopher Lee as the Count Dracula of virtually all the Hammer
Dracula films to follow.   But as each succeeding film in the
series went before the cameras, the footage devoted to Dracula himself seemed to lessen; Lee became too expensive.
Also, Hammer's writers proceeded to emphasize characters
that should have been in supporting roles, and to pull fangs
in order to insert the Count into these other characters'
stories.   The result was diminishing quality.

In 1968 Warner Brothers-Seven Arts released the next
Hammer Dracula film, with fewer scenes of Dracula than in
the previous entry, but with the most commercial title in the
entire series: DRACULA HAS RISEN FROM THE GRAVE.*
The film was directed by Freddie Francis and the script, as
written by "John Elder" (a nom de plume for Anthony Hinds,
one of Hammer's top producers) finally permitted Christopher
Lee to use his resonant voice.   The film marked Lee's first
dialogue in a Dracula film since the opening scenes of HOR-
ROR OF DRACULA.

*DRACULA HAS RISEN FROM THE GRAVE was originally
announced under the less original title of DRACULA'S RE-
VENGE.

DRACULA HAS RISEN FROM THE GRAVE was actually the story of Paul, played by Barry Andrews, a curly haired young man who spent most of his time on camera grinning like a Cheshire cat, and his relationship with Maria, played by blonde and bosomy Hammer starlet Veronica Carlson. With this film Hammer attempted to orient their horror films to a more youthful audience, making this the story of two young lovers, with Dracula reduced almost to the role of a supporting character. Nevertheless, DRACULA HAS RISEN FROM THE GRAVE was more successful financially than any Hammer Dracula film to date. One reason for this was the sensational title. Another was the advertising campaign launched to exploit the picture. Posters flooded cities depicting Ms. Carlson--principally the area between the cleavage exposed by a low-cut gown and her panting mouth--with two bandaids placed over the area of the jugular vein. The caption on the posters was "Dracula has risen from the grave ... obviously!" Yet another poster showed a snarling Dracula in his coffin, clutching the large wooden stake impaling his chest. The caption read, "When we last saw him ... Dracula was dead with a stake through his heart --- but you just can't keep a good man down." These exploiting posters, obviously, lured into theatres patrons who might not otherwise attend the screening of a Dracula movie.

This film was the first in the series in which Christopher Lee wore an exact duplicate of the ring Bela Lugosi wore in his Dracula films. The ring was given to Lee by Forrest J Ackerman, editor of Famous Monsters of Filmland magazine, during one of the actor's visits to Hollywood. Lee continued to wear the ring in subsequent films in the series. He also now sported a cloak with a scarlet lining.

The body of a young girl slain by the bite of a vampire is discovered in a village church. Much later, no one attends services at the church since it is crossed by the shadow of Castle Dracula. The Monsignor of the church, portrayed by Rupert Davies, and his assistant priest, played by Ewan Hooper, journey to the dreaded castle to perform an exorcism. Upon arriving at the castle, the priest becomes terrified. The Monsignor then leaves his assistant on the mountain slope while he proceeds to perform the exorcism himself. The Monsignor enacts the religious rites, which include placing a large golden cross upon the door to Castle Dracula. Suddenly the sky is alive with lightning and thunder, further terrifying the priest and causing him to fall down an incline. The priest stops by a frozen stream beneath which

lies the dormant Count Dracula.   In horror films, no monster remains frozen for long, especially when characters like
the priest are governed by coincidence.   As blood from a
wound acquired by the priest trickles into Dracula's mouth,
the King of the Un-Dead revives.   The priest sees the Count's
reflection in the water (a contradiction since BRIDES OF
DRACULA had established that vampires do not have mirror
images) and is promptly placed under the vampire's power.
When Dracula sees the cross which bars his entry to the castle, he swears revenge against the Monsignor, thus setting
the theme for the rest of the picture and justifying the originally announced title, DRACULA'S REVENCE.   Actually,
Dracula could have commanded his new slave to remove the
cross from his castle door, but that would have ended the
picture during those early scenes.

    The film proceeds with the priest robbing a grave in
order to provide his master with a coffin, and with the ever
grinning Paul attending the birthday party of Maria, the Monsignor's nubile niece.   Paul shocks everyone at the party
with the admission that he is an atheist and is asked to leave.
Dracula's next victim is Zena (Barbara Ewing), whom he
later commands to fetch Maria, whose blood he will take in
order to avenge himself upon the Monsignor.   When Zena
fails because of the intervention of Paul, Dracula brutally
kills her.   The Count then goes to Maria personally, entering her bedroom and attacking her.   In these scenes, Lee attempted to show that Dracula also possessed human, non-
sanguinary cravings, by not wearing the red contact lenses.
When the Monsignor observes the wounds on Maria's throat,
he decides to trap the vampire.   The Monsignor waits in the
shadows of Maria's room as Dracula returns, then drives the
vampire away with a crucifix.   Later, the Monsignor is fatal-
ly wounded by the priest, but before he dies he instructs
Paul on how to destroy the un-dead.

    During the day, the priest temporarily escapes Dracu-
la's power through the crucifix and takes Paul to the cellar
where the vampire reposes in his stolen casket.   As the sun
begins to set, Paul rams a large wooden stake through Dracula's heart.   In this scene Hammer added a bit of their own
vampire lore which contradicted that of their other Dracula
films.   Now, in an attempt to remove the prosaism from
driving a stake through the heart, certain prayers were also
required to keep the vampire pinned to his grave.   But Paul
is an atheist and cannot pray, and thus Dracula is able to
yank the stake from his own chest.   Dracula then escapes
and abducts Maria, fleeing with her in a hearse.

In this scene from DRACULA HAS RISEN FROM THE GRAVE (1968), the infamous Count (Christopher Lee) yanks a wooden stake from his own chest.

Back at his castle, Count Dracula compels Maria to remove the gilded cross from his door. The cross falls to the valley below. Paul arrives upon the scene and attacks the vampire physically in an attempt to save the woman he loves. During the struggle Paul trips his inhuman adversary off the mountain wall. The cloaked form plunges downward and is impaled upon the cross below. The priest, now free of Dracula's control, manages to blurt out the proper prayers. Writhing helplessly like an insect pinned in a box, Dracula begins to cry tears of blood, then crumbles to reddish powder. The ending was again spectacular, but "Elder" provided himself with another "death" scene which would prove difficult in surmounting in the next film.

Although Dracula's footage in the picture was brief, Christopher Lee's scenes were worth awaiting. Director Freddie Francis created some lasting images of the Count, as in the sequences in which he brutally drives his horse-drawn hearse through a dark forest and when he pulls the wooden shaft from his chest, leaving the wound miraculously to heal.

DRACULA HAS RISEN FROM THE GRAVE was so successful that Hammer Films began to make sequels on a yearly basis. Studio executives claimed that their Dracula films were more popular and lucrative than their Frankenstein productions, and in 1969 Hammer finished a film with a title almost as exploitable as that of their 1968 entry. Warner Brothers released the film, TASTE THE BLOOD OF DRACULA, which was directed by Peter Sasdy from another script by "John Elder" and again starred Christopher Lee.

The film opens with the climactic scenes from the previous movie. Like the preceding film, TASTE THE BLOOD OF DRACULA was founded upon a plot of revenge. The story introduced Lord Courtley, a practitioner of the black arts and another of Dracula's disciples, portrayed by Ralph Bates, a handsome young actor Hammer was grooming as a horror films star with special appeal to youthful audiences. Courtley seeks all that remains of his master Count Dracula--the black cloak, the royal ring and a vial containing the powdered red blood of the King Vampire, which had been salvaged by a merchant who had witnessed his demise. Not having the finances to purchase these items, Courtley enlists the aid of three supposedly respectable (but actually degenerate) men: William Hargood (Geoffrey Keen), Jonathan Secker (John Carson) and Samuel Paxton (Peter Sallis). The three men, always game for some new depravity, join Lord Courtley in a clandestine ritual in which each holds a chalice containing some of Dracula's powdered blood. Courtley then cuts his hand and lets his own blood flow into each chalice. Dracula's blood mixes with his own, the concoction beginning to bubble. Courtley is the first to taste the revitalized blood of Dracula. Overcome by the madness of the situation, the three men do not drink from their cups. Instead, they kill Lord Courtley and flee. Presently, something astounding happens to the Lord's corpse. A kind of unnatural cocoon envelops the body, then splits apart to reveal Count Dracula himself, reborn from the remains of his disciple. Now Dracula seeks revenge anew, this time against the three slayers of his protégé.

Count Dracula's vengeance is enacted through the

Opposite: The cross, a symbol of goodness on which the vampire cannot look, terrifies Dracula (Christopher Lee) in the 1969 Hammer film, TASTE THE BLOOD OF DRACULA.

30037

children of the three men--another attempt to capture a youthful audience.   Concealing his coffin in a desecrated church,
the master vampire proceeds to place beautiful Alice Hargood
(Linda Hayden) under his hypnotic control.   Alice then kills
her father by slashing his neck with the edge of a shovel.
The Count then places his bite upon Lucy Paxton (Isla Blair),
transforming her into a vampire.   When Lucy's father comes
to the long-abandoned church, Lucy and Alice trap him in
one of the pews.   Upon Dracula's command the two girls
gleefully drive a stake through Paxton's heart.   Lucy then
lures Jeremy Secker (Martin Jarvis) out of his house and
bites him with her fangs.   Jeremy completes Dracula's vengeance by stabbing his own father to death.

In the church, Dracula attempts to destroy the vampirized Lucy by draining off all her blood.   Lucy's boyfriend,
Paul Paxton (Anthony Corlan), enters the church, placing a
crucifix upon the door.   When Lucy is attacked by Dracula
she also seizes a cross, which she uses to fend off the vampire.   Dracula now finds himself trapped in the church by
more crosses and sacred white candles.   Realizing that the
forces of Goodness which originally inhabited the church have
returned, the King of Vampires attempts to climb to safety.
High above the altar, Dracula is totally overcome by these
positive forces and falls to his doom, again decomposing to
dust.

TASTE THE BLOOD OF DRACULA did not approach
the excellence of HORROR OF DRACULA but it did surpass
DRACULA HAS RISEN FROM THE GRAVE in quality.   Since
the Count could not have been revived without the death of
his disciple, it seems unlikely that he should desire revenge
against the men who killed him, or that he would choose such
a complicated method of achieving that revenge.   Lee was
given more footage as Count Dracula in this latest entry of
the series but he did not possess all the youthful vigor that
he displayed in HORROR OF DRACULA and his scenes in
TASTE THE BLOOD OF DRACULA provided him with little
to do.

TASTE THE BLOOD OF DRACULA was supposed to
be Christopher Lee's final appearance as the Count in a Hammer film.   The actor resented the fact that his agency had
signed him to do the picture without his first reading the
script, and he announced that he would not do the next film
in the series.   About this time Michael Carreras commented
upon the youthful actor who had played Lord Courtley in

TASTE THE BLOOD OF DRACULA: "... we gave birth to
Christopher Lee and Peter Cushing who play our monsters.
Right now they're getting a little bit long in the tooth, so
we're developing new talent. We're building up a boy called
Ralph Bates who should make an excellent Dracula...." But
Christopher Lee had reconsidered his refusal of the Dracula
role and went on to star in the next entry of the series,
SCARS OF DRACULA, directed by Roy Ward Baker and re-
leased by Continental in 1970.

SCARS OF DRACULA was an attempt to reinstate the
Count as the central character of the film. The Elder screenplay alloted Christopher Lee more footage and dialogue than
any other film in the series. The film also attempted to recreate some characteristics of the old Universal Dracula
films, so that SCARS was replete with angry torch-bearing
villagers and oversized vampire bats while still catering to
audience demands for more sex and gore. Unfortunately,
this latest Dracula picture had a stringent budget, a factor
that showed in the production. The irate villagers stormed
a castle exterior that was obviously hastily constructed on an
indoor soundstage, and the awkward vampire bat prop was
far from convincing. Such shortcomings notwithstanding,
SCARS OF DRACULA was an attempt to place the series' emphasis back on the bloody Count. There was also an attempt
at returning to Stoker with a scene of Dracula scaling the
castle wall in the fashion of a human lizard.

When a vampire bat with loyalties to the Count splashes
blood on his powdery remains, Dracula returns to his life in
death. The villagers of the Transylvanian town of Kleinenburg
soon learn that Count Dracula has returned to his castle and
decide to destroy him and his sanctuary for all time. After
leaving their loved ones in the village church, the men storm
the castle, setting fire to the ancient structure. Convinced
that the castle cannot endure the fire, the villagers return to
the church. To their horror they discover that all of their
loved ones have been savagely killed by Dracula's pet bat.
To make matters worse, both Dracula and his castle survive.

When philanderer Paul Carlson (Christopher Matthews)
is discovered making love to the burgomaster's daughter, he
flees and inadvertently arrives at Castle Dracula. Paul meets
Count Dracula and the beauteous vampire Tania (Anoushka
Hempel). Paul is invited to spend the night in the castle and
is delighted to find Tania a willing recipient of his affections.
When Dracula discovers his mistress in bed with Paul, he

kills her with a knife and makes her lover a prisoner of the
castle.   Paul attempts to escape through a window on a rope
of tied together bedsheets, but only succeeds in entering
Dracula's hidden resting place.

Paul's brother Simon (Dennis Waterman) and his girlfriend Sarah (Jenny Hanley) go off in search of the missing
young man, and they also become the night guests of the
Count.   Dracula enters Sarah's room with sanguinary intentions but is repelled by the crucifix worn about her neck.
The Count then commands his servant Klove (who has mysteriously returned as a derelict, in the person of Patrick
Troughton, after his apparent death in DRACULA, PRINCE
OF DARKNESS) to get rid of the miniature cross.   But, as
is the case with so many unsavory assistants in horror films,
Klove falls in love with Sarah and helps her and Simon escape.   In an unpleasantly vivid scene, Dracula punishes Klove
for his traitorous actions by branding his back with the red-
hot blade of a sword.   The resulting scars authenticate the
movie's title.

Leaving Sarah with the village priest, Simon returns
to Castle Dracula in hopes of learning the fate of his brother.
Simon discovers Dracula's resting place and also the hanging
and bloody corpse of Paul.   As Simon prepares to drive a
stake through the heart of the slumbering vampire, Dracula's
red orbs blaze through his shut eyelids.   A mesmerized Simon slumps into unconsciousness.   Dracula then proceeds to
command his bat to kill the priest and drive the fleeing Sarah
back toward the castle.   The climax of SCARS OF DRACULA
occurs atop the castle, with the Count about to make a vampire out of Sarah.   A vengeful Klove suddenly appears, attempting to kill his master with a knife, but instead he is
hurled by the Count to the valley below.   Seizing upon the
confusion, Simon launches a metal pike into Dracula's side.
But the Count yanks out the pike and prepares to use it as
a spear to impale his human enemy.   An electrical storm begins to brew overhead and, as Dracula prepares to release
his missile, the pike is struck by a bolt of lightning, which
sets the vampire ablaze.   In the form of an unconvincing
dummy provided by Hammer's prop department, Count Dracula, now a flaming inhuman torch, plunges from the rooftop
of his castle.

Opposite: The King of Vampires (Christopher Lee) in a moment of murderous rage in SCARS OF DRACULA (Hammer,
1970).

The same year as SCARS OF DRACULA, Hammer
made a film with the misleading title, COUNTESS DRACULA.
Actually not a part of their Dracula series at all, this was
a horror film based on the life of Countess Elizabeth Báthory
(see Chapter 2).

Hammer returned to the original Count Dracula in
1972 when they began filming DRACULA TODAY, again starring Lee.   Just prior to the film's release by Warner Brothers, the title was changed to the dating DRACULA A.D.
1972.*   As is evident from the title, this film was Hammer's
attempt to bring the series out of its nineteenth century period setting and into the modern world.   Perhaps the studio's
writers had exhausted their abilities to devise new plots during the time period in which the King of Vampires was most
comfortable and DRACULA A.D. 1972 was a last gasp effort
to inject new life into the series.   While none of the Hammer Dracula sequels has matched, let alone surpassed, HOR-
ROR OF DRACULA in quality, many Hammer devotees agree
that DRACULA A.D. 1972 marks the series' nadir to date.
Essentially, writer Don Houghton produced a script centering
upon the supposed counter-culture of 1972 Chelsea and inserted Count Dracula somewhere between the rock music and
the pseudo-hip dialogue.   The film probably should have been
entitled "Dracula A.D. Late 1960s," since the life styles depicted by the youthful characters belong more to that decade.
Alan Gibson's direction of these carryovers from mod London
is laughable; they rock about society parties to the shock of
England's confused upper class, and mouth clichés that would
even embarrass today's staunchest would-be "freaks."

Mercifully, the scenes in which Dracula himself appears convey a sense of period gothic, as the Count never
is shown to leave the desecrated church he has made his lair.
Furthermore, Dracula's female victims, who also haunt the
gothic church, are dressed in a manner which suggests the
previous century.   In this sense Dracula himself remains un-
changed and in his element while a modern world carries on
oblivious to his existence, thereby obviating the problems of
pitting the vampire against twentieth century technology.
Separating Dracula from the trappings of the modern world
was done upon the insistence of Lee.   "I think it's all wrong,
mind you," said Lee.   "I think it's totally and completely
wrong to take it out of context, out of the historical period,

---

*For a while the titles DRACULA CHELSEA '72 and DRACU-
LA CHASES THE MINI GIRLS were also contemplated.

out of the gothic period, and put it in modern times. But from what I'm told, in a weird way, it quite works. "

DRACULA A. D. 1972 marked the return of Peter Cushing to the role of Professor Van Helsing, his first such appearance since BRIDES OF DRACULA. (One wonders why Van Helsing did not continue his crusade against Dracula until now.) Not only did Cushing recreate his former role of Van Helsing, he also portrayed his modern day descendant.

Though Lee again portrayed Dracula and Cushing once more played Van Helsing, DRACULA A. D. 1972 is not a direct sequel to any of its predecessors. The film opens with the two foes struggling atop a runaway coach somewhere in nineteenth century London. The battle ends as the coach overturns and Dracula is impaled by one of the wooden spokes of a broken wheel. Soon afterwards Van Helsing dies. During the Professor's funeral another disciple of Dracula buries his master's collected ashes in that same graveyard. The story then abruptly cuts to 1972, introducing young and long-haired Johnny Alucard (a name which by 1972 had become a movie cliché; its first use was in Universal's SON OF DRACULA), a hedonist always on the search for new and illicit thrills and, not surprisingly, a descendant of the Count. Alucard was portrayed by Christopher Neame, not because of his modicum of acting ability but probably because of his physical resemblance to Malcolm McDowell, who was enjoying popularity after his performance in the 1971 film, A CLOCKWORK ORANGE. Johnny acquires the powdered remains of Dracula, then calls his group of rowdies to the ruined church near the graveyard where Professor Van Helsing is buried, for the purpose of celebrating a Black Mass. This also happens to be the anniversary of Van Helsing's death. Adding to the coincidences is the fact that one of the group is Jessica Van Helsing (Stephanie Beacham), granddaughter of the Professor's grandson (Cushing). After his cohorts have left the church upon realizing that he is not joking, Johnny pours a mixture of his own blood and the Count's remains over his sacrificial victim (Caroline Munro), a ritual which brings a fully restored Dracula out of the graveyard earth. Again Dracula swears revenge, this time against the family of Van Helsing.

To slake his thirst, Johnny brings a beautiful black girl (Marsha Hunte) to his master, then later asks that the Count make him one of the un-dead. Reluctantly Dracula bares his fangs as the scene tastefully cuts to another.

Hammer Films starlet Stephanie Beacham, as Jessica Van
Helsing, poses with Christopher Lee, as Count Dracula in
DRACULA A.D. 1972.

Dracula's intended revenge upon the Van Helsings is the supreme Irony: he means to make the lovely Stephanie a vampire. Gradually the current Dr. Van Helsing discovers that
Count Dracula, the creature whom his ancestor had fought in
the past, has returned from the grave and is menacing his
granddaughter. First, Van Helsing encounters the vampire
Johnny Alucard, and after a fierce battle in the latter's apartment, destroys him by turning on the running water when
Johnny falls into the bathtub. Van Helsing then proceeds to
the ruins of the church, where he finally encounters the ancient enemy of his lineage. Dracula is apparently doomed
when a silver blade is thrust into his heart. But the knife is
promptly removed, and Dracula again stalks Van Helsing.
After a one-sided struggle with Van Helsing, mostly in the

vampire's favor, Count Dracula falls backwards and is impaled upon a trap of wooden stakes, which again reduces him to dust. The vampire's intended irony is reversed, for he perishes upon the grave of the original Van Helsing. *

Despite the absurdities of DRACULA A.D. 1972, Christopher Lee managed to retain his dignity as the Count. Even in so late a sequel the actor inserted a line taken from Stoker: "You would play your brains against mine ... against me who has commanded nations," says Dracula as he stalks Van Helsing through the old church.

"I did so deliberately," Lee informed this writer, "in a desperate attempt at putting in one line from the original Stoker book, as a tribute to the author to show him that, as far as I was concerned, his original characterization is very much alive to me. It's a marvelous phrase. But that line wasn't properly covered. It was too far away in the distance. But people who know the book and respect it immediately got it, right away. It was my tribute to the author as a desperate cry from the heart that at least I'm trying to get something original into this."

Prior to releasing DRACULA A.D. 1972 in the United States, Warner Brothers filmed a brief short subject entitled HORROR RITUAL, which served as a type of comic prologue to the feature. HORROR RITUAL featured actor Barry Atwater (the vampire of Las Vegas in THE NIGHT STALKER, a motion picture made for television) as a Dracula-type vampire who rises from a slab in a foggy crypt to initiate audiences into the Count Dracula Society. "I'm sorry I did that," Atwater told me. "I liked the money. But I was really upset by it. I didn't like doing it. I was very embarrassed. The make-up, I thought, was atrocious. I complained about the make-up but there was nothing I could do. They wouldn't listen to me. They wanted to do it very fast and get it over with and the make-up man had all his ideas in his head before he even showed up. I'm glad they didn't show it very much. Vampires don't wear pankake!"

Prior to the release of DRACULA A.D. 1972 word leaked out in various film publications that the next Hammer film in the series would be DRACULA WALKS THE NIGHT. Supposedly, the film had gone into production, with Lee again

---

*In Italy the film became 1972: DRACULA COLPISCE ANCORA! ("1972: Dracula Strikes Again!")

as Dracula and Cushing as Van Helsing. The story began
with Vlad the Impaler eventually becoming the vampire Count
Dracula during the fifteenth century. Then, in London, circa
1895, Van Helsing, Sherlock Holmes and Dr. Watson band together to fight the King of the Un-Dead. The basic plot was
to follow that of Stoker's novel. Jimmy Sangster and Richard
Matheson were to have co-authored the script and Terence
Fisher was to have directed this Brockridge/Russ Jones production. Included in the impressive cast were James Donald
and Michael Ripper (a familiar face in many a Hammer film)
as Holmes and Watson respectively, with Jack Palance as
Dracula's servant Macata, and Michael Gough, Barbara Shelley, Andrew Keir, Thorley Walters, Ferdy Mayne, Suzan
Farmer, Hazel Court, Michael Gwynn, Jack McGowran,
Ronald Lewis and Duncan Lamont. Warner Brothers was supposed to release the film. What sounded like Hammer's most
ambitious Dracula effort, however, was finally exposed as a
hoax; in fact, it was one of several similarly announced
Dracula films that will probably never go before the cameras.

Hammer continued its policy of making one Dracula
film each year when DRACULA IS DEAD ... AND WELL AND
LIVING IN LONDON, under Alan Gibson's direction, went before the cameras in 1973. A very reluctant Christopher Lee
starred.

While DRACULA A. D. 1972 was going into American
release, the actor said, "I'm doing the next one under protest. I just think it's fatuous. I can think of twenty adjec-
tives--fatuous, pointless, absurd. It's not a comedy. At
least with me it's not a comedy. But it's a comic title. I
don't see the point. I don't see what they hope to achieve.
I think it's playing down to people. I don't think people like
it. I don't think people appreciate it either, because people
who go to see a character like this go to see him seriously.
They don't laugh at him. That I know. They may laugh at
some of the things in the pictures, but they'll never laugh at
me to my knowledge.... The next one takes place not in a
ruined church but in a modern building, while the character
can only be described as a mixture between Howard Hughes
and Dr. No. And it's getting further and further and further
away from the original conception of the character, which I
have always said is totally wrong. People say to me, 'Well,
then, why do you do it?' My answer to that is that as an
actor I have to appear on the screen. I also have to make
a living. And there are millions of people all over the world
who want to see me play that part. In whatever context I

play it, I don't change.   I remain the same.... It's the old, old story.   Whenever they do one of these things they write the story first, then rack their brains to think of a way of inserting the main character into the framework of that story, instead of the other way around.   Well this, of course, is ludicrous.   You've got a modern story which, by itself, is probably quite good and quite well-written.   And then somebody says, 'My God! How are we going to put Dracula into this? What are we going to give him to do? What are we going to give him to say!' The result being that I invariably cut out all the lines because they're so appalling.   I'd rather say nothing than say some of the lines in the original scripts.   They never seem to bother about the central character.   It's, 'Oh, we'll fit him in someway and people will come to see him.' They concentrate on the rest of the story where they do their good writing.   But on the presentation of the central character I feel they fall down very badly.

"... I just hope that people, whenever they see me play this character, which hopefully won't be for very much longer because I've become so disenchanted with the way the character is presented in the films, I hope they realize that I am struggling against insuperable odds on occasions to remain faithful to the author's original character."

The new Dracula film again reunites Lee and Cushing in their familiar roles and involves the Count's attempt to take over the world by unleashing a terrible plague upon mankind.   After finishing this film, Lee stated in a letter written in Spain during the filming of a new version of THE THREE MUSKETEERS: "... I am not prepared to do any more films of this kind, including Count Dracula films, unless the quality of script, direction and production is considerably raised. Unless I am offered Bram Stoker's book 'in toto' I shall almost certainly not play Dracula again ... "

Hammer had the foresight to change the title of this film to THE SATANIC RITES OF DRACULA.   When a high government official takes part in a Black Mass held at an old mansion, Van Helsing (Cushing) is summoned by the authorities to intervene.   Within the house are youthful guards dressed in black, like Nazi soldiers.   The basement is inhabited by a colony of vampire girls.   Presently, Van Helsing's daughter Jessica (Joanna Lumley) is to be Dracula's victim on the altar of the Black Mass.   At the end of the film, Van Helsing stakes a number of the female un-dead and traps Dracula in a deadly hawthorn bush before the Count suffers a fiery demise.

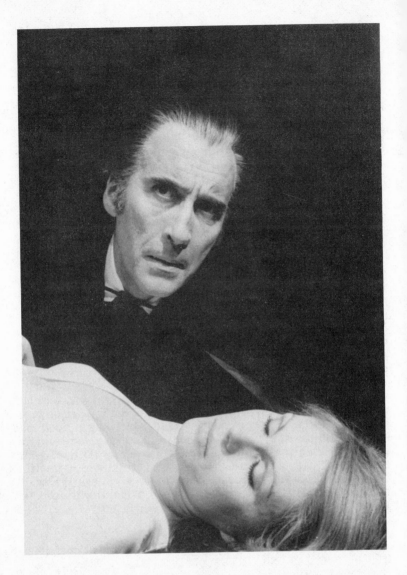

The Lord of the Un-Dead (Christopher Lee) prepares to place the vampire's bite upon Jessica Van Helsing (Joanne Lumley) in THE SATANIC RITES OF DRACULA (Hammer, 1973).

In 1974 Peter Cushing as Lawrence Van Helsing made a comeback in THE LEGEND OF THE SEVEN GOLDEN VAMPIRES (also known as DRACULA AND THE 7 GOLDEN VAMPIRES), a co-production between Hammer and the China-based Shaw brothers, made in color and directed by Roy Ward Baker.   John Forbes-Robertson played Dracula while Christopher Lee remained faithful to his vow of leaving the series. During the early 1800s, a Chinese emissary awakens Dracula, after which he is attacked and possessed by the Count.   Now appearing Oriental, Dracula journeys to China and establishes a vampire cult which adds reviving the dead to their debaucheries.   Van Helsing, in China on a lecture tour, and a group of martial arts experts then proceed to battle the undead.

After completing this film, Hammer announced KALI: DEVIL BRIDE OF DRACULA in 1974, with Cushing again as Van Helsing.   Based upon the Indian religious cult, the film furthers the new direction of the Hammer Dracula films.

The Hammer Dracula films are frequently damned by horror movie purists who prefer the atmospheric (and tamer) product made by Universal.   But Hammer has portrayed Count Dracula more as the figure envisioned by Stoker--sanguinary, feral, noble, confident and dynamic.   The studio also removed the vampire from his stereotyped image of the suave continental in tuxedo and opera cape and characterized him more according to tradition.   And, shortcomings notwithstanding, Hammer managed to produce a series of generally entertaining and quite profitable Dracula films without having to pit the Count against any of the studio's other monsters. Hammer's Dracula series continues on the popularity of Dracula himself.

Chapter 9

DRACULA FLIES AGAIN

> There's only one reality, Rachel, and that is death
> --a living death. I bring you the darkness of cen-
> turies past and centuries to come. Eternal life--
> and eternal death. Now do you fear?--Francis
> Lederer in THE RETURN OF DRACULA (1958)

Relatively few Dracula motion pictures were made between the last of the Universal series and the debut of the
series made by Hammer. This hiatus may perhaps have
been because studio executives thought that Universal had exhausted the possibilities of stories about the old Count. No
one apparently predicted the veritable wave of Dracula films
that would eventually descend upon the world like a swarm
of bats in the 1960s and 1970s. During the fifties Dracula's
movie appearances would be few until the advent of Christopher Lee.

DRAKULA ISTANBULDA ("Dracula in Istanbul") is a
curious Turkish motion picture, made in 1953 by And Film
and directed by Mehmet Muhtar. The film was based both
upon Stoker's Dracula and upon the novel Kastgli Voyvoda,
by Ali Riga Seifi. Turgut Demirag produced the film and detective novelist Umit Deniz wrote the screenplay. "Drakula"
was portrayed by a gray and balding Atif Kaptan, bearing
somewhat of a facial resemblance to Hamilton Deane. Kaptan haunted a castle made up of rather inexpensive looking
sets. A significant aspect of his portrayal is that Kaptan
sported canine fangs. Not since NOSFERATU had the Count
been shown on screen with sharp or elongated teeth.

The plot of DRAKULA ISTANBULDA generally follows
that of the original Stoker book. An accountant named Amzi
is the film's version of Jonathan Harker. Amzi arrives at
Count Drakula's Carpathian castle to become the nobleman's

Atif Kaptan as "Drakula" in the rare Turkish film of 1953, DRAKULA ISTANBULDA.

personal secretary, not heeding the warnings of the peasants that the Count is directly descended from the terror of the Turks, Vlad the Impaler. Amzi is greeted by the Count's hunchbacked servant and later, at sunset, by Drakula himself. Soon, Amzi discovers that Drakula exhibits vampiric qualities, including an aversion to the sacred book of Islam, the Koran. He also finds three coffins, one of which contains the reposing body of Drakula, the others holding two beautiful vampire women. When the accountant is awakened from his night's slumber by the girls' voices, he finds the female vampires luring him to the castle wall. Drakula himself appears and Amzi flees the evil place, finally rejoining his friends and ballerina fiancée (played by Annie Ball) in Istanbul (which was substituted for London). In Istanbul, Count Drakula is attracted to Amzi's intended bride and uses his mesmeric abilities to entice her to his bite; she is transformed into a vampire as a result of Drakula's attacks. Amzi, accompanied by a Turkish version of Van Helsing, searches out the Count's resting place. In the ruins of an old section of the city, Drakula is impaled with a stake and then beheaded.

That same year a man wearing an enormous Dracula headmask appeared during a festival scene in I VITELLONI ("The Young Men"), a film made in Italy by Federico Fellini.

Count Dracula apparently did not appear again in a feature-length film until 1955 when he was featured with the Frankenstein Monster in a satire of horror films entitled EL FANTASMA DE LA OPERETA ("The Phantom of the Operetta"). This Argentinian film made by Gral Belgrams was directed by Enrique Carreras and featured Amelita Vargas, Alfredo Barbieri, Tono Andreu, Gogo Andreu and Inez Fernandez. A still photograph from EL FANTASMA DE LA OPERETA shows the Frankenstein Monster about to strike Dracula over the head with a vase.

American-International Picture's BLOOD OF DRACULA (1957) was a double misrepresentation, for it featured neither Dracula nor his blood. This was the era of teenage monsters in films, a cycle which began with the same studio's box-office success, I WAS A TEENAGE WEREWOLF, made earlier that year. Naturally there would have to be a similarly youthful version of the vampire to fit in with the rock 'n' roll idols and hubcap thefts that were so popular at the time. BLOOD OF DRACULA was directed by Herbert L. Strock and was released as the second half of a nation-wide double program headed by Strock's I WAS A TEENAGE FRANK-ENSTEIN.

The teenaged vampire of BLOOD OF DRACULA was not even the same sex as the infamous Count from Transylvania. Sandra Harrison played Nancy Perkins, who would become the vampire of the film. But Nancy would not become the un-dead species of vampire; she was a mostly normal young student who periodically transformed into an almost werewolf-like, living vampire.

Neurotic Nancy Perkins arrives at an all-girls school where she encounters Miss Branding (Louise Lewis), a suspicious old maid chemistry teacher. Miss Branding's interest in the girls is more than grades and term papers. Expectedly Nancy retains her naiveté even as Miss Branding mentions an extraordinary scheme to end future wars. She possesses a medallion which might, according to the implication of the title, have once belonged to Count Dracula (although this fact is never confirmed or denied). Apparently it did belong to some extremely powerful vampire, though, for when Miss Branding concentrates upon the jewel and utters her arcane spell, it transforms Nancy into a blood-thirsty human vampire.

Nancy's version of the vampire was new to motion pictures. Make-up artist Philip Scheer gave her a marble-white face, long uneven fangs, high shooting eyebrows and a mass of coarse hair that began as a sharp widow's peak on her forehead. Nancy metamorphoses into this monster during the day or at night, and sometimes at the most inopportune moments as in a parked car with an amorous young man.

When one of the vampire's victims is discovered drained of blood, a janitor who had spent much of his life in the "Old Country" identifies the marks on the throat as being those of a vampire or a "Dracula." Perhaps this was scriptwriter Ralph Thornton's justification for the film's title. In the final scenes of the picture Nancy savagely turns upon her creator and Miss Branding perishes at the fangs and claws of the once pretty student. Nancy meets her destruction shortly afterwards when she falls upon an upright piece of wood (conveniently resting on the floor) which impales her through the heart. The vampire features fade away and Nancy's soul is at peace. *

During that same year producers Arthur Gardner and

---

*BLOOD OF DRACULA was released in England as BLOOD IS MY HERITAGE and in Canada as BLOOD OF THE DEMON.

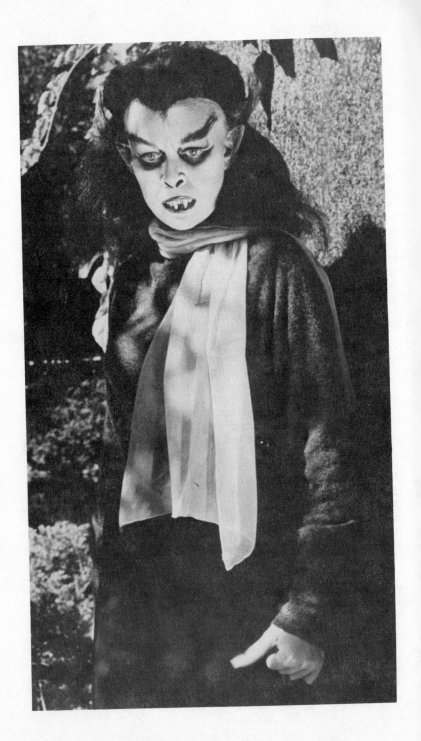

Jules Levy of United Artists made a film entitled simply THE
VAMPIRE, directed by Paul Landres. THE VAMPIRE starred
John Beal as a scientist whose use of a new type of pills
causes him regularly to transform into a puffy-faced living
vampire whenever the full moon rises. *

    Gardner, Levy and Landres followed THE VAMPIRE
with a more traditional vampire film in 1958, even returning
to the infamous Count himself. THE RETURN OF DRACULA
was United Artists' contribution to the King Vampire's film
career. Handsome Czechoslovakian actor Francis Lederer
portrayed a curly-haired Count Dracula. As Dracula, Lederer did not parade about in conspicuous tuxedo and cape. Instead he wore a standard business suit, a hat and an overcoat
which, when draped over his shoulders, suggested a cape. This
change in attire was not so much an attempt to remain incognito
as it was not to infringe upon the copyrighted image owned by
Universal. Lederer's lack of distinctive costuming was not enhanced by the overall low-budget appearance of the film.

    THE RETURN OF DRACULA begins in the Balkans
with a group of vampire exterminators entering the current
tomb of Dracula, hoping finally to drive the destructive stake
through his heart. When they open the vampire's coffin it is
empty. At a railroad station, Bellac Gordal (Norbert Schil-
ler) prepares to leave for the first part of a journey which
will eventually bring him to relatives living in the United
States. While on the train Bellac encounters Dracula, whom
he recognizes immediately. Bellac screams as the menacing
figure approaches him.

    Dracula, having assumed the identity of Bellac, ar-
rives in America to be greeted by his new "family." The
train is half an hour early and Bellac (like Count Alucard in
SON OF DRACULA) is never seen to step off. The sun is
still in the sky and the only baggage taken from the train and
identified as belonging to Bellac is a box the size of a casket.
Bellac's relatives are disappointed, having made elaborate
preparations for his arrival. After sunset, a mist, unseen

---

*THE VAMPIRE was also known under the title IT'S ALWAYS
DARKEST BEFORE THE DAWN and was released to television under the title MARK OF THE VAMPIRE.

Opposite: During the height of the 1950s' "teenage monster"
craze, Sandra Harrison transformed into a vampire in American-International Pictures' BLOOD OF DRACULA (1957).

Incognito as a Balkan immigrant named Bellac, Count Dracula
(Francis Lederer) meets his demise in a pit of wooden shafts.
From United Artists' 1958 motion picture, THE RETURN OF
DRACULA.

by the group, issues from the crate and solidifies into "Cousin Bellac." The continental visitor is then taken to the family's house. The next day Bellac is not to be found in his
room. The scene changes to a dark cave in the nearby hills
which harbors the coffin of Dracula. The casket opens to
reveal the Count immersed in dense mist. The scenes of
Lederer emerging from his coffin were double printed (every
frame printed twice) to impart an ethereal quality.

Dracula's first victim is a blind girl named Jenny
(Virginia Vincent) who is able literally to see him during his
attacks. Jenny finally dies, calling out for him to return.
After the girl's funeral, a man from the United States Immi-
gration Department named Mac Bryant (Ivan Young), investigating the death of the man thrown from the train, visits the
family adopted by Dracula. Dracula visits Jenny's mausoleum,
summoning her. Mist changes into the white-clothed girl and
before long she, now in the form of a white wolf, kills
Bryant. Only when "Bellac" is not visible on a photograph
are the authorities convinced that vampires are at large.
Jenny is seen returning to her tomb and lying as if asleep in
the mist-filled casket. In the first graphic scene of its kind,
a wooden stake is driven through Jenny's heart, with artificial blood overflowing in close-up. Simultaneously, Dracula,
in the cave, experiences the same pain, buckling forward before he can place the damning bite on Bellac's cousin Rachel
(Norma Eberhardt). Rachel's boyfriend Tim (Gage Clark)
fends off Dracula with a cross before he can complete his attack, and drives the vampire through the cave toward a deep
pit filled with wooden shafts. Stumbling backwards, Dracula
falls, impaling himself through the back and chest and fading
away to bones.

Francis Lederer was a refreshing Dracula. Though
obviously influenced by Lugosi (with lights focused upon his
eyes à la the 1931 DRACULA), Lederer did not imitate the
Hungarian actor and brought something of the foreign spy to
his Dracula. Despite his performance THE RETURN OF
DRACULA* seemed even more anemic in the light of another
genre picture released that same year, Hammer Films' HOR-
ROR OF DRACULA.

A semi-Dracula film made in 1959 was NIGHT OF

*THE RETURN OF DRACULA was released in England as
THE FANTASTIC DISAPPEARING MAN and to television as
CURSE OF DRACULA.

THE GHOULS, an extremely low-budget production produced, written and directed by Edward D. Wood, Jr. Dracula did not appear in NIGHT OF THE GHOULS, a sequel to Wood's 1956 release, BRIDE OF THE MONSTER.* But veteran Western actor Kenne Duncan did wear a turban for his role as a phony swami named "Dr. Acula." The plot of this film involves Dr. Acula's attempts to swindle gullible customers into believing that he can conjure up the spirits of the dead. Dr. Acula's faked seances are in the same house as shown in BRIDE OF THE MONSTER. Among his ghostly effects troupe are the White Ghost, the slinky Black Ghost as portrayed by Vampira,** the dummy of a vampire and the mountainous Lobo (Tor Johnson), who had escaped his death in BRIDE OF THE MONSTER with a scarred face. NIGHT OF THE GHOULS (also known as REVENGE OF THE DEAD) opened with television prophet Criswell rising from a coffin. The heroes of the film, two police detectives, encounter the Black Ghost in the swamp and then the White Ghost in the house; then they meet Dr. Acula, who is faking the resurrection of a corpse. But Dr. Acula's phony rituals achieve more astounding results than anticipated. He inadvertently

---

*BRIDE OF THE MONSTER (re-released as BRIDE OF THE ATOM) was a pitiful attempt to return Bela Lugosi to the screen after his long bout with drugs. Lugosi portrayed a mad doctor trying to develop a race of supermen from human guinea pigs in his Frankenstein-like laboratory. In the process, he tried to use the old Dracula staring eyes and waving hands to hypnotize a victim.

**Vampira (real name Maila Nurmi) achieved her greatest fame on television during the 1950s. Patterning her image after a vampiric female appearing in the Charles Addams cartoons, Vampira had a pale white face, gaunt features, Satanic eyebrows, dark lips and long black hair. She wore a tight fitting black dress with a plunging neckline. On television, Vampira introduced old horror films, interrupting them with her own ghoulish remarks. In 1959 she appeared in another Wood film, PLAN 9 FROM OUTER SPACE, essentially portraying her television image. Yet another film role for the actress as a vampire was THE MAGIC SWORD (first announced as ST. GEORGE AND THE SEVEN CURSES and then ST. GEORGE AND THE DRAGON), directed by Bert I. Gordon and released in color by United Artists in 1962. In the film the knight George (Gary Lockwood) is seduced by a beautiful young vampire in the bright daylight. Before she can sink her fangs into his throat she transforms into an old hag (played by Vampira).

revives some corpses who seize him and toss him into a grave. NIGHT OF THE GHOULS has still not been theatrically released. Apparently, an unpaid laboratory bill forced the picture into storage after its completion. The film was made in black and white, making it even more difficult to market at some possible future date. Perhaps it is all for the best. The same year NIGHT OF THE GHOULS was made, Dracula appeared in the form of a teenager attending a masquerade party in GHOST OF DRAGSTRIP HOLLOW, a film made by American-International Pictures which went into production under the title, THE HAUNTED HOTROD.

DIE STUNDE WENN DRAKULA KOMMT ("The Hour when Dracula Comes") was the German title for the 1960 Italian horror film, LA MASCHERA DEL DEMONIO ("The Mask of the Demon"), which was released in the United States by American-International Pictures under the title BLACK SUNDAY. It was also known under the title HOUSE OF FRIGHT, and was released in England as REVENGE OF THE VAMPIRE. The Galatea-Jolly production was based on Nicolai Gogol's story "The Vij" (also known as "Viy") written in 1835, the climax showed the corpse of a young witch rising vampire-like from her coffin while the church which sheltered it was bombarded by the demons of Satan.

LA MASCHERA DEL DEMONIO starred Barbara Steele in the dual role of an evil vampire witch and her mortal descendent. Ms. Steele, a striking beauty with high cheekbones, sensuous mouth and magnificently large eyes, managed to contrast the two portrayals, one totally corrupt, the other virtuous, but both extremely desirable in different ways. She continued to enjoy a successful career as the unexcelled sex goddess of the horror films. Her performances were enhanced by real acting ability and a powerful screen presence.

The film is based on the premise that Satan walks the Earth every hundred years on the dark night of Black Sunday. LA MASCHERA DEL DEMONIO opens with a Moldavian inquisition of a combination witch and vampire named Princess Asa (Barbara Steele). Found guilty, Asa is bound to a large cross and executed by a spiked mask which is pounded into her face. There is no Dracula in the film despite the German title. Apparently, the Dracula character is Asa's lover, Prince Javutich (Arturo Dominici), whose appearance includes long hair and a lengthy cloak. Javutich is given the same grisly death. But before Asa dies she swears to return from the grave for vengeance.

Two centuries later a doctor and his assistant come upon the tomb of the vampiress and remove the spiked mask. When an enormous bat swoops down upon them, the doctor kills it, letting the creature's blood drip upon the cratered face of Asa. This is Black Sunday. And the prince of the nearby castle fears that his vampiress ancestor might return from the dead. His daughter Katya (also Barbara Steele) is an exact double for Asa. Asa steps out of her coffin and summons Prince Javutich, who rises from his unmarked grave and yanks off the impaling demon mask.

While Javutich sets out to destroy the ruling prince, Asa's vengeful plans include taking the place of Katya. After defeating the supernaturally strong Javutich in a physical battle, the young doctor discovers the secret passage leading from the castle to the tomb of Asa, and there finds two identical women each claiming to be Katya. The doctor is mistakenly about to impale the real Katya with a wooden shaft when he notices her crucifix. Realizing the truth, the doctor pulls away Asa's cloak, revealing the rotting ribs of a corpse. The vampire witch is then taken by the irate villagers and is burned at the stake.

LA MASCHERA DEL DEMONIO, though not really a Dracula film, remains one of the finest and most terrifying pictures of its kind. Certainly it is the best Italian horror film to date. The motion picture was the first directorial assignment of Mario Bava,* who wisely chose to make the

---

*Mario Bava had previously served as cameraman on such Italian horror films as I VAMPIRI, which Roccardo Freda (Robert Hampton) directed for Titanus-Athena in 1957. The film is the tale of a countess whose youth is restored, similarly to that of Elizabeth Báthory, by the blood of a young girl. This time, however, the blood is acquired through a doctor's injections. The film is also known as THE VAMPIRE OF NOTRE DAME and LUST OF THE VAMPIRE. In 1963 it was edited and dubbed for United States release as THE DEVIL'S COMMANDMENT.

Continuing to direct horror films, Bava often returned to the vampire subject, creating impressive products but never equaling his triumphant premiere effort LA MASCHERA DEL DEMONIO. In 1963 Bava directed the color film, I TRE VOLTI DELLA PAURA ("The Three Faces of Fear"), also known as BLACK CHRISTMAS and THE THREE FACES OF TERROR. The Galatea picture was released in the US by American-International under the title BLACK SABBATH.

(cont. on p. 201)

film in black and white.   Bava's gothic atmosphere is stunning, his relentless succession of scenes of darkness and demons a veritable tour de force of all that is unholy.   Such scenes as Prince Javutich's coach drawn silently by horses and moving in slow motion through the vaporous woods convey an authentic sensation of unreality.   And the performance of the sultry Barbara Steele completed the finished visual nightmare which was LA MASCHERA DEL DEMONIO.

Korea contributed to the Dracula film mythology with the 1961 production, AHKEA KKOTS ("The Bad Flower"). This remake of Hammer's HORROR OF DRACULA was directed by Yongmin Lee and starred Chimi Kim and Yechoon Lee.   AHKEA KKOTS was released by Sunglim Film.

Dracula's first in a long line of sex films was the 1962 color production of THE HOUSE ON BARE MOUNTAIN, directed by R. Lee Frost for Olympic International Films. This was one of the "nudies" so popular in the Sixties, quite innocent by today's standards.   Dracula (Jeffrey Smithers) and the Frankenstein Monster (Warren Ames) crash a nude party thrown by Granny Good (Bob Cresse), terrifying the numerous unclothed girls.   After a police raid both horrors are revealed as being quite human.   But the werewolf present at the affair proves to be genuine.   The film was apparently

---

The film featured three separate stories, all introduced by Boris Karloff.   In the last of the three, "The Wurdalak" (based on the story by Alexei Tolstoy) Karloff portrayed a man who goes off to slay a wurdalak, a vampire that finds his own family's blood particularly delectable.   He beheads the sanguinary fiend, then returns to his family as a wurdalak himself, eventually changing all of them into creatures like himself.   Two years later Bava directed TERRORE NELLO SPAZIO ("Terror from Space"), a color film for Castilla. The movie was known in Spain as TERROR EN EL ESPACIO, in the United States (released by American-International) as PLANET OF THE VAMPIRES, on American television as THE DEMON PLANET, and was also given such titles as PLANET OF THE DAMNED, HAUNTED PLANET, HAUNTED WORLD and OUTLAW PLANET.   Not a real vampire film, TERRORE NELLO SPAZIO is a science fiction story about ghostly entities attempting to leave their dead world by possessing the bodies of alien astronauts.   Bava's later films were often slow moving, but were always extremely atmospheric and elegantly photographed.

also known as NIGHT ON BARE MOUNTAIN. In Belgium the title became LA COLLINE DES DESIRS ("The Hill of Desires").

ESCALA EN HI-FI ("Scale in Hi-Fi") was made by the Spanish company Documento and Izaro and directed by Isidoro Martinez-Ferry in 1963. The musical comedy included a nightmare sequence set in Castle Dracula. That same year Dracula returned to the world of the sex film, appearing in a vignette in an Italian pseudo-documentary on the striptease entitled SEXY PROIBITISSIMO ("The Most Prohibited Sex"), a movie directed by Marcello Martinelli for Films Marbeuf. In his sequence Count Dracula enters the bedroom of a stripper and is about to sink his fangs into her throat when she begins to remove her clothes. The lecherous vampire decides it is better to watch than attack. SEXY PROIBITISSIMO was known in France as SEXY SUPER INTERDIT and SEXY INTERDIT.

A film entitled MGA MANUGANG NI DRAKULA ("The Secrets of Dracula") was made in the Philippines in 1964. But at present nothing more is known of the production. The same year Dracula appeared in the person of a party-goer wearing a commercially available Ellis Burman mask in THE CANDIDATE, an English film from Atlantic Cosnat, directed by Robert Angus.

Barbara Steele returned to bewitch audiences the following year in the Italian-Yugoslavian co-production, LA SORELLA DI SATANA ("The Sister of Satan"), a film directed by Mike Reeves for Europix and Leith and known in the United States as SHE BEAST. A witch, dead two centuries at the bottom of a lake, returns to life to haunt a Communist-occupied Transylvania. Although Dracula does not appear in the film, "Von" Helsing (John Karlson) boasts how he had once battled and destroyed the King of Vampires. Utilizing his knowledge of the supernatural, Von Helsing destroys the evil witch. At the end of the film the witch's spirit inhabits the shapely body of Ms. Steele. (LA SORELLA DI SATANA was known in England as REVENGE OF THE BLOOD BEAST.)

A proposed film with the absurd title of BILLY THE KID VS. DRACULA had been appearing in print since the beginnings of the 1960s. Horror film purists prayed that so ludicrous a conflict would never actually materialize on film, but BILLY THE KID VS. DRACULA was finally made in color by Embassy Pictures in 1966.

After a hiatus of twenty-one years as a motion picture Dracula, an aging John Carradine returned to the role. Among Carradine's additions to his Dracula portrayal were a satanic mustache and beard, a bright red ascot and a salient contempt for the role he had somehow been cajoled into desecrating in this combination Western and horror film. Carradine's true regard for the film may be evident in one scene during which he opens wide his eyes and mouth and lets out an animal-like "Raaaaaaaaa!"

On the other hand, the actor did manage to exhibit some fondness for the part. When I visited the set at Producer's Studio in Hollywood during the filming of BILLY THE KID VS. DRACULA, Carradine was doing a scene in which he was trying to seduce a pretty victim with his talk of a world of vampires. Carradine insisted that Count Dracula would be averse to using the term vampire, and substituted the word un-dead. When the shooting halted for lunch it was amusing to see Carradine, in full Dracula costume, relaxing in the bright sun and then crossing Melrose Avenue to enter a nearby bar.

Like the Carradine of former Dracula films, the Count threw no mirror image and could transform into a bat. Yet somehow, he had apparently discovered an antidote for sunlight, as evidenced by scenes of the Count parading about on the brightest of days. Never was Dracula shown rising from a coffin, although he did enjoy the occasional privacy of a mine where he could rest. In one scene the Count reveals that he "just might sleep all day."

Dracula (whose name is never mentioned in the film, although it does appear throughout Carl K. Hittleman's script) arrives via stagecoach at Papago Wells. In bat form, the Count takes the blood of an Indian girl named Nana (played by Charlita). When the Indians discover Nana's corpse they blame the white people and massacre the occupants of the coach. Dracula then assumes the identity of one of the passengers, James Underhill (William Forrest), and quickly sets his glaring eyes upon Underhill's niece, Betty Bentley (Melinda Plowman). Since Betty and her uncle have never met, the vampire's disguise is a success.

Unknown to the Transylvanian on American vacation, Betty's ranch foreman and fiancé is the notorious outlaw Billy the Kid (Chuck Courtney), who had been whitewashed and reformed so that the film would have a hero. Meanwhile,

In one of the least prestigious Dracula films of all time,
BILLY THE KID VS. DRACULA (Embassy, 1966), the Count
(John Carradine) brings Betty Bentley (Melinda Plowman) to
his lair.

some European immigrants contend that a vampire was responsible for the deaths of the stagecoach passengers and
that one of these bloodsuckers nearly killed a girl on their
wagon train.   The victim, Lila Oster (Hannie Landman),
faints upon seeing Dracula but he convinces the girl that her
accusation is a case of mistaken identity.

Through a series of complications, including an attack
on sheep by some unknown predator and a shootout in which
Billy kills the ex-foreman of Betty's ranch, the outlaw is
jailed by Marshal Griffin (Roy Barcroft).   Dracula then takes
Betty, who had already been bitten and placed under his control, to the abandoned silver mine which serves as his lair,

intending to make her his bride. Escaping jail, Billy reaches the mine, but his well-aimed bullets have no effect on the fiendish Count. After a battle between them, Billy transfixes Count Dracula with a surgeon's scalpel. Dracula's corpse disintegrates and Betty is released from the vampiric spell.

BILLY THE KID VS. DRACULA was directed by William Beaudine, a veteran of numerous "B" Westerns. Although the film was cheaply made, Beaudine made a reasonably honest, old-fashioned cowboy picture, of the type which was so popular during the thirties and forties. The picture just happened to include Count Dracula. The film was appropriately designed for Saturday kiddie matinees, with scenes in which a youthful audience could cheer out loud for Billy and hiss the bad guy in the cape. To strengthen the tradition of the old-style Western, Beaudine's hero and villain were appropriately attired in light and black clothing. In this respect BILLY THE KID VS. DRACULA is not entirely the atrocity it is labeled by most critics.

That same year Dracula made appearances in KISS ME QUICK and GHOST IN THE INVISIBLE BIKINI. KISS ME QUICK (also known as DR. BREEDLOVE) was a nudie made in color by Russ Meyer's Fantasy Films. Dracula, a Frankenstein Monster and a mummy are the creations of the mad Dr. Breedlove (spoofing Dr. Strangelove). An alien named Sterilox (Frank Coe) journeys from a planet lacking women and comes to Earth, discovering that Breedlove is now creating beautiful naked women. After falling in love with a vending machine, Sterilox takes one of the pretty creations and rockets back to his native planet. Dracula's appearance in the color film, GHOST IN THE INVISIBLE BIKINI, was in the form of a life-sized manikin. The film was directed by Don Weis and released by American-International. *

Dracula made a number of screen appearances in 1967. The Philippines plagiarized the two most popular bat-like creatures in the world in BATMAN FIGHTS DRACULA. The film will probably never be legally screened in the United States because of copyright infringements.

MAD MONSTER PARTY? was a feature-length

---

*GHOST IN THE INVISIBLE BIKINI had a number of shooting titles including SLUMBER PARTY IN HORROR HOUSE, BIKINI PARTY IN A HAUNTED HOUSE, BEACH PARTY IN A HAUNTED HOUSE and PAJAMA PARTY IN A HAUNTED HOUSE.

children's film produced by Arthur Rankin, Jr., directed by
Jules Bass and released by Joseph E. Levine's Embassy Pictures. Count Dracula, Baron Frankenstein, the Monster and
his Mate, the Werewolf, the Mummy, the Invisible Man, Dr.
Jekyll and Mr. Hyde, the Creature and myriad other fiends
cavorted about the screen as puppets designed by Jack Davis
and brought to life through stop-frame animation.

When Boris von Frankenstein (with Karloff's voice)
invents a new explosive, he decides to celebrate with a party
at his island castle. During the party he also plans to announce his nephew Felix Flanken as his successor and leader
of all the monsters. Among the guests invited to the special
gathering is Count Dracula, wearing formal attire including
spats, a cape cut like bat wings and a large monocle. Dracula transforms into a vampire bat and flies toward the vessel
that will bring all the monsters to Baron Frankenstein's island. At the gala party Dracula conspires with Francesca,
the Baron's daughter, to eliminate Flanken and thus secure
the explosive and the leadership for himself. The Monster's
Mate witnesses the clandestine alliance. When Dracula tries
to place the woman under his hypnotic control, her husband,
the Frankenstein Monster, tosses him across the room.

Dracula and the other monsters secretly attempt to
get rid of Felix, but all of them fail. Dracula then makes
an alliance with the Monster and his mate and turns on Francesca. But she holds them off with wolfbane and a torch and
escapes. Felix and Francesca realize they love each other
and prepare to flee the island. Dracula organizes the other
monsters to stop Felix and Francesca, but the Count's plans
are interrupted by the arrival of a giant gorilla called "It,"
who picks all the monsters up in his enormous arms. Baron
Frankenstein uses his explosive to destroy It, Dracula and
all the other creatures, while Felix and Francesca escape in
a speedboat. As the film ends, both of them are revealed
to be robots invented by Frankenstein.

Jules Bass was careful in his direction of MAD MON-
STER PARTY? to allow the classic monsters to retain much
of their dignity throughout the humorous situations of the film.
The film is one of the few satires of the Dracula genre made
with integrity. To children and Dracula film aficionados with
a sense of humor, the two audiences for which it was intended, MAD MONSTER PARTY? is entertaining and genuinely
funny.

In the form of an animated puppet, Dracula conspires with Francesca in MAD MONSTER PARTY?, released by Embassy Pictures in 1966.

That same year Dracula prowled again in the incredibly inept DR. TERROR'S GALLERY OF HORRORS, a color film made by Dora Corporation-Borealis Enterprises and released by American General. The picture was comprised of five individual horror stories--an attempt to capitalize not only on the title but also on the format of Amicus' earlier success, DR. TERROR'S HOUSE OF HORRORS. The attempt was unsuccessful, however, due to an inept comic book-type script by David Prentiss, Gary Heacock and Russ Jones, shoddy production values, mostly amateurish acting and poor direction by David L. Hewitt. The final product was so inferior to the horror films being made by other studios that DR. TERROR'S GALLERY OF HORRORS had a short theatrical run and presently was sold to television under the new title RETURN FROM THE PAST. *

---

*The film went into production as simply GALLERY OF HORRORS and was later re-released to theatres as THE BLOOD SUCKERS.

Two of the segments of DR. TERROR'S GALLERY OF HORRORS were vampire stories. The first, with the misleading title "King Vampire," concerned a vampire in nineteenth century London who is finally revealed to be the female secretary of the police inspector investigating the case. The final story in the film was entitled "Count Alucard" (although it was listed as "Count Dracula" in the end titles), the starring role originally being intended for John Carradine. The lean actor was forced to abandon the role due to another commitment, leaving behind his tailor-fitted Count Dracula formal wear. Mitch Evans, an actor who had once played cub reporter Jimmy Olsen on the SUPERMAN radio program, replaced Carradine in the role, but Evans' heftier physique forced a large rip up the back of the outfit and only the flowing Dracula cape (and some discreet camera angles) concealed the embarrassing truth. Carradine did return to the production, wearing the tuxedo intended for him, to introduce each of the individual stories.

Mitch Evans as "Count Alucard" and a lovely vampire woman in American General Pictures' DR. TERROR'S GALLERY OF HORRORS (1966).

"Count Alucard" adheres somewhat to the opening chapters of Dracula. Harker journeys to the castle of Count "Alucard" (Dracula showing a lack of originality) to sell him the Carfax property in London. Alucard, sporting a devilish mustache and beard, speaks the expected Dracula lines. Harker is later attacked by a vampire woman who presently becomes the prey of a band of torch-wielding villagers. Harker and the vigilantes track her to a graveyard crypt and destroy her with a stake. Harker then returns to the castle, where he accuses Alucard of being a vampire. In an ending typical of the horror comic book, Harker transforms into a werewolf and attacks the Count, growling that he must eliminate some of the bloodthirsty competition.

The same backwards spelling of Dracula appeared that same year in A TASTE OF BLOOD, also known as THE SECRET OF DR. ALUCARD, a film made in color by Creative Film Enterprises. A TASTE OF BLOOD was produced and directed by Herschell Gordon Lewis, a Chicago-based film maker specializing in tasteless orgies of gratuitous gore. In such films as the 1963 atrocity, BLOOD FEAST, Lewis acquired his most important props from butcher shops and slaughter houses. A TASTE OF BLOOD, made in the same grisly style, was a variation on the Dracula theme.

John Stone (Bill Rogers) receives a mysterious package from England containing two archaic bottles of a Yugoslavian brandy called Slivovitz. The brandy has been bequeathed by his deceased mother who had requested that he consume it in toasting one of his ancestors. After a few weeks, Stone has drunk all of the brandy. During this time he becomes strangely melancholic and nocturnal, sleeping during the day and prowling about at night. Visiting England to claim his lands, Stone learns that certain men are being murdered with wooden stakes thrust through their bodies. He visits a young man named Lord Gold (Ted Schell) and discovers the incredible truth. Stone is the descendant of Count Dracula and the brandy was in actuality the King Vampire's blood. Now a living vampire himself, Stone must have vengeance for Dracula, driving stakes through the descendants of the Count's executioners, all of whom have shortened their names. Stone rams a pool cue through Lord Gold's heart.

Stone returns to the United States where he assumes the role of a vampire, sleeping by day in a casket and using the Count's ring to keep his wife mesmerized. First he kills a burlesque stripper named "Vivacious Vivian" (Gail

Janis) when the sight of blood oozing from her cut finger
arouses him.   Then he mutilates and kills another descendant
of Dracula's foes, Sherry Morris, whose corpse he dumps in
a swimming pool.   Stone's wife Helene (Elizabeth Wilkinson)
enlists the aid of the European Dr. Howard Helsing (Otto
Schlesinger), who tracks the vampire to his coffin at sunrise
and drives a stake through his heart.

Dracula made a brief appearance also that year, in
the guise of a man wearing a Burman mask at Mardi Gras
time, in the Elvis Presley film: DOUBLE TROUBLE (MGM).

Count Dracula has become a part of the Spanish series of werewolf movies starring Paul Naschy (real name
Jacinto Molina), the first of which was made in 1968 under
the title LA MARCA DEL HOMBRE LOBO ("The Mark of the
Wolfman").   This was undoubtedly the most ambitious film
of the series, having been made by Maxper in color, stereo-
phonic sound, 70mm and in three dimensions.   LA MARCA
DEL HOMBRE LOBO spared nothing and included two werewolves and a pair of vampires.   The confusion which this
film causes in trying to catalogue all Dracula films centers
upon the question: Is the male vampire in the film Count
Dracula or not?

When the picture was released in Southeast Asia the
title became THE WOLFMAN OF COUNT DRACULA; in Ger-
many, either DER WOLFSMENSCHE DES DR. DRACULA or
DIE VAMPIRE DES DR. DRACULA ("The Wolfman ... The
Vampire of Dr. Dracula") and in Belgium, both HELL'S
CREATURES and DRACULA EN DE WEREWOLF ("Dracula
and the Werewolf").   To add to the confusion, Spain also
knew the film under the alternate title of EL HOMBRE LOBO
("The Wolfman"), while yet another name for the film is
TOTEN AUGEN DES DR. DRACULA ("Dead Eyes of Dr.
Dracula").   In 1970, Independent-International released the
film in the United States under the thoroughly misleading title,
FRANKENSTEIN'S BLOODY TERROR.   The Dracula-type vampire in this version was named "Dr. Mikelhov," and I wonder why, the releasing company having taken the trouble to
market this as a Frankenstein epic, they did not retain the
then even more commercial name of Dracula.

For the nonce I will assume LA MARCA DEL HOM-
BRE LOBO features Count Dracula and will refer to the vampire character as such.   Two gypsies seek shelter from a
storm in the ancient castle of the Daninsky family.   As they

are looting the place they happen upon the casket of a man
with a silver-cross dagger imbedded in his heart. The greedy
couple remove the gleaming object, only to revive a long dead
werewolf and die by its fangs. Later, young Waldemar Daninsky (Paul Naschy) joins the villagers in a hunt for the werewolf, his father. Waldemar is attacked by the beast in the
woods and apparently kills it with the silver dagger. Now
Waldemar has inherited the curse that changes him into a
man-beast when the moon is full. Waldemar's girlfriend Janice and friend Rudolph chain him in the castle cellar, then
send for a strange doctor who might be able to cure him.
The doctor and his wife arrive at night, bringing with them
two coffin-like boxes. Instead of trying to cure the hapless
Waldemar, the doctor reveals himself to be a vampire, apparently Count Dracula, who intends to use the forces of the
Devil to increase the strength of the wolfman. To augment
Waldemar's horror, Dracula has also revived his wolfish sire.
The two vampires then prepare to seduce and attack Janice
and Rudolph while the two werewolves break their chains and
battle until the shaggy Waldemar emerges the winner. A
stake finally impales the heart of the vampiress. After a final confrontation between Dracula and his snarling opponent,
the vampire is destroyed, bursting into flames. A silver bullet apparently kills Waldemar, returning him to human form until the first sequel in the series. E. L. Eguiluz directed.

      Despite the comic bookish plot of LA MARCA DEL
HOMBRE LOBO the film is extremely atmospheric, especially in such scenes as the Dracula character beguiling his female victim with his swirling cloak as he almost dances
through the enveloping mists. The battle between the two
werewolves is a motion picture first, especially exciting in
the 3D process. Naschy's growling and leaping portrayal of
Waldemar endeared him to the hearts of Spanish horror film
fans and precipitated a lengthy list of horror film assignments.

      EL HOMBRE QUE VINO DE UMMO ("The Man Who
Came from Ummo") was the second of Naschy's werewolf pictures, made in 1970 by Jaime Prades/Eichberg Film/Inter-
national Jaguar and directed by Tulio Demicheli. This Span-
ish/West German/Italian co-production is, thankfully, absolutely established as a Dracula film. The color picture is
also known as DRACULA JAGT FRANKENSTEIN ("Dracula
Hunts Frankenstein") and was released in Great Britain as
DRACULA VS. FRANKENSTEIN.* Paul Naschy not only

---

*EL HOMBRE QUE VINO DE UMMO is also known under the
                                          (cont. on p. 212)

portrayed the werewolf Waldemar Daninsky in this film but
also doubled as Frankenstein's Monster.   Michael Rennie,
perhaps capitalizing on his role as the alien Klaatu in the
1951 science fiction classic, THE DAY THE EARTH STOOD
STILL, played a scientist from the distant planet Ummo.
The scientist arrives on Earth with a seemingly impossible
ambition--to conquer the entire universe.   The alien mind
must function in strange ways, for the Man from Ummo plans
to conquer our world by reviving the four most infamous monsters of history: Count Dracula, the Frankenstein Monster,
the Werewolf and the Mummy.   Though two of the film's
titles suggest a battle between Frankenstein's creation and
the Count, such a fight never happens.   A secret agent
(played by Craig Hill) prevents the realization of the alien's
mad plot.

        Waldemar Daninsky howled through two more films,
LAS NOCHE DEL HOMBRES LOBOS ("The Night of the Wolf-
men") and LA FURIA DEL HOMBRE LOBO ("The Fury of the
Wolfman"), before again becoming associated with the name
of Dracula.   LA NOCHE DE WALPURGIS ("The Night of Walpurgis") was made in color in 1970 by Plata Films as a Span-
ish/West German co-production, directed by Leon Klimovsky.
Although Count Dracula does not appear in this film, the
French title is DANS LES GRIFFES DE DRACULA ("In the
Claws of Dracula"). *   Actually this is another of the many
films based on the historical figure, Countess Elizabeth
Báthory, though liberties have been taken with the original
character.

        Two young students named Elvire and Genevieve search
for the grave of Countess "Wandesa" de Nadasdy, a vampiress who maintained her youthful beauty by consuming the
blood of virgins.   Lost somewhere in the mountains of France,
the girls come to the house of Waldemar Daninsky, who has
been revived since a doctor removed the silver bullets that
were imbedded in his heart.   Since the Countess was impaled
on a cross of silver, which might also end a werewolf's
curse, Waldemar also hopes to find her tomb.   After the
grave is discovered, Genevieve removes the cross and accidentally cuts her wrist.   The flowing blood revives Wandesa.

Spanish title LOS MONSTRUOUS DEL TERROR ("The Mon-
sters of Terror").
        *In the United States the film was re-titled THE
WEREWOLF VS. THE VAMPIRE WOMAN; in Belgium, LA
NUIT DES LOUPS-GAROUS ("The Night of the Werewolves").

The Countess proceeds to vampirize Genevieve, who then goes on to attack Elvire until Waldemar impales her with a stake. Elvire soon becomes the victim Wandesa intends to sacrifice to her master, Satan, as if forsaking vampirism for witchcraft. Waldemar is overcome by the curse of the full moon and attacks the vampiress in his werewolf form, while Elvire stabs him through the heart with the silver cross. *

Dracula's other motion picture appearances in 1968 were few and unimpressive. DRACULA MEETS THE OUTER SPACE CHICKS was an independently produced sex film in which the vampire's alien victims wore little more than the marks of his fangs. MONDO KEYHOLE, probably made that year, was another sexy entry that included a Dracula sequence. ISABELL, A DREAM was an Italian film made by Luigi Cozzi in which Dracula, Frankenstein's Monster and the Mummy (actors wearing Don Post masks) are hunted in the woods. The footage was then included in Cozzi's 1970 film TUNNEL UNDER THE WORLD, which was made from a science fiction story written by Frederik Pohl. TUNNEL** also featured a scene with Count Orlock, the Dracula character of the silent NOSFERATU. THE MARK OF DRACULA (also known as THE CURSE OF THE HEADLESS DEMON) was announced for filming in 1968 but never went into production. The Russ Jones script did not feature the original Dracula but another cloaked vampire who is beheaded, then surgically made whole again. The result is a Frankenstein Monster type of vampire, unsightly stitches joining the head to the body, its severed vocal cords permitting only inarticulate grunts. Famous Monsters of Filmland editor Forrest J Ackerman was to deliver a eulogy over a grave in the artificial language Esperanto.

---

*A paperback novel of The Werewolf vs. the Vampire Woman, written by Arthur N. Scram, was issued in 1972 by the Guild-Hartford Publishing Co. Purportedly an adaptation of the motion picture story, the novel, though retaining the names of most of the main characters, became a sex comedy in which Wandessa de Nadasdy and "Waldo" the werewolf go to Hollywood to accept parts in a monster film. At the end of the novel, the two fiends kill each other, Waldo utilizing a silver stiletto and Wandessa firing silver bullets.

**Cozzi included scenes from TUNNEL UNDER THE WORLD in his film IL VICINO DI CASA ("The Man Upstairs"), made in the early 1970s.

The following year was hardly more impressive for the endurable King of Vampires. Producer Al Adamson's BLOOD OF DRACULA'S CASTLE for the A & E Film Corporation, released by Crown-International, was actually filmed two years earlier. The picture was directed by Al Adamson and Jean Hewitt. By consensus of the horror films buffs who have seen it, BLOOD OF DRACULA'S CASTLE is one of the poorer adventures of the King of the Un-Dead. The film featured John Carradine, but not in the role of Dracula. Carradine portrayed Dracula's murderous butler, a moonlighting high priest of a selenology cult. Dracula himself was portrayed by a younger actor, Alex D'Arcy.

Count Dracula and his Countess wife (played by Paula Raymond) displayed a bit more ingenuity than former Draculas. In attempting to conceal their true identities they did not change their names to the conspicuous "Alucard." Instead they adopted the names of Count and Countess Townsend and rented a castle in the Mojave Desert. These Draculas have oriented themselves to the twentieth century. They sleep in coffins placed in the bedroom. No longer is there any need to hunt down victims to satiate their thirst for blood. George (Carradine) the butler sees that his master and mistress are sufficiently fed. The "wine cellar" is stocked with an ample supply of chained and well endowed maidens whom George taps for their blood. Then Dracula and wife drink down their literal bloody marys from cocktail glasses. This practice seems to give the Draculas an excuse to sit at their dining table making sick puns about blood. The Draculas' victims are then given to their preverted handyman who is appropriately named Mango. BLOOD OF DRACULA'S CASTLE continues with the arrival of a werewolf who has recently escaped from prison and then of a young couple who claim to have inherited the Townsend estate. After a series of overly violent murders and human sacrifices, the young wife is almost burned at the stake. Mango is disposed of by an axe imbedded in his back. The Count and Countess also suffer an ignoble demise: tied to chairs, they are struck by the rising sun and reduced to dust. But phoenix-like, two bats rise from the ashes and fly away. Perhaps they would have continued their bloodthirsty careers had Adamson actually filmed DRACULA'S COFFIN, the sequel he planned to make in 1969.

TALES OF BLOOD AND TERROR was a color film made in 1969 by Maurine Dawson, director of the play I'M SORRY THE BRIDGE IS OUT, YOU'LL HAVE TO SPEND THE

NIGHT. The movie was then sold to Titan Films in England, where it was expanded to feature length. TALES OF BLOOD AND TERROR traces the origins of various supernatural characters and presents more than one version of Dracula.

The Dracula myth plunged to new lows in 1969 with such films as DRACULA (THE DIRTY OLD MAN), a color film produced, written and directed "in Dripping Color" by William Edwards for Whit Boyd Productions. The picture was made as a reasonably serious sex film. But Edwards later realized that through the proper dubbing it might be transformed into a comedy. Again Dracula (Vince Kelly) assumes the name of Count Alucard, which by now should not have fooled anyone. Other bizarre characters in the film included Dracula's mother (literally an old bat), a man hypnotized into becoming a werewolf and a servant named Irving Jekyllman whose job it was to bring young girls to his lusting master. Dracula again meets his demise by the dawn sun.

There was also DOES DRACULA REALLY SUCK?, the first homosexual Dracula film, made in color by an independent film company. The film was advertized in the newspapers as DRACULA AND THE BOYS and as DRACULA ... DOES HE? A film entitled DRACULA SUCKS was announced in the fifth issue of Live Naked, a nudist magazine. The film was to have Georgio Dracula emerge from his coffin to vampirize a group of nudists staying at his castle, now strangely located in Italy. Georgio Dracula wears a cape, fangs and a frown. He perishes by the traditional stake in the heart. It is doubtful that DRACULA SUCKS ever went into production.

The Philippines offered two Dracula films in 1969. DRAKULITA was an RJF Brothers production directed by Consuelo P. Osorio and featuring Lito Legaspi, Rebecca, Gina Laforteza, Joseph Gallego, Rebecca Rocha and Rossana Ortiz as a vampire, possibly Drakulita herself. The film is a vampire comedy set in a haunted house. MEN OF ACTION MEET THE WOMEN OF DRAKULA, directed by Artemio Marquez, was a confrontation between human tumblers and the Count and his vampire women. The film featured Dante Varona, Eddie Torrento, Ruben Obligacion, Norman Henson, Ernesto Beren and Angelito Marquez.

IL RISVEGLIO DI DRACULA ("The Revival of Dracula") was made in Italy during the late 1960s. The picture was

directed by U. Paolessi and written by L. Mauri with a cast
including Gabby Paul and Gill Chadwich. No other information is available concerning this obscure title.

Two Dracula films were announced in the late 1960s.
DRACULA RETURNS was a project planned by a film company in France. In the United States, tall and thin actor
Paul Kalin was considered to portray Count Dracula in a nudie
film that was never made.

The Dracula legend again became a prestigious motion
picture subject with the 1970 film, JONATHAN, a West German production made in color by Hans W. Geissendörfer.
The controversial vampire film, though including scenes and
dialogue taken directly from Stoker's Dracula (and so credited
in the titles), depicts little vampirism and is more of a political motion picture. JONATHAN is an allegory in which
the Dracula figure is compared to Germany's own real monster, Adolf Hitler, and the relationship between the vampire
and the town he dominates is presented as a grim lesson in
the consequences of fascism.

A European town is under the domination of a black-
cloaked nobleman who is also the leader of a cult of vampires. Though presumably Dracula, this vampire (played by
Paul Albert Krumm) is not referred to by name and is characterized as an un-dead precursor of Hitler. His face and
hair style resemble those of the Nazi beast and his manner
of speaking recalls the Führer's compelling oratorical style.
Dracula's un-dead minions are clothed in either red, black
or white (the colors of the Nazi swastika flag) and his human
Gestapo-type soldiers keep the villagers contained under
threat of gunfire. An old crone urges some of the vampire's
soldiers to break into a room occupied by a pair of human
lovers. The young man leaps from the window to his death
while the girl becomes the victim of the vampire's blood-
hounds. Dracula later makes his only on-screen attack,
drinking the blood of a woman, then forcing her to drink
blood from a wound in his chest. The villagers decide that
they have suffered long enough under the domination by the
vampires and send a young man named Jonathan (Jürgen Jung),
the "Jonathan Harker" of this film, to the castle of the un-
dead to destroy them. As Jonathan travels to the castle of
the vampires, he learns the results of Dracula's fascist rule
over the villagers: the townspeople have become as perverse
and monstrous as their vampiric overlord. Jonathan is
robbed of his stakes and crosses, which become the property

of a strange young girl and her mad hunchbacked accomplice.
Among the other acts perpetrated by the villagers are the
kicking to death of a man, the hanging of a nun, a child de-
lightedly setting a fire outside the church, and a group of
townspeople crowding about to gawk at a couple engaged in
sexual intercourse. It is only much later in the film, after
beholding the villagers at their worst, that Jonathan enters
the castle of the vampires and is taken prisoner by them.

In the castle, Jonathan goes through the actions that
Harker wrote about in the Stoker novel. But when he opens
one of the doors forbidden him by Dracula and discovers the
human captives of the un-dead, he is chained to a wall and
graphically tortured. Finally, the villagers come to Jonathan's rescue, relishing their slaughter of the vampire's
armed henchmen, and finally driving Dracula and his un-dead
minions, at cross point, into the sea to drown. At this point
it is quite obvious that the vampires are the victims and the
villagers are the fiends. The final scene shows Jonathan attempting to touch the young woman who previously made love
to him, only to be stabbed by her. Though the vampires
have been destroyed, the effects of their tyranny remain.

JONATHAN is replete with strange images, including
the vampires appearing during the daylight hours and proces-
sions of white-clad flower girls who are in reality vampires
themselves. Geissendörfer's direction is often slow and boring, but at the same time fascinating, if such a seeming contradiction is possible. His work has been compared to that
of Murnau and Polanski and the film itself has been praised
by critics who would normally deride a horror film. To
Geissendörfer's chagrin, however, the Iduna-Film production
company chopped twenty minutes from his edited version of
the picture, including much of the scenes involving the torture of Jonathan and the villagers' brutal onslaught at the
castle. "This is no longer my film," Geissendörfer said at
the time. Left in the film, however, was much gratuitous
violence, such as a vampire stomping to death a white rat.
In censoring the picture, Iduna-Film hoped not only to tone
down the violence but to also assuage the picture's political
message. Two years after the film's completion it was released under the title JONATHAN, VAMPIRE STERBEN
NICHT ("Jonathan, the Vampire Does Not Die"). In France
the film was released as JONATHAN, LE DERNIER COM-
BAT CONTRE LES VAMPIRES ("Jonathan, the Last Combat
Against the Vampires").

Hardly comparable to the above film was the "sex-
ploitational" picture, GUESS WHAT HAPPENED TO COUNT
DRACULA, a color film released that year by Merrick International and directed by Laurence Merrick.   In this entry
Dracula (Des Roberts) attempts to retain the old ways of
Transylvania while also adapting to the pseudo-hip styles of
1970.   On formal occasions the Count, now sporting a Van
Dyke beard, wears the full formal wear so familiar to Dracula fans.   But since his new haunting ground is modern day
Southern California, he also wears turtleneck sweaters and
double-breasted suits.   Dracula is in the United States incognito and has displayed the foresight to select the alias
"Count Adrian" instead of the usual "Alucard."   The main
target of his sanguinary attacks is the hippie-inhabited Sunset
Strip.   Actor Roberts not only played the part of Dracula in
this film, he also composed the music and conducted the
orchestra.

Dracula desires a pretty young woman named Angelica
(Claudia Barron).   If he sucks her blood three times she will
become a vampire.   Angelica's boyfriend Guy (John Landon)
is an ambitious actor who agrees to exchange his girlfriend
in return for Dracula's making him a movie star.   The King
Vampire enters Angelica's bedroom and makes his first
bloodthirsty attack.   Dracula's second attack is interrupted
by another vampire named Imp (Frank Donato) who promptly
battles the Count for leadership of all the supernatural forces
in Hollywood.   Naturally, Dracula emerges from the battle
victorious.   The second bite is inflicted upon Angelica when
Dracula, in the guise of Count Adrian, becomes her blind
date.   Then the vampire recites a weird incantation over his
victim (made more weird when the director decided to record it backwards).   Having suffered two bites, Angelica begins to shun sunlight and crave raw meat.   Soon she becomes
a resident of Dracula's castle.   Guy eventually realizes the
folly of his bargain with Dracula and ventures to the vampire's abode.   There he encounters such menaces as a boa
constrictor and a Bengal tiger, a Negro hunchback, a man
with the features of a corpse and a woman with matted hair
and glowing eyes.   To Guy's horror, Angelica has already
received the third and final bite which has transformed her
into a vampire.   Count Dracula, surprisingly, is not destroyed
but survives along with his new un-dead bride, begging for a
sequel that was, perhaps fortunately, never made.   (The film
was originally titled WHATEVER HAPPENED TO COUNT
DRACULA? and later became known under the alternate title,
THE MASTER OF THE DUNGEON.)

GUESS WHAT HAPPENED TO COUNT DRACULA

COLOR BY MOVIELAB

A GIANT TERRORAMA

SEE IT WITH SOMEONE YOU TRUST.

A MERRICK INTERNATIONAL FILM STARRING
DES ROBERTS · CLAUDIA BARRON · JOHN LANDON

The year 1970 also included such films as the Swiss
DRACULAS LÜSTERNE VAMPIRE ("Dracula's Vampire Lust"),
directed by Mario D'Alcala for Monarex and again starring
Des Roberts as the Count.   VAMPYROS LESBOS--DIE ERBIN
DES DRACULA ("Lesbian Vampires--The Heiress of Dracu-
la"), a German/Spanish co-production from Telecine and
Fenix, directed by Jesus Franco and starring Dennis Price,
Susann Korda, Paul Müller, Ewa Stroemberg and Soledad
Miranda, was reputedly based on 'Dracula's Guest," by
Stoker.   The film is about a girl dreaming that she is being
menaced by a lesbian vampire. *

In THE BODY BENEATH, a color film by Nova International directed by Andy Milligan, a vampire comes to London to prey upon a particular family and eventually comes to
Dracula's Carfax Abbey.   The film starred Gavin Reed,
Jackie Skarvellis, Susan Clark and Colin Gordon.   Jason Ro-
bards, Jr. portrayed an aging horror actor in a Dracula role
in FOOLS, a color film made by Translor and directed by
Tom Dries.   Mention should also be made of Russ Meyer's
BEYOND THE VALLEY OF THE DOLLS, made in color for
20th Century-Fox, in which a character attired in black theatrically refers to himself as Count Dracula.

Dracula's motion pictures of 1971 include a film which
began as a mundane low-budget horror movie and resulted in
the confrontation of the screen's two most infamous monsters.
THE BLOOD SEEKERS went into production in 1971, a color
film from Independent-International.   It was to star J. Carrol
Naish as Dr. Durea, Lon Chaney as the slow-witted Groton
the Mad Zombie, and Angelo Rossito as an evil dwarf named
Grazbo, but when the final version of the film proved to be
too short and confusing, the film company's Sam Sherman
concocted a scheme not only to lengthen and clarify the picture but to increase its box office appeal.   Count Dracula
and the Frankenstein Monster were written into the lineup of
bizarre characters and the film was re-titled BLOOD OF
FRANKENSTEIN.   Dr. Durea was explained as an alias used
by the incognito Dr. Frankenstein.   The film, directed by
Al Adamson (BLOOD OF DRACULA'S CASTLE), was released

---

*VAMPYROS LESBOS--DIE ERBIN DES DRACULA is also
known as VAMPYROS LESBOS (THE STRANGE ADVENTURE
OF JONATHAN HARKER).   The film was released in Spain
as EL SIGNO DEL VAMPIRO ("The Sign of the Vampire")
and was originally announced as THE HERITAGE OF DRACU-
LA.

Zandor Vorkov in the role of the un-dead nobleman in
DRACULA VS. FRANKENSTEIN, an Independent-International
picture of 1972.   Photo by Hedy Dietz.

in 1972 under the even more descriptive title DRACULA VS. FRANKENSTEIN (not to be confused with the British title for EL HOMBRE QUE VINO DE UMMO). In Europe, it was released in 1973 under its former title, BLOOD OF FRANKENSTEIN, and is also known as SATAN'S BLOODY FREAKS.

In the role of Count Dracula was Zandor Vorkov, a name given to a curly-haired actor on the very set of the film by Forrest J Ackerman, who also enacted a small role. Zorkov's Dracula had a bluish gray face, mustache and beard, a mouthful of sharp fangs and a ring emblazoned with the head of a demon. When he spoke, his words resounded through an echo chamber. Zandor's performance as the Count was adequate but the film itself was shoddy from every artistic and technical standpoint and maintains the distinction of being one of the very worst of the "straight" Dracula/Frankenstein films ever made.

Count Dracula desires to revive the long dormant Frankenstein Monster. Taking the Monster's body from its secret tomb in Oakmoor Cemetery, the King Vampire takes it to the local amusement park's "House of Horrors." The laboratory behind the horror ride is operated by Dr. Durea, who, as Dracula knows, is really Dr. Frankenstein. The mad scientist has been working on a new blood serum, utilizing the corpses of young girls axed by Groton and Grazbo. Many of their victims were secured in the darkness of the horror ride. Dracula hopes that the blood serum will allow him to endure sunlight. He also convinces Dr. Frankenstein to revive the Monster. The Monster's first victim is Dr. Beaumont (Forrest J Ackerman), who had discredited Dr. Frankenstein years before. (Originally, Dracula was to have transformed the Monster into a lumbering vampire, but the make-up was so designed that the fangs would not stay in the creature's mouth.)

Dracula and Dr. Frankenstein then decide to use their monstrous henchmen to procure more victims for the blood serum experiments. Before the climax of the film, Dr. Frankenstein is beheaded in his own "Horror Chamber" guillotine and Groton is shot from the rooftop of the building by the police. Dracula, meanwhile, takes Judith (Regina Carrol), a young girl who had traced her missing sister to the House of Horrors, to the chapel where his coffin is hidden. But when the Monster sees the girl about to perish at the vampire's fangs, he attacks the King of the Un-Dead. A raging battle between the two monsters ensues, with Dracula's superhuman strength ripping the Monster into its individual pieces. Yet even as he gloats over his victory, the sun rises, reducing Count Dracula to a rotted corpse.

For a while in 1972 Independent-International toyed with the idea of filming a sequel to DRACULA VS. FRANK-ENSTEIN. A proposed followup film I had written was brief-ly under consideration by the company. Entitled FRANKEN-STEIN--DEMON OF DRACULA, the story opens with Dracula surprised by an angry mob as he is attacking young Linda Trask. Dracula is pursued to the graveyard. Near the mausoleum where the dull-minded Bruno protects his master's coffin, the vigilantes attack. Bruno receives the stake in-tended for Dracula's heart. Infuriated over the death of his servant, Dracula summons the Wolves of Hell, who attack the mob under the moonlight. After the ghoulish massacre Drac-ula chops off Bruno's head for reasons of his own. At dawn, however, Carter Starrett, one of the group and Linda's lover, has survived, his wounds miraculously healed. Carter is also the laboratory assistant to Dr. Gustav Frankenstein. Gustav receives parcels containing the segmented yet living remains of his ancestor's creation, which he hopes to reas-semble, give a new brain and use in environmental experi-ments. Dracula, through his victim Linda, manages to sub-stitute the good brain for that of loyal Bruno, in the hopes of acquiring a superhuman slave. Carter soon discovers that Dracula's wolves have made him a werewolf and Linda soon becomes a vampire herself. The climax of the proposed film was to have Dracula and the Monster attempt to kill the sav-age werewolf, with Linda destroying all three horrors by dynamiting the cave in which they are fighting. Weeping over her lost love, Linda willfully steps into the fatal light of dawn. FRANKENSTEIN--DEMON OF DRACULA never went beyond the treatment stage as Independent-International de-cided against continuing with these traditional characters.

A Spanish/French answer to the other "Dracula vs. Frankenstein" films of the early 1970s was DRACULA CON-TRA EL DR. FRANKENSTEIN ("Dracula vs. Dr. Franken-stein"), made in color by Comtoir Francais de Film and Fenix and directed by Jesus Franco (who seems to have a particular affection for the Count, judging by the number of Dracula motion pictures to his credit). Count Dracula (Howard Vernon) and Lady Dracula (Britt Nichols) return to their haunt in the Carpathian Mountains and initiate a new wave of vampirism. To combat this terrible situation, Dr. Frankenstein (Dennis Price) and Morpho (Luis Barboo), his

assistant, create a monster (Fernando Bilbao) which will be
invincible against Dracula. Dr. Seward (Alberto Dalbes),
however, wants Dracula for a guinea pig, hoping to cure his
vampiric condition. The two doctors, then, each attempt to
reach the King Vampire first. * Franco made what appears
to be a sequel film, LES EXPERIENCES EROTIQUES DE
FRANKENSTEIN ("The Erotic Experiences of Frankenstein"),
with virtually the same cast as DRACULA CONTRA EL DR.
FRANKENSTEIN. Howard Vernon also appeared in this film,
but Count Dracula did not.

Ferdy Mayne, who appeared as the vampiric count in
DANCE OF THE VAMPIRES and was featured in THE VAM-
PIRE LOVERS, donned the mantle of Count Dracula himself
in the 1971 West German horror comedy, GEBISSEN WIRD
NUR NACHTS--HAPPENING DER VAMPIRE, which is known
in English-speaking countries as THE VAMPIRE HAPPENING.
The film was made in color by Aquila Enterprises and directed by Freddie Francis, who is best known for his horror
films made for Amicus and Hammer. Betty Williams, a motion picture star, journeys to claim a castle situated in the
Balkans but encounters Dracula and her own vampiric double.
The King Vampire's evil encompasses all manners of perver-
sions. But unlike most Dracula films, this one has the Count
escaping while the vampire twice attacks the mayor of Los
Angeles. The means by which Dracula escapes shows that he
has changed with the times. For, as if influenced by the
Batman comic books and television series, Count Dracula flies
off in a sleek helicopter emblazoned with the sign of a large
vampire bat.

NELLA STRETTA MORSA DEL RAGNO ("In the Grip
of the Spider"), made that same year as an Italian/French/
West German co-production, is another example of a movie
which confuses any attempt to list all of the Dracula films.
Whether or not Count Dracula actually appears in the film is
unknown to this writer. Yet the picture was released in
Germany as DRACULA IM SCHLOSS DES SCHRECKENS
("Dracula in the Castle of Terror"). NELLA STRETTA
MORSA DEL RAGNO (originally announced as E VENNE
L'ALBA ... MA TINTA DIROSSO ["And Comes the Dawn ...
But Colored Red"]) is based on Edgar Allan Poe's "Danse

---

*In France the film was given the title DRACULA, PRISON-
NIER DU DOCTEUR FRANKENSTEIN ("Dracula, Prisoner of
Doctor Frankenstein").

Macabre" and is a remake of the film LA DANZA MA-
CABRA,* neither of which featured a Dracula figure. The
plot involves Poe's wager with a man, betting that he will
not spend the night in a haunted castle. Apparently the film
also refers to the ignominious Elizabeth Báthory. NELLA
STRETTA MORSA DEL RAGNO was directed by Antonio
Margheriti (Anthony Dawson), who also directed the original
version LA DANZA MACABRA. It featured Anthony Fran-
ciosa, Michele Mercier, Karin Field, Klaus Kinski, Paolo
Goslino and Irinia Maleva.

Japan contributed its first Dracula film in 1971.
CHIOSU ME ("Bloodthirsty Eyes") was made in color by Toho
and directed by Michio Yamamoto. When the film was released the following year in the United States it bore the in-
triguing title, LAKE OF DRACULA. The opening scenes follow a girl child as she pursues her dog through a cave and
past a lake under a red sky, until she comes upon a castle
hidden in the woods. There she encounters an old man, a
pale girl and a strange young man with golden eyes. Years
later the same girl, now an adult, considers the experience
to have been a nightmare and proceeds to paint a picture of
the golden-eyed man. When a coffin is delivered, a pale-
faced vampire, Oriental in appearance, breaks his chains and
emerges, placing a number of mortals under his spell, including the sister of the heroine. She dies and comes back
to an un-dead existence while in the morgue. The heroine
and her boyfriend, a doctor who had been investigating the
vampire's victims, wonders if the dream of the golden-eyed
man could actually have been reality. Locating the castle,
the doctor finds the corpse of a man whose writings reveal
that his son is a descendant of Count Dracula and a Japanese

---

*LA DANZA MACABRA was an Italian/French co-production
made by Vulsina and Woolner in 1964. The film was directed
by Antonio Margheriti (Anthony Dawson) and starred Barbara
Steele as one of a family of vampires, portrayed more like
sanguinary ghosts whose powers included transforming into
vapors. Edgar Allan Poe challenges a man to spend the night
in a house which is reputedly haunted. He proceeds to meet
the lovely Ms. Steele and then her bloodsucking kin. In the
morning he is discovered bloodless, hanging on the fence just
outside the house. LA DANZA MACABRA is also known as
LA LUNGA NOTTE DEL TERRORE ("The Long Night of Terror"), TOMBS OF HORROR and COFFIN OF TERROR. It
was released in the United States as CASTLE OF BLOOD
and to American television as CASTLE OF TERROR.

woman.   The boy had been born with golden eyes and a cruel
bloodthirsty nature.   After the boy died the old man chained
him in a casket but he later returned to un-death as a vampire.   As the doctor concludes his reading, the offspring of
Dracula appears with the girl's vampire sister.   There is a
fight between the doctor and the superhumanly strong male
vampire.   Then, as if possessing enough "life" to perform
one final noble act, the corpse of the old man reaches out
and trips the Dracula figure, causing him to plunge through
a bannister to be impaled on a wooden post.   In an overly
long scene, obviously inspired by the climax of DRACULA
HAS RISEN FROM THE GRAVE, the vampire writhes con-
vulsively, impaled through the back and chest, until he perishes.   Her evil master no longer influencing her, the vampiress dies.   CHIOSU ME, despite its Oriental origin, is
mostly a modern gothic horror film.   In many ways, as with
the numerous scenes of blood and the portrayal of the vampire as a dynamic figure, it imitates the style established by
the Hammer Dracula films.   Some of the photography is extremely satisfying, especially the scenes of the lake itself,
enhanced by the unreality of a blood-red sky.   CHIOSU ME
is also known as DRACULA'S LUST FOR BLOOD.

Dracula sank to new lows in THE MAD LOVE LIFE
OF A HOT VAMPIRE, a sex film in which the Count (Jim
Parker)* utilizes the services of a hunchback and has his
vampire girls draw blood from the penises of male victims.
Dracula's demise is by the reliable rays of the sun, an ending which could not happen early enough in the film.   THE
LUST OF DRACULA was another sex film made in 1971.   In
the British comedy, EVERY HOME SHOULD HAVE ONE, a
color film directed by Jim Clark and released by Lion International, comedian Marty Feldman fantasizes that he is Dracula and battles the Frankenstein Monster.   Also about 1971

---

*Jim Parker was a television personality in Las Vegas, the
star of a program called THE VEGAS VAMPIRE.   Wearing
a beard and long hair, and dressed in a cloaked outfit of
some earlier century, Parker as the Vegas Vampire introduced old horror films and interrupted the films at the commercial breaks.   His popularity grew to the extent that he
made personal appearances even as far away as Los Angeles,
where he introduced the sneak preview screening of a 1972
vampire film entitled VOODOO HEARTBEAT, in which a man
periodically transforms into a crazed bloodsucker.   There
have also been such items as a Vegas Vampire comic strip,
fan club, etc.

Hawthorn Productions announced a film entitled DRACULA'S
CASTLE OR WILL THE REAL COUNT DRACULA PLEASE
STAND UP?, to be directed by Anthony Cardoza and to star
Thor Nielsen, Valda Hansen and Joy Wilkerson. Thus far
the film has apparently not been made.

A new variation on the Dracula theme was manifested
in 1972 with the growing popularity of films starring black
performers. BLACK DRACULA was announced by Dimension
Productions and Meier-Murray and was to be directed by
Paul Nobert. Had the film been made it would have been
the world's first motion picture to feature a Negro Dracula.

Power Productions did, however, proceed with a similar film for release by American-International. BLACULA
was first conceived as a horror film in which an undistin-
guished character named Andrew Brown (named after Andrew
H. Brown of radio and television's AMOS 'N' ANDY) somehow blunders into Dracula's Transylvanian castle and becomes
a vampire. Producer Joseph T. Naar interviewed "teams of
black athletes," hoping to find a suitable star for his film,
but found no one. Afterwards Naar attempted to hire Raymond St. Jacques for the part, but the fine black actor declined. Eventually the project was presented to the Shakespearean actor, William Marshall.

William Marshall is an impressive six-foot five-inch
actor with a powerful physique and even more powerful bas-
so voice. He was born and raised in Gary, Indiana, where
he worked for a time in the steel mills. Before his acting
career Marshall worked as a commercial artist, a waiter and
a soldier. First appearing as a chorus singer in a 1944 production of CARMEN JONES, Marshall went on to become
Boris Karloff's understudy as Captain Hook in PETER PAN
and to star in the role of "De Lawd" in THE GREEN PAS-
TURES. But the actor achieved his most noted success in
the title roles of OEDIPUS REX and of Shakespeare's
OTHELLO. The London Sunday Times said of Marshall's
performance, "The best Othello of our time." A myriad of
stage, film and television parts followed (during a time in
our history in which black actors playing black characters
other than Negro stereotypes was a rarity), including such
roles as the Haitian patriot King Dick in the motion picture
LYDIA BAILEY and the Nubian converted to Christianity in
DEMETRIUS AND THE GLADIATORS.

For an actor of Marshall's stature to assume the title

In American-International Pictures' BLACULA (1972) Count
Dracula was portrayed superbly by Charles Macaulay (above).
The distinguished Shakespearean actor, William Marshall (opposite) played Prince Mamuwalde, the first black counterpart
of Count Dracula.

role in a film with the seemingly ludicrous title of BLACULA, it was understandable that some changes would necessarily be made in the original "Andy Brown" conception of the script. Marshall saw potential in the Blacula theme, especially if it were not presented as merely another "black exploitation" picture. Horror films enjoy a universality of audiences, and BLACULA would probably be seen by almost as many white people as black.

During a visit I made to the home of William Marshall, the actor revealed that he wanted to justify the presence of the eventual "Blacula" in nineteenth century Transylvania. Since slavery was still operative at that time, Marshall changed the character to Mamuwalde, an African prince, hoping to convince Count Dracula to use his influence in helping to place an embargo on the slave trade. Despite studio opposition, the slave issue was included in the script.

Marshall also wrote in a scene in which Mamuwalde is drawn to a beautiful young woman, a reincarnation of his former love, and the embodiment of all the virtues and riches that represented Africa to him. The scene established the human side of the vampire, made him someone with whom the audience could empathize. Though the moving scene was callously abbreviated by the studio editors, it does remain the most memorable part of the film.

Count Dracula appears in the opening scenes of BLACULA, expertly portrayed by Charles Macaulay, with gray hair, mustache and beard, and nineteenth century garb. Prince Mamuwalde and his beautiful wife Luva (Vonette McGee) have journeyed to Castle Dracula in 1815 on a cultural exchange and in an attempt to put an end to the European slave trade. In the past, Dracula had been portrayed as every kind of fiend and deviate; but now he was also a racist. (Yet perhaps we might regard the Count as prejudiced against any mortal, regardless of color.) Dracula returns bigoted remarks to all of Mamuwalde's questions and statements. When the Prince decides to leave the castle, the vampire forbids it. After a struggle between the African Prince and the Transylvanian Count, Dracula and his un-dead accomplices attack the two visitors. Mamuwalde and Luva are forced into a tomb-like chamber. There, the Prince is sealed in a coffin while Count Dracula intones, "You shall pay, black prince! I will place a curse of suffering on you that will doom you to a living hell. A hunger, a wild, gnawing animal hunger, will grow in you--a hunger for human blood! But I will seal you in this living tomb, you and your princess, and here you will starve for eternity, torn by an unquenchable thirst. I curse you with my name. You will be ... Blacula! A vampire like myself. A living fiend!"* Then Dracula locks Luva within the chamber so that she will die a lingering death.

One hundred and fifty years after Mamuwalde's imprisonment, two gay interior decorators visit Castle Dracula to buy some souvenirs. They learn that Dracula and his cohorts were destroyed long ago by Van Helsing. Among the items which the boys ship to a Los Angeles warehouse is Blacula's coffin. When one of the boys gashes his arm with a crowbar in attempting to pry open the casket lid, his flowing blood revives the black version of Dracula. Now in the vampire state, Mamuwalde (who is never again referred to as Blacula) sports bushy eyebrows, a widow's peak, hairy cheeks and sharp fangs. The vampire satisfies his craving for blood on the young man.

Mamuwalde then prowls the streets of Los Angeles, searching for victims. He places the vampire bite upon a black woman taxicab driver, who is promptly taken to the morgue. There she returns to "life" and attacks the hook-handed attendant (Elisha Cook, Jr.). She is repelled by crosses and then staked through the heart.

When Mamuwalde is not overcome by the bloodlust, he appears as his normal handsome self, sans fangs and shaggy hair. It is in this identity that he meets Tina (Denise Nichols), the beautiful reincarnation of his lost Luva, in a discotheque. Mamuwalde becomes disturbed when a photographer flashes a photograph of him. When the photographer later develops the picture and discovers that the noble-looking black man does not appear on film, the vampire destroys her for her knowledge. Mamuwalde begins to woo Tina in the extremely tender scene written by William Marshall himself. While Mamuwalde's unearthly craving forces him to continue to drink the blood of the living, a black and a white police detective deduce that a vampire is responsible for the bizarre goings on.

The climax of BLACULA is staged in a sewage disposal plant, through which the police stalk Mamuwalde, who is fleeing with Tina, the woman who loves him for the man he

---

*Some of these scenes with Dracula appeared in the sequel film SCREAM BLACULA SCREAM.

truly is. One of the officers fires his gun, hitting Tina.
As she dies in the arms of her prince, Mamuwalde expresses
his deep remorse, then destroys the policemen. Having lost
his only reason to exist, Mamuwalde voluntarily marches onto the roof to be destroyed by the fatal rays of the sun. *

Upon the basis of an advance screening of BLACULA,
the Count Dracula Society praised the film and supplied a
quotation to enhance the advertising posters: "BLACULA is
the most horrifying film of the decade. " And after receiving
a print of the film, that organization gave BLACULA its annual Mrs. Ann Radcliffe Award. Well, such praise was not
entirely deserved. William Crain's direction, added to an
economy budget, gave the picture a cheap look. Often, the
supporting actors' performances were almost amateurish.
BLACULA is replete with pseudo-hip cliché dialogue. As
with so many past horror films, the sophisticated detectives
slowly make their "brilliant" deduction that an authentic vampire is the culprit at large. Despite the flaws of BLACULA,
the performance of William Marshall as Mamuwalde is sheer
delight. Marshall's serious portrayal of the "Blacula" character is one of the finest vampire performances in motion
picture history. Certainly, his Mamuwalde is one of the
most noble and sympathetic of all Dracula figures; his Mamuwalde is a star-crossed African of royal heritage whose need
for human blood is akin to the cravings of the heroin addict.
The actor elevated a mediocre film by the sheer weight of
his performance.

BLACULA was a highly profitable venture for American-International, having grossed more money than any film
the studio has made since its inception. When a film of this
type rakes in such profits there is usually little question in
the minds of studio executives that a sequel will also make
money. Marshall was approached to appear in a Blacula
cameo in BLACKENSTEIN, the 1972 horror film from that
studio, but declined. The following year, however, Prince
Mamuwalde returned to the screen in a film that Marshall had
hoped would be titled THE NAME IS BLACULA. Marshall's

---

*The concept of the suicidal vampire exposing himself to sun-
light is relatively new. "Death Is a Lonely Place," a short
story by Bill Warren, published in the first issue of Worlds
of Fantasy (1968), might possibly be the first. Miklos, a
modern day vampire, awaits the dawn rather than change the
woman he loves into a horror like himself. Warren later
adapted his story to the comic strip format in Creepy no. 32
(April 1970).

title was not used when it was announced that the black vampire would rise again. Blacula's second motion picture was originally announced as BLACULA II. After American-International considered the more commercial titles BLACULA LIVES AGAIN! and BLACULA IS BEAUTIFUL, the sequel was finally named SCREAM BLACULA SCREAM.

Vampirism and the arcane rites of voodoo are mixed in SCREAM BLACULA SCREAM. When a local voodoo high priestess dies, her son Willis (Richard Lawson) claims that the throne is now rightfully his. But after the voodoo cult rejects him in favor of a young woman named Lisa (Pam Grier), Willis vengefully purchases a strange bag of bones from an equally vengeful dethroned voodoo priest called Ragman (Bernie Hamilton). Willis secretly performs an ancient voodoo ritual. The bones burst into fire and Mamuwalde is inadvertently resurrected. Willis becomes the first victim of the black Prince and transforms into a vampire himself. In an amusing scene, neo-vampire Willis dresses to the hilt and prepares to go to a party, but then discovers he has no reflection. "Tell me," he says to Mamuwalde, who sits and watches him warily, "how do I look?"

It is not Willis but Mamuwalde who attends the party. There he befriends an ex-policeman named Justin (Don Mitchell), who is now a collector of African art and artifacts, and Justin's girlfriend Lisa. At the party Mamuwalde claims one of the guests as his victim. Then, raising his cape, he transforms into a bat and flies away.

The bat transformation scenes in SCREAM BLACULA SCREAM were accomplished through an animated cartoon, all in black, in the fashion of those created by Fulton for the Universal Dracula films. The effect was mildly successful, but lacked Fulton's masterful touch. And the scenes in which the superimposed bat flaps about, semi-transparently, over the traffic-crowded streets of Hollywood were not very convincing.

Mamuwalde proceeds to recruit a group of young people to his vampire legion, all of whom now inhabit Willis' old mansion. As Lisa watches over the corpse of the girl killed at the party, the latter rises as a vampire. Lisa is about to fall prey to her fangs when Mamuwalde enters the room in a burst of wind. Not realizing quite what is happening, Lisa lets the pleading Mamuwalde convince her that she might cure him through her powers of voodoo.

The police believe the strange murders are the workings of the voodoo cult, since the wounds on the victims' necks could have been made by the serpents used in the voodoo ceremonies. Justin intends to prove that the murders are being committed by a vampire and manages to convince the skeptical police detective only when he shows that the corpses of the unknown killer do not photograph.

During the final scenes of the film, Lisa performs the voodoo rite that will hopefully drive the demon out of Mamuwalde's body. But as the ceremony nears a successful completion, it is interrupted by the entrance of Justin and the police. Police and vampires clash, the un-dead being destroyed by the lawmen's wooden stake. Mamuwalde reverts to his fanged and hairy identity and begins to destroy the policemen one by one. When Lisa sees Mamuwalde in this form, she panics and refuses to continue with the ritual. The Prince then attacks Justin and when the latter addresses him as Mamuwalde, the vampire bares his fangs and growls, "The name is Blacula!" Lisa then impales the voodoo doll of Mamuwalde, which she had been using in the ceremony, with a wooden arrow. Blacula screams, apparently dying, and at the same time authenticating the title and intimating another sequel.

SCREAM BLACULA SCREAM was directed by Bob Kelljan, who three years earlier had directed the highly successful COUNT YORGA--VAMPIRE. The direction is slicker than in the original BLACULA and there is an over-all professional quality that the first film lacks. But some scenes might better have been left out, for they detract from the nobility of the Mamuwalde character. These include a scene in which the black Prince is accosted on the street by two pimps who spout the latest jive and profanities and call him a faggot because he wears a cape.

The second film was not as popular or profitable as the original BLACULA and Marshall ascribes this to a weak script. Marshall would like to see further Blacula films made, in order to raise Prince Mamuwalde out of his predicament. As of this writing, no such decision has been made by American-International.

Paul Naschy, moonlighting from his role of werewolf Daninsky, appeared in two color Dracula films in 1972, playing the Count himself. EL GRAN AMORE DEL CONDE DRACULA ("The Great Love of Count Dracula") was made in

Madrid by the Spanish Eva/Janus Productions and was directed by Javier Aguirre.   Count Dracula makes the fatal
error of falling in love with a mortal woman, becomes emotional and then, rather than endanger her life, rams a stake
through his own chest.   Naschy also portrayed the Count in
LE MESSE NERE DELLA CONTESSA DRACULA ("The Black
Harvest of Countess Dracula"), an Italian film of 1972.

Narciso Ibañez Menta played Dracula in LA SAGA DE
LOS DRACULAS ("The Saga of the Draculas," also known as
DRACULA'S SAGA), a Spanish film of 1972, made by Pro-
filmes and directed by Leon Klimovsky.   Another film of that
year, GO FOR A TAKE, was made in England and directed
by Harry Booth.   The film was set in a motion picture
studio and featured Dennis Price in a Dracula role.

As if the Dracula films of 1972 were not numerous
enough, more of them were announced but apparently never
made.   THE SECRET SEX LIFE OF DRACULA was a project
of Kirt Film International.   Marlene Productions announced
DRACULA IN THE YEAR 2000, DRACULA IN THE REALM
OF TERROR: DRACULA VS. THE TERROR OF ATLANTIS
and DRACULA VS. THE BEASTS OF ZARCON, the latter to
star John Carradine.   There is also the mysterious title,
THE HORRIBLE ORGIES OF COUNT DRACULA, OR BLACK
MAGIC--RITES--REINCARNATIONS, directed by Ralph Brown.
Whether or not this Italian film was actually made is unknown.

THE DEVIL'S WEDDING NIGHT (a film originally intended for release by Roger Corman under the title COUNT-
ESS DRACULA) was made in color in 1973.   Mark Damon
portrayed twin brothers, Karl and Fritz, the former on the
trail of the magical Ring of the Nibelungen (from the opera
Die Nibelungen).   Karl has traced the ring to Castle Karnstein and now to Castle Dracula, and sets off for Transylvania, taking with him an Egyptian medallion to ward off evil.
At a Transylvanian inn, Karl learns from the innkeeper's
daughter that once every fifty years five young virgins are
summoned from the village to Castle Dracula, never to return (recalling Elizabeth Báthory).   Proceeding to the castle,
Karl first meets "The Zombie," an entranced servant girl,
and then a noblewoman who is later identified as Countess
Dracula (Sara Bey).   Karl and the Countess go to bed, during
which she transforms into a gigantic (and real) bat.   Meanwhile, Fritz journeys to the castle after his brother.   The
innkeeper's daughter also goes there, to return the medallion

which Karl lost. Fritz drinks some drugged wine and envisions the Countess with fangs, being bathed by The Zombie
in blood (à la Báthory). After this dream, the real Countess
stands atop her castle and uses the mystic ring to summon
the five virgins from the village. Karl, meanwhile, has been
possessed by the spirit of Dracula himself and appears wearing the garb of the Count. Now sporting fangs, Karl engages
Fritz in a battle while a mysterious man (perhaps Dracula
himself or, more likely, Satan) watches. Downstairs, the
virgins' throats have been cut to satisfy the lusts of Countess
Dracula. Then Fritz, disguised as the "Dracula" Karl, enters the room, beheading the Countess' robed accomplices.
The Countess escapes, pursuing the innkeeper's daughter to
the battlements of the castle. In the shape of an enormous
bat, the vampiress confronts the girl. But she resumes human form when Fritz arrives. Protected by the Egyptian
charm, Fritz lops off the Countess' hand with the ring, while
lightning suddenly destroys her. Even with Countess Dracula
obliterated, the horror has not yet ended. Fritz impales his
brother with a stake, then drops the medallion atop his grave.
Riding off in a coach with the innkeeper's daughter, Fritz
discovers that she is now a vampire. As she fangs him,
Fritz drops the Nibelungen into the hand of the mysterious
stranger, who is also the coachman. The stranger vanishes,
and Karl's hand emerges from the grave to grasp the medallion.

That same year Spain contributed EL RETORNO DE
LA DREQUESSA DRACULA ("The Return of Duchess Dracula"),
directed by Javier Aguirre, while the French LE CIRCUIT
DE SANG ("The Blood Circuit") involved modern day vampires
in Dracula's castle.

Ringo Starr abandoned his Beatle image to portray
Merlin the Magician in Apple Film's SON OF DRACULA (originally announced as COUNT DOWN), a 1973 color film directed in tongue-in-cheek style by Freddie Francis. Count
Down, Dracula's son, was played by singer Harry Nilsson,
who incorporated music from his albums Nilsson Schmilsson
and Son of Schmilsson (the latter showing him in a Dracula
outfit) into the film. Born a vampire, Count Down is also a
musician who performs with his rock band in the basement
of his castle. Count Down awaits the time in which he will
become Overlord Of The Netherworld (a realm occupied by
such horrors as mummies, werewolves, Baron Frankenstein
and his monstrous creation). When Count Down begins to
regret the upcoming coronation, Dr. Van Helsing, now a

friend of Count Dracula, offers the vampiric son an operation
to cure him and, at the same time, destroy the gruesome inhabitants of the Netherworld, a proposition particularly op-
posed by the Baron. SON OF DRACULA was released by
Cinemation Industries.

BLOOD FOR DRACULA, a film by former underground
movie-maker Andy Warhol, was made in 1973 and released
the following year. Directed by Paul Morissey, the picture
introduced the concept that Dracula (Udo Keir) can only
stomach the blood of virgins. With virgins becoming more
difficult to find during these promiscuous times, even in
Transylvania, the Count determines to seek victims elsewhere.
Reasoning that Italy is a Catholic country and, consequently,
abundant in nubile virgins, Dracula fastens his coffin to the
roof of his car and drives off for some untainted Italian blood.
There Dracula preys upon a number of girls. But when he
discovers that the women are, in fact, not virgins, he vomits
their stolen blood. BLOOD FOR DRACULA was outrageously
graphic in depicting gore, especially in the climax. As Dracula descends the stairs, the hero of the film hacks off his
arms and legs, then impales him through the heart.

A comedy entitled VAMPIRA (originally announced in
the trade publications under the already owned title VAM-
PIRELLA) was also made that year. Produced by Jack
Wiener, the film starred ultra-suave leading man David Niven
as Count Dracula, complete with fangs, mustache and widow's
peak. Vampira, Dracula's Countess, was portrayed by
Teresa Graves. The story takes Count Dracula away from
Transylvania and sets him in modern day London, where he
becomes involved with a number of lovely young women.
Among Dracula's London adventures are a visit by personnel
from Playboy magazine and a chivalrous rescue of a woman
from a mugger in a crowded parking lot.

Other Dracula titles announced in 1973 were FRANK-
ENSTEIN'S DRACULA and DRACULA DE FRANKENSTEIN,
the latter starring Dennis Price as Dr. Frankenstein and
Howard Vernon as Dracula. One or both of these titles may
be synonymous with the 1971 production, DRACULA CONTRA
EL DR. FRANKENSTEIN. A Japanese film titled, predictably, JAPULA emerged in 1973. There was also an announcement for a color film THE HOUSE OF DRACULA'S DAUGH-
TER, to be directed by Gordon Hessler and to star Peter
Lorre, Jr., John and David Carradine, Broderick Crawford
and Lorraine Day.

TENDRE DRACULA OU LES CONFESSIONS D'UN BUVEUR DE SANG ("Tender Dracula or The Confessions of a Bloodsucker") was announced in 1973 and went into production in France in January of 1974, ushering the Count right into the New Year. Originally, Christopher Lee was approached to star in this horror satire presenting vampires in a sympathetic light. "And I turned down the offer very firmly," the actor told me in a letter. "It is perhaps ironic that Peter Cushing starts this film at the end of this month." The film was directed by Alain Robbe-Grillet. Cushing played the role of Count Dracula.

DRACULA'S BLOOD, a color film starring Tina Sainz, was released in 1974 by Cannon. That same year Creative Entertainment Corporation made a musical called ROCKULA, RVQ Productions in the Philippines made DRACULA GOES TO RP, and Peter Cushing appeared as Dracula for a masquerade party sequence in MADHOUSE, a co-production made in color by Amicus and American-International. (The film was shot under the title THE RETURN OF DR. DEATH.) Also in 1974, Tyburn Films in England announced DRACULA'S FEAST OF BLOOD; an American producer announced ALLEN AND ROSSI MEET DRACULA AND FRANKENSTEIN, with Bernie Allen and Steve Rossi the villains, and the titled monsters, the heroes.

Other Dracula films have presented problems. THE GREEN MONSTER was an Italian film presumably featuring Dracula. A horror comedy simply called DRACULA was announced by Sam Bischoff and David Diamond, with no other data available. Sometime during the 1960s or 70s, Milton Subotsky of Amicus Productions planned a film of several Bram Stoker tales with the title DRACULA'S GUEST, but the project was abandoned due to Hammer's domination of the Dracula field in England.

Count Dracula's appeal to all age groups has warranted his appearance in a number of animated cartoon short subjects. In 1933 Dracula sat with Frankenstein's Monster and Quasimodo in a motion picture theatre to watch the on-screen antics of Mickey Mouse in the Walt Disney cartoon MICKEY'S GALA PREMIERE, a cartoon released by United Artists.*

---

*Hollywood Film Enterprises later issued a home movie of MICKEY'S GALA PREMIERE under the new title MOVIE STAR MICKEY. Scenes from the Disney cartoon showing Count Dracula also appeared in UNCLE WALT, an independently made animated satire of Disney.

Paul Terry's Terrytoons, which were released in color by 20th Century-Fox, first presented a cartoon Dracula in a Gandy Goose short subject, THE GHOST TOWN, directed by Mannie Davis. A vampire bat leads the obedient Frankenstein Monster before Gandy and transforms into the human form of Count Dracula. "He knows too much," Dracula says profoundly. Gandy then goes into hysterics and awakens from his nightmare. In THE JAIL BREAK, a 1946 Mighty Mouse cartoon, Dracula and the Frankenstein Monster are prisoners at Alcatraz.

BATULA was a short subject starring Al Capp's comic detective Fearless Fosdick, released in 1952. Not really a cartoon, it was made with puppets. In 1960 Bugs Bunny met Count Bloodcount in a Warner Brothers color cartoon, TRANSYLVANIA 6-5000. The Count's evil ambition is to transform Bugs into a bat. THE MAD BAKER was an award-winning color cartoon made in 1972 by the Crunch Bird Company. The cartoon spoofed the old Universal horror films. A Dracula-type mad doctor creates a monster made of chocolate cake.

RETURN OF THE MASTER VAMPIRES

Bela Lugosi never managed to shirk his Dracula image. It yet lingers to the extent that his estate won a lawsuit in 1974 against Universal for the studio's continued use of his image in selling Dracula merchandise. Although the Hungarian actor only portrayed the original Count in two Universal motion pictures, Lugosi's name would always be associated with the role.

One reason for this association is the fact that Lugosi's version of the Count established the image of the vampire on the screen. A second reason is that Lugosi continued to enact his Dracula role in other studios' motion pictures, changing only the name. Lugosi often consented to act in motion pictures of little merit and accepted parts that were designed to capitalize on his Dracula image of 1931. These other studios were confronted with one problem, however, which prohibited them from making new Dracula films molded in the Lugosi image. Universal retained the copyright on their conception of Dracula. Lugosian Draculas did star in a number of independent productions which ignored Universal's copyright or in films made in foreign countries where American copyrights did not necessarily apply. But most reputable American

producers chose rather to present Dracula in some other image
(à la THE RETURN OF DRACULA) or to present their vampire
in the Lugosi image but give him an altogether new name.

MARK OF THE VAMPIRE (MGM 1935) was director
Tod Browning's remake of his silent film, LONDON AFTER
MIDNIGHT. But since Browning had directed the extremely
successful DRACULA four years earlier, he tried to reclaim
the glory of that classic by attempting to make another. He
hired Lugosi to recreate his Dracula characterization in this
first of the imitation Dracula films. With Browning directing
and Lugosi starring, MARK OF THE VAMPIRE certainly
brought DRACULA to the minds of audiences in 1935.

Bela Lugosi portrayed Count Mora in MARK OF THE
VAMPIRE, but he might as well have been called Dracula.
His formal wear was virtually the same, the only real differ-
ence being his ruffled shirt. There was also a bullet wound
with dried blood at his right temple to show how he died before returning from the grave. Count Mora does not speak
in MARK OF THE VAMPIRE until the very end of the film,
which is surprising considering the popularity of Lugosi in
1935. He merely stalks through the fog-enveloped sets, accompanied by his daughter Luna (played by teenaged Carol
Borland with long black hair and clad in shroud-like white).

Carol Borland (now known as Carroll Borland) was a
fan of Bela Lugosi after seeing his performance in the film
DRACULA. In tribute to the actor, she wrote a sequel to
Dracula entitled Countess Dracula. (Carroll Borland attempted to sell the story as a film project as late as the mid-
1960s.) She submitted the manuscript to Lugosi who considered it but replied that the original Dracula was still in
copyright with the Bram Stoker estate. Her Countess Dracula never saw publication or filming, but a positive result of
the correspondence between Lugosi and Borland was her finally acquiring the role of Lucy in one of the Hungarian's stage
runs of DRACULA. Lugosi and Borland worked well together
on the stage and this contributed to her winning the part of
Luna in MARK OF THE VAMPIRE. *

*On Halloween, 1965, Carroll Borland reenacted her role of
Luna in an amateur production of MY FAIR ZOMBIE,
(cont. on p. 242)

Opposite: Bela Lugosi as Count Mora and Carol Borland as
Luna in Tod Browning's MARK OF THE VAMPIRE (MGM
1935).

The film was to be Tod Browning's comeback. He
had not made a film since FREAKS (MGM 1932) and therefore determined that MARK OF THE VAMPIRE would be a
class production with an impressive budget, an impressive
script and an equally impressive cast. Certainly the production began with the correct intentions. A lavish castle set,
with its gossamer spider webs and beclouded with fog,
equaled that of DRACULA in authenticity and realism. The
excellent cinematography was the work of James Wong Howe.
The cast, including Lugosi, Borland, Lionel Atwill, Lionel
Barrymore and Jean Hersholt, was more than capable.
Browning's direction, in my opinion, was not as static as it
had been in DRACULA, and the result was a far more entertaining film than its 1931 predecessor. However, MARK OF
THE VAMPIRE was not the complete success that Browning
and MGM envisioned. Perhaps the reason was that the public demanded another authentic DRACULA but, more likely,
the story itself was the problem.

Guy Endore, author of the classic lycanthropy novel
The Werewolf of Paris (1933), was originally hired by MGM
to write the script to the film, then titled VAMPIRES OF
PRAGUE. But after the intervention of others, Endore was
displeased with the final script. What could have been a film
surpassing DRACULA in chills was destroyed by an ending
that smacked of the horror and fantasy films of the silent era
of motion pictures.

MARK OF THE VAMPIRE was set in Czechoslovakia
at a castle now inhabited by Sir Karrell Borotyn (Holmes
Herbert) and his daughter Irena (Elizabeth Allen). The castle
had originally been occupied by the evil Count Mora and his
daughter Luna, an almost feline beauty. The Count was shot
through the temple and Luna drowned, but their vampiric
forms are still said to haunt the castle, violently killing off
the members of the Borotyn family. When the last Borotyn
dies, the people believe, the vampire Count and his daughter
will reclaim their castle. Presently Sir Karrell is found
dead in the castle, his blood drained and two puncture marks
on his neck. Three men look at the corpse--Dr. Doskil
(Donald Meek), Baron Otto von Zinden (Jean Hersholt) and
Inspector Neumann (Lionel Atwill), the latter not believing in
vampires. During the following year Irena remains in Otto's

which she also wrote. The play was a short spoof of MY
FAIR LADY and featured Eric Hoffman as Count Dracula and
Manny Weltman as Frankenstein's Monster.

home and prepares to marry a young man named Count Fedor (Henry Wadsworth). Apparently Fedor and Irena are to be the next victims of the vampires. Professor Zelan (Lionel Barrymore) comes to the Baron's house to destroy the un-dead. According to the Van Helsing-like professor, the vam-pires leave their bodies at night and it is these bodies that must be destroyed. Inspector Neumann takes Baron Otto to the castle, where they hear organ music emanating from the chapel. Peering through the window they behold Count Mora watching as the previously dead Sir Karrell plays the organ and Luna gracefully flies overhead on bat-like wings.

Carroll Borland reported that the bat harness she wore in this brief scene was built in two weeks. Browning shot the scene many times until, after several days, he achieved the desired effect. To this day the effect is stunning. The cost of the scene, according to Carroll Borland, was about $10,000. Count Mora transformed from a prop bat only un-der the concealment of the dense studio fog.

That night Luna lures Irena to the castle. Baron Otto then becomes the apparently intended victim of the vampires, encountering Mora and Luna and the threatening Sir Karrell. Zelan hypnotizes the terrified Baron and sends his mind back to the night that Sir Karrell died. The stage having been set, the Baron reveals that he murdered Sir Karrell so that the latter would not be able to arrange a marriage between Irena and Fedor and so that Otto could have her for himself. Otto shows how he first doped Sir Karrell's wine, then punctured his neck and siphoned out the blood, using a heated drinking glass. The vampires and "Sir Karrell" are all actors hired to prey upon Otto's gullibility. The final scene, the only one in which Lugosi speaks, shows him packing up his vampire paraphernalia and telling "Luna" that someday he will truly play a great vampire.

The ending was a throwback to an earlier generation in which the supernatural content of a film would only be ac-cepted by an audience if it were explained away as a dream or hoax. Browning ignored the fact that his DRACULA pre-sented vampires as real within the context of the story. Perhaps, since MARK OF THE VAMPIRE was his comeback film, he was taking no chances and reverted to a more con-servative approach. At any rate, audiences felt cheated and MARK OF THE VAMPIRE, despite its merits, left DRACULA unchallenged.

Lugosi's next Dracula-type role was in a film hardly as meritorious as MARK. By 1941 the actor was working for studios like Monogram. In that year he made SPOOKS RUN WILD for Monogram, an East Side Kids vehicle produced by "Quckie King" Sam Katzman and directed by Phil Rosen. Lugosi appeared in full Dracula attire and was photographed in some close-ups emphasizing his staring, piercing eyes, as in the 1931 Universal classic. There was little plot in the film and even less production value. A bizarre killer, known only as the Monster, is at large. This criminal is said to sleep in a coffin by day and come out to drink human blood by night. The fact that Lugosi parades about in tuxedo and black cloak and possesses three oblong boxes resembling coffins immediately implicates him. The East Side Kids (played by Leo Gorcey, Huntz Hall, Bobby Jordan, and others) become involved in the case, and after undergoing the stock "haunted house" comic scare routines in the old building where Lugosi and his assistant (played by Angelo Rossito) live, the East Side Kids discover that the suspected Monster is actually an innocent stage magician and the real vampiric murderer is some one else. *

The success of its horror films of the 1940s made Universal the target of imitation by other studios. Columbia Pictures produced during this period a number of horror films which astoundingly resembled the Universal product, and in 1944 Columbia made an impressive "B" film for which they elicited the services of Bela Lugosi, at least for a while removing him from the shoddy productions of Poverty Row. The film was entitled THE RETURN OF THE VAMPIRE. But it was such an imitation of the Universal films--not only in story content, but also in direction, lighting, cinematography, music and casting--that had Universal produced it instead of Columbia, it would most likely have been called DRACULA MEETS THE WOLF MAN. Lew Landers' direction is reminiscent of such horror films as Universal's SON OF DRACULA and HOUSE OF FRANKENSTEIN.

While John Carradine was playing Dracula at Universal, Bela Lugosi played a role virtually identical to Count Dracula in THE RETURN OF THE VAMPIRE. Again dressed in immaculately clean formal wear with long black cape, Lugosi changed only his name for this 1944 performance. ** Though

---

*SPOOKS RUN WILD was released in England as GHOST IN THE NIGHT.

**Lugosi so resembled the Count in this film that

(cont. on p. 245)

he appeared to be Dracula he was really Armand Tessla, a former student of occult lore who eventually became a vampire himself.   The actor never wore fangs for his vampire portrayals; yet for some unknown reason his teeth were blackened for his role as Armand Tessla, the effect being a strangely toothless vampire.

THE RETURN OF THE VAMPIRE opens in a graveyard in 1918.   A werewolf named Andreas Obry (played by Matt Willis, a husky actor who resembled Universal's Lon Chaney, Jr. in both appearance and performance) enters a crypt to summon his master, the vampire.   (Unlike Universal's Wolf Man, Andreas can speak.)   The cloaked figure rises, spreading his cape at the hilltop to become one with the swirling fog.   The vampire's victim is a young girl named Nickie, who is in the nearby sanitarium of Lady Jane Ainsley (Frieda Inescort).   Sir John Ainsley (Roland Varno), Nickie's grandfather, consults a book on vampirism by Armand Tessla, then locates the vampire's crypt.   His identity revealed when his face does not reflect in a mirror, the vampire is impaled with an iron spike.   As the werewolf returns, Andreas experiences the same pain and regains his human form.   Twenty-five years later the German blitzkrieg over London wrecks the old cemetery.   Two Civil Defense guards happen upon the impaled body, remove the spike and re-bury the budy.   That night, in an effective scene, the vampire's hand claws its way out of the dirt.   Now back to his former power, Tessla summons the cured Andreas by telepathic command and reverts him back to his werewolf existence.   Tessla then vows vengeance on those who destroyed him.

The vampire summons Nicki in a room filled with rolling mist.   Later, Tessla visits Lady Jane and she brandishes a crucifix and forces him to vanish in an explosion of smoke. Toward the climax of the film, Tessla places the unconscious Nicki on a bier in the ruins of the crypt.   But when he tells Andreas that he no longer needs him and that he plans to make Nicki his own, Andreas rebels, touching a discarded crucifix and regaining his human form.   Andreas saves Nicki by warding Tessla off with the cross as another bombing raid buries the tomb in rubble.   When Andreas revives the sun is shining.   Hastily he drags the dazed vampire outside where Tessla is rendered powerless by the solar rays.   Then the

scenes from THE RETURN OF THE VAMPIRE were said to be of Dracula in the HOLLYWOOD AND THE STARS television documentary of 1964.

mortally wounded Andreas impales him with another metal spike. The former werewolf himself dies as Armand Tessla, perhaps due to the combination of spike and sunlight, perishes, his face melting from the bone like hot wax.

In 1947 Bela Lugosi was back to performing in a shoddy film with the title SCARED TO DEATH. This Lippert/ Golden Gate/Screen Guild production, directed by Christy Cabanne, has the distinction of being one of Lugosi's only films made in color. The story, about a woman who literally dies of fright, includes Lugosi as a "red herring" who stands about draped in a black cape, looking guilty although he is innocent all the time.

Returning to his Dracula image in 1952, Bela Lugosi co-starred with British transvestite comic Arthur Luncan in a film which began as VAMPIRE OVER LONDON but was finally released in England as OLD MOTHER RILEY MEETS THE VAMPIRE. The comedy was made by Fernwood and Renown and was directed by John Gilling. Because of the heavy British humor, the film was not released in the United States until the 1960s, when the title was changed to MY SON, THE VAMPIRE, * with a title song performed by Alan Sherman.

Lugosi portrayed Baron Von Housen, a master criminal who claims to be descended from a vampire and is now that ancestor's reincarnation. To support his own fantasies, Von Housen appears with a chalky complexion, sinister-looking eyebrows, and a black outfit complete with long cloak. He sleeps in a coffin, calls himself "The Vampire" and refers to the framed picture of a bat on his wall as a portrait of his brother. Baron Von Housen's delusions are those of most super-criminals. He wants to conquer the world. To accomplish this ambitious feat "The Vampire" plans to utilize a robot slave, his "perfect man. " But the robot is delivered

---

*In England this film was also known under the abbreviated title, MOTHER RILEY MEETS THE VAMPIRE. Walton Home Movies in England also issued two condensed versions of the film in 8mm with the titles MOTHER RILEY IN DRACULA'S DESIRE (though the vampire character is definitely not Dracula) and MOTHER RILEY RUNS RIOT.

Opposite: Werewolf Andreas Obry (Matt Willis) and a very Dracula-like Armand Tessla (Bela Lugosi) menace an entranced Nickie (Nina Foch) in THE RETURN OF THE VAMPIRE (Columbia, 1944).

by mistake to the home of Mother Riley (Luncan), who eventually rips it to pieces of junk metal with her bare hands. Von Housen leaves the heroine tied to an operating table in his old house, sets a time bomb to explode and then goes to the shipping yards where he hopes to obtain a chart that he needs in his plans. But the police arrive at the docks and capture "The Vampire."

In the 1960s American film producer Alex Gordon thought to salvage the Lugosi footage from the unseccessful OLD MOTHER RILEY MEETS THE VAMPIRE. His plans were to shoot new footage to incorporate with that of Lugosi and create a new film with the title KING ROBOT. But this version was never made.

Lugosi's mere presence in a film could spark off dialogue associating him with vampires, as in the 1952 comedy, BELA LUGOSI MEETS A BROOKLYN GORILLA, directed by William Beaudine for Jack Broder Productions. (This film is often seen on television as THE BOYS FROM BROOKLYN and is also known as THE MONSTER MEETS THE GORILLA and the shortened LUGOSI MEETS A BROOKLYN GORILLA.) The following year the Hungarian actor again donned his Dracula cape in a personal appearance stunt to publicize the film, HOUSE OF WAX, which was premiering at Hollywood's Paramount Theatre. Against his better judgment, Lugosi led an actor in a gorilla suit by a chain. Then he pretended to bite the neck of a nurse working at a Red Cross milk stand. According to film director Alex Gordon who was present at the event, Lugosi was supposed merely to pose for a photograph, drinking milk instead of the expected blood. But the actor, in the commotion, did not know this. "They (the nurses) were so surprised and shocked," said Gordon, "they threw the milk all over him!"[*]

The actor's last excursion into the realm of the vampire movies was in 1956, shortly before his death. Edward D. Wood, Jr., of BRIDE OF THE MONSTER fame, had been planning to film TOMB OF THE VAMPIRE with Lugosi starring, and actually shot some scenes of Lugosi in his Dracula outfit. Lugosi was photographed lurking about the forest, entering a house and raising his cape over his sleeping victim. When Lugosi died, TOMB OF THE VAMPIRE was shelved -- at least for a while and in its original form.

[*]Alex Gordon, "My Favorite Vampire," Fantastic Monsters of the Films, no. 5 (1963), p. 48.

Wood could not let his Lugosi vampire footage go to waste, however. Thus he devised another plot into which the Lugosi footage could be reworked. The new film, GRAVE ROBBERS FROM OUTER SPACE, went into production that same year, combining old-style horror with science fiction. A double impersonated Lugosi for the new scenes, cautiously hiding his face behind a cloak-draped arm. Wood also hired television personality Vampira to reenact her famous slinky portrayal and Tor Johnson to play a police detective.

Alien invaders attempt to conquer the Earth by resurrecting a few corpses. Lugosi and his double silently stalk through the picture in imitation of Count Dracula. Finally, the impersonator of Lugosi, seen from behind, is blasted with a raygun and reduced to a skeleton. The film was not released until 1959, with the new title, PLAN 9 FROM OUTER SPACE. It is infamous among monster film buffs as the worst horror film ever made. This is surely hyperbole; yet with its cardboard sets, amateurish acting, shoddy special effects and Wood's uninspired direction, PLAN 9 is certainly a contender.

Although these were Bela Lugosi's only other Dracula-type films, the actor did star in another picture which brought visions of vampires before the public. DEVIL BAT (Producers Releasing Corporation, 1941), directed by Jean Yarbrough, worked the vampire theme not into the film but into the advertising with such catchlines as "Your blood will freeze in your veins as these bloodthirsty monsters bring death in the dead of night! ... Beware of these vampires of the night, this scourge of mankind! ... He lets loose a horrible monster to satisfy his thirst for human blood! ... Fangs of flying doom sink into the bare throats of those marked for death!" Lugosi actually played Dr. Paul Carruthers, a mad scientist working for a cosmetics company. When the executives of the firm cheat Carruthers out of the profits from his own discoveries, he avenges himself with a killer bat enlarged to monstrous proportions via electricity. The "Devil Bat" attacks anyone wearing Carruthers' special after-shave lotion. As expected, Carruthers is finally splashed with his own lotion and attacked by the Devil Bat. DEVIL BAT is fun to watch, especially the scenes showing a hammy Lugosi enticing his victims-to-be to wear his after-shave lotion on the "tender parts" of their necks and the scenes of the enormous rubber Devil Bat prop flying through the air. *

*DEVIL BAT went into production as KILLER BATS. In 1946

(cont. on p. 250)

Lugosi's successor, Christopher Lee, refused to spoof
his Dracula roles unless the character was changed to be
other than a carbon copy of the Count. These changes were
often subtle but they were apparent to viewers who looked beyond the flowing cloak and sharp fangs. Lee's first vampire
role following HORROR OF DRACULA was for Maxima in
Italy. In 1959 the studio wanted Lee to play the Count in
HARD TIMES FOR DRACULA, a spoof of horror films made
in color and directed by Stefano Steno. Lee consented to do
the film providing the vampire he was to portray was not
Count Dracula.

"That was supposed to be a gag," Christopher Lee
told me. "But I didn't play Dracula in it. No, I refused to.
It was not supposed to be a parody on Dracula. But the idea
was that I'd do this picture with this very well known comedian. He was Italy's top comedian at the time. I would play
an unnamed vampire called the Baron. It was almost done
for comedy, as you know. But I did very much resemble
Dracula, except that the wig was very dark instead of gray;
it was black. And there were other subtle differences which
I insisted on, which stopped it from being too much of a resemblance to the character I've been associated with ... too
often."

There were other differences, including a high-col-
lared cloak and a voice dubbed through an echo chamber.
The final outcome of Lee's characterization was a German
vampire named Baron Rodriguez. Although the film was basically a comedy, showcasing Italian comedian Renato Rascel
as Baron Oswald, Lee maintained a serious portrayal of his
vampire. And Marco Scarpelli's photography, along with
Steno's direction, resulted in some fine vampire footage, especially in scenes showing Baron Rodriguez prowling the rooftop of the castle with cape majestically flowing.

PRC made a sequel, DEVIL BAT'S DAUGHTER, directed by
Frank Wisbar. This film actually was about vampires. Rose-
mary LaPlanche played the title role. According to this film,
Dr. Carruthers was an altruistic scientist whose experiments
with bats led him to be called the Devil Bat and prompted
people to believe that he was a vampire. Now his daughter
has weird dreams (with scenes of the flying Devil Bat from
the earlier film) which add to her belief that she has inherited
the vampire taint. Actually, the whole affair is revealed as a
plot (and a quite boring one) to discredit her.

Christopher Lee insisted that he not play Count Dracula in
the Italian spoof of horror films, TEMPI DURI PET I VAM-
PIRI (1959), released in the U.S. as UNCLE WAS A VAM-
PIRE.

The title of the film eventually became TEMPI DURI
PET I VAMPIRI ("Hard Time for Vampires"). The picture
was released by Embassy in the United States as UNCLE
WAS A VAMPIRE.

Baron Oswald loses his fortune and is compelled to
sell his family castle; it is converted into a hotel, with the
Baron as bellboy. Oswald learns that his Uncle Rodriguez
is arriving for a visit, but only his uncle's luggage arrives,
including a trunk shaped not unlike a coffin. Baron Rodriguez
appears at midnight, emerging from the trunk as a vampire.
Rodriguez begins to attack the beautiful women staying at the
castle, fleeing when the father of one of his victims wards

him off with a coathanger.   When Oswald later decides to
destroy his uncle with a stake he becomes the vampire's next
victim.   Oswald dons his uncle's cloak and becomes a fanged
vampire by night, attacking women and leaving them begging
for more.   In one amusing scene he deliberates whether or
not to follow his new life, spoofing Shakespeare with a "To
bite or not to bite" soliloquy.   By day, Oswald knows nothing
of his nocturnal escapades, even while being chased by his
adoring victims.   TEMPI DURI PET I VAMPIRI ends at dawn
with Oswald warning his uncle to get back into his coffin.
But Baron Rodriguez declares that he is weary of spending
eternity getting in and out of such boxes.   Now he has a new
destiny to pursue.   The final scene shows the vampire unaf-
fectedly riding by coach into the sunrise, accompanied by two
beautiful girls from the hotel, while the soundtrack of the
film plays the Italian hit song, "Dracula Cha-Cha-Cha." This
song also figured in the film, TWO WEEKS IN ANOTHER
TOWN (MGM 1962).

Christopher Lee played Lico in a variation of the vam-
pire theme in the Italian ERCOLE AL CENTRO DELLA TER-
RA ("Hercules at the Center of the Earth"), made in color
by Omnia S. P. A. Cinematografica and directed by Mario
Bava.   Three years after its completion the film was re-
leased in America by Woolner Brothers as HERCULES IN
THE HAUNTED WORLD.   It was released in England as HER-
CULES AT THE CENTER OF THE EARTH and in France as
HERCULE CONTRE LES VAMPIRES ("Hercules vs. the Vam-
pires"), and is also known as WITH HERCULES TO THE
CENTER OF THE EARTH.

Lico is a vampire who will become immortal providing he drinks the blood of a beautiful princess.   Hercules
(Red Park) learns that he can save the princess by obtaining
a certain mystical plant.   The musclebound demigod literally
goes to Hell in search of the plant, overcoming such obstacles
as wispy vampires who fly from their ancient stone coffins.
At last Hercules battles Lico himself and pins him beneath a
boulder.   Trapped beneath a lunar eclipse, Lico bursts aflame
and perishes.   Thanks to its atmospheric sets and Bava's
direction, the film was better than most of the Italian muscle-
man epics.

In 1967 Lee played Count Regula in the West German
film, DIE SCHLANGENGRUBE UND DAS PENDEL ("The
Snake Pit and the Pendulum"), made by Constatin, directed
by Harald Reinl and released in color in the United States by

Hemisphere as THE BLOOD DEMON. (The film is also known as THE SNAKE PIT and, in southeast Asia, as THE TORTURE CHAMBER OF DR. SADISM.) In this variation on Edgar Allan Poe's "Pit and the Pendulum," Regula was a fiend revived from the dead by blood.

Lee played the "Ship's Vampire" in THE MAGIC CHRISTIAN (Commonwealth United), based on the Terry Southern novel. The British film was made in color in 1969 and was directed by Joseph McGrath. Lee first appears as a vampiric waiter. As he is clearly seen reflecting in a mirror he is revealed to be not a real vampire but an actor hired by Sir Guy Grand (Peter Sellers) to haunt his ship, The Magic Christian. In one magnificent scene, Lee, dressed more like the Lugosi Dracula, strides majestically down the corridors in slow motion, his cape billowing behind him. "I didn't wear the gray wig," said Lee. "And I wore a black tuxedo with a bow tie, if you remember. I didn't play Dracula."

Although Lee did not portray Count Dracula in THE MAGIC CHRISTIAN, he did enact the role in the British film, ONE MORE TIME, directed by Jerry Lewis for Crislaw and Trace-Mark and released in color by United Artists in 1970. In this sequel to the film, SALT AND PEPPER, Sammy Davis, Jr. inadvertently enters a room occupied by Count Dracula, Baron Frankenstein (Peter Cushing) and his Monster.

What at the time seemed to be the most ambitious Dracula project to date was the 1970 color film, EL CONDE DRACULA ("Count Dracula"). The Spanish/Italian/English/West German co-production was to be a faithful adaptation of Bram Stoker's novel, given an impressive budget, directed by Terence Fisher and co-starring Vincent Price as Van Helsing. Producer Harry Alan Towers, however, eventually cast Herbert Lom in the part originally intended for Price, assigned the directorial position to Jesus Franco and cut a good portion of the budget.

Nevertheless, Lee was to portray Dracula as Stoker envisioned him. "As far as my own performance is concerned," the actor told me, "with regards to the script, which was pretty dismal, it is Stoker's character. It is an old man in a black frock coat, with white hair and a white mustache, getting progressively younger during the film as he gets stronger and stronger because of blood. In that respect, I

am the only person who has ever presented that character
correctly on the screen, as the author described him completely. Old. Getting younger. The clothes are correct.
The make-up is correct. I don't have the pointed nails or
the hair on the palms of my hands because these are details
that could hardly ever be picked up. But otherwise it is correct. And my part of it, I believe, is all right. The production values, I've been told, are extremely bad. But it is
the only time--I can say this--that Stoker's character has
been presented authentically, as he described him, on the
screen. The only time. Ever. "

   EL CONDE DRACULA does follow the Stoker book with
reasonable accuracy. The film was made in Barcelona and
took advantage of eerie forests and an authentic castle. Jonathan Harker (Fred Williams) proceeds through the early scenes
in the film, encountering Dracula disguised as a coachman.

In the Spanish EL CONDE DRACULA, Christopher Lee appeared as the King Vampire as described by Bram Stoker.
The 1970 film followed the original novel rather closely.

Lee's Dracula is slow-paced, unlike his Hammer characterization, as he drives away the wolves by gesturing with his
hands.   At the castle, the credulity of the Dracula character
is tested in one scene where he stands with Harker before a
full-length mirror and does not reflect.   It is not explained
why the Count, first, would possess such a mirror and, second, why he would so obviously stand before it.   Much of the
dialogue between the Count and Harker during the scenes set
at Castle Dracula was taken directly from Stoker, as were
the scenes involving the three vampire women and the woman
who cries for her missing infant.

Arthur Holmwood was eliminated entirely from the
story.   And the sanitarium in which Harker becomes a patient
now belongs to Dr. Van Helsing.   Count Dracula proceeds
with his vampirizing of Lucy (Soledad Miranda), his control
of Renfield (played with extreme restraint by Klaus Kinsky)
and finally of Mina (Maria Rohm).   Van Helsing takes precautions in his sanitarium against Dracula's final attacks on
Mina and confronts the King Vampire alone in his study.   In
one line of dialogue Van Helsing recalls the earlier Hammer
film by referring to the Count by the title usually reserved
for Satan, "Prince of Darkness."

Count Dracula, now appearing to be a young man,
books passage on a ship and returns to his native Transylvania.   Jonathan Harker and Quincey Morris arrive at the
castle first, and there destroy the three vampire women.
Blood splashes in Harker's face as he drives a stake through
one of them.   Then the two men ascend to the castle rooftop,
rolling down heavy rocks upon the approaching Gypsies who
are transporting their vampiric master to his home.   Scaring
off the Gypsies, Harker and Quincey open Dracula's coffin
and set his body ablaze with a torch.   As the Count burns,
his face becomes old again and then decomposes.

EL CONDE DRACULA was a disappointment, especially after all the advance publicity.   Franco's direction was
slow, often tediously so, and his preoccupation with the zoom
lens caused the audience to anticipate its repeated use.   The
color and lighting were poor and I was glad when the film
was finally over.   Nevertheless, Lee and Lom portrayed
Dracula and Van Helsing masterfully.   And EL CONDE DRAC-
ULA, for its attempt to recreate Bram Stoker's novel on the
screen within the limitations of the low-budget motion picture,
is of extreme importance in the history of the Dracula film.

Christopher Lee, disappointed with the results of EL
CONDE DRACULA, still hopes someday to present the story
as it should be.   "It has never been done on the screen,"
said the actor, "exactly as Stoker described it, physically
and in every other way.   It would cost a fortune, with all
the shipwrecks, the Bay of Whitby and everything.   And locations, with very mountainous country.   With many mountains
and gorges.   It would cost a tremendous amount of money,
particularly in today's inflated price range.   It would cost
about three or four million dollars, I would think.   And nobody would make it for that figure because they wouldn't get
proportionately greater profits; which they do, you see, if
they make it for half a million dollars or something like
that."

EL CONDE DRACULA was the victim of courtroom
procedures when Commonwealth United Releasing Company,
which was to issue the film, was bought by American-International.   The question of ownership arose and the film had
only limited engagements in the United States, under the title
of COUNT DRACULA, even though it was quite successful in
Europe.   EL CONDE DRACULA has a rather involved history
as far as titles are concerned.   In Germany the film is
known as NACHTS, WENN DRACULA ERWACHT ("Nights,
When Dracula Arises").   In England the title became BRAM
STOKER'S COUNT DRACULA.   France knows the film as
LA NUITS DE DRACULA ("The Nights of Dracula").   American-International considered two earlier titles before settling
on COUNT DRACULA for the United States release: DRACU-
LA '71 and DRACULA #1.

During the filming of EL CONDE DRACULA Christo-
pher Lee became associated with Spanish film-maker Pedro
Portabella.   The latter had come to the set of EL CONDE
DRACULA to make a documentary on the shooting of the picture.   Portabella used footage of Lee from EL CONDE
DRACULA and shot new film of the actor as himself behind
the scenes.   To this footage Portabella added scenes taken
from NOSFERATU, from Dreyer's VAMPYR and from the
Universal Dracula films.   The final product was entitled
VAMPIR and was issued not as a documentary but as a tribute to the tradition of the vampire.   "That was a Spanish
director's personal presentation in film form of his impres-
sions about the vampire in the cinema only," said Lee.   "It
was shown at the Metropolitan Museum of Modern Art and to
the best of my knowledge has not been shown in the commercial cinema.   It's in black and white and very strange in

many respects. I mean, it shows me arriving at location before I'm made-up. And then playing in the picture. I didn't even know half the time they were shooting. "

Also in 1970 Christopher Lee appeared in another Portabella film, EL UMBRACLE ("The Shady Place"). This film, which protested censorship, included a scene in which a vampire hands Lee a copy of Bram Stoker's Dracula.

During the seventies Warner Brothers had considered making an entire series of Dracula films in India. Christopher Lee was to portray the Count if the series got underway. The project, certainly an odd idea, was never begun.

Lugosi and Lee both put forth their efforts to keep the eternal Count alive. But there was a country south of the American border that would borrow from both of their Dracula images in its own contributions to the genre.

DRACULA MEXICO STYLE

The Dracula character has been given considerable attention by Mexican film-makers, so much, in fact, that their contributions are assigned a special section of this book. The Mexican Draculas and Dracula-type vampires have advanced only slightly with the times, usually in the elements of sex and gore. Otherwise they closely imitate the Dracula movies made by Universal during the thirties and forties and when seen today by American audiences, they tend to create a sort of pseudo-nostalgia for those earlier productions.

The Mexican vampire cavorts with the most exaggerated Lugosian mannerisms. He pursues screaming heroines with his eyes wide and black cloak fluttering wing-like from raised arms. Unlike Lugosi, he also boasts a set of long, sharp canine teeth. By means of simple scene cuts, the Mexican vampire transforms into an enormous (and thoroughly unconvincing) prop bat, often with light bulb eyes and dangling awkwardly from wires. Some of the elements that other countries have abandoned in their vampire films, Mexican producers dwell upon. Sets are usually extremely cheap and scripts ludicrous. The Mexican Dracula films, nevertheless, are usually beautifully atmospheric, with their heavy blankets of mist drifting about old tombs and castles, and are most often quite entertaining to anyone who has not forgotten how to sit back and enjoy horror films with a smile on his face.

In 1957 the Mexican film company, Producciones Soto-
mayor, made a satire of American horror movies with the
title, EL CASTILLO DE LOS MONSTRUOS ("The Castle of
the Monsters"), directed by Julian Soler.   The film boasted
shoddy Mexican versions of Frankenstein's Monster (here
called "Frentestein"), the Creature from the Black Lagoon,
the Wolf Man, the Mummy and a gorilla.   Also among the
cast of ghouls was a formal-attired, caped vampire, presumably Count Dracula himself (played by German Robles who,
we shall see, remains Mexico's most prolific screen vampire).   The story is the typical haunted house comedy plot.
A newlywed couple, played by Mexican comedian Clavillazo
and Evangelina Elizondo, are forced to stay at a sinister-
looking castle when their automobile runs out of gas.   Within
the castle lurk the infamous monsters, with Dracula and
Frentestein paying particularly fascinated attention to the girl.
Yet after many encounters with the creatures, the young
married couple manage to escape the Castle of the Monsters.

Cinematografica Calderón borrowed Count Dracula in
1961 for the comedy film FRANKESTEIN, EL VAMPIRO Y
CIA ("Frankestein, the Vampiro and Company"), directed by
Benito Alazraki.   The reason I use the term "borrowed" is
that the film was really an unauthorized Mexican version of
ABBOTT AND COSTELLO MEET FRANKENSTEIN.   Though
the Vampire performs much as the caped nobleman in the
Abbott and Costello film, he is never referred to as Count
Dracula.   The supposedly wax figures of Frankestein and the
Vampire are assigned to an express agency at which Paco
and Agapito are employed.   These two zanies deliver the
bodies to a spooky-looking old house where they are revealed
to be the authentic characters, who presently return to life.
The Vampire plans to give Frankestein the simple brain of
Agapito and use the resulting obedient monster in his scheme
to conquer the United States.   The appearance of the Wolf
Man interrupts the operation, with the werewolf and the Vampire fighting each other until they are destroyed in a fire,
leaving Frankestein to sink into a bog of quicksand.   The
film is also known under the title FRANKESTAIN, EL VAM-
PIRO Y COMPAÑIA.

EL IMPERIO DE DRACULA ("The Empire of Dracula")
was a color film directed by Federico Curiel for Filmica
Vergara in 1966.   Advertising posters for the film also list
a subtitle, LAS MUJERES DE DRACULA ("The Women of
Dracula"), and depict a handsome Count Dracula surrounded
by beautiful vampire women.   Stills from the film reveal a

"El Vampiro" appears to be Count Dracula himself in FRANK-ESTEIN, EL VAMPIRO Y CIA, a 1961 Mexican remake of ABBOTT AND COSTELLO MEET FRANKENSTEIN.

woman being bitten by a vampiress, Dracula leaping to attack a man in a horse-drawn buggy, and the Count being fought in his coffin by a man wielding a crucifix. The press sheet for the film mentions orgies of blood to satisfy the lusts of Count Dracula. The film starred Lucha Villa, Cesar Del Campo, Eric Del Castillo and Ethel Carrillo.

John Carradine returned to the role of Count Dracula in the 1967 film, LAS VAMPIRAS ("The Vampire Girls"), made in color by Filmica Vergara and directed by Federico Curiel. "I don't remember much about it," Carradine told me. "I did these so fast. You see, I was working with Spanish-speaking actors. I was the only one in the picture who spoke English. And it was very difficult for me to

An athletic Count Dracula from EL IMPERIO DE DRACULA
("The Empire of Dracula"), a Mexican film of 1966.

figure out what the hell was going on. " Apparently the plot
of LAS VAMPIRAS involves the imprisonment of Count Dracula in a cage with bars. His vampire wife takes over the un-
dead operations, commanding a cult of vampire women, each
clad in tights and capes cut into the shape of bat wings. The
hero of the film is one of Mexico's numerous real-life masked
wrestlers who portray themselves in super-hero roles upon
the screen. In this film the hero is Mil Mascaras ("Thousand Masks"), who appears in his various scenes with different concealing masks. Eventually he enters the vampire
queen's throne room to battle her muscular henchman and the
un-dead girls under her command. John Carradine learned,

Opposite: John Carradine portrayed Count Dracula again in
the Mexican film, LAS VAMPIRAS (1967).

in Spanish, his famous line about having to go to the bath-
room, which he used to accompany his final bow in the DRACU-
LA stage play (see Chapter 5). Carradine proceeded with a
scene in which he was to emerge from his coffin, then, with
all sobriety, Carradine looked toward the camera and spoke
the line in Spanish, shocking almost every member of the
crew.

A wax dummy of Dracula was seen the following year
in another Mexican film starring Carradine, LA SEÑORA
MUERTE ("Madame Death"), made in color by the same studio. The dummy stood among others including the Wolf Man
and Frankenstein's Monster, in a chamber of horrors exhibit.
Count Dracula also appeared, along with such American fiends
as Frankenstein's Monster and the Creature from the Black
Lagoon, in the juvenile film, CHABELO Y PEPITO CONTRA
LOS MONSTRUOS, ("Chabelo and Pepito vs. the Monsters"),
made in color in 1973.

Most popular of the Mexican masked wrestlers and
super-heroes was Santo, En Enmascarado de Plata ("The
Mask of Silver"). Santo (meaning "Saint") has faced a long
line of monstrous adversaries upon the motion picture screen
and has battled his share of Draculas and Dracula-type vampires. EL SANTO CONTRA LAS MUJERES VAMPIRAS
("Santo vs. the Vampire Women") was made in 1961 by Alfonso Corona Panamericana and directed by Alfonso Corona
Blake. Santo battles a group of vampire henchmen cloaked
in Dracula-style capes and all ruled by an evil vampire
queen. Since the Santo films are patterned after the American movie serials of the past, these male vampires prefer
using their fists to their fangs. In one sequence Santo
wrestles one of these vampires, disguised as another masked
wrestler, in the ring. When Santo unmasks his opponent he
reveals the face of a werewolf! If that were not enough, the
monster then transforms into a bat and flies out of the ring.
Later, Santo physically battles a group of these henchmen,
one of them bursting into flame beneath a large crucifix.
The climax of the film shows Santo battling the male vampires as the sun rises and incinerates them. The masked
hero then rushes to the murky den of the vampire women and
sets their bodies aflame with a torch. The film was released to American television by American-International as
SAMSON VS. THE VAMPIRE WOMEN. The film is also
known as LA MUJERES VAMPIRO ("The Vampire Women")
and EL SANTO CONTRA LAS VAMPIRAS. In Argentina the
film became EL SANTO VS. LAS MUJERES VAMPIRAS and

in France, SUPERMAN CONTRE LES FEMME VAMPIRES
("Superman Vs. the Female Vampires").

In 1965 Santo battled a kind of poor man's Dracula in
SANTO CONTRA EL BARON BRAKOLA, a Vargara film directed by Jose Diaz Morales. Although the name of the vampire was Brakola he resembled Count Dracula. Posters for
the film actually pictured Lugosi in his most famous role.
The stills from the film intimate that perhaps SANTO CON-
TRA EL BARON BRAKOLA is a Mexican version of HORROR
OF DRACULA, with Santo substituting for Van Helsing.
Brakola claims a female victim who is saved by blood transfusions. The vampire grins with bloody fangs and later digs
a grave for his entranced victim. Finally, he and Santo
battle each other until the wrestler destroys the vicious vampire. (The film is also known under the simpler title, EL
BARON BRAKOLA.)

Santo did not encounter the actual Count Dracula himself until 1968, in Calderon's SANTO EN EL TESORO DE
DRACULA ("Santo and the Treasure of Dracula"), a film
which is also widely known under the title EL VAMPIRO Y
EL SEXO ("The Vampire and Sex"). This was one of the
new image Santo pictures, filmed in color and showcasing a
line of almost totally nude chorus girls. The film, as directed by Rene Cardona, proved that Santo and his comic
book heroics could also appeal to adults.

Through a revolutionary scientific device, a girl is
regressed to a previous incarnation where she had been the
victim of Count Dracula. Santo follows her escapades of a
century ago on a time-television screen, observing Dracula
incognito (again) as Count Alucard. The vampire is unmasked
when someone astutely notices that he does not have a mirror
image. Presently he is staked through the heart. Back in
the present, the masked wrestler locates Dracula's grave and
takes his royal ring (the treasure of the title). Villains remove the stake fastening Dracula to his grave, thereby freeing him. After a physical battle with the burly Santo, Dracula again receives a stake through the heart.

The following year Santo teamed up with Mexico's second most popular masked wrestler to battle another Dracula-
type vampire who preferred not to use the name of the famed
Count. SANTO Y BLUE DEMON CONTRA LOS MONSTRUOS
("Santo and Blue Demon vs. the Monsters") was a color film
made by Cinematografica and directed by Gilberto Martinez

Solares. Simply called the Vampire (David Alvizu), this
Dracula-like character and his bride joined forces with a
Mexican version of Frankenstein's Monster, the Wolf Man,
the Mummy, the Cyclops and a creature from another world
to battle the two masked heroes.

The villainous Bruno Halder (Carlos Ancira) is revived
from the dead and proceeds to make an evil duplicate of Blue
Demon who has gotten into his castle. The mad scientist
then goes on to revive the most famous monsters in the world
to be his slaves. The Vampire is discovered in a cave below the castle, first appearing as a bat on the wall. Later
he bites a number of girls, transforming them into his bare-
breasted vampire harem. In a later scene, not unlike the
one in Santo's first vampiric adventure, the Vampire is made-
up as a human wrestler scheduled to fight the silver-masked
hero in the arena. When the Vampire reveals his true nature
and attempts to fang Santo, he is repelled by a cross, then
flies away in bat form. Pandemonium follows as the other
monsters enter the ring. In the final reel of the film, Santo
goes to the castle, where he defeats the false Blue Demon
and brings the real hero back to consciousness. The two
masked men then defeat the band of monsters, staking the
vampires in their subterranean haunt and using the laboratory
apparatus to blow up the castle, in the tradition of many horror films. SANTO Y BLUE DEMON CONTRA LOS MON-
STRUOS suffered from an apparently lower budget than some
of Santo's earlier black and white films. The eerie atmosphere of such films as EL SANTO CONTRA LAS MUJERES
VAMPIRAS was also lacking, with much of the action ludicrous even for Santo. *

Blue Demon was also the star of his own series of
action films, including LA SOMBRA DEL MURCIELAGO ("The
Shadow of the Bat"), a 1966 film directed by Federico Curiel
for Vargara. The posters for the film intimate that vampires might be featured. The blue-masked hero encountered
not only Count Dracula (Cesar Silva) but also the Frankenstein Monster (Tarzan Moreno) and a zombie (Luis Mariscal)
in the 1972 film, LA INVASION DE LOS MUERTOS ("The Invasion of the Dead"), directed by Rene Cordona.

Next year both masked wrestlers were again fighting
side by side in Calderon's SANTO Y BLUE DEMON CONTRA

*The film is also known under the title SANTO CONTRA LOS
MONSTROS DE FRANKENSTEIN.

DRACULA Y EL HOMBRE LOBO ("Santo and Blue Demon vs. Dracula and the Wolf Man"), made in color and directed by Miguel M. Delgado. A scientist who possesses a knife with mystic properties is a friend of both Santo and Blue Demon. Dracula is revived when the scientist's throat is cut and blood allowed to spill into the vampire's coffin. The Count, along with his cane, materializes in the casket, while the Wolf Man returns to life in a second coffin. The two monsters then become involved with a gang of crooks, one of whom is a hunchback. Dracula later tries to vampirize Santo's girlfriend but is driven back by the magical knife. The hunchback, holding the knife, also confronts the girl. But the weapon turns in his hand and stabs him in the stomach. Dracula, meanwhile, has created a horde of vampires while the Wolf Man has produced a number of werewolves, all of whom inhabit the house where the two master fiends are hiding. Even the slain scientist, his throat still cut, haunts the premises. Blue Demon battles some vampires and werewolves, tossing one of the latter into a pit of stakes. The hero almost suffers the same doom but Santo rescues him. After a fierce battle, Santo and Blue Demon kick Dracula and the Wolf Man into the stake pit, after which the other monstrous creatures of the house mysteriously disappear.

In 1974 the wrestling Santo continued to battle against the un-dead, including a Dracula-style vampire, in the color film SANTO EN LA VENGANZA DE LA MUJERES VAMPIRO ("Santo and the Vengeance of the Vampire Women").

Most Mexican vampires are portrayed in the image of Count Dracula regardless of their names. German Robles, Mexico's answer to Lugosi and Lee, enacted his first of many vampire roles in 1956. The film was EL VAMPIRO (seen in the United States under its translated title, THE VAMPIRE), directed by Fernando Mendez for Cinematografica. As Count Lavud, Robles was a carbon copy of Lugosi's Dracula, dressed in tuxedo and cape and with a royal medallion hung over his chest. But Count Lavud also boasted a set of canine fangs, apparently the first ever shown in a Dracula-type motion picture.

In EL VAMPIRO a young girl named Marta (Ariadna Welter) visits the farm owned by her two elderly aunts. Marta and Dr. Enrique (Abel Salazar, who also produced the film), who is attending her aunts, ride in the cart of a man who says he is delivering a box of dirt to a Mr. Duval (another backwards spelling). At the house Marta learns that one of her aunts has died. But the other aunt, Eloisa (Carmen Montejo), resembles a young woman. Eloisa is actually under the power of Count Lavud, who rises from his grave to receive the box of earth. Then he swears to bring his vampire brother back to life, so that the two of them can prey upon the countryside. Count Lavud enters Marta's room in bat form and takes her blood. When Marta later discovers that Eloisa casts no reflection, the aunt slips her a drug which gives her the semblance of death. Marta is nearly buried alive before Dr. Enrique saves her. In the final scenes, Count Lavud takes Marta's body to a secret chamber where the other aunt still lives. Lavud and Dr. Enrique battle one another while the old aunt strangles Eloisa, causing her to revert to her true age. Then, after Count Lavud returns to his coffin, the woman long believed dead shoves a long wooden shaft through his heart. *

Despite the gothic atmosphere of EL VAMPIRO, the film pales beside American films of the same nature. The picture was popular in its native country, though, enough so for producer Salazar to make a sequel in 1957, EL ATAUD DEL VAMPIRO ("The Vampire's Coffin"), again directed by Méndez. A mad scientist and his assistant (played by Mexican horror films star, Yeire Beirute) steal the impaled body of Count Lavud, proving its identity by the skeletal reflection it throws in a mirror. Later, the assistant removes the stake in order to steal the vampire's medallion, inadvertently reviving Count Lavud and becoming his slave. Little happens in this film, other than some impressive shadow work while Lavud determines to recapture his Marta (Ariadna Welter again). Lavud abducts the girl and takes her to his lair, a dark wax museum. The final confrontation between Count Lavud and Dr. Enrique (Salazar) is in the museum, where she falls beneath the raised blade of a guillotine. Enrique attempts to destroy the vampire with a spear, but Lavud continues to vanish. At last Count Lavud transforms into a bat which the doctor manages to pin against the wall with a thrust of his javelin. Regaining his human form, the vampire remains fastened to the wall. Marta, naturally, revives and slips out of the guillotine only moments before the deadly blade comes crashing down.

Count Lavud did not return to the screen. Yet German Robles' vampire career was only beginning. In 1960

---

*EL VAMPIRO was released in France as LES PROIES DU VAMPIRE ("The Prey of the Vampire").

Robles starred in four Mexican films chronicling the adventures of the vampire Nostradamus, a descendant of the original Nostradamus who made his famous predictions.   The vampire Nostradamus was clothed entirely in black, with the usual black cloak, a small hat, and with a face sporting a Satanic mustache and beard.   Nostradamus was totally evil and ruthless in his attempts to establish a vampire cult.   He was aided in his endeavors by a ludicrous hunchbacked assistant named Leo who had the distinction of being one of the most slovenly and unsavory characters ever to lope across the screen.

In LA MALDICION DE NOSTRADAMUS (THE CURSE OF NOSTRADAMUS) the vampire is established as a creature who must sleep in a coffin containing the ashes of his ancestors. It is also stated that the only bullets that can destroy him are those made of platinum, thereby making him a bit more expensive to eliminate than Count Dracula himself.   Nostradamus intimidates the Van Helsing-like Professor Dolan (Domingo Soler) and threatens to claim the lives of thirteen unlucky people unless the man of science cooperates.   This first film in the series ends with Nostradamus trapped in a tunnel cave-in.   The film was made with little imagination and on an incredibly low budget, as were all the entries to this series.

The second film: NOSTRADAMUS Y EL DESTRUCTOR DE MONSTRUOS ("Nostradamus and the Destroyer of Monsters"), is known on American television as MONSTER DEMOLISHER.   This time Nostradamus returns from his previous entrapment to enslave a condemned murderer.   He is foiled when Dolan uses an electronic device that employs sound waves to torment bats (and human vampires).   In NOSTRADAMUS, EL GENIO DE LAS TINIEBLAS ("Nostradamus, the Genius from the Dark"), seen on American TV as GENII OF DARKNESS, the vampire destroys his ancient enemy Igor and eventually falls in love.   Dolan and a group of townspeople storm the vampire's tomb and steal the ashes from his coffin.   Later Dolan scatters the coveted ashes to the wind.   But in the final entry, LA SANGRE DE NOSTRADAMUS (THE BLOOD OF NOSTRADAMUS), the vampire reveals that he substituted the ashes with others.   This longest (and, hence, most unbearable) of the Nostradamus films ends with the police pursuing the vampire with platinum bullets.   Finally Nostradamus comes to a welcomed doom by the timeless stake through the heart.   All of the Nostradamus films were ploddingly directed by Frederick Curiel.   The series seems to have been compiled from episodes of a Mexican television series.

Another blatant imitation of the American Dracula films was EL MUNDO DE LOS VAMPIROS ("The World of the Vampire"), directed in 1960 by Alfonso Corona Blake for Cinematografica. As in the Count Lavud films, the producer was Abel Salazar. The carbon-copy Dracula is now called Subotay and commands a horde of cloaked and cowled vampires beneath an old house. Subotay uses a huge pipe-organ composed of human bones to control his un-dead. Eventually he hopes to completely exterminate mankind. But first he must have vengeance upon the Colman family whose ancestors once fought the vampires. In his Dracula-like outfit, Subotay visits the Colman house during a party when a young man named Rudolpho plays music which affects the living dead. The vampire puts Leonor Colman under his spell and then flees the strange musical strains. Subotay continues his attacks on the Colmans until Rudolpho tracks him to his lair and destroys his minions with his specialized music. Rudolpho then battles Subotay physically, maneuvering him to plunge into a pit of stakes (though why a vampire would reside near such a pit is never explained). EL MUNDO DE LOS VAMPIROS was one of the better Mexican vampire films, especially in the atmosphere created with the monk-like undead parading before the awesome organ. *

Yet another Mexican Dracula imitation that became a short-running series character was Count Frankenhausen, portrayed by Carlos Agosti. In quality the Count Frankenhausen films lie somewhere between the Count Lavud and Nostradamus series. Count Frankenhausen wore satiny black and a flowing cape, which would trail behind him as he ran, with arms raised, down the murky corridors of his chateau.

---

*The Italian magazine Malia, which during the 1960s published a series of fumettis based on frame blowups from horror films, included an adaptation of EL MUNDO DE LOS VAMPIROS under the title, "La Vendetta del Vampire" ("The Revenge of the Vampire"). Among the other adaptations in Malia of Dracula and Dracula-type vampire films were "Il Risveglio di Dracula" ("The Revival of Dracula"), based on THE RETURN OF DRACULA; "Dracula Nella Casa Degli Orrori" ("Dracula in the House of Horror"), based on HOUSE OF DRACULA; "Il Vampiro dell'Opera"; and "L'Amante del Vampiro."

The first film of the series made by Tele-Talia was EL VAMPIRO SANGRIENTO (THE BLOODY VAMPIRE), made in 1961. There are some atmospheric scenes at the beginning of the film showing a black coach, driven by a cowled skeleton, silently rolling through the mists in slow motion (obviously inspired by a similar scene in Bava's MASCHERA DEL DEMONIO). Otherwise, the film was tedious and mundane. Count Frankenhausen rises from his "trunk," which is set before a rather Halloween-looking skull emblem. The vampires' trunks in this film might have made Houdini envious, for at a mere command the sides flap open. Count Frankenhausen goes to great lengths to transform his wife into a vampire. The ending of the film is strange, showing the dead wife lying upon the beach, and Frankenhausen, in bat form, escaping unharmed. The film is also known simply as COUNT FRANKENHAUSEN.

The second and final Count Frankenhausen film was LA INVASION DE LOS VAMPIROS (THE INVASION OF THE VAMPIRES), which was made the next year. Count Frankenhausen now plans to invade the world with an army of vampires under his command. A scientist opposes the vampiric nobleman with a mysterious black flower called the Mandagora, which has a toxic effect upon the un-dead. When Frankenhausen is finally staked in bat form, his former victims return to pseudo-life with their stakes still protruding from their chests. Both EL VAMPIRO SANGRIENTO and LE INVASION DE LOS VAMPIROS were written and directed by Miguel Morayta. Their only real asset, as with many of the Mexican horror films, is atmosphere.

Another Dracula-type vampire menaced the famous hero and heroine of CAPURCITA Y PULGARCITO CONTRA LOS MONSTRUOS ("Little Red Riding Hood and Tom Thumb vs. the Monsters"), a film also known simply as LITTLE RED RIDING HOOD AND THE MONSTERS. * The picture was made in color during the early 1960s by Peliculas-Rodriguez and was directed by Roberto Rodriguez.

ECHENME AL VAMPIRO ("Throw Me to the Vampire"), a 1965 Clasa-Mohme film, seen on American television as

_____
*The film is a sequel to LA CAPURCITA ROJA ("Little Red Riding Hood") and CAPURCITA Y SUS TRES AMIGOS ("Little Red Riding Hood and Her Three Friends") known in the US as LITTLE RED RIDING HOOD AND HER FRIENDS. Both films were made in 1959.

BRING ME THE VAMPIRE, was a rather unfunny comedy in which a group of heirs must remain for some time in a haunted castle to collect their fortune. The owner of the castle is a vampire in the Dracula mold who engages his guests in some obvious situations. The film was directed by Alfredo B. Cravenna. In 1966 a Dracula-style vampire, along with a werewolf and some headless horsemen, fights a cowboy hero in EL CHARRO DE LAS CALVERAS ("The Rider of the Skulls"), a Western horror film directed by Alfredo Salazar and released by Columbia. A character in a black cloak is buried alive and then returns from the grave seeking revenge in the Mexican nudie of 1969, LOVE AFTER DEATH, directed by Glauco Del Mar. At the end of the film the fiend flashes away to nothingness. LOVE AFTER DEATH is also known under the French titles, DE VANPIER VAN NEW YORK and LE VANPIRE DE NEW YORK ("The Vampire of New York"). Still another Dracula-type vampire was prominently featured in Cinematografica's 1971 color film, CHANOC CONTRA EL TIGRE Y EL VAMPIRO ("Chanoc vs. the Tiger and the Vampire"), directed by Gilberto Martinez Solares and starring comedian Tin-Tan. Producciones Zacarias' CAPULINA CONTRA LOS VAMPIROS (color, 1973) also upheld this tradition.

DRACULA UNDERGROUND

Dracula's "underground" adventures do not necessarily refer to his spending the daylight hours in some dank grave. The Count has been the subject of a number of "underground" movies, or independently produced motion pictures usually made in 16mm by a single film-maker. Underground movies are most often released through a network of independent film-makers to specialty theatres or are rented for public or private use through film cooperative organizations.

Andy Warhol, at one time considered to be the king of both the cinema underground and the "Pop Art" movement of the sixties, delved into the Dracula film in 1964. But Warhol's Dracula ventures leave the question: Did he make one, two, or even three underground Dracula productions?

The first Warhol title in this line was simply called DRACULA, a film starring Naomi Levine. That same year Warhol made a two-hour film in black and white, titled BATMAN DRACULA. Shot in New York City, the film starred

Jack Smith as Dracula and featured Warhol discovery, Baby Jane Holzer. The picture was noted for Warhol's first use of the zoom lens for its own sake. Warhol never completed BATMAN DRACULA. But there is a listing for yet another Warhol title of 1964, BATMAN, with Smith again as Dracula. Whether or not these three titles actually refer to the same film is not known. DRACULA, BATMAN DRACULA and BATMAN were all released through Film-makers' Cooperative.

THE EYE OF COUNT FLICKENSTEIN was a Dracula parody made by Tony Conrad in 1966. The short subject moved for a close-up to show television static in the Count's eye. Mike Jacobson made DRACULA'S WEDDING DAY the following year. This black and white film, tinted purple, shows Dracula entrancing a girl and leading her to his cave at sunset. About 1967, Harrison Marks starred as Dracula III along with Wendy Luton as Carmilla in VAMPIRE, a film made by Tony Roberts. The film combined sex and vampire lore.

Another American underground film, entitled A TRIP WITH DRACULA, was made in 1970. That same year Forrest J Ackerman guided a tour through his museum home of science fiction, fantasy and horror history, pointing out his Dracula memorabilia, in SCIENCE FICTION FILMS, made at the University of Kansas. In 1971 Tom Baker included some Dracula imagery in his dramatic documentary, BONGO WOLF'S REVENGE, a film about William Donald Grollman (known in real life as Bongo Wolf). The feature-length film included footage taken at a Count Dracula Society meeting and showed some of its members wearing capes and medals. RENDEVOUS, a 1973 film by Cortlandt B. Hull, took appropriate scenes from films like DRACULA (1931), SON OF DRACULA, HOUSE OF DRACULA, HORROR OF DRACULA and NOSFERATU and set them to the music of Frank Sinatra's "Strangers in the Night."

Often, the line between underground films and student or amateur films is virtually invisible. Student and amateur films are often shown on television or in theatres and have been deemed important enough by Walt Lee for inclusion in his Reference Guide to Fantastic Films. Among such films are CURSE OF DRACULA, made by Anthony Brezezinski's Adventure Films Productions about 1957. Brezezinski followed this production with BLACK INFERNO, which included a scene in which Dracula lures a female victim to himself in a cemetery. After this, Brezezinski attempted an amateur feature-length film of the original DRACULA.

Bob Greenberg, who has since become a professional film-maker, made PAWNS OF SATAN (color, about 1959), starring Richard Christy as Dracula. The Count menaces the neighborhood until Van Helsing tracks him to his crypt and stakes him. One of the most ambitious amateur Dracula films was Glenn Sherrard's 1966 remake of HORROR OF DRACULA. Sherrard (who played Dracula) imitated the make-ups, costumes, sets and storyline of the original. After this Sherrard planned to film REVENGE OF DRACULA, his own remake of DRACULA, PRINCE OF DARKNESS. The Delta SF Film Group made CASTLE OF DRACULA, a British color film of 1958. SHADOW OF DRACULA, an hour-long amateur film made in 1973 in Toronto, may be released theatrically.

Before becoming a writer I made amateur films, many of which featured Dracula. In a number of these I assumed the role of the Count or of his teenaged son. In FRANKEN-STEIN MEETS DRACULA and RETURN OF THE WOLFMAN (both color, 1957) Dracula (Victor Fabian) revives the Frankenstein Monster but is eventually staked through the heart. REVENGE OF DRACULA (1958) again had the Count reviving the Monster before his blood-craving drives him out seeking a victim at dawn. THE TEENAGE FRANKENSTEIN (1959) showed Dracula (Gene Gronemeyer) again getting staked, while SLAVE OF THE VAMPIRE (1959) had the Count battling and being staked by his slave, the Wolf Man.

Teenage monster movies were popular in the late fifties, and since I was a greasy teenager in those days, I turned to making a series of films starring the Count's greasy vampire son. I WAS A TEENAGE VAMPIRE (color, 1959) brought the young Dracula in contact with a typical 1950s leather-jacketed gang before futilely trying to reach the graveyard (via motorcycle) before sunrise. In MONSTER RUMBLE (color, 1961) the same vampire becomes involved with a horde of monsters before reviving the Teenage Frankenstein and perishing by stake and sun. DRAGSTRIP DRACULA (part color, 1962) had him revived again, only to meet doom beneath the morning sun.

DRACULA BY ANY OTHER NAME

The vampires of folklore are rarely noblemen of Dracula's stature. They usually spend their daylight hours in some dirty grave rather than in the opulence of a castle crypt. Yet the un-dead continue to appear in films wearing immaculate formal wear and long opera capes in order to capitalize on Count Dracula's reputation. Instead of wearing some more practical garb, motion picture vampires prefer to resemble the Count so obtrusively that any sub-teen monster fan can identify them on the spot.

CRY OF THE WEREWOLF (Columbia 1944), which went into production as DAUGHTER OF THE WEREWOLF, included a scene set in a horror museum showing a vampire exhibit with a manikin resembling Count Dracula. The year 1960 offered the Italian film, L'ULTIMA PREDA DEL VAMPIRO ("The Vampire's Last Victim"), directed by Piero Regnoli for Nord Film Italiana. Released in the United States as THE PLAYGIRLS AND THE VAMPIRE, the film starred Walter Brandi in a dual role as Count Gabor Kernassy and his twin brother who happens to be a vampire. In this "sexploitation" film a group of showgirls stays at the Castle Kernassy, where the Dracula-like vampire finds them to be delectable prey. In France the film was titled DES FILLES POUR UN VAMPIRE ("The Daughters of the Vampire"), and in Belgium, DESIRS DE VAMPIRE ("Desires of the Vampire"). On television the film plays as CURSE OF THE VAMPIRE.

An Italian film made by Pao in the early sixties was L'URLO DEL VAMPIRO ("The Cry of the Vampire"), directed by T. Fec. This time the vampire, including hat and cape in his attire, disintegrates much as Christopher Lee did in his first vampire epic.

Yet another Italian Dracula-type film was IL VAMPIRO DELL'OPERA ("The Vampire of the Opera"), directed by Renato Polselli and made by NIF in 1961. Giuseppe Addobati portrayed the vampire. Since the vampire was a devotee of the opera he was one un-dead character who had reason to appear in tails and opera cape. The film was a type of combination DRACULA and THE PHANTOM OF THE OPERA. When a theatrical troupe reopens the Paris Opera House, a ghost interrupts their rehearsals and warns them to leave. The ghost's master, a vampire, begins to attend the rehearsals and attack the various performers. The vampire takes the play's star down to his subterranean haunt, where his female vampire slaves are chained to the wall. The hero of the film tries to destroy the vampire by burning his portrait but succeeds only in burning the fiend's skin. The vampire is finally trapped upon the stage as the performers set

him ablaze with their torches.   IL VAMPIRO DELL'OPERA
is also known as MONSTER OF THE OPERA.

That same year Polselli directed L'AMANTE DEL
VAMPIRO ("The Vampire's Lover") for the Italian company,
CIF.   The film had a typical plot.   Two female members of
a ballet troupe are caught in a rainstorm and forced to take
refuge in a castle inhabited by two vampires, the Contessa
(Maria Luisa Rolando) and her cloaked servant (played by
Iscaro Ravajoli).   But a unique aspect of the film was in the
manner that the servant drank the blood of the ballerinas,
then offered his own neck to the Contessa.   As she drains
off his stolen blood he reverts to an ancient, withered man.
The climax of the film was directly inspired by HORROR OF
DRACULA.   The hero forms a cross from a knife and a can-
dlestick then drives the vampires out into the brightening sky.
The two vampires melt and crumble much as Lee did in
1958, to be finally blown away as dust in the morning wind.
The film is also known as VAMPIRE AND THE BALLERINA.

LA STRAGE DEI VAMPIRI ("The Slaughter of the Vampires"), an Italian film of 1962, written and directed by Roberto Mauri, was a blatant imitation of Dracula.   Two vampires, one resembling Dracula and the other being his female
companion, are pursued by irate villagers.   The vampiress
is impaled by a pitchfork while the mule escapes.   The story
proceeds with the Dracula-like vampire making attacks on a
woman who soon becomes un-dead.   Her husband, a doctor,
seeks the aid of a Van Helsing-type vampire hunter.   The
two of them hunt down the vampires and the husband presses
the spikes of an iron gate into the Dracula-type character's
chest.   The film was released to television as SLAUGHTER
OF THE VAMPIRES and shown in American theatres years
later as CURSE OF THE BLOOD-GHOULS.   In France it was
known as VAMPIRE, HOMME OU FEMME? ("Vampire, Man
or Woman?").

American films also perpetuated the Dracula image
under different names.   PARIS WHEN IT SIZZLES (Paramount 1964) was a color film directed by Richard Quine.   The
movie included a fantasy sequence in which William Holden as
a Dracula-style vampire chased Audrey Hepburn about a cave.
The film is also known as THE GIRL WHO STOLE THE
EIFFEL TOWER.

Vampirism and Black Magic were mixed in DEVILS OF
DARKNESS, a film made in color in 1965 by the British

company Planet. It was directed by Lance Comfort and released in the United States the following year by 20th Century-
Fox. During the sixteenth century a Gypsy girl named Tania
(Carole Gray) dies when a mysterious flash of light appears
at her own wedding. Later, a bat flies over her coffin and
metamorphoses into the cloaked Count Sinistre (Hubert Noel),
who commands her to awaken and follow him through time.
In the twentieth century the Count, known as Armond, wears
modern clothing and commands "The Devils of Darkness," an
occult group hoping to attain immortality through Black Magic,
voodoo and Satanism. Sinistre is about to cut a girl's wrists
for the blood ritual when lightning strikes the old mansion
where the group is meeting, destroying the Count and his followers.

ORGY OF THE DEAD (Astra 1966), directed by A. C.
Stevens, was a nudie made in color by Edward D. Wood, Jr.
Although the film is also known as ORGY OF THE VAM-
PIRES, it has no real vampires. Criswell appeared as the
"Prince of Darkness," clad Dracula-like in black cloak, rising from a coffin to join the Princess of Darkness, a werewolf and a mummy in their harassment of a young couple one
moonlit night. A beam of light from a skull-tipped magic
wand finally decomposes both Prince and Princess to bones. *

Ironically, one of the finest vampire films ever made
also happened to be a satire of the genre. DANCE OF THE
VAMPIRES, a color film made in 1967 by Cadre and Film-
ways, was Roman Polanski's tribute to the Dracula film.
Polanski wrote, directed and starred in this superb black
comedy which, humor notwithstanding, was also a superb horror film. (Perhaps it is also ironic that two of the most
outstanding vampire pictures of all, DANCE OF THE VAM-
PIRES and NOSFERATU, were made by directors not usually
associated with the horror film.)

The Transylvania that Polanski created in the motion
picture is so atmospheric and replete with meticulous detail
that the viewer gets the impression that the film was shot on

---

*The original shooting title of ORGY OF THE DEAD was the
less obtrusive REVENGE OF THE DEAD. Edward D. Wood,
Jr., the writer of the film, also prepared a novel, Orgy of
the Dead, complete with photographs from the movie. The
book was published in 1966 by Greenleaf Classics, with a
special introduction by Forrest J Ackerman, using both his
real name and nom de plume, "Dr. Acula."

location.   Again there is the vampiric count; not Dracula,
but Count Von Krolock, played with a masterful touch of grim
humor by Ferdy Mayne.   Polanski managed to take Count Von
Krolock and the numerous other vampires infesting Transylvania through all the old vampire clichés.   Yet the clichés
seemed to vanish amid the new humorous situations that Polanski derived from the old vampire trappings.   The film
was the first to show the Jewish vampire who, when his victim attempts to ward him off with a cross, laughs and remarks, does she ever have the wrong vampire.

DANCE OF THE VAMPIRES co-starred Sharon Tate,
who would eventually marry Polanski, as Sarah, the beautiful
young daughter of the innkeepers.   While bathing in wooden
tub, Sarah looks to the overhead transom and sees Count Von
Krolock, baring his fangs and watching her with feral delight.
Leaping down upon her, the Count makes her his victim and
his captive.   Rescuing Sarah becomes the task of the Van
Helsing-like Professor Abronsius, a skinny wild-haired old
man who is an authority on vampires.   The Professor, accompanied by his boyish assistant Alfred (Polanski in a role
that seems to have been visually patterned after the character Hutter in NOSFERATU), journey across the snow-blanket-
ed hills and arrive at the castle of Count Von Krolock (a
name perhaps based on Orlock in NOSFERATU).   The Count
self-consciously covers his mouth when he reveals too much
fang.   Herbert Von Krolock (Iain Quarrier), the Count's
blond homosexual son, tries to seduce Alfred.   As Alfred
runs from the anxious vampire he again encounters Sarah,
once again in the midst of a bubble bath.   The Professor and
Alfred then set out to save the girl before Count Von Krolock
can summon all the other vampires together for the special
ball to be held at the castle, during which Sarah will be in-
itiated into the ranks of the un-dead.   The vampires that arrive are all dressed in the garb of past centuries, one hunchbacked member seeming to be Richard III.   During the dance
Abronsius and Alfred surreptitiously mingle among the gray-
faced creatures, but their reflections betray them in the large
ballroom mirror.   After an exciting escape over the snow-
covered hills, the Professor drives a sled, with the loving
couple, Alfred and Sarah, riding in back.   Then Sarah looks
toward Alfred, bares her new vampire fangs and bites.

Polanski became engaged in a feud with co-producer
Martin Ranschohoff, who insisted on releasing his own cut of
the film to the United States and also dubbing someone else's
voice into Polanski's mouth.   The move prompted Polanski to

demand his name be removed from the picture.   Ranshohoff's
shorter version of the film was released to American theatres as THE FEARLESS VAMPIRE KILLERS, OR PARDON
ME, BUT YOUR TEETH ARE IN MY NECK.   Having never
seen Polanski's cutting of the film, I find little, if any, fault
with what was shown on the American screens.   The original
shooting title of the film was YOUR TEETH IN MY NECK.
On television the title became merely THE FEARLESS VAM-
PIRE KILLERS.

A Dracula-style vampire appeared in the American
nudie, VAMPIRE'S LOVE, made by an independent producer
in 1969.   That same year Dan Rowan and Dick Martin starred
in THE MALTESE BIPPY, made in color by MGM, spoofing
old mystery and horror films.   Fritz Weaver played Ravens-
wood, a phony werewolf who looks and dresses like Dracula.
During a dream sequence Rowan also appears in the same
tuxedo and cape and brandishes a wooden stake.   Norman
Panama directed.   The shooting title of the film was THE
STRANGE CASE OF ... !#*%? and was also known before
release as THE INCREDIBLE WEREWOLF MURDERS and
WHO KILLED COCK RUBIN?

Dracula-type vampires also left their toothy marks in
TORE NG DIYABLO ("Tower of the Devil"), directed in the
Philippines by Lauro Pacheo.   Based on Nela Morales' serial
appearing in Lagim Komiks, the movie concerned vampires
attempting to get a strange pregnant woman who sucks the
blood of lizards to bear a vampire son.   The vampire leader
(played by Ramon D'Salva) leads his followers against a pack
of werewolves until all the monsters are destroyed by an
earthquake in this preposterous film.

The Dracula-type vampire returned to marvelous comedy in THE HOUSE THAT DRIPPED BLOOD (Amicus, 1970),
a color film directed by Peter Duffell.   The British movie
was scripted by Robert Bloch and showcased four individual
episodes based on his previously published short stories.
There was a frame story in which Detective Inspector Holloway (John Bennett) comes to a house in search of missing
horror-films actor Paul Henderson (Jon Pertwee).   Included
were such characters as "A. J. Stoker" (the house proprietor,
played by John Bryans) and "Theo Von Hartmann" (named in
part after Dr. Franz Hartmann, a nineteenth century occult
scholar, writer and vampire hunter) and such props as a
copy of the novel Dracula.   The first episode, "Waxworks,"
numbered among the wax exhibits a figure in the image of
Christopher Lee's Count Dracula.

The film also presented an adaptation of Bloch's vampire story, "The Cloak." Aging Paul Henderson is about to star in a quickie horror film, CURSE OF THE BLOODSUCKERS, and pines for the days of the original DRACULA. "The one with Bela Lugosi, of course," he says. "Not the new fella." (Christopher Lee starred in an earlier segment of the film.) In a rage, Henderson pokes his cane through the cardboard set and rejects the shoddy cape he is to wear in the film. The actor hunts down an old curio shop where the weird proprietor, Theo Von Hartmann (Geoffrey Balydon), sells him a rather authentic-looking cape. At home Henderson dons the cape and discovers that his mirror image is gone. During the filming of his movie, the actor really bites leading lady Carla (Ingrid Pitt). That midnight, Henderson, still wearing the cloak, grows fangs and floats off the floor. When he eventually confesses to Carla what the cloak has made him, she bares her fangs and rises toward the ceiling to meet him, saying that the vampires had so admired his performances that they wanted him to become one of them. The film concludes with the skeptic Holloway searching the house and encountering the vampiric Henderson rising from his casket. After shoving a stake through the creature, the detective is attacked by Carla.

Two years before BLACULA, American-International Pictures released the first of a new series of Dracula-like movies made by Michael Macready's Erica Productions. The film went into production as VAMPYRE but when previewed for AIP executives, was changed to include the name of its leading vampire, THE LOVES OF COUNT IORGA. Seeing the financial possibilities in this low-budget film, the studio shortened a number of the scenes and released the picture in 1970 with the new title, COUNT YORGA, VAMPIRE (Iorga and Yorga being pronounced the same).

Count Yorga was portrayed by Robert Quarry, with pale face, upper and lower fangs, black clothing and cape. "After all these years, I thought it'd be great fun to play a vampire," Quarry said during an interview conducted by Al Satian and myself. "There's been no enduring character to come along. I think that's one of the reasons COUNT YORGA caught on--he's sort of the first new kind of horror figure, even though he's a direct steal from Dracula. But at least the action is in a modern setting, he's a little more with what's happening today than poor old Dracula, who's always lurking around with coach and horses." Count Yorga was charming, humorous, sarcastic and cynical. And he enjoyed some genuinely chilling scenes, stalking in slow motion with fangs bared, eyes wide, hands outreaching, as the soundtrack whined with blaring effects.

A coffin is driven through modern day Los Angeles in the back of a truck and taken to an old mansion. Later, Count Yorga conducts a seance at a gathering of young people. The vampire arranges for two of them, Paul (Michael Murphy) and his girlfriend Erica (Judith Lang), to be stranded in the woods in their camper. Erica becomes Yorga's victim and gradually reverts to a vampiric state, going so far as to devour a pet cat. Inevitably Paul, his friend Michael (Michael Macready) and young Dr. Hayes (Roger Perry) consult old texts to learn what any movie-going child would know--that a vampire is at large. Erica and Michael's girlfriend Donna (Donna Anders) are at Yorga's mansion. The mortal intruders battle Yorga and his vampire harem, with the Count receiving a broomstick through the chest. Michael and Donna are the only people left alive and she attacks him with her new fangs (a scene inspired by DANCE OF THE VAMPIRES and fast becoming cliché).

COUNT YORGA, VAMPIRE proved that a profitable and impressive film could be made on an economic budget. The script was well written and Quarry's performance was memorable. Bob Kelljan directed the vampire Count in accordance with modern times. AIP executives were sufficiently impressed to order a sequel.

THE RETURN OF COUNT YORGA, again directed by Kelljan, was released in 1971. No explanation was given as to how Count Yorga (Quarry again) survived from the last film. (Obviously someone removed the broomstick between movies.) Now the Count resides in a chateau neighboring an orphanage. A young orphan named Tommy (Phillip Frame) encounters the Count and his female vampires in the woods. Later, Yorga attends a masquerade party at the orphanage, where he takes an immediate dislike to a man in a shabby Dracula costume. He also takes an immediate romantic interest in Cynthia Nelson (Mariette Hartley), an orphanage employee whose fiancé is Dr. David Baldwin (Roger Perry). In a scene capitalizing on the Manson murders, Yorga sends his vampire harem to invade the Nelson home. Cynthia is spared the blood orgy and is taken to the mansion, where the Count professes his love and offers her immortality. The film ends with a police raid on the vampire mansion. Baldwin fights Yorga who is stabbed through the chest with a knife and plummets off the balcony. In an imitation of its predecessor, the final shot shows the vampiric Baldwin attacking Cynthia. CURSE OF COUNT YORGA and THE ABOMINABLE COUNT YORGA were two titles considered for the film before its release.

For a while AIP considered making another Yorga film, also guest-starring Quarry as the Count in DR. PHIBES RISES AGAIN (1972). But the final decision was to cast the actor in the role of a near immortal man. Yet Quarry did wear his Count Yorga fangs to star as a vampire washed ashore in California to become a hippie guru in THE DEATH-MASTER, a film announced as KHORDA and made in 1971 by R. F. Productions and World Entertainment Productions. American-International released it the following year. Quarry did, however, make a guest appearance as Count Yorga in a costume-party sequence of the Vincent Price film, MAD-HOUSE (1974).

Perhaps not to be outdone by AIP's first Yorga film, Lobo Productions released a sex movie in 1971 with the title COUNT EROTICA VAMPIRE. The film was made in color, directed by Tony Teresi and starred John Peters, Mary Simon and Paul Robinson.

That same year Hammer Films did a variation on their own Dracula films in VAMPIRE CIRCUS, a picture directed by Englishman Robert Young and released in color by 20th Century-Fox. In a Serbian village, circa 1810, Anna Mueller, wife of one of the villagers, lures a child victim to the castle of Count Mitterhouse (Robert Tayman), a handsome and virile vampire with, thus far, the longest fangs in Hammer history. Discovering this, Anna's husband leads the villagers to storm the castle. Mitterhouse is staked but before dying, curses the village and whispers to Anna to summon his cousin Emil. Fifteen years later the town is beset by a strange plague and is also visited by the mysterious Circus of the Nights, led by an earthy Gypsy woman (played by Adrienne Corri) and Emil (Anthony Corlan), a curly-haired, dark-complected character who looked more like a rock musician than a vampire. This circus of vampires enacts the Count's revenge and finally revives him with the blood of the burgomeister's daughter. But Mitterhouse's revival is short-lived, for the villagers soon return to start a blazing fire. VAMPIRE CIRCUS could have been one of Hammer's best vampire films. Tayman's feral performance as the Dracula-like Count Mitterhouse was magnificent but too brief. The film also suffered from choppy editing resulting from the censorship of nude scenes.

THE BLUE SEXTET was an independent American film of 1971 about a man who makes 8mm horror films, one of which shows Dracula-style vampires chasing naked girls through a dungeon. VIERGES ET VAMPIRES ("Virgins and Vampires") was a French sex film made by Jean Rollin in 1972, featuring Phillipe Gaste as a green-faced Dracula-type vampire, only one of a cult that preys upon young women. Two girls dressed as clowns flee their school on New Year's Eve and are eventually hypnotized by two vampire bats and lured to the castle of the un-dead. The film is also known as REQUIEM POUR UN VAMPIRE ("Requiem for a Vampire") CRAZED VAMPIRE and SEX VAMPIRES. CASUAL RELA-TIONS, a 1973 film by Mark Rappaport, included a satire of vampire films titled "A Vampire's Love," featuring Mel Aus-ton with fangs and black cape.

Count Dracula and his kin have demonstrated the im-mortality of the vampire to demanding motion picture audi-ences. Thus it was logical that people willing to pay money to see the Count on the screen would also welcome him with-out cost into the living room.

Chapter 10

STAY TUNED FOR DRACULA

> The one you love is mine already. I have known
> her. Already my mark is on her throat. Flesh
> of my flesh, blood of my blood. --Orson Welles,
> in DRACULA, on THE MERCURY THEATRE ON
> THE AIR (1938)

While Dracula's appearances were not as prolific on
radio and television as in motion pictures, Stoker's novel
was dramatized a number of times in both the audio and
video media. Coincidentally, two dramatic radio adaptations
of Dracula in the 1930s starred actors who were also associated with the voice of The Shadow, the mysterious hero who
clouded men's minds and brought criminals to justice. Both
Bret Morrison and Orson Welles brought a Shakespearean feeling to the role with their commanding resonant voices. Morrison's DRACULA, the first ever to be aired on the radio,
was a half-hour adaptation of the 1931 movie, broadcast from
Chicago radio station WCFL that same year.

The hour-long version of DRACULA which opened THE
MERCURY THEATRE ON THE AIR anthology series on the
Columbia Broadcasting System in 1938 remains the most faithful radio adaptation of the classic. Orson Welles, still a
youthful prodigy, who later that year would terrify a nation
with his WAR OF THE WORLDS broadcast of THE MERCURY
THEATRE, produced, directed and acted in DRACULA. In
the prologue of the drama Welles addressed the listening
audience:

> WELLES: Good evening. THE MERCURY THEA-
> TRE faces tonight a challenge and an opportunity to
> which we are grateful.... We are starting off to-
> night with the best story of its kind ever written.
> You will find it in every representative library of

classic English narrative. It is Bram Stoker's
Dracula. The next time I speak to you I am Dr.
Arthur Seward. George Colouris plays Jonathan
Harker. And Martin Gable plays Dr. Van Helsing.
It is Dr. Seward who tells the story, and so for
the moment, goodbye, ladies and gentlemen. I'll
see you in Transylvania.

DRACULA was presented, like Stoker's novel, as a
series of journals, diaries and letters. Much of the dialogue
was quoted directly from the book. The drama was one of
the most faithful adaptations of Dracula in any medium, with
alterations made only where necessary to condense the story
into an hour and yet retain the basic plotline and mood of
the original. Arthur Holmwood and Dr. Seward's roles were
combined into a single character while Renfield was eliminated
altogether. And the ending differed slightly from that of
Stoker.

Welles not only portrayed Dr. Seward, but also demonstrated his versatility by doubling as Count Dracula. Bor-
rowing a gimmick from The Shadow, Welles spoke Dracula's
lines through a filtered microphone which, added to his use
of a "Transylvanian" accent, presented the Count as a foreign
nobleman seemingly speaking from some nether world of the
un-dead.

Welles' DRACULA proceeds according to the plot devised by Stoker, the climax approaching when the Count is
thrust from his coffin just before sunset. Mina, hypnotically
entranced by the vampire, stares at her master. Yet before
Harker can drive home the stake, Dracula speaks.

DRACULA: Claw. Wing. Tooth. Scale. 'Tis your
flesh, death of my death, dead and un-dead. The
hand of the living is over your master. Console
ye, my children. This instant is no longer than
the space between two heartbeats. But the night
is not here. And I am lonely. Come to your
master, my children. Beguile him now in the instant of his peril. Beguile him with the sound of
your names. Claw. Wing. Tooth. Scale. Tissue of flesh.

VAN HELSING: Too late, Harker! Strike!

DRACULA: There is one very dear to me who

would not answer. My love, Mina. There is less
than a minute between me and the night. You must
speak for me. You must speak with my heart.

Then, as the eyes of Dracula turn to see the sinking
sun and the hate in them becomes a look of victory, the King
of Vampires makes a final effort to triumph.

DRACULA: Flesh of my flesh, come to me ... my
love. Come into the night and the darkness. You
have served me well, my love ... my bride.

Unexpectedly, Mina (played by actress Agnes Moore-
head) then grabs the stake from Jonathan Harker and performs the final grisly act herself.

VAN HELSING: When Mina Harker seized the stake
and hammer from her husband, I believe she was
under some form of hypnosis. She herself remem-
bers nothing. But whatever influence was at work
on her, she must, at the last moment, have re-
jected it. For at the exact instant the sun disappeared, it was Mina Harker who drove the stake
through the heart of the thing that called itself ...
Dracula.

The wounds on Mina's neck instantly vanish and the
corpse of Dracula crumbles to dust and passes from sight.
Orson Welles makes a final appearance as himself in an epilogue to remind listeners, in the tradition of Hamilton Deane
and Edward Van Sloan, "There are werewolves. There are
vampires. Such things do exist."

DRACULA, as presented by Welles on THE MERCURY
THEATRE, remains one of the finest dramatic adaptations of
Stoker's novel to date and copies of the program have fortunately been preserved. Welles not only recreated the mood
and power of Dracula, but also delved into the symbolism of
the original story. Leonard Wolf, in his book A Dream of
Dracula, discusses the sexual symbolism of the Stoker book,
explaining the Count's attack on Mina as constituting an unholy marriage, consummated through the act of vampirism.
Welles also realized this aspect of Stoker's tale and made it
as obvious as 1938 radio would permit. Thus Dracula announces in the biblical sense, "I have known her," to the
mortals who seek to destroy his resting place. His final
word, directed to Mina, is "bride." Welles, then, confronted

the sexuality of vampirism while most films were concerned
with black cloaks and black bats.

A spoof of <u>Dracula</u> was presented over the Canadian
Broadcasting Company in the 1960s.

A radio adaptation of "Dracula's Guest," written and
announced by this author and starring Paul Kalin as Jonathan
Harker, was among the episodes of the radio series, MINI-
DRAMA, produced and directed by Jim Harmon in 1968. The
series of five-minute dramas was never officially released,
though individual episodes occasionally play over the air.

There was also a version of DRACULA presented by
Henry Mazzo at Columbia University.

A new fifty-two-minute version of DRACULA was
adapted by George Lowther for the dramatic series, CBS
RADIO MYSTERY THEATRE and aired in 1974. The adaptation was disappointing, especially in that it made little use
of its length and told only a little of Stoker's tale. The story
was updated and presumably set somewhere in the United
States. The narration was through the diary of Mina Harker
(Mercedes McCambridge).

After Mina and Dr. John Seward arrive by automobile
at the country estate of Lucy Westenra, they discover that
she is suffering from a strange loss of blood. Neighbor
Count Dracula (Michael Wager) is on hand and reveals accidentally that he has no mirror image. Later, in Lucy's
room, a conversation between her and Mina is interrupted by
a disturbance at the window.

> MINA: Oh, good lord! At the window -- (<u>sound
> of bat</u>)
>
> LUCY: It--it's nothing! Go! It's nothing!
>
> MINA: Nothing? It's that bat ... that huge bat
> that followed my car!
>
> LUCY: Go! I beg of you!
>
> MINA: Lucy, that thing is trying to get in! Look,
> it's clawing at the window! Is that locked? Is
> that window locked?

LUCY (hysterical): Yes, yes, it's locked.

DRACULA (calm): But locks are useless against Count Dracula.

MINA: Oh, good lord!

DRACULA: Mirrors do not reflect my image, Miss Harker. Nor do locks keep me out.

MINA: You ... you were that bat.

DRACULA: As the wolves you hear are not wolves --but like myself. Vampires!

MINA (gasps): Vampires!

DRACULA: The dead ... who live by night. The dead un-dead. (sound of wolves)

This DRACULA proceeded with very little happening. Count Dracula is exposed when John holds a Bible to his face, compelling him to assume bat shape and disappear. Lucy becomes a vampire thirsting for the blood of children as per Stoker. Count Dracula did not even appear in the third and final act of the play. Lucy's former fiancé John regretfully drives home the stake while Van Helsing later severs her head with a surgical knife. With the hour almost exhausted, the listener wondered how Dracula would meet his destruction in the final moments. Announcer E. G. Marshall provided that disappointing bit of information at the end of the play: "You will want to know that, later on, Professor Van Helsing freed Count Dracula from his earthly bondage, and in so doing, brought his bloody career to an end. Unhappily, I must add that Count Dracula was only one vampire among, er, how many? I don't know. Hope I never find out. Hope you don't either." Rather than experiencing the unequaled horror promised by the announcer, this listener only felt cheated. The cast of DRACULA also featured Paul Hecht, Stefan Schnabel and Marian Sanders. Radio veteran Himan Brown directed.

Dracula's radio voice (actors doing impersonations of Bela Lugosi) was also heard on commercials for Baskin Robbins ice cream and Turtle Wax (middle 1960s), Remington electric shavers (1969), the Movieland Wax Museum and Arrowhead Puritas Water (1972), radio station KRLA, Raid insect spray and, in the early 1960s, to promote safe driving.

DRACULA TELEVISED

Count Dracula's appearances on television outnumber those on radio. John Carradine recreated his role of the vampiric Count in a version of DRACULA which was presented in 1957 on the dramatic anthology series, MATINEE THEATRE. Carradine included a mustache in his Dracula characterization for this live color presentation which was telecast over the National Broadcasting Company. DRACULA was based more upon the Bram Stoker novel than the Hamilton Deane play.

DRACULA, as an adaptation of the original story, remained dormant on American television until 1967, when writer Steven Brocho prepared a forty-nine page treatment for a proposed film with that title for Universal Pictures. This DRACULA (dated December of that year) closely follows Stoker's storyline, differing mainly in the ending. For the first time in his dramatic career, Count Dracula escapes unstaked and unscathed to battle Jonathan Harker and Van Helsing another time. DRACULA was to be a feature-length motion picture made for television. At the same time, it would double as a pilot film which, if well received, would develop into a regular DRACULA television series. Whether or not the series will ever materialize is moot, for the project never progressed beyond the treatment stage.

Another never made television production of DRACULA was planned by Milton Subotsky of Britain's Amicus Productions in the late 1960s or early 1970s. The production was in two parts and to last for three hours, but it never went beyond the stage of Subotsky's outline. Discussions for DRACULA had already commenced between Subotsky and a television station in the United States.

Even with two television dramatizations of DRACULA stifled so prematurely in America, the story was televised abroad and in Canada. A version of the story entitled TREMPLIN was telecast in France in 1969. The play was directed by Henri Dassa and Bernard Soulie, the latter also assuming the part of Dracula. Another version of DRACULA was televised in England as an installment of the anthology series, MYSTERY AND IMAGINATION (English ABC). The story followed Stoker's and featured a graphic disintegration scene at the end. Patrick Dromgoole directed the production, with Denholm Elliott as Count Dracula, Corin Redgrave as Jonathan Harker, Suzanne Neve as Mina, Bernard Archard as

A new dramatic adaptation of Bram Stoker's story was presented on Canada's PURPLE PLAYHOUSE. Norman Welsh played the vampire Count.

Van Helsing, James Maxwell as Seward and Susan George as
Lucy.   During the early 1970s another dramatization of
DRACULA was presented on the PURPLE PLAYHOUSE television series in Canada.   Norman Welsh portrayed the Count
in characteristic garb and in make-up which included long
white hair combed back and a set of vampire fangs.   The
videotaped production followed the Stoker novel rather closely,
including a scene in which Dracula scales a wall (accomplished by turning the camera sideways as Welsh walked along
on hands and feet).   The vampires vanish as they are attacked by mortals.   At the end of the play, Dracula is staked
by Van Helsing (Nehemiah Persoff) with a good amount of
graphic blood.   Jack Nixon Browne directed the Rod Coney-
beare script.

     With so many Draculas flitting across the videowaves
it was inevitable that a new American version of the novel
would go into production.   Thus a feature-length film entitled
DRACULA was made by MGM in 1973 from a script by Richard Matheson.   "It was shot in England and Yugoslavia,"
Matheson wrote me.   "I followed the novel as closely as possible and I think it's more faithful to it than most of the
films have been."   Dan Curtis produced and directed DRACU-
LA, having been announcing plans to make a legitimate version of the classic since his DARK SHADOWS days.   Hurd
Hatfield was considered to star as the Count but the role finally went to an actor I had been touting as the perfect Dracula ever since the publication of the Dell Publishing Company
edition of the book in 1965.   The cover artwork depicted the
Count as Stoker described him and also bore a resemblance
to Jack Palance as the actor looked during the early 1950s,
with high cheekbones accenting an almost skeletal countenance.
The actor's portrayal of Attila in SIGN OF THE PAGAN in
1954 suggested the fine Vlad the Impaler he would have made
in those days.   His association with Dan Curtis commenced
in 1967 with a special dramatization on video tape of THE
STRANGE CASE OF DR. JEKYLL AND MR. HYDE, in which
Palance played the dual role.

     DRACULA (or BRAM STOKER'S DRACULA as the title
appears on the screen) was originally scheduled to be aired
over the CBS network on October 12, 1973.   However, due to
a special televised speech by Richard M. Nixon concerning
the resignation of Vice President Spiro T. Agnew, DRACULA
was pre-empted, thereby making the already unpopular President even more unpopular with the many horror film buffs
who stayed home that Friday night to watch it.   The reviews

of the film that appeared in that day's newspapers were extremely favorable, and when the film was rescheduled for February 8, 1974, there was no pre-emption. DRACULA starring Jack Palance proved worth the long wait.

Jack Palance played the role of Dracula with quiet strength, often moving with the extreme lassitude or the deathlike rigidity of Lugosi, and then lashing out with a ferocity and power even beyond that of Lee. This clean-shaven Count Dracula was depicted as the victim of a sadistic Fate, forced into acts that revolt him but which he cannot overcome. Personally, I prefer to see Dracula portrayed as the truly vicious character of Bram Stoker's novel and not as a pathetic figure who scowls with revulsion every time he is about to sink his fangs into a victim's throat, but Palance was superb in the role and when he tossed his attackers about with superhuman strength, the viewer could believe it.

Matheson's script retained the overall atmosphere and story of Stoker's Dracula. The motion picture begins with Jonathan Harker's (Murray Brown) journey to Castle Dracula, with much of the dialogue adapted from the original novel. Count Dracula is fascinated by a photograph that Harker possesses showing Lucy Westerna (Fiona Lewis). Later, Harker, alone in the Count's library, finds such items as an empty coffin and a fifteenth century painting depicting a warrior resembling Dracula mounted on a charging horse. The horseman is identified by a plate as Vlad Tepes. Also in the picture is a woman who bears a startling resemblance to Lucy. Three vampire women then enter the room and threaten to attack Harker, but Dracula, now clothed in black and draped by a flowing cloak, enters the room and stops them, as in the book. The Count is then plagued by a memory (shown in flashback) of a time when he was a living man, enjoying a romantic interlude in the sunlight with his beloved Maria, a double for Lucy. When Harker later finds Dracula's crypt and is about to strike him with a shovel, he is restrained by the Count's loyal Gypsies. Presently, the Englishman becomes the victim of the trio of vampire women.

Matheson condensed much of Stoker's plot and eliminated a number of characters, including Renfield, Dr. Seward, and all the male leading figures with the exception of Arthur

Opposite: In 1973, screen villain Jack Palance donned the black mantle to star in DRACULA, a motion picture made by Don Curtis for CBS Television.

Holmwood (Simon Ward). Van Helsing (Nigel Davenport) became an Englishman who seemed to be a combination of that
character and Seward. Matheson also eliminated most of the
supernatural elements of the original story, removing all
references to bats and transformations and presenting Dracula more as a physical and real being, which he felt would be
more readily accepted in the world of the 1970s.

When Dracula lures the entranced Lucy out of her
house and onto the dark lawn, he sees her as his Maria.
But though he tries to kiss her, his thirsty mouth fights
against him, a battle which he cannot win. When Van Helsing attempts to protect Lucy from the nosferatu, Dracula
frees a wolf from the zoo, has it kill the zoo keeper, and
then sends it crashing through Arthur Holmwood's window.
While Arthur struggles with and finally shoots the wolf,
Dracula enters Lucy's room and takes the last of her blood.

After her funeral, Lucy returns to Arthur as a vampire and is about to bite his neck when Van Helsing enters
the room and repels her with a cross. The next morning
the two men enter her crypt and find her asleep in her coffin; Van Helsing impales her with a stake. When Dracula
comes back to Lucy, calling her "Maria" and then finding her
truly dead, he suffers a memory of soldiers dragging him
from the bedroom of his former love. Dracula then goes
wild with animal rage and wrecks the inside of Lucy's tomb.

Dracula then begins his attacks on Mina Murray (Pe-
nelope Horner). When he goes to the hotel which she has
already left, he is confronted by the manager, whom he
promptly chokes to death. Another man fires a bullet into
the vampire without effect and is promptly hurled out the window. Dracula effortlessly tosses another man off the stairs
and charges through the other human beings who seek to de-
tain him, taking their blows without even flinching and tossing
the men aside as if they were nothing.

Meanwhile, Van Helsing and Arthur find nine of Dracula's ten boxes of earth at Carfax (the number had been de-
pleted since Stoker's book) and destroy them. Dracula goes
to Mina and uses his supernatural strength to break open the
door to her bedroom. Van Helsing and Arthur enter the
room and see him forcing her to drink blood from his chest,
thereby uniting her with the King of Vampires. When Dracula
later finds his nine earth boxes burned, he again goes on a
destructive rampage.

The final scenes showed Van Helsing and Arthur at Castle Dracula. First the doctor impales the hearts of the three slumbering vampire women. Jonathan Harker, now a vampire himself, leaps to attack Arthur, but the latter maneuvers his un-dead opponent into a pit of upstanding stakes (presumably left from Dracula's days as the Impaler). The two vampire hunters then find the picture of Vlad and Maria, just as Dracula himself bursts into the room. Furious, the Count upsets a table on the two men and throws Van Helsing through the air and crashing into a suit of armor. He is about to strangle Arthur when Van Helsing pulls open the drapes, letting in the sunlight, à la HORROR OF DRACULA. The Count grimaces from the pain of the light illuminating his pale face. Van Helsing continues to open curtains and doors, until Dracula is transfixed by the excruciating rays. Then, performing the coup de grace, Van Helsing rams a long wooden javelin, apparently one of Vlad's own impaling stakes, through the vampire's heart, pinning him against the surface of the overturned table. A look of relief appears on Dracula's face before he dies. (Again Matheson attempted to de-emphasize the supernatural qualities of the vampire legend by not having the Count decompose as in the established ending for most Dracula stories.) The camera then dollies over the impaled Dracula and to the portrait of Vlad Tepes, where superimposed titles roll upward to explain that this former warrior, ruler and statesman did, in fact, exist.

DRACULA, though not as close to the Stoker novel as the Franco adaptation, EL CONDE DRACULA, is certainly a more entertaining film. Dan Curtis' direction is not only atmospheric but also dynamic and exciting. And his choice of locations, including real castles and dark woods, give the picture an air of authenticity. The film surely ranks with the best movie adaptations of Stoker's Dracula and firmly established director Curtis and actor Palance among the genre's upper echelon.

DRACULA BECOMES A GRANDFATHER

Although the Universal Pictures television movie of DRACULA was never filmed, that studio did revive their original property in 1964. However, to purist fans of the venerable old Count, the manner in which Dracula returned was sheer blasphemy. For Dracula had settled down to be affectionately known as Grandpa in a situation comedy on

CBS-TV entitled THE MUNSTERS, a series produced by Joe Connelly and Bob Mosher.

The Munster family consisted of the Frankensteinian Herman (played by Fred Gwynne), his vampiric wife Lily (Yvonne de Carlo), their lycanthropic son Eddie (Butch Patrick), their blonde and beautiful neice Marilyn (Beverly Owen, later to be replaced by Pat Priest), and Lily's lovable old father, Count Dracula (Al Lewis).

Grandpa, or Dracula as he occasionally identified himself, had mellowed over the centuries. He was not the same diabolical menace of former years. Time and domestic life with this typical American family (as they regarded themselves) had given him a Jewish accent and a taste for cigars. The old Dracula tuxedo had seemingly helped sustain the lives of more than a few moths over the years. Black leather gloves had become a part of his permanent wardrobe. And the bluish green face and the weight he had accumulated since his prime attested to the fact that Dracula had seen better nights.

Grandpa had also lost some of the supernatural powers that had once made him a feared creature of the night. Luckily, he had become adept at mad science, for his transformation into a wolf or bat usually required a special magic pill or a puff of smoke. His powers had declined to performing small parlor tricks, and even these usually backfired. Grandpa did manage to learn how to cast a reflection and walk about in broad daylight. Perhaps the reason is revealed in Eddie's classroom composition in which he states that his Grandpa used to be known as Count Dracula and has been irregularly dead or alive. Now he is alive, and therefore no longer needs the safety of a coffin to sleep in during the day. He slept when it suited him, usually either stretched upon a stone slab or hanging batlike from the rafters.

This retired Count Dracula apparently never actually drank blood anymore, although the implication existed that he might someday want to renew his old sanguinary practices. Grandpa frequently referred to "putting the bite on" someone, or said, "I'll bite 'em in the neck, " perhaps to remind the television audience that this comedian was once a murderous fiend. No one seemed to mind his past, however, since THE MUNSTERS premiered during a "monster craze" in the United States in which many of the popular terrors of old were presented as either humorous or lovable characters.

Count Dracula, as played by Al Lewis, settled down to family life in Universal's comedy series for CBS-TV, THE MUN-STERS.

The pilot film of THE MUNSTERS was never shown on television. Running only fifteen minutes, this initial episode of the series presented the Munster family as slightly more gruesome creatures than those which finally made their way into thousands of living rooms. The very first televised episode of THE MUNSTERS was entitled "Munster Masquerade," directed by Lawrence Dobkin and broadcast in September of 1964. When Grandpa is not invited to a masquerade party at the home of "homely" Marilyn's boyfriend, he threatens to change himself into chopped liver and sneak in with the hors d'oeuvres.

The Munsters lived in a dreary old "haunted house" type mansion at 1313 Mockingbord Lane. The basement of the house served as both a dungeon and laboratory where Grandpa performed his weird experiments and kept company with his pet bat Igor (a prop left over from Universal's old Dracula movies). The humorous situations of the series frequently involved Herman's getting into trouble and Grandpa attempting to rescue him by some feat of magic or pseudo-science. Still, Grandpa's abilities and experiments were also often the cause of monstrous trouble.

In one episode Grandpa transforms himself into a bat and inadvertently becomes caged among the test animals at a government laboratory. Complications arise when a female bat falls in love with him. Another time, Grandpa in bat form becomes stranded in a girl's dormitory, with only Herman to rescue him. Once, in an effort to impress Herman's employer, an undertaker named Gateman (played by former movie Dracula John Carradine), Grandpa attempts a spell to transform young Eddie into a trumpet virtuoso. In yet another installment, entitled "Hot Rod Herman," the bumbling Frankenstein Monster loses the family car (a combination hearse and hot rod called the Munster Koach) in a drag race. Grandpa retaliates by building his own car, the coffin shaped "Dragula," which he races to win back the Munster Koach. (Both custom automobiles were designed by George Barris.)

The early episodes of THE MUNSTERS paid particular attention to atmosphere, with the make-up and eerie sets enhanced by some impressive black and white photography and low-key lighting. Despite the fact that this was a comedy series, these early installments retained much of the mood of the old Universal horror films of the thirties and forties. Such care was not taken in the later episodes, particularly during the second season of the program. Plots became a combination of slapstick, horror and mundane situation comedy. Virtually every new television series at the time was being made in color but, to remain more or less faithful to the films it was spoofing, THE MUNSTERS was photographed in black and white. Eventually the show's stars, especially Yvonne DeCarlo, tired of wearing the make-ups. Furthermore, humorous monsters were being ousted in popularity to secret agents and super-heroes. As a result, THE MUNSTERS left the air, save for reruns, in 1966.

But THE MUNSTERS would not suffer so ignoble a defeat as cancellation without Universal making one final effort to make profits. In 1965 the Munster family was shown on the cover of Monster World magazine in a brief scene of the Morgan-Steckler spoof of comic book super-heroes, RAT PFINK A BOO BOO. (The film went into production under the title MURDER A GO GO.) The same year that the television series left the air, Universal made a feature-length motion picture entitled MUNSTER, GO HOME! for theatrical release. The film was directed by Earl Bellamy and, to insure its future sale to television after its theatre run, was made in color. MUNSTER, GO HOME! repeated many of the comedy situations already seen in black and white by the video audience, and starred the same cast with the exception of Pat Priest. Marilyn was now played by Universal starlet Debby Watson.

MUNSTER, GO HOME! opens with Herman learning that his uncle has died and that he must journey to the ancestral Munster Hall in England to claim his inheritance. Aboard the ship bound for England, Grandpa produces his seasick pills, which inadvertently induce rather than prevent seasickness. When Grandpa's pills transform him into a wolf, he is placed in the kennels by the ship's officers, one of whom makes a remark associating the caged canine with Lon Chaney, Jr. This time Grandpa is saved by his vampiric daughter Lily, who drapes him over her shoulders as if he were a furpiece. The "stole" complemented her lengthy straight black hair, her satanic jutting eyebrows and the bat medallion worn on a chain about her neck.

The conniving Freddie Munster (Terry-Thomas) schemes to claim the inheritance for himself and rigs Munster Hall with weird effects in an effort to frighten off the visiting family. But Freddie does not realize that the Americans are something other than entirely human. The Munsters are delighted by the ghostly manifestations. There is some terrible secret harbored in the ancient manor involving the transport of coffins in and out of the dungeons of Munster Hall. The secret also involves a mysterious criminal mastermind known as the Griffin.

Herman Munster agrees to drive Grandpa's invention, the Dragula, against Marilyn's current boyfriend Roger Morsby in the annual automobile race. The Griffin replaces Roger and nearly dooms Herman, but Herman wins the race despite the Griffin's efforts, finally exposing the criminal as the daughter of Cruikshank (John Carradine), the butler at Munster Hall.

MUNSTER, GO HOME! marked the end of that bizarre American family's career on television or in film. But Grandpa, alias Count Dracula, had also made other television appearances, such as participating in the annual Macy's Thanksgiving Day parade in New York. During the heyday of THE MUNSTERS Universal built, as part of its studio tour, a special exhibit in which Grandpa flapped about his laboratory in bat form.

There were three Munsters novels published while the television series was being aired. In 1964 Avon Books published a novel by Morton Cooper simply entitled The Munsters. Cooper seemed not as familiar with the characters as most home viewers, for he described Grandpa and Count Dracula as being two distinct characters. Dracula, according to the novel, was a publicity seeking gourmet who chose his blood carefully, but he gradually reverted to an overrated gourmand. According to the novel, Grandpa was one of Dracula's most adoring students, who finally managed to overcome his craving for blood without having to resort to Bloodsuckers' Anonymous. Cooper's Grandpa had also amassed more centuries than on television, being a spry 3,700 years old.

The Munsters follows Herman as he attempts to win the "Family of the Week" award given by a television program. Grandpa, meanwhile, strives to perfect his two dream inventions, the Tomorrow Television and the Munster Mud Marvel, the latter being a facial treatment that "beautifies" women according to the distorted Munster outlook. The Munsters miraculously win the contest and appear on television, becoming immediate celebrities. Grandpa then sells his Mud Marvel to a large corporation and travels to Washington, D. C. where he magically defeats some spies who are out to steal his Tomorrow Television. Grandpa returns home to

learn that the Munster Mud Marvel has made the nation
wrinkle-conscious and begging to look older.   He also discovers that fame is ruining the Munsters' family life, a problem which Herman finally rectifies.

The Whitman Publishing Company issued two Munsters
novels, the first being The Munsters and the Great Camera
Caper (1965), by William Johnston.   The Munsters investigate
when a movie company tries to film a romantic comedy next
door to their mansion.   When the director and the male star
begin to bicker, Grandpa changes them into a dog and cat.
In order to rid the neighborhood of the film group, Grandpa
makes a concoction from the contents of three bottles labeled
"Dracula," "Mr. Hyde" and "The Blob," creating a monster
to stop their activities.   Grandpa then transforms himself
and Eddie into facsimiles of the producer and his Pekingese
(the latter fooling none of the Munsters).   The film company's
final accomplishment is a combination romantic comedy and
horror movie.   The next year Whitman published a second
Munsters book, The Last Resort.   Both novels were written
for young readers.   Whitman is part of Western Publishing
Company which, in turn, has a line of comic books under the
Gold Key banner.   From 1964 through 1968 Gold Key published The Munsters comic book which lasted for sixteen issues.

Grandpa also appeared in a comic strip advertisement
for Aurora plastic model kits and in a black and white strip
of The Munsters published during the late 1960s in the British
paper, TV Century 21.

Twin Hits published a magazine called The Munsters in
1965, with a number of features about the celebrated family.
"The Life of a Lady Vampire" and "Have Crypt, Will Fly"
were alleged interviews with Lily and Grandpa.   (Herein
Grandpa acquired his son-in-law's surname.)   In Eando (Otto)
Binder's short story, "The Munsters Go House-Haunting," the
brood tries to frighten the man who has acquired the deed to
their mansion, but succeeds only in making him happy.   "A
Visit to Grandpa's Crypt" had Grandpa reveal his furnishings;
"The Day Lily Went Shopping" followed her through various
stores, shocking the clerks with her weird requests; and
"Grandpa in a Time Machine" took him through the prehistoric past, Seventeenth-Century Salem, the ship of Captain Kidd
and Ancient Egypt (the latter actually a set for a modern
Cleopatra movie).   The Munsters was edited by Roger Elwood
and lasted only one issue.

Grandpa's image has been captured on masks, model kits, ballpoint pens, dolls, coloring books, lunch boxes, puppets, a View Master stereo set of the episode in which he invents an electricity-making device, and other merchandise. There were Munsters phonograph records, including the show's theme song by Billy Strange and two albums. The first album, At Home With the Munsters (Golden Records), featured the voices of the television cast and included such selections as "Meet Grandpa," "Grandpa's Lab," "Lily's Favorite Story," "Grandpa's Favorite Recipe" and "Herman's Favorite Story," which recounted the television episode in which Grandpa becomes nostalgic for his homeland, transforms into a wolf and is caught by forest rangers. A second album titled The Munsters (Decca, 1965) featured music by a rock group using the name The Munsters. Some of the numbers on this album were "Vampire Vamp," "Ride the Midnight Special" and "Down in the Basement."

The Munsters returned to television in a special hour-long animated cartoon, MINI-MUNSTERS, which premiered October 27, 1973 on ABC-TV's SATURDAY SUPERSTAR MOVIE. Al Lewis spoke the words of Grandpa while Richard Long and Bob Diamond did the voices of Herman and Eddie. MINI-MUNSTERS opened with a Dracula-type relative of the Munsters in Transylvania sending his two teenagers, the Frankensteinian Igor and the vampiric Lucretia, to Mockingbird Heights. Herman buys a hearse for the expanded family and the kids discover that it runs on music. After the music-driven hearse beats a gangster's car in a road race, Grandpa develops a machine that allows any vehicle to run the same way, thereby eliminating the pollution caused by exhaust fumes. The gangsters, who had been forcing customers to buy their own polluting gasoline, kidnap the Munsters' reptilian pet Spot and then the children in an attempt to get Grandpa's device. Grandpa defeats the villains by remote control.

THE MUNSTERS is still popular in television reruns. The comedy of the show and its feature-length offspring, MUNSTER, GO HOME!, is often hilarious, at least for those horror fans who realize that no one, not even so revered a character as Count Dracula, is beyond healthy spoofing.

DRACULA IN THE LIVING ROOM

Dracula's television appearances seem as eternal as the Count himself. In feature length motion pictures made

for television, he has continued to raise his ebony cloak.
GIDGET GETS MARRIED, a film made by Universal and aired
in 1971, featured Paul Lynde as a tenant who impersonates
various movie characters including Count Dracula. The Walt
Disney studios contributed to the lore of the Count with the
feature-length television film, THE MYSTERY IN DRACULA'S
CASTLE. Shown in two parts on the NBC-TV series, WORLD
OF DISNEY, in 1972, the film starred Johnny Whitaker and
Scott Kolden as a pair of young amateur movie makers in the
process of filming their own Dracula epic. Their black cloak
and fangs, however, do not provide the realism they desire,
so they decide to use a nearby lighthouse as Dracula's castle.
To the boys' dismay, the lighthouse proves to be a hideout for
jewel thieves.

In 1974, Vincent Price portrayed horror films star
Michael Bastion in a Universal SNOOP SISTERS feature-length
film entitled BLACK DAY FOR BLUEBEARD. Bastion, in the
guise of Dracula, arrives in a coffin at a festival of his old
films and finds himself falsely accused of his wife's murder.

Bela Lugosi played Dracula on YOU ASKED FOR IT,
over ABC-TV in 1954. Upon a viewer's request, Lugosi, as
Dracula, is summoned by his servant to rise from his coffin.
Then he proceeds to perform a magic illusion. Afterwards,
Lugosi steps out of character and tells master of ceremonies
Art Baker that he will soon star in a television series called
DR. ACULA. The program never materialized.

Rod Serling's NIGHT GALLERY series, which aired
over NBC-TV in 1971-73, featured a number of Dracula vignettes, usually ending on a joke and featuring such actors as
Cesar Romero and Victor Buono as the Count. "The Funeral,"
by Richard Matheson, who adapted his own short story to the
NIGHT GALLERY format, showed Dracula and another cloaked
vampire attending yet a third vampire's belated funeral. The
most important Dracula segment of NIGHT GALLERY was a
dramatization of Manly Wade Wellman's story, "The Devil Is
Not Mocked," starring Francis Lederer (who played the Count
in THE RETURN OF DRACULA). When asked by a youthful
descendant what he did during World War II, Dracula reveals
how he destroyed a patrol of Nazi soldiers who tried occupying his castle. Lederer played the Count with humor and
dignity in one of the series' finest episodes. In 1972 Serling
announced an upcoming version of the original Dracula on
NIGHT GALLERY but the project never went into production.

In 1974 THE EVIL TOUCH presented an episode

starring and directed by Vic Morrow. He played Purvis
Green, a horror film star who is "collected" by two old women, drugged and made-up to look like Dracula (one of his
screen roles). He is eventually found with a sword impaling
his chest, his body lying near a poster from one of his
Dracula movies.

Count Dracula has been spoofed on such television programs as YOU'LL NEVER GET RICH (Joe E. Ross dressed
as Dracula), THE LUCY SHOW (Gale Gordon as Dracula in
a dream sequence), THE MAN FROM U.N.C.L.E. (Martin
Landau as a Dracula-type spy), THE MONKEES (several episodes; one with Ron Mosk as Dracula preparing Monkee Davy
Jones to be his daughter's vampiric husband), F TROOP
(Vincent Price as a suspected vampire), GILLIGAN'S ISLAND
(Bob Denver as the Count in a dream sequence), GET SMART
(several episodes; one featuring Robert Ridgely as a spy masquerading as Dracula), LOVE, AMERICAN STYLE (Tiny Tim
in Dracula get-up), LIDSVILLE (Dracula in the form of a
living red hat), THE MOUSE FACTORY, CIRCLE OF FEAR
(the ghostly incarnation of "Count Vampire" and scenes from
DRACULA HAS RISEN FROM THE GRAVE) and LOVE STORY
(scene of Dracula on a movie screen).

The Lugosi Dracula character has often been the subject of impressionists like Will Jordan in nightclubs, on
radio and on television. Gabe Dell, long associated with the
Dead End Kids and East Side Kids films, had long been a
fan of the elder Lugosi. When Dell and his youthful actor
friends performed with Lugosi in the movies and on the stage,
he began to mimic the former portrayer of the Count. After
Lugosi's death, Dell proceeded to imitate his voice and mannerisms and appeared as Count Dracula on many television
occasions, usually on the STEVE ALLEN SHOW. Allen, himself a fan of old horror films, once presented a musical
comedy spoof of Dracula on his variety show, starring Dell
as the Count. Frank Gorshin and John Byner are two more
of the numerous impressionists who have imitated Lugosi's
distinctive Dracula characterization on television. Some of
the best impressionists in the entertainment industry grouped
together for THE KOPYKATS segments of THE ABC COME-
DY HOUR in the 1970s and, on April 8, 1972, presented a
musical spoof of horror films with Tony Curtis impersonating
the Count.

Other variety and information programs involving
Dracula are THE GARY MOORE SHOW (Durward Kirby as

Dracula), THE SPIKE JONES SHOW, THE JERRY LEWIS SHOW, CAROL BURNETT SHOW (several appearances; one in which Vincent Price played the role), DEAN MARTIN SHOW, ROWAN AND MARTIN'S LAUGH-IN, THE JOE PYNE SHOW, SESAME STREET, THE COLGATE COMEDY HOUR, THE NEW PHIL SILVERS SHOW, JUVENILE JURY, THE GOLDDIGGERS, THE ELECTRIC COMPANY, CURIOSITY SHOP, SCREAMING YELLOW THEATRE (Chicago) and the SONNY AND CHER COMEDY HOUR. In 1967 a Dracula-type character with a skull-like face, appearing under the name Count Shockula (Dick Bennick), presided over the MESS AMER-ICA CONTEST in North Carolina, broadcast over television station WGHP.

The Dracula figure has also been prominent in animated cartoons made for television. THE GROOVIE GOOLIES was a sixty-minute cartoon series featuring caricatures of the famous old horrors like Frankenstein's Monster, the mummy and the werewolf. Among the weird looking group was Cousin Drac, who would sometimes transform from bat to man in mid-air and fall crashing against the floor. The series featured music, gags and stories, the latter starring Sabrina the Teen-age Witch, from the comic books published by the Archie Mu-sic Corporation. A rock band calling themselves the Groovie Goolies and wearing appropriate costumes performed at Holly-wood's Magic Castle nightclub when the show began on CBS-TV in 1970. The show's success resulted in a considerable amount of licensed merchandise, including Groovie Goolie coloring books, masks, costumes and miniature dolls. After one year, however, THE GROOVIE GOOLIES was cancelled. But the characters, like the almost immortal counterparts they represented, did not die. Cousin Drac and his brood immediately became supporting characters in a half-hour car-toon series entitled SABRINA, THE TEENAGE WITCH. The Goolies' latest appearance was in 1972, in their own "movie" on the SATURDAY SUPERSTAR MOVIE, an hour-long animated anthology on ABC-TV. The film, entitled PORKY PIG AND DAFFY DUCK MEET THE GROOVIE GOOLIES, was a unique pairing of the old Warner Brothers cartoon folk with the char-acters of another company. It was disheartening to see Porky, Daffy and other Warner Brothers characters now go-ing through antics via television's extremely limited animation. The story required the Groovie Goolies to save the Warner Brothers stars from a PHANTOM OF THE OPERA-type vil-lain who was terrorizing the movie studio. Toward the cli-max Cousin Drac, Frankie and Wolfie burst into the real world and suddenly appear in the form of flesh and blood actors.

Yet another Dracula appearance on the SATURDAY SUPERSTAR MOVIE was in the film MAD, MAD, MAD MONSTERS, which first played on September 23, 1972. This was actually a type of television sequel to the theatrical motion picture, MAD MONSTER PARTY? Virtually all the same characters, looking as they had in the feature, returned for this television cartoon in order to attend the gala wedding of the Frankenstein Monster and his newly built bride. Dracula had settled down since MAD MONSTER PARTY? and was now the proud sire of a young vampire named Boobula.

Dracula has also made appearances on such animated cartoon series as UNDERDOG (Battyman), THE BEATLES, TOM SLICK, THE FLINTSTONES, SCOOBY DOO--WHERE ARE YOU?, THE THREE STOOGES (Count Dunkula), ABBOTT AND COSTELLO, LAUREL AND HARDY, THE FUNNY COMPANY (Belly Lagoona), BEANY AND CECIL, MILTON THE MONSTER, SPUNKY AND TADPOLE and CRUSADER RABBIT.

While Count Dracula was appearing on television programs, he also helped to sell some of the sponsors' products, appearing in commercials for Sucrets (Count Soar Throat Pain), Colorforms, Wohl Shoes, Straw Hat Pizza Palace, Movieland Wax Museum, the Dairy Council (Count Alucard), the American Land Title Association (Jim Boles as Dracula), Der Wienerschnitzel restaurants ("Dracula" with Tom Basham), Colonel Sanders' chicken, Clackers, and the breakfast cereal, Pebbles (a two-headed monster resembling both Dracula and Frankenstein's Monster). General Mills began a series of commercials in 1971 advertising their new breakfast cereal, Count Chocula, represented by a comic Dracula-type character with brown hair and cloak. Perhaps the Dracula figure had turned full circle, for now his young fans could devour him. Merchandise followed the popular commercials: Count Chocula posters, coloring sets, a coloring book titled How to Be a Good Monster, masks, stick-ems, glow-in-the-dark stickers, animated rings, bath mittens, towels, mini-mugs, mobiles, erasers, "spooky speedster" cars, bicycle safety flags, boy "mini-monsters," puzzles and dart games.

A chapter representing Dracula on television could not be terminated without mention of DARK SHADOWS, an afternoon soap opera which debuted over ABC-TV in the late 1960s and flourished until 1971. Although Count Dracula himself never appeared on this Dan Curtis-produced Monday through Friday serial, there were enough elements borrowed from his old movies to please his devoted fans. DARK SHADOWS starred Shakespearean actor Jonathan Frid as Barnabas Collins, a vampire introduced to boost the gothic serial's waning ratings. Barnabas is resurrected when neurotic Willie Loomis (John Karlen) opens his chained coffin while searching for the Collins family jewels. From that point onward DARK SHADOWS' ratings skyrocketed. Writer Sam Hall took his vampire through many of the plot trappings of Stoker's Dracula, with Barnabas making his nocturnal attacks on young and beautiful Maggie Evans (Kathryn Leigh Scott). Willie eventually becomes Barnabas' "Renfield." Later, an elderly student of the occult, with the obvious name of Professor Timothy Elliott "Stokes" (Thayer David), became the show's Van Helsing. In a scene inspired by the film HORROR OF DRACULA, a vampiress named Angelique (Lara Parker) begs a visitor to free her from the imprisonment of her demonic master Nicholas Blair (Humbert Allen Astredo). A temporarily cured Barnabas even imitated a scene from that film by repelling another vampire with an ersatz cross formed by two candlesticks.

While the television show was in its final months, Dan Curtis collected his players to make a feature-length film. Originally announced as simply DARK SHADOWS, the film became HOUSE OF DARK SHADOWS (MGM 1970) and was directed by Curtis himself. The color film adapted the first Barnabas plotline from television, with Barnabas freed by Willie, then introducing himself at the Collins mansion as a cousin from England. Carolyn Stoddard (Nancy Barrett), Barnabas' "cousin," becomes his victim and is eventually staked by the police in an excellently staged scene. By the end of the film almost the entire cast has been changed into vampires. Barnabas, wearing the clothing of the eighteenth century during which he lived (including a black cloak), is about to wed Maggie Evans and make her a vampire when Willie impales him through the back with an arrow. Barnabas dies in one of the most vivid stakings ever recorded on film. The fast-paced, atmospheric and graphic film proved that Curtis was capable of transforming a television soap opera into one of the finest horror films of the year.

The Barnabas legend was perpetuated by a barrage of paperback books like the novel Barnabas Collins (1968) and an adaptation of the movie (1970), all of which were published by Paperback Library. There were Dark Shadows comic books from Western Publishing Company, games and all manners of paraphernalia. On television the villainous Barnabas eventually mellowed into a tragic hero. Then, one afternoon

in 1971, DARK SHADOWS left the air, having demonstrated
once again that there is always a niche for the Dracula-type
character, even if only for a while on the television screen
during a brightly lit weekday afternoon.

On Halloween night, 1974, KTLA in Los Angeles un-
leashed its own Dracula-inspired vampire on THE HILARIOUS
HOUSE OF FRIGHTENSTEIN special. The vampiric Count
Frightenstein has been exiled from Transylvania for failing to
bring his Frankenstein monster (named Bruce) to life. Billy
Van played Frightenstein (and most of the other bizarre characters) in this potpouri of generally non-hilarious vignettes.
The show promptly became an unbearably repetitive series,
shown five nights a week. Miraculously the series survived
into 1975.

Dracula had become a radio and television personality.
But he also gained notoriety on the printed page many years
after his immortalization by Bram Stoker. Not surprisingly,
Dracula's new literary escapades never quite reached classic
calibre.

Chapter 11

OTHER DRACULA BOOKS

> I am sorry, general ... Sorry--my servants were
> too eager within and without. Wolves and vampires
> are hard to restrain. After all, it is midnight--
> our moment of all moments. --"The Devil Is Not
> Mocked," by Manly Wade Wellman

Although Bram Stoker wrote but one novel chronicling
the sanguinary escapades of Count Dracula, the King of Vampires has managed to escape the apparent total destruction
detailed by that writer and flee to the safety of other works
of fiction. None of Dracula's subsequent adventures, under
the auspices of later writers, has approached the greatness
of Stoker's original novel, and some, indeed, have declined
to the level of pulp fiction. The name of Dracula, though,
continues to appear on the covers of novels, and most of
them sell on the strength and popularity of the name alone.

The original Dracula novel has been reedited and re-
written on numerous occasions in order to lure diverse read-
erships to the famous story. Monsters was a book for young
readers published in 1965 by Wonder Books, presenting condensed and simplified versions of the novels Frankenstein,
Dracula and The Strange Case of Dr. Jekyll and Mr. Hyde,
adapted by Walter Gibson and illustrated by Tony Tallarico.
Gibson titled his well-written and faithful adaptation of
Stoker's work, "Dracula the Vampire."

Children were not the only readers to receive a new
version of Stoker's Dracula. Sex scenes were added to the
original text for a version entitled Valuto Infernale ("Satanic
Desire"), published in Italy in the late 1960s as part of the
"I Grandi Romanzi" series of novels. Valuto Infernale was
tame compared to The Adult Version of Dracula, written
anonymously and issued by Calga Publishers in 1970. The

307

back cover audaciously asserted, "Everything is as close to
the original as possible ... except that our adaptation has
been written as it might have been originally ... if the author
had the literary freedom of today's mores and standards."
Now Dracula is revealed to be a bisexual maniac, indulging
in orgies interwoven through Stoker's basic plotline, until he
is tracked to his vault and then destroyed in the manner described in the original novel.

Another lurid adaptation of the Stoker novel appeared
in three parts under the banner of a publication entitled Monster Sex Stories, issued by the Gallery Press in 1972. The
first story of the trilogy, "Castle of Dracula," by Chester
Winfield, follows a reporter to the ancient castle where he
has sex with the Count's three wives. The women attack him
with their fangs, after which Dracula himself appears, with
the reporter going insane. The second story "Voyage of
Dracula," by Roy Hemp, is the story of the Demeter, with
the Count and a vampiress preying upon the crew. The captain escapes Dracula's lusts with a crucifix, then ties himself
to the ship's wheel. Finally "Lust of the Vampire," by Dudley McDonly, reveals that the reporter in the first story had
escaped from Castle Dracula. Now an inmate in an insane
asylum, he is forced into sex acts by a nurse, after which
he, now a vampire himself, attacks her. The poorly written
Monster Sex Tales did not even measure up to the standards
of The Adult Version of Dracula.

A satire of a scene from the original Dracula was included in Jack Sharkey's "I Want a Ghoul ... " in the September 1971 issue of Playboy. In a successful imitation of
Stoker's prose, Sharkey has Jonathan Harker write in his
journal how he has made it appear as though he has fled the
castle. Only as Dracula himself approaches his room does
Harker realize that he has been recording the incidents of
his ruse on a quite noisy typewriter.

A number of novels adapted from Hammer Dracula
films have been published, the earliest being The Brides of
Dracula, dressed with mildly erotic scenes, written by Dean
Owen for Monarch Books in 1960. Unlike the film, the novel
climaxes with Van Helsing summoning a swarm of bats from
hell which destroy the vampire Baron because of his incestu-
ous attack upon his mother.* The Second Hammer Horror

*The possibility exists that the ending involving the judgment-
dealing bats was originally intended for the film but was

(cont. on p. 309)

Omnibus, published in 1967 by Pan Books in London, included a novel by John Burke, Dracula--Prince of Darkness. In 1971 Beagle Books issued novel adaptations of The Scars of Dracula by Angus Hall and Countess Dracula by Michael Parry. There was also a novel, One More Time, by Michael Avallone, published in 1970 by Popular Library, based on the United Artists film and featuring a scene of Christopher Lee as Dracula.

The King Vampire has been the star of numerous original novels. Ali Riga Seifi, a Turkish writer, contributed Kastgli Voyvoda ("The Impaling Voivode"), a novel published in Istanbul in 1928. The book was mostly based on Stoker's Dracula but referred to the vampire as the Impaler, portraying him as a vampiric ghost who journeys to Istanbul in search of blood and is finally impaled by a stake.

Count Dracula's Canadian Affair, by Otto Fredrick, was published in 1960 by Pageant Press. Mary Sallow, a homesteader in Canada during frontier times, is attacked by a wolf which transforms into a man and back to a wolf again. On a "taboo" island, Mary finds a cabin with three coffin-like boxes, one containing a girl who had previously convinced her to discard her crucifix. Before long, Mary has an affair with a mysterious captain and lieutenant who also drain off some of her blood. Paul, a French-Indian guide, later finds the coffins in a cave on the island, two being empty and one containing the sleeping lieutenant, whom he promptly impales. The two other boxes are dragged out into the sunlight as a pair of bats (one being Dracula) swoop down for the attack (since the sky is not overly bright) but are driven away by Paul's cross. When Dracula, dressed in the uniform of the captain he had previously slain, returns for Mary, she states that she has changed her decision about going away with him. Surprisingly, the Count flies off without contesting her. The

---

changed because of censorship existing at the time. This more grisly ending did, in fact, climax the 1963 Hammer film, KISS OF THE VAMPIRE (released to television as KISS OF EVIL), which concerned an entire cult of vampires. These were not vampires in the "Dracula" sense, but living beings who lived normal lives during the day and acquired their fangs at night. KISS OF THE VAMPIRE was directed by Don Sharp and released by Universal. Leader of the cloaked band was the sinister Count Ravna, played by Noel Willman.

quaintly written novel was published in a limited edition and copies are now extremely rare.

The Vampire Affair (Act Books, 1966) was a novel by David McDaniel based on the popular television super-spy series, THE MAN FROM U. N. C. L. E.   Agents Napoleon Solo and Illya Kuryakin venture to Transylvania to investigate the strange death of fellow agent Carl Endros, whose body was completely drained of blood.   Solo and Illya meet a man who is being pursued by villagers--a Count Zoltan Dracula, descendant of Vlad Tsepesh, who was the grandson of Petru Stobolzny and whose family acquired the name of Drakula or Dracula in 1658.   When Illya sees a figure with dead white face and winglike cloak hovering over U. N. C. L. E. agent Hilda Eclary, he futilely shoots at the apparent vampire (presumably Vlad Tsepesh), who leaps from the third story window and vanishes in the fog.   Zoltan then leads the three agents into the ancestral Stobolzny castle, where they discover an empty coffin.   When Illya shoots one of a pack of obedient wolves, he discovers an electronic controlling device in its brain.   In the castle, Solo and his friends discover that "Vlad Tsepesh" is actually an agent of the international criminal organization, Thrush, which has discovered the lost treasure of Atilla and is smuggling it out of Transylvania to use in their plans of world conquest.   Make-up, acting and a helicopter contributed toward creating a "Dracula" that kept the Transylvanians indoors at night while Thrush went to work.   The Thrush agents are defeated, and Solo and his friends learn that someone else has killed Endros and left the empty coffin in the castle.   "Thank you.   I return to my rest" is a message written in the snow.

The Dracula theme was incorporated into So What Killed the Vampire?, one of the "Carter Brown Mystery Series" of novels published in 1966 by Signet.   A production company plans to film a vampire movie in an authentic castle starring Nigel Carlton, referred to repeatedly as the "Dracula-type. " Hero Larry Baker sees Carlton lying corpse-like upon a slab and must prove that the "Dracula-type" was murdered for his knowledge of an archaic treasure.

A series of Dracula novels was published in Paris by Editions Bel-Air in 1966 under the general title, "Les Aventures de Dracula. " The novels in this series included Terreur au Chateau ("Terror at the Castle"), by Max Dave; Les Loups de la Violence ("The Wolves of Violence") by Michael Shiofy; and two more by Dave, Le Monstre de Preston ("The

Monster of Preston") and L'Homme de L'au-Dela ("The Man on the Other Side of Death").

A paperback entitled Dracula's Curse and the Jewel of the Seven Stars, by Bram Stoker, was issued in 1968 by Tower Publications. But the book actually contained Jewel and "Dracula's Guest," now titled "Dracula's Curse."

The Orgy at Madame Dracula's, by F. W. Paul, was one of "The Man from S. T. U. D." series of moderately sexy spy novels published in 1968 by Lancer Books. Secret agent Bret Steele is given the job of delivering a million-dollar insurance voucher to one Bram "Stroker." Steele arrives at a gloomy old house where he meets a gorgeous vampiress named Placenta (the "Madame Dracula" of the title) and her nymphomaniac maid Bridgette. Learning that Stroker is in Transylvania, Steele and Bridgette go there and upset the filming of a movie, DRACULA'S FAMILY MEETS THE WOLF-MAN'S ESTRANGED WIFE, encounter American gangsters attempting to start a brothel, and find a classroom for vampires with rows of coffins instead of desks. Dracula does not appear but is described as a publicity hound and author of a "vampire rulebook." At Placenta's castle Steele learns that Stroker is dead and that the vampiress wants the million dollars. Only the agent's masculine prowess saves him from Placenta's electrical assaulting machine.

Another series of Dracula novels, titled "I Racconti di Dracula" ("The Story of Dracula"), was published in Italy in 1968. Despite the vampires depicted on the lurid covers, not all the stories featured Dracula or the un-dead. Included in the series were La Notte di Dracula ("The Night of Dracula"), Il Destino dei Taskett ("The Destiny of Taskett") and Goran Ritorna Dall'Inferno (original Title: Goran Returns from Hell), all by Red Schneider; Dracula Anno 2000 ("Dracula in the Year 2000"; original title: Lux), by Alan Preston; and L'Abbraccio Dell'Ombra ("Embrace of the Shadow"; original title: And the Death Said), by Morton Sidney.

Dracutwig, by Mallory T. Knight, a travesty on Stoker, was published in 1969 by Award Books in an attempt to capitalize on the current popularity of model Twiggy and what remained of the 1960s monster craze. After raping a nymphomaniac in Transylvania, Dracula is forced into a marriage. Though the mother dies, Dracutwig is born and, in Dracula's custody, grows into a lovely young woman. Dracutwig clings to the old ways, sleeping in a coffin, for example, but is

also swept into the fashion world of mod England. A photographer named Harry cajoles her into modeling and she becomes a world sensation with her vampiric styles. After
Harry falls in love with Dracutwig she gradually becomes a
vampire, losing her mirror image and no longer showing on
film. The lithe model becomes the bloodthirsty terror of
London and is finally staked by Harry's dominating and jealous mother. Harry meets a blonde at Dracutwig's funeral
and as they drive away, Count Dracula pursues them in the
form of a bat.

Germany had its own series of Dracula novels in the
early 1970s, written by Dan Shocker and published by Zauber-
kreis-Verlag. The first two titles were Draculas Höllenfahrt
("Dracula's Trip to Hell") and Draculas Liebesbiss ("Dracula's
Love Bite").

The Dracula Archives, a novel by Raymond Rudorff
published by David Bruce & Watson (London, 1971), was a
serious attempt to provide an origin for Stoker's Count while
linking the King of Vampires to the historical lineage of Vlad
the Impaler and Countess Elizabeth Báthory. Rudorff imitated
Stoker's style with astounding accuracy, interconnecting a collection of first-person accounts. He wrote the novel in the
fashion of a nineteenth century novelist who also happened to
be an authority on vampirism, on the geography of Transylvania and on the history of Southeastern Europe. An obvious
love for Stoker and Dracula is evident in Rudorff's novel, and
there is a feeling of such authenticity in The Dracula Archives
that the reader can almost believe it to be a "prequel" to the
Stoker novel. Rudorff's work remains to date the most important Dracula novel since the original, and the only one ap-
proximating its over-all scope and atmosphere.

Providing a detailed plot synopsis of The Dracula Archives would necessitate a chapter in itself, as it ingeniously
weaves an incredible series of events weighted by so many
proper names that one feels as if he were reading a history
book. In brief, The Dracula Archives is based on the thesis
that both the Báthorys and Draculas were linked in antiquity.
Vlad "Dracul" had married a Gypsy woman and their offspring became Vlad's sole heir. Miklos, the great-grandson
of Countess Elizabeth Báthory, had claimed to be a descendant of Vlad's heir and had desired to acquire the fortune and
property which were rightfully his. But in venturing to the
Báthory castle, Miklos encountered the Countess whose body,
so many years after dying in solitary confinement, was now

in the vampire state.   Miklos inadvertently became a vampire himself and, with his wife Mirea, begot a wave of vampirism which persisted even after their destruction.

The main plot stream of The Dracula Archives, based upon the preceding "history," involves young Stephen Morheim, a descendant of "Dracul," and Elizabeth Sandor, whose ancestor and look-a-like was the infamous Countess Báthory. Stephen courts and marries Elizabeth, thereby again uniting the two ancient families.   Then apparently deserting his bride, Stephen goes off in pursuit of one of her possessions, the battle-worn castle of Vlad Dracul.   Shortly thereafter, Elizabeth receives psychic callings to join her husband ... and Master.   Elizabeth is nocturnally attacked by her "Master" and becomes one of the un-dead, to be inevitably staked through the heart by her former fiancé.   In the final demouement the reader learns that the old man now inhabiting the castle is Count Dracula, in actuality Stephen's spirit occupying the resuscitated body of Vlad Dracul through some unknown supernatural process.   Presumably, Bram Stoker's Dracula follows.   Yet this is not the end of The Dracula Archives. Rudorff has provided a frame story, written "in an Unknown Hand," which concludes with the writer's venturing to Castle Dracula in hopes of realizing his destiny in that house of vampires.

A science fiction novel, Project Dracula, written by Alan Scott, was published in London by Sphere Books in 1971. The story has nothing to do with vampires, but involves a biological research station where scientists have developed capsules containing spores capable of destroying whole populations.   The capsules are carried by bats which, during an explosion, escape to unleash the new plague upon mankind.

Count Dracula also appeared in "The New Adventures of Frankenstein" series of novels, written by this author, the first two of which were published in Spain in 1971 by Buru Lan de Ediciones.   But Spanish censorship regulations halted the series prematurely, even though three of the books had already been announced under the titles of Frankenstein y Dracula ("Frankenstein and Dracula"; original English title: Frankenstein Meets Dracula), El Horror de Frankenstein ("The Horror of Frankenstein"; original title: Tales of Frankenstein) and Frankenstein y el Vampiro ("Frankenstein and the Vampire"; original title: Frankenstein and the Evil of Dracula).

The announced but never published Spanish edition of the
novel, Frankenstein Meets Dracula, with cover artwork by
Esteban Maroto.

Frankenstein Meets Dracula was a sequel to Stoker's
original novel, written as a connected series of journals,
diaries and the like.   Based on the authentic tradition that a
vampire can escape his destruction in the form of an insect
that crawls from his crumbling flesh, Dracula is revived.
A page in the Ruthvenian, the "Bible of the Vampires," reveals the secret whereby Dracula, in insect form, is restored
to his full powers through human blood.   Dracula then decides to avenge himself on those who destroyed him in the
last century, first by having the brain of the current Van
Helsing transplanted into the skull of the Frankenstein Monster.   The Monster revives in time to shove a wooden post
through the vampire's chest.

Tales of Frankenstein was a collection of short stories,
one of which was entitled "A Man Called Frankenstein," featuring an ice pick-wielding assassin whose nickname is Dracula.

The eleventh book in the series, Frankenstein and the
Evil of Dracula, concerns a scientist named Nathan Kane and
his attempt to rid the world of the curse of vampirism.   His
work brings him into contact with the Frankenstein Monster,
a werewolf and Count Dracula, the latter being revived when
a former (and quite mad) rival scientist removes the wooden
shaft from his heart.   Dracula's desire is now to have revenge on the Frankenstein Monster, and he first attacks him
with a swarm of bats and later makes arrangements to dis-
sect him alive.   But the Monster splashes flammable chemicals over the vampiric Count while Kane fires a burning arrow into his chest, thus creating a blazing inhuman torch.

In 1973 "The New Adventures of Frankenstein" series
was placed with the Schorpoien publishing house in Holland.

A Dream of Dracula, a non-fiction study of Dracula,
vampirism and the significance of blood, written by Leonard
Wolf, was published in 1972 by Little, Brown and Company.
Wolf interviewed subjects to whom blood, blood-letting and
the consumption of blood held particular significance, in an
attempt to illustrate that the Dracula figure is yet with us.
Wolf also presents his analysis of Dracula and his opinions as
to the mental, sexual and emotional state of Bram Stoker, all
of which are open to debate.   Wolf also created and taught a
college course in "Dracula."

A new series of American Dracula novels debuted in
1973 from Pinnacle Books.   Dracula Returns! by Robert Lory

was the first in "The Dracula Horror Series." The story opens with Dracula being staked in his castle by "the Dutchman" and his intrepid group of "Englishmen" (apparently Van Hensing and company). Almost a century later, wheelchair-ridden Professor Damien Harmon is approached by Ktara, a strange ageless woman who can transform herself into a cat and who wants him to help her mysterious master. Through old documents, one describing a vampire accepting victims in Mexico during the time of Cortez, Harmon deduces her master to be Count Dracula. Other writings reveal that Dracula and Ktara originated in lost Atlantis. Harmon and the muscular Cameron Sanchez, both ex-members of the New York police force, venture to Dracula's castle, finding the vampire staked but not decomposed in any way. Before Cam removes the stake, Harmon implants his own invention next to the vampire's heart. By a single mental command the Professor can send a sliver from the stake into Dracula's heart, returning him to his deathlike state. Before Dracula makes his attacks, his nose flattens and the nostrils widen, upper and lower fangs appear, ears become pointed and enlarged, beginning at the lower jaw, eyebrows grow thicker, and the eyes, with black and purple centers and streaks of pink and red crosshatching over the whites, enlarge abnormally, all giving him the semblance of a human bat. Smuggling Dracula back to the United States, Harmon compels him to brutally eliminate a gang of crooks. Dracula almost destroys Harmon when the battery powering his heart implant begins to wear down, but Ktara adds her mental power to the Professor's and Cam produces a torturous sound in the communicator which was placed in the Count's ear. Dracula Returns! has more the feel of a pulp detective novel than a horror story, and thus it was with all the books in this mediocre series.

The Hand of Dracula! was the first sequel to Dracula Returns! Harmon's niece Jenny tells her uncle about Roy Ambers, a young man arrested for the murder of Derek Williams, a man who vanished after Roy had threatened him. Dracula bargains that if Harmon proves Roy's innocence within sixty hours he will obey the Professor without resistance for six months; otherwise, Harmon will remove the implant. Their handshake authenticates the novel's title. Cam investigates the Manson-inspired family of which both Roy and Derek had been members. Dracula intervenes as Jenny is about to be the cult's next human sacrifice, compelling their leader to set himself and the members on fire, but also learning that the family had nothing to do with Derek's murder. The search leads to a mortuary into which Cam delivers Dracula's coffin under pretext of wanting a funeral. Cam discovers that the thanatophile undertaker Yorge disposes of murder victims by burying them in occupied graves. The Count emerges from his coffin to save Cam and Jenny from the mortician's hunch-backed assistant Peter, then turns to kill Yorge before he can reveal the truth about Derek. Again Ktara intervenes, compelling Yorge to reveal how Derek was killed because he had discovered the undertaker's clandestine activities. Dracu-la then kills Yorge with his fangs (only those chosen by the Count becoming vampires themselves) and resolves to fulfill his end of the bargain.

In Dracula's Brothers the mad brothers August and Adrian Abelard have cross-bred the vampire bat with a larger and more intelligent genus, the result being a new species of bloodsucker which is receptive to their commands. When the bats make a number of attacks, using sharp metal sheaths to slash their victims apart, Harmon reminds Dracula of their wager. After the bats retrieve some bugged ransom money, Cam tracks them to the Adrian's house, where he is almost killed by the winged monsters. The bats fly off to attack Harmon. Futilely the Professor fires his pistol at the bats, killing only a few of them. Only the timely arrival of Count Dracula saves him. Reluctant to harm one of his "little brothers," Dracula points a finger at their leader, causing the creature to burst into a glow of pale green. The Count then leads the trained killers after Adrian, forcing him to stop his car and taking just enough blood to keep the maniac alive. In the presence of Cam and the police, Adrian is ripped apart by his own creations. Dracula then enters the cave where August awaits his brother's return. Though August pleads with Dracula to make him a vampire also, the Count chooses merely to take his blood and let him die.

Dracula's Gold was a more traditional vampire story. While climbing "Dracula Mountain," upon which stands the Count's castle in Transylvania, a young couple meet an aging, white-clad beauty named Dava who commands wolves to kill them. Dava claims to be the sister of Radu Conescu (named after Radu Florescu), a man overseeing the excavation of the mountain. Radu is a self-proclaimed descendant of the Count and is working to clear the family name. In the United States, Dracula denounces Radu as an imposter seeking his gold treasure and vows vengeance (he does not appear again until nine chapters later). Radu, actually an international spy who wants the gold for himself, and Dava, a homicidal actress

who knows how to train wolves, promote the vampire scare
to keep away the villagers. Dava finally gains access to the
treasure room of the castle and, shortly afterward, in the
tunnels beneath the ancient fortress, Cam battles three of the
madwoman's wolves. When Count Dracula finally does make
his reappearance to enact his vengeance, it is with lingering
passages of gratuitous sadism. He crushes the bones in
Conescu's wrist, forces him to slice out his own tongue,
then, as the villagers storm the castle, hurls him off the roof
to be blown up by a hidden charge of dynamite. Dracula then
returns to the treasure room, torturing Dava and hanging her
as a permanent guard to his gold. Before Dracula, Harmon,
Cam and Ktara leave Transylvania, the latter moves a sculp-
tor to create a statue called The Vampire Count, to be placed
as a warning atop Dracula Mountain.

The Count continues to make a limited number of appearances, finally enacting a grisly revenge on behalf of his
enemy Damien Harmon, in The Drums of Dracula, the first
novel of the series to be published in 1974. Harmon's neice
Jenny goes to the estate of Atwood Garth in Jamaica to research a paper she is writing on voodoo. Jenny is promptly
captured by a band of zombies and held for ransom by voodoo
houngan Daddy Bones. Cam becomes a prisoner when he
tries to rescue her but, as usual, Count Dracula arrives like
the ubiquitous U.S. Cavalry. Dracula cracks one zombie over
the voodoo sacrificial altar; two more burst aflame when the
Count, exhibiting some unexplained power, merely stares at
them. The voodoo priest, Daddy Bones himself, is engulfed
by his own sacred serpent, now under Dracula's control,
while his priestess Euleila, now a vampire herself, gives him
the fatal bite. Ktara destroys the rest of the voodoo cult by
fire while Dracula goes off to kill Atwood Garth, the real
guiding force behind the group. The Drums of Dracula concludes with Cam staking the un-dead Euleila.

The next novel, The Witching of Dracula, brought Elizabeth Báthory, the Blood Countess, into the series. Having
gone through many incarnations, including Lilith and Circe,
Elizabeth (now using her "real" name of Sabor) is revealed to
be a sadistic immortal who lives on by draining away the
thoughts of her victims. Sabor is also an ancient enemy of
Dracula. A Hungarian peasant is led by a wolf to a secret
chamber in Sabor's castle, where he finds the red-haired
beauty lying naked in a glass-sealed box, in which she had
been imprisoned by the senior Dracul. The peasant frees
her, allowing Sabor to use her powers to find Count Dracula,

creating an army of mindless slaves in the process. In Germany, Harmon becomes her prisoner and Cam is tortured by her rack and branding iron. Dracula finally confronts her, but is warded off with crosses. Only Harmon's disrupting the crosses with a toss of his wheelchair frees Dracula. Cam stabs Sabor with a lance while the Count finishes her off with his fangs. Later, again lying dormant in her glass-topped receptacle, Sabor is sunk beneath the Rhine River.

Xerox Education Publications issued Dracula's Guest and Other Stories in 1973. This was an anthology edited by Vic Ghidalia, presenting the Bram Stoker tale, "Dracula's Guest," along with short stories by other noted authors.

The Beast with the Red Hands, by Sidney Stuart, published in 1973 by Popular Library, concerned a fiend known as the Redhead Killer, who strikes while certain films play at a local theatre. One of these pictures, described in some detail, is the 1931 DRACULA. That same year Popular Library issued The Vampire Women, a novel which deals more with Count Drakula (explained as the correct spelling before Stoker tinkered with it) than it does with any vampire women. A scientist named John Hamilton, his wife Victoria and her sister Carolyn travel to Transylvania to investigate earthquakes, but are forced to take residence in the old Drakula castle. As the Americans ride to the castle via horse-drawn coach, three women in white appear and are apparently replaced by wolves. Somehow Hamilton remains naive to the implications of Drakula's name with vampirism. The story proceeds in routine fashion, with the Americans' removing the stake from a skeleton's ribs and presently meeting a man calling himself Count Drakula (a descendant, he says, of the original Count). Hamilton, Victoria and Carolyn also meet three women resembling those seen on the road. Victor Samuels borrowed from Stoker's novel, lifting descriptions (especially that of the Count), actions and dialogue, with Hamilton remaining ignorant while mimicking the actions of Jonathan Harker. After Drakula places Carolyn under his spell, the brilliant scientist finally deduces that he is a vampire. Learning of Drakula's plan to return with the Americans to the United States, Hamilton uses explosives to blow open the door leading to the vampire's coffin. Drakula rises from his coffin, summoning Carolyn and the vampire women to his aid, but Hamilton finally thrusts the stake through his chest, reducing the Count to bones. Carolyn dies and the vampire women fade away, leaving Dracula buffs with little they had not read before.

Dracula continued to haunt novels in 1974, as in Dracula's Triomf ("Dracula's Triumph"), by R. Michael Rosen, in which the Count returns from the dead to punish the mortals who have converted his castle into a hotel. The novel was published in Holland by De Schorpioen as part of its Horror series.

The Night Stalker, a novel originally titled The Kolchak Tapes, written by Jeff Rice, was published in 1973 by Pocket Books. The novel concerned vampire Janos Skorzeny, loose in modern and glittery Las Vegas. The story frequently referred to Count Dracula with details about Vlad the Impaler. In one scene Skorzeny attacks one of his female victims near a motion picture theatre which is appropriately running a film entitled DRACULA RETURNS. A motion picture announced as THE KOLCHAK TAPES but finally changed to THE NIGHT STALKER was made for ABC-TV in 1971 and shown in 1972. The film was scripted by Richard Matheson who adapted Rice's then unpublished manuscript. Dan Curtis (of DARK SHADOWS fame) produced the film while John Llowellyn Moxey directed. Darren McGavin starred as Kolchak, the newspaperman who tries to convince the world of the vampire's existence and who eventually stakes his heart. Barry Atwater portrayed Janos Skorzeny without dialogue. THE NIGHT STALKER was the highest rated feature film ever made for television and won a number of awards.

Many non-Dracula vampire novels owe their existence to Stoker. Eugene Ascher's To Kill a Corpse, published by World Distributors (London, 1965), was the story of Count Chesley (also known as Asper), who is finally destroyed by a surgical knife through the heart. Ascher's narrator attributed the vampire's destruction to medical reasons, theorizing that piercing the heart with anything or severing the external carotid jugular arteries would sufficiently bring the creature true death.

The Vampire Cameo, a gothic romance by Dorothea Nile, published in 1968 by Lancer Books, brought the virginal American schoolteacher Rosalie Lindquist to the Transylvanian Alps. When her coach overturns, Rosalie is rescued by the handsome Count Alexander Darkus who stands before her in complete Dracula regalia. Due to their strange behavior, the Count and his wife seem to be vampires, but their actions are eventually explained as a complicated series of highly unlikely circumstances. After the Countess commits suicide, Rosalie marries the man of her dreams and becomes the new lady of Castle Darkus.

Peter Saxon's Vampire Moon (Belmont Books, 1970) featured the vampire Count Zapolia. Frequent references to Dracula are made in this Transylvania-set novel. The Count menaces two American girls visiting his domain, transforming one into a vampire and eventually suffering decapitation while grappling with the story's hero atop his castle.

Brother Blood, by this writer, followed the basic plot structure of Dracula, with a black vampire named Preston Duval establishing a nest of vampires and finally meeting destruction by fire. Written two years before BLACULA, the novel was published in 1974 as Broeder Bloed in De Schorpoien's Horror.

... AND OTHER STORIES

Dracula was the subject of short stories as early as 1930, when "Another Dracula," by Ralph Milne Farley, was published in two parts in the September and October issues of the pulp magazine Weird Tales (Popular Fiction Publishing Co.). "Another Dracula" was set not in Transylvania but Pennsylvania, in the town of Yangton, and concerned a newly arrived Frenchman named Peter Larousse, whose appearance and actions seemingly betray him as a vampire. (There was good reason for this. The description of Larousse was lifted almost verbatim from Stoker's description of Count Dracula.) More evidence convicts Larousse as one of the un-dead when he buries a coffin in a vacant lot and when a young girl apparently dies from loss of blood. The girl, having been buried alive, is rescued by a doctor just as villagers are about to stake her through the heart. Larousse then reveals that the coffin in the lot contains the corpse of his father, who had promised him a fortune providing he was some day buried in the soil of his home town. The explanation for the clandestine burial was that Larousse's father was once wrongly accused of theft in that town. Another pulp story published in the thirties was "Little Miss Dracula," written by Ralston Shields.

"The Cloak," by Robert Bloch, published in the May 1939 issue of Unknown, is the story of a young man named Henderson, who stops by a costume shop on the way to a Halloween party and asks for an authentic vampire cloak. Wearing the cloak, Henderson attends the party and learns that his face has seemingly taken on the features of a vampire. He also discovers that he no longer throws a mirror

image and that he has a sudden thirst for human blood. The
guests begin to call him Dracula or Dracula Henderson and
he appears to authenticate the name by trying to bite one of
them on the neck. Henderson's Dracula career is quelled
when a young woman, who purchased a similar cloak from
the same shop, sinks her fangs into his neck.

"Dracula's Brides," by Wayne Rogers, in the February 1941 issue of the pulp magazine Horror Stories (Popular
Publications), was more a hardboiled detective story than
what the title of the magazine implied. A bloodless corpse,
barely flesh and bone, is discovered during a time when a
gang of criminals called the Wolf Pack terrorizes the city,
robbing and killing. Private investigator Jim Hanley becomes
involved in the case when a girl dies shielding him from bullets, just after giving him a business card publicizing a
strange cabaret called the Dracula Club. There the detective
witnesses the main act, a masked performer called Dracula
attacking girls and drinking their blood. When Hanley is
captured by the Wolf Pack, he learns that their leader is a
mad scientist who has created living vampires in his gunmen,
arousing in them a craving for blood, which he gives them
in exchange for their loot. Finally, Hanley dons one of the
Wolf Pack's claw gloves and slashes the doctor's throat.

More of a traditional Dracula story was "The Devil Is
Not Mocked," by Manly Wade Wellman, which appeared in the
June 1943 issue of Unknown Worlds (Street & Smith Publications). The tale answers the question, "What did Count
Dracula do during the Second World War?" The most literate
of the early Dracula pulp magazine stories despite its pulp
magazine origin, "The Devil Is Not Mocked" is the tale of a
troop of Nazi soldiers who occupy an old castle in Transylvania. General von Grunn is invited into the castle by a
pale-faced man in black. While Herr General is treated to
a sumptuous meal, some of his men explore the castle. To
his horror, General von Grunn discovers that the men outside the castle are being devoured by wolves, while those within are the victims of vampires. The sinister host explains,
"I am Count Dracula of Transylvania," then moves toward
him for his own meal.

Richard Matheson's tragic story "Drink My Red Blood
..." was published in the April 1951 issue of Imagination
(Greenleaf Publishing Company). The tale concerns a young
idiot boy named Jules, who not only is pale in complexion
and hates the sunlight, but also desires to become a vampire.

After discovering the movie DRACULA and then the original
novel, Jules carries his fascination with the vampire to the
extremes of morbidity. In school he writes a paper under
the name Jules Dracula, professing an ambition to be a vampire. He steals a vampire bat from the zoo, appropriately
naming it the "Count." Eventually, Jules hacks at his own
throat with a pen knife, forcing the winged creature to drink
the flowing blood. As Jules dies he beholds a dark man with
red eyes looming over him and addressing the boy as "son."
"Drink My Red Blood ... " was reprinted in 1967 with the
new title, "Blood Son."

        A number of short stories featuring Count Dracula have
been printed in the magazine Famous Monsters of Filmland,
which is edited by Forrest J Ackerman (who occasionally uses
the pseudonym "Dr. Acula") and issued by the Warren Publishing Company. In "Sun of Dracula," by Lima da Costa,
in Famous Monsters, no. 12 (June 1961), the infamous Count
is on his way to the North Pole (where the nights are six
months long) but is destroyed when his train pauses in Nor-
way, the "Land of the Midnight Sun." Famous Monsters no.
22 (April 1963) presented "The Undead," a story paralleling
a scene in the 1931 DRACULA film. The Count kills a peasant boy, then proceeds to attack Mina in her bedroom, only
to be forced into retreat in the form of a bat by Van Helsing
and Seward. After daybreak, the heroes find Dracula asleep
in the Crypt beneath Carfax Abbey, and stake him. Richard
Benda and Henry Hamarck's story "Transylvania, Here We
Come!" in Famous Monsters no. 26 (January 1964), was a
story about two visitors to Castle Dracula who share a pic-
nic in the graveyard with the Count. Dracula commits suicide
by stake in "Rip Van Dracula," by G. John Edwards, in issue
no. 36 (December 1965), after being tricked into believing
that aliens have invaded the Earth with a blood-evaporating
ray. "Dracula 2000," by Sathanas Rehan (G. John Edwards)
and Viktor Vesperto (Forrest J Ackerman), in Famous Monsters, no. 55 (May 1969), brings Dracula to the planet Pluto
where he is arrested for breaking into a "water bank" and
charged with vampirism (water, not blood, flows in the
Plutonians' veins). Monster World, a companion magazine to
Famous Monsters, featured "Count Down to Doom," by
Charles Nuetzel and Vesperto in its eighth issue (May 1966).
Dracula searches an Earth ravaged by atomic war for a victim but finds his manlike victim to be a bloodless vegetable,
the obvious joke being that you can't get blood from a turnip.

        In 1963 the final pages of Stoker's Dracula were

published as "The Death of Dracula" in The Vampire, an
anthology edited by Ornella Volta and Valeria Riva. (The collection was published in England by Neville Spearman, while
a 1960 edition was issued in Italy as I Vampiri tra Noi; "The
Vampire in Us. ")

Robert Bloch's story, "The Plot Is the Thing," in the
July 1966 issue of The Magazine of Fantasy and Science Fiction (Mercury Press), concerned a lobotomy recipient sent
into the world of such movie characters as Dracula. "Bruce,"
a story by Salitha Grey in Witchcraft and Sorcery, no. 5 (Jan-
uary-February 1971), issued by the Fantasy Publishing Company, was about a dragon named Bruce who is bitten on his
scaly neck by Dracula. Woody Allen included a humorous
story called "Count Dracula" in his book, Getting Even (Ran-
dom House, 1971). Dracula, tricked by a solar eclipse into
thinking night has fallen, arrives early for a dinner party.
After making various unsuccessful attempts to leave, Dracula
hides in the closet until the visiting mayor opens the door and
the returning sunlight reduces him to ashes.

Again, Dangerous Visions (Doubleday, 1972), edited by
Harlan Ellison, included the James Blish story, "Getting
Along," in which the author, through a series of letters, tells
a story of fantasy, horror, comedy and sex. Each letter is
written in the style of some former author of imaginative fiction. "Letter the Third" successfully imitates Stoker and the
early scenes of Dracula. The female narrator visits an
"aunt-in-lieu" named Mrs. Vrolok, whose description could
almost be that of the Count himself, right to the mustache.
Mrs. Vrolok shares her bed with the narrator, then attacks
a servant girl. Finally, the narrator finds the woman in the
woodshed, sleeping upon a layer of mothballs in a coffin-like
hope chest, her mouth darkened with blood.

The Monster Times, a newspaper of horror, science
fiction and fantasy, published "An Interview with Count Dracula" in its eleventh issue (June 14, 1972). This piece by
Roger Singleton was a veritable short story with the inter-
viewer going to the New York hotel where Dracula, bitter
over the way the films have distorted his image, resides incognito.

A series of generally mediocre short stories starring
the Count were included between comic strips in Marvel's
magazine Dracula Lives! "Who Is Bram Stoker and Why Is
He Saying Those Terrible Things About Me?" was written by

Chris Claremont for <u>Dracula Lives!</u> no. 2 (1973) and had
Dracula swearing revenge against Stoker for the latter's vicious "lies." "I Was Once a Gentle Man," in the third issue
(October 1973), again by Claremont, had Van Helsing discover
that his new bride Elisabeth is the victim in a Black Mass
being conducted by Dracula. Inevitably forced to destroy his
wife, now a vampire, Van Helsing beings his war against the
Count. "Demons of Darkness," by Gerry Conway, in <u>Dracula
Lives!</u> vol. 2, no. 1 (March 1974), brought Dracula, incognito as "Drake," to an old mill to summon forth hellish demons. A young boy, working at the inn where Dracula left
his coffin, fends off the vampire with a cross, sets fire to
the former demon haunt and receives the Count's threat to
return for him some night. Dracula called himself "Mr.
Vlad" in "Blood Moon," by Thomas O'Rourke, in the sixth
and seventh issues (May and July 1974), and hired a burglar
to break into a blood bank, only to discover the liquid to have
been broken down into its constituents. The Count is then
forced to capture the bank's receptionist and set a pack of
coyotes upon the priest who is chasing after him. There is
an eventual automobile wreck in which the priest and receptionist are saved when Dracula's coffin protects them from
the overturning vehicle. Claremont's "Child of the Sun," in
<u>Dracula Lives!</u> no. 8 (September 1974), had a vampire called
Dragon attack a female spy in her wooden airplane. Forcing
the plane down in the Transylvanian Alps, she becomes a vampiress who refuses to accept her fate, opposing Dragon and
fighting off his vampire minions. The story concludes with
her crashing the plane a second time in an attempt to destroy
herself and Dragon. One vampire survives, however--Dragon,
who not surprisingly reveals himself as Dracula.

Other Dracula-style vampires have haunted short
stories, an amusing example being the Baron in Arthur
Porges' "Mop-Up," first published in the July 1953 issue of
<u>The Magazine of Fantasy and Science Fiction.</u> The last man
on Earth after the nuclear war happens upon a witch, a ghoul
and the vampiric Baron who are contemplating destroying him
when suddenly the forest animals attack. Trying to escape,
the Baron transforms into a bat but is felled by birds of prey
and impaled by the forest creatures with a sapling, the meek
having inherited the planet. "Fresh Guy," another post-nu-
clear war story by E. C. Tubb, published in 1958, featured
Count Boris, one of several monsters pondering the potential
human victims living underground to escape the surface's
atomic fallout.

The January 1963 issue of Midi-Minuit Fantastique, a French magazine devoted to fantastic films, was devoted entirely to Dracula. There is also The Count Dracula Society Quarterly, the journal of that organization, edited by Gordon R. Guy. The first issue was published in 1967.

The Count has even invaded poetry. In Edward Moss' poem "Horror Movie" (originally published in Harper's Bazaar), the poet expresses his fondness for the old monster films, describing Count Dracula pursuing a female victim.

Dracula's literary career continues to endure. Back in the 1950s the King Vampire's fame had spread to illustrated fiction. Twenty years later the virtually immortal Count would become the most popular fiend in the comic books.

Chapter 12

DRACULA MEETS THE COMICS

> ... and most of all, I yearn for that most pleasing
> taste ... the sweet nectar of life itself!
> --Tomb of Dracula, no. 1 (1972), by Gerry Conway

Count Dracula seems almost made for the comic books.
His many powers--his ability to change form and command
the elements--are extremely visual in their conceptions.
Those abilities can be more easily drawn on a sheet of comic
art board than they can be created on the motion picture
screen or in the theatre.

Bram Stoker's Dracula was abundant in visual imagery
and was first adapted to the comic book medium in the twelfth
issue of Eerie (August 1953), published by Avon Periodicals
(not to be confused with the Warren magazine of the same
title). The version was faithful to Stoker but ended with Van
Helsing driving a stake through Dracula's heart. Classics
Illustrated had considered doing a Dracula adaptation but abandoned the idea because of the Eerie version appearing at the
same time. Russ Jones prepared two paperback books featuring graphic adaptations of Stoker's works in 1966. In the
first, simply titled Dracula, writers Otto Binder and Craig
Tennis and artist Alden McWilliams created a masterful adaptation of the novel. The second book, Christopher Lee's
Treasury of Terror (Pyramid Books), included a comic strip
version of "Dracula's Guest," adapted by E. Nelson Bridwell
and drawn by Frank Bolle. Another adaptation of Dracula,
titled Dracula il Vampiro and identifying the Count as the un-
dead Impaler, was presented in the Italian illustrated paperback, I Classici a Fumetti (January 1969). A superb adaptation of Dracula, written without the more grisly scenes by
Naunerle Farr and drawn stunningly by Nestor Redondo, was
published in 1973 in a black and white edition in the Now Age
Illustrated (Pendulum Press) series. Pendulum soon made a
color poster available of the splash page artwork.

During the 1950s horror comic book craze, the name
of Stoker's novel was changed to Tracula for the story, "Pages
of Death," in the eighth issue of Superior Publishers' Journey
into Fear (July 1952).   A scientist invents a chemical that
sends him and his girlfriend into the fictional world of the vampire Tracula.   The antidote saves them moments before Tracula's wolves can attack.

After the inauguration of the Comics Code Authority in
the mid-1950s, which banned vampires from the color comic
books, Dracula went into retirement from the medium.   Dell
Comics, a company which did not subscribe to the Code,
resurrected the Count in a Dracula comic book published in
October-December 1962.   The story itself, "The Vampire's
Curse," takes artist Bruce Shawcross to Transylvania where
he meets a beautiful girl named Irina who becomes his model.
Bruce's father Sir Basil Shawcross and vampire authority
Janos Tesla journey to Transylvania where Irina and Bruce,
now a vampire himself, take them to Castle Dracula.   The
Count wants Sir Basil, a doctor, to supply the vampires with
blood.   But the doctor suffers a fatal heart attack while Janos
drives the un-dead away with wolfbane and garlic, Dracula
swearing vengeance against his new enemy (intimating a series).

But Dell's Dracula remained unseen for four years.
With the mid-1960s super-hero craze incited by television's
BATMAN, Dell revamped their book to present their own bat-
oriented costumed crime-fighter.   Dracula no. 2 (November
1966) featured poor artwork by Tony Tallarico and poorer
writing.   A descendant of the original Count Dracula attempts
to clear "the blight of history on my ancestors" and at the
same time find a means "to aid the healing of brain damage"
with a serum derived from "the supersensory portions of the
brains of bats."   Accidentally consuming the potion (which
had somehow gotten into his drinking glass), Dracula gains
the ability to transform into a bat.   When a fascistic army
moves into his castle Dracula uses his powers to expel them.
The last story, "Dracula's Pledge," showed the Count developing his body to physical perfection, donning a purple super-
hero costume complete with bat ears and vowing war on evil
(all à la Bruce Wayne becoming The Batman).   In America,
using the secret identity name of Al U. Card, Dracula gains
an underground headquarters in "The Secret Cave" and a girl

Opposite: Cover of the first comic book adaptation of Dracula.
Copyright 1953 by Avon Periodicals, Inc.

. . . .and also unseen.

But. . .I can't see him in the mirror!

I frightened you. . .you've cut yourself!

Suddenly the Count's eyes filled with fury and he grabbed my throat!

There is blood on your throat!

But, sir. . . it is nothing. . . .

A cross!

At sight of the landlady's gift, Dracula's strange fury passed.

Be careful how you cut yourself. It is dangerous in this country!

partner in "The Origin of Fleeta," both in the fourth issue
(March 1967). Dracula no. 4 was the last issue of this magazine, although it was revived in reprints during the 1970s to
capitalize on the Dracula comics being published by other companies. In addition to Dracula, Dell also published a comic
book adaptation of the film, MAD MONSTER PARTY? in 1967.

Dracula frequently appeared in the comic books published by ACG (American Comics Group) during the mid-six-
ties. "Pass a Piece of Pizza, Please!" in Herbie no. 20
(September 1966) had the Count unable to cope with the modern world and developing an unnatural craving for pizza.
During the late 1960s a series of sexy Dracula comic books
was published in Brazil by Taika, Ltd., often with the images
of Lugosi or Lee on the covers and taking the Count through
many black and white adventures in many time eras. The
first issue sent Dracula to the Egypt of Rameses III, where
he enjoys the blood and beds of many nubile women before escaping as a bat from a raging fire. In succeeding issues the
Count fights a sword duel in the eighteenth century, becomes
a knight during the Middle Ages and takes the blood of a
young witch during the Spanish Inquisition. These comics
were abundant in sex and sadism, often depicting the Count
staking his victims to avoid creating his own competition.
The same publisher also brought out several issues of Alma-
naque de Dracula with new stories, one of which brought the
Count into conflict against a tribe of Incas. Equally sexy and
sadistic was Jacula, an Italian comic of the late sixties starring a beautiful Transylvanian vampiress.

National Periodical Publications (DC Comics) kept
Dracula as a tame comedic figure in "Scared Silly!", written
by Arnold Drake and drawn by Bob Oksner for the eighty-
third issue of The Adventures of Jerry Lewis (July-August
1964). Count Drinkula and his monster friends are replaced
by their actor counterparts, including Bela Le Ghoul, until
the supposedly real monsters are exposed as gangsters. The
same writer and artist created a virtually identical set of
monsters for "Super-Hip, the Sickest Super-Hero of 'em All,"
in The Adventures of Bob Hope, no. 95 (October-November
1965). The Dracula character, now called Dr. Van Pyre,
was principal of a high school run by monsters in this book
that continued for almost three years.

Opposite: A page from the "Now Age Illustrated Series" of
graphic stories. Reprinted from Dracula by Bram Stoker,
by permission of Pendulum Press, Inc. Copyright 1973.

A more serious Dracula-type story was written, drawn and edited by Jack Kirby for the two-part tale, "The Man from Transilvane!" in Superman's Pal Jimmy Olsen, no. 142 (October 1971), and "Genocide Spray," in the next issue (November 1971). But Count Dragorin and his monstrous cohorts are revealed as inhabitants of the miniature, artificially-created planet Transilvane who had so developed because of a relentless dosage of old earthly horror films. A more serious DC story was "Captain Dracula," in Weird War Tales no. 18 (October 1973), by Drake and artist Tony DeZuniga. Captain Paul Blake becomes the victim of a beautiful vampiress named Angela. After destroying her with the leg of a broken chair, he makes his own vampiric attacks on Nazi soldiers, then destroys them with rifle stocks and other makeshift stakes until he himself falls upon an impaling crucifix. In contrast to the fine scripting and artwork of "Captain Dracula" was "Vampire in the White House," a fatuous, demeaning story by editor Joe Simon and drawn by Jerry Grandenetti for the fourth issue of Prez (February-March 1974). Dracula was now a legless and previously tortured travesty of himself, wheeling about on a little platform. Smuggled into the White House by a werewolf ambassador from Transylvania, Dracula makes a futile attempt to invade America with rabid bats. Finally he is driven into the sea when trained birds enter his bat-shaped plane. Count Dracula operated tours to vampire-ridden Transylvania in "Flight into Fright," a story by George Kashdan and drawn by Ernie Chua in DC's Weird Mystery Tales no. 14 (October-November 1974). The Count, and his hunchbacked servant Quasimodo, would fly jaded jet-setters to his native land, where they would be promptly attacked by vampire bats and transformed into Dracula's obedient, un-dead slaves.

A large sized Dracula comic magazine was issued by Buru Lan S. A. de Ediciones in Spain, the first issue appearing in February, 1972. The series lasted for a dozen issues, terminating in August of that year. The title was misleading. Except for "The Messenger" in the sixth issue, in which the Count emerges from his coffin to receive a letter, and except for a few covers showing Dracula or other vampires, the book showcased a variety of quite different characters. After its original publication, Dracula was reprinted in Spain as a complete volume. That same year the New English Library in London published all twelve issues in English and later (1974) as a single volume titled Dracula Annual, while Warren Publishing Company, in 1972, reprinted the first six issues as one impressive volume. Dracula himself was the villain of the twenty-sixth issue of the Mexican mini-comic book, Conchita la Detective (May 1972), in the story "Conchita vs. Dracula" which climaxed with his falling upon a jagged piece of wood.

In 1973 an unauthorized Blacula comic book was published independently in black, white and red. Blacula, now presented as a former student of the occult, becomes a vampire by night and eventually grinds his victims into dog food in one of the poorest of the comic books in script, art and taste. Count Rudolf, first cousin to Count Dracula, was dismayed in "The Curse of the Vampire," written by Joe Gill and drawn by Tony Williamsune (Talarico), in The Many Ghosts of Dr. Graves, no. 44 (January 1974), published by the Charlton Comics Group. For Rudolf's castle becomes a tourist site while he has become a celebrity, feared by no one and forced to hitch-hike to spend some time recuperating with Dracula.

Gold Key Comics (a division of Western Publishing Company) published "The Flintstones Meet Frankenstein and Dracula" in the thirty-third issue of The Flintstones (September 1966), wherein the famous monsters travel through time and apprehend a Stone Age burglar. A serious Dracula and other personalities took revenge on a prima donna mimic, causing him to assume his own cowardly personality in "The Impressionist," in The Twilight Zone, no. 66 (November 1966). "The Vampires," in Gold Key's Ripley's Believe It or Not! no. 4 (April 1967), showed Bram Stoker along with the Count and the historical Drakula. "Ghost of Dracula" was written by Mark Evanier and drawn by Dan Spiegle for Scooby Doo--Where Are You? no. 25 (April 1974), a gangster masquerading as Dracula tries to discredit mayoral candidate Sidney Ladacur (anagram for Dracula) by claiming to be his ancestor. The Occult Files of Dr. Spektor, a comic book created and scripted by this writer and illustrated by Jesse Santos, brought Dracula into the fifth (December 1973) issue's "Little Ol' Coffin-Maker." A wanted criminal hides from the police in a handmade casket, only to be carried off by its owner, Count Dracula (still sporting the scar given him by Jonathan Harker's shovel). "Dracula's Vampire Legion," in Spektor, no. 8 (June 1974), had the Count use the Ruthvenian to revive Sir Francis Varney, Countess Mircalla Karnstein and Lord Ruthven to join his un-dead ranks. The story introduced Valdemar Van Helsing, a type of bounty hunter who tracks down supernatural creatures for payment.

When Dracula attempts to enlist the cured vampire Baron
Tibor* in his legion, occult hobbyist Dr. Adam Spektor intervenes and defeats the evil un-dead with a counter-spell from
the ancient book. Dracula himself escapes as a bat.

THE TOMB OF DRACULA

The Marvel Comics Group has to date published more
Dracula stories than any other American comic book company.
During the early 1950s, when Marvel was known as Atlas,
the company issued a number of pre-Comics Code magazines
with Dracula stories, all of which led to shock or surprise
endings.

"Dracula Lives!" was published in the seventh issue
of that company's Suspense (March 1951). A man named
Tartoff reveals to horror writer Sandor Xavier that Dracula
has been preying upon his family for years and that if the
Count fails to take his blood this night, the vampire will die
forever. Just before dawn Tartoff hands Xavier his wooden
stake when the writer shows his fangs and reveals his true
identity. "Behind Locked Doors," in Mystic, no. 17 (February 1953), was the story of an unscrupulous psychiatrist
named Denby who meets a blonde-haired nobleman with an in-
feriority complex stemming from existing in the shadow of his
father. Through hypnosis Denby obviates the man's fears and
finds himself confronted by the thirsty son of Dracula. A
third Atlas story, "Of Royal Blood," in Journey into Unknown
Worlds, no. 29 (July 1954), showed Phineas Kroner breaking
up his daughter's romances, murdering one suitor and letting
the blame fall upon a vampire preying in the area. Insisting
that she marry only one of royal blood, Kroner is delighted
to meet her next fiancé, Count Dracula.

*Baron Tibor first appeared as an evil vampire in "A Tree
Grows in Transylvania," in Mystery Comics Digest, no. 4
(January 1972), and was impaled by the limb of a dead tree,
the roots of which had grown among the bones of his victims.
He was revived in "Cult of the Vampire," in the first issue
of The Occult Files of Dr. Spektor (1973), and reformed when
Spektor cured him of his craving for blood, a side-effect be-
ing the loss of his vampire powers. Both stories were writ-
ten by the present author and drawn by Jesse Santos. Baron
Tibor has since become a semi-regular character in the
Spektor series.

With the inauguration of the Comics Code Authority vampire stories could not be published in the regular color comic books.   The Code was revised in 1971, premitting vampire stories if they were presented in the classic tradition of Dracula.   In 1972 the Marvel Comics Group published "Blechhula!", a spoof of the movie BLACULA, in the fourth issue of Spoof (March 1973).

But Marvel took further advantage of the laxity of the Code that same year with a comic book entitled Tomb of Dracula.   First announced as an upcoming large-sized black and white magazine, the book became a standard color comic book in April.   Gerry Conway penned the script over Gene Colan's artwork.   The first story, "Dracula," set in the present time, brought Frank Drake to Transylvania to claim Castle Dracula, which he had inherited.   (The Drake family name used to be Dracula.)   Accompanying Drake to the castle are his girlfriend Jeanie and his questionable friend and Jeanie's former lover, Clifton.   The latter discovers the coffin containing the staked skeleton of Dracula and revives him. Dracula, portrayed with dead white face and Satanic mustache and beard, confronts Drake and transforms Jeanie into one of the un-dead.

"The Fear Within!" in the second issue (May 1972), had Dracula visiting a former doctor friend who makes the vampire more human in appearance.   Drake is forced to stake Jeanie through the back and watch her crumble to dust in the sunlight, demonstrating just how lenient the Code had become. Beginning with the third issue (July 1972), Archie Goodwin, who had just left the Warren Publishing Company where he had been scripting other Dracula stories, assumed the writing chores on Tomb.

With the arrival of Goodwin, Dracula lost his beard and gained new adversaries in beautiful Rachel Van Helsing and her East Indian servant Taj, who continued her great-grandfather's war against the Count.   Goodwin brought Dracula to a fading beauty who asks to become un-dead to restore her lost youth in "Through a Mirror Darkly!" in issue no. 4 (September 1972).   When her new vampiric state does not provide rejuvenation, she willingly lets Rachel fire a wooden arrow into her heart.   The next two issues of Tomb were written by comics veteran Gardner F. Fox who, in the sixth issue (November 1972), sent the Count back to nineteenth century Transylvania where he unsuccessfully tries to destroy his original Van Helsing Adversary.

An atmospheric page from "Fear Is the Name of the Game!" in Tomb of Dracula, no. 15, written by Marv Wolfman and illustrated by Gene Colan. Copyright 1973 by Marvel Comics Group.

Most of the stories in <u>Tomb of Dracula</u> were written by Marv Wolfman, whose first story in the series, "Night of the Death Stalkers!" was for the seventh issue (March 1973). Wolfman introduced wheelchair-ridden Quincy Harker, son of Jonathan. Harker continues the war against the Count with such innovations as a flying net weighted with garlic balls to ensnare bats and a wheelchair that fires poisoned wooden darts. The story brought Count Dracula to control a group of entranced children.

A surprising fact about Marv Wolfman's version of <u>Tomb</u> is that at the time he began to script the series he had never seen a Dracula film. "Whatever background I have on Dracula comes from the original Stoker novel, which I enjoyed very much," he told me. "I first read this about a month before I began writing <u>Tomb of Dracula</u>. Dracula, as Stoker wrote him, had a certain aristocratic feel to his being. He was also the Devil incarnate. Secondly, the novel, since it was told in diary form from several people's points of view, interested me--because of the human side of the story against the evil side of life. Thirdly, I've always been fascinated by the subjects of fear and death. The vampire and Dracula legend fit in perfectly with whatever warped views I possessed. Therefore, the topic of life and death, the idea of a story dealing with people facing such, and a character that epitomized life, death and fear were absolutely perfect.... Dracula is arrogant, bestial, hot-tempered. He has no reason to calm himself. But sometimes his arrogance can be his weakness. He is so sure of his abilities, he sometimes overlooks those of lesser men."

Among the "lesser men" that Dracula would meet under Wolfman's authorship was Blade, the Vampire-Slayer. Blade was a hip 1970s black man with a peculiar immunity to the bite of the vampire because his mother's blood had been tainted by Dracula. "His Name Is ... Blade!" in issue no. 10 (July 1973), introduced the character who tries to destroy the hated Count with his accurately thrown wooden knives.

"Dracula Is Dead!" was a rather unique Wolfman story which appeared in <u>Tomb of Dracula</u>, no. 14 (November 1973). Dracula, his skeleton impaled by one of Blade's knives, is revived by a misanthropic preacher before an awed congregation; the preacher then faces the consequences. Count Dracula was introduced as a special guest star to boost the sales of <u>The Frankenstein Monster</u>, another Marvel comic book. In "The Fury of the Fiend!" in issue no. 7 (November 1973), the Monster witnesses the revival of the staked Count during the 1800s. (By now Marvel had established that Dracula had been destroyed and revived many times before his resurrection in Tomb no. 1.) The two horrors battle in the next issue's "My Name Is ... Dracula" (January 1974), with the Count being simultaneously staked by the Frankenstein Monster and bathed in sunlight. Dracula next encountered Jack Russell, the lycanthropic protagonist of Marvel's Werewolf by Night, another book written at the time by (appropriately) Marv Wolfman. "Enter: Werewolf by Night," in Tomb no. 18 (March 1974), brought Jack to Transylvania and into conflict with Dracula. The story concluded that same month in Werewolf by Night no. 15, in "Death of a Monster!" with artwork by Mike Ploog. The Werewolf hurls the Count off a balcony but the vampire saves himself by metamorphosing into a bat.

Tomb of Dracula was a well written and illustrated magazine, far above the calibre of many comic books, and it remains the best Dracula comic series to date. Marvel's attempt at producing a prestigious Dracula book was appreciated by the paying readers. Tomb became one of the company's top sellers and publisher Stan Lee knew that the best way to profit from Dracula's popularity was to feature him in more magazines.

Marvel's second Dracula magazine, entitled Dracula Lives!, was published in the oversized black and white format originally planned for Tomb. Unaffected by the Comics Code, the Dracula Lives! stories could be on a more adult level, with sex and gore graphically displayed. The first issue was released in 1973 with the Count consistent with the Dracula of the color magazine but also taking the reader back through time to show his earlier adventures. The first story of the premiere issue, "A Poison of the Blood," written by Gerry Conway and drawn by Gene Colan, brought Dracula in search of his enemy Cagliostro, but finding only an imposter. "Suffer Not a Witch," written by editor Roy Thomas and drawn by Alan Weiss, was set in 1691, with Dracula precipitating the witch scare in Salem after the woman he loves is hanged for witchcraft. Dracula was herein pictured in the dashing garb of a seventeenth century lord. "To Walk Again in Daylight," the last story in the issue, written by Steve Gerber and illustrated by Rich Buckler, placed Dracula in nineteenth century Vienna, stepping out of character to seek a cure for his vampiric state.

Cover of Dracula Lives! no. 3, with artwork by Neal Adams. Copyright 1973 by Marvel Comics Group.

Dracula Lives! no. 2, also published that year, gave the Count an origin. "That Dracula May Live Again!", written by Wolfman and drawn by Neal Adams, followed Vlad the Impaler through a battle against the Turks in which he is mortally wounded. A vampiric Gypsy hag, vengeful for what the Impaler had done to her people, gives him the bite of the un-dead. Dracula then becomes a prisoner in his own castle, now occupied by the Turks and their leader Turac. When he learns that his wife Maria has been raped by the Turks, Dracula realizes what he has become, breaks his chains and destroys the enemy. Eventually Dracula flies off with his infant son Vlad and Maria's corpse. Later he vows upon her grave, "This world took you from me--and now all the world shall pay! So swears--DRACULA!"

Dracula Lives! no. 3 (1973) concluded the origin in "Lord of Death... Lord of Hell!" by Wolfman and artist John Buscema. Neo-vampire Dracula is taken to the lair of the un-dead where he engages Nimrod, the burly King of Vampires, in a duel with stakes, emerging as the victorious "Lord of the Undead." Another story, "Castle of the Undead," by Roy Thomas and artist Alan Weiss, pitted the Count against Solomon Kane, Robert E. Howard's Puritan, swashbuckling righter of wrongs. The Count saves Kane from wolves and then invites him to Castle Dracula. When Kane learns the true nature of Dracula he fights the vampire in a sword duel. The hero is about to behead the Count with an ax, but is unable to destroy the man who saved his life and leaves knowing that every life taken by Dracula will henceforth weigh upon his conscience.

"Fear Stalker," by Wolfman and artist Mike Ploog in Dracula Lives! no. 4 (January 1974), brought a vengeful Dracula into conflict with a temperamental, alcoholic and quite mad actor named Louis Belski, who is portraying the Count in a film, THE FANGS OF DRACULA! After a drunken Belski, thinking he is Dracula, commits a murder, he and his leading lady are changed into real vampires by the real Count. Both of them are finally staked by a lycanthrope in Werewolf by Night, no. 19 (July 1974), in the story "Vampires on the Moon!" by Mike Friedrich and artist Don Perlin.

The finest adaptation yet of Stoker's Dracula began in the vol. 2, no. 1 issue of Dracula Lives! (March 1974). Continuing over a number of issues, the adaptation was drawn by Dick Giordano and written by Roy Thomas, a master of transferring literary works to the graphic story medium.

Dracula prepares to duel for the title, Lord of the Undead, in "Lord of Death ... Lord of Hell," written by Marv Wolfman and drawn by John Buscema, in <u>Dracula Lives!</u> no. 3. Copyright 1973 by Marvel Comics Group.

Even with two Marvel Dracula books, the readers
wanted more.   Marvel then announced another magazine, The
Victims of Dracula, a book which never saw print.   The project was replaced by a color comic book, Giant-Size Chillers,
in June 1974, introducing a new series The Curse of Dracula.
The series unveiled Lilith, a sultry, black-haired vampiress
and the Count's daughter.   "Night of the She-Demon," the
origin tale by Wolfman and Colan, revealed that Lilith was
Dracula's daughter by an earlier and undesired marriage ar-
ranged by his father.   Banished by Dracula, this wife en-
trusted their daughter to the same old Gypsy woman responsible for making the Count a vampire, then stabbed herself to
death.   When the vampire Dracula killed the Gypsy's son,
she vengefully transformed Lilith into a living vampire unaffected by sunlight or the cross.   Lilith's spirit gained the
power to survival though her body perished, existing through
the centuries to possess "an innocent like yourself who wishes
death to her father."   The story showed Lilith possessing, at
intervals, the body of red-haired Angel O'Hara, a young woman fitting the Gypsy's requirements.

With the second issue (September 1974), the title of the
magazine was changed to Giant-Size Dracula.   Lilith was absent from the issue; in her place was a Count Dracula tale,
"Call Them Triad ... Call Them Death!" written by Chris
Claremont and drawn by Don Heck.   The story brought Dracula in conflict with the Elder Gods that once inhabited the
Earth and also had him meet an apparent modern day reincarnation of his lost wife Maria.   Lilith returned in a black and
white strip of her own, Lilith, Daughter of Dracula, in the
sixth issue (August 1974) of Vampire Tales.   Plotted by Wolfman, scripted by Steve Gerber and drawn by Bob Brown, the
story had Lilith possess the body of blonde Angel O'Hara and
destroy an axe murderer with her fangs.

Marvel bridged the worlds of the vampire and the
super-hero with "Ship of Fiends!" in the first issue of Giant-
Size Spider-Man (July 1974), originally announced as Super-
Giant Spider-Man.   In this story by Len Wein and artist Ross
Andru, both Dracula and Spider-Man seek a scientist who has
developed a new vaccine.   But since this was technically
Spider-Man's magazine, the Count fails to destroy both the
vaccine and its creator.

THE VAMPIRES OF DRAKULON

Famous Monsters of Filmland, the original and most successful magazine of its type, edited by Forrest J Ackerman for the Warren Publishing Company, published a comic strip adaptation of the film HORROR OF DRACULA by Russ Jones and Joe Orlando in its thirty-second issue (March 1965). The previous year publisher James Warren had tested a short-lived companion magazine, Famous Films, featuring "comic strips" made from movie stills and blown-up film frames and supplemented with captions, dialogue balloons and sound effects. The second issue featured such a fumette of HORROR OF DRACULA, by Jones and Orlando. Seeing the potential in the comic strip medium, Warren gambled by pioneering a new magazine featuring the graphic adventures of vampires and other monstrous creatures. Creepy was a large-sized black and white magazine, technically not a comic book and therefore not restricted by the Comics Code Authority. The magazine debuted in 1964 and established a new format in which the old Count could return unfettered by censorship.

"The Coffin of Dracula," written by editor Archie Goodwin and illustrated by Reed Crandall, was a two-part tale in Creepy nos. 8 and 9 (April 1965 and June 1966). In nineteenth century London, Lord Adrian Varney, dressed in a Dracula outfit for a costume party, reclines in the dust-filled casket which once belonged to the Count and which was recently purchased at auction. Adrian is possessed by the spirit of Dracula, becomes a vampire himself and kidnaps Mina Harker from the masquerade party. Jonathan Harker, Van Helsing and Seward pursue him to his castle. Adrian flees but his escape ends prematurely when his funeral coach plunges off the cliffside to the rapids below, the vampire getting impaled on a wheel spoke and the coffin sinking to the bottom of the sea.

"The Monster from One Million B. C. " by Tom Sutton, in the eleventh issue of Warren's second comic magazine Eerie (September 1967), was about a mad special effects genius who resurrects the actual bodies of Dracula and other monsters to star in his movies.

The third Warren illustrated horror magazine, Vampirella, debuted in September 1969 and was similar to Creepy and Eerie, with an emphasis on female nudity. Vampirella (affectionately known as "Vampi") was the creation of Forrest J Ackerman, publisher Warren having asked him to invent a

"mod witch" in the fashion of France's Barbarella. Ackerman's origin story, written in humorous style, was illustrated
by Tom Sutton for the premiere issue. Vampirella was revealed as an incredibly endowed inhabitant of Draculon, a
planet of vampires where water has the same chemical make-
up as blood. Vampirella has long black hair, a bat-shaped
birthmark over her right breast, and wears a revealing outfit that stays on by what can only be secrets known to Dracu-
lonian clothing designers. She can either sprout bat wings or
change into an entire bat. An Earth spaceship crashes on
Draculon during a drought and, to the thirst-crazed Vampirella's delight, its crew members have "water" flowing in their
veins. Vampirella drinks her fill ("Smorgasblood" being one
of the many blood puns in this first story), then proceeds to
introduce the other tales in the book.

The second issue's (November 1969) "Down to Earth!"
was by Ackerman and artist Mike Royer. The story, told by
Vampirella's blonde twin sister Draculina, brought the dark-
haired vampiress to our world where she wins a "Monsterella"
contest and is one of the victims of an airline crash. Vampirella's adventures halted with this issue, the lovely Dracu-
lonian serving to introduce the other stories in the books.

The series was revived as a serious strip in Vampirella no. 8 (November 1970), a story called simply "Vampirella,"
written by Goodwin and drawn by Sutton. After the plane
crash, Vampirella is rescued by Dr. Tyler Westron who is
forced to amputate her wings but also gives her a blood sub-
stitute serum to obviate her need for human victims. Conrad
Van Helsing, a blind psychic fanatically carring on the family
vampire-hunting tradition, is introduced, vowing to destroy
Vampirella. The surprise in "The Resurrection of Papa Vou-
dou," by Goodwin and artist Jose Gonzalez in the fifteenth issue (January 1972), was that the supreme leader of a group
called the Companions of Chaos was a very handsome Count
Dracula. In the following issue's (April 1972) "And Be a
Bride of Chaos," Dracula overpowers Vampirella and offers
her to the demon-god Chaos. Then the Count reveals what,
perhaps, had been in writer Goodwin's mind for many a month.
This was to be Goodwin's last story in the series and he decided to leave behind him the complete Dracula mythology as
far as Warren magazines were concerned.

Dracula was once a hunter on the planet Drakulon (new
spelling) and followed the long outlawed tradition of drinking a
man's blood to absorb his strength. Sentenced to die in a

disintegration chamber, he was instead displaced to Chaos'
dimension and then transported to Earth. Chaos' power
caused the hunter's victims to become infected by his bite,
while traveling through dimensions altered Dracula so that he
could not survive the sun's rays. Other traits were lost or
gained through the abilities of Chaos. In the fifteenth century the hunter became the notorious ruler whose name was
derived from that of Drakulon. Then Dracula went through
Stoker's adventure, followed by his possession of Adrian
Varney. The Count's undying spirit then possessed other men
who curiously entered his coffin, such as a ship's captain
and a Count Mordante, another follower of Chaos. After his
story, Dracula leaves Vampirella to the approaching god.
Meanwhile, Van Helsing learns that Chaos has made the
Count immune to the stake. Vampirella revives and saves
Van Helsing from Dracula, while Chaos, in revenge for Drac-
ula's failure, lets him perish from the stake wound. At the
end of the story a human scavenger contemplates lying in
Dracula's coffin.

"Dracula Still Lives!" in the eighteenth issue (August
1972), was drawn by Gonzales, who had become the regular
artist on the strip, and written by T. Casey Brennan. The
scavenger enters the coffin, is attacked by vampire bats and
finally transforms into Dracula reborn. The Count then meets
the Conjuress, a beautiful goddess who inflicts guilt feelings
upon him, changing him to a sympathetic character forced to
atone for his past misdeeds. Vampirella is about to kill
Dracula by draining his blood when he reveals yet more of
his new origin (one not unlike Superman's). Now Dracula was
described as a scientist who discovered that Drakulon's blood
rivers were drying. After bringing his conservation program
to the planet's high council, he was derided as a prophet of
doom. Dracula resorted to witchcraft to summon the Conjuress but inadvertently contacted Chaos, who compelled the
scientist to hunt down his fellow men. Moved by this story,
Vampirella is unable to destroy Dracula.

In "When Wakes the Dead," in Vampirella, no. 20
(October 1972), Dracula and Vampirella journey to meet Van
Helsing and the other characters in the Stoker novel at the
time of Lucy's staking. The Count, temporarily cured by the
Conjuress, saves Lucy with the blood-substitute serum but,
like a drug addict, reverts to his former ways and vampirizes her a second time. The story ends with Vampirella's
realization that she loves Count Dracula. Yet Vampirella's
feelings change in the next issue (December 1972), after she

finds that Dracula is as evil and bloodthirsty as ever.   After
a battle in the air between the two vampires in bat form, she
realizes that she has mistaken homesickness for love.   The
Conjuress then removes Dracula from the strip, on a journey
to "realms unknown. "

That unknown realm materialized as Dracula's own
series in Eerie, the first story being in the forty-sixth issue
(March 1973), by Bill Dubay and artist Sutton.   The cover,
a magnificent painting by Sanjulian depecting Dracula carrying a woman in his arms, was so well received that Warren
made it available as a poster.   "Dracula, " this first installment, brought the Count to the Barbary Coast in the early
1900s.   A blind witch named Elizabeth utilizes a prostitute
named Josephine to lure men to her shack where she bludg-
eons them with a club and eats their hearts to perpetuate her
eternal life.   Dracula is the next intended victim but the
Conjuress appears and receives the fatal blow to the head.
Dracula and the two women escape to a ship as the San Francisco earthquake begins, the story climaxing with Josephine
becoming his victim.

"Enter the Dead-Thing!" in Eerie, no. 47 (March
1973), again by Dubay and Sutton, brought Dracula through a
shipboard adventure involving a walking corpse and finally
back to Castle Dracula.   As the Count opens the door an old
man fires a shotgun which sends Dracula falling back over a
precipice.   The following issue's (June 1973) entry, by Dubay
and artist Rich Buckler, was "The Son of Dracula. "   The
Count's slayer is revealed as the illegitimate son of the King
Vampire and a woman who had once saved him from the sunlight.   The story promised a follow-up installment, "Blood
Princess of Bathory Castle, " but the series did not continue,
perhaps because of the competition of the Marvel and other
Dracula series which were so prevalent at the time.

Eerie no. 50 (August 1973) included "Genesis of Depravity, " by Doug Moench and drawn by Ramon Torrents, a
story which was not really part of the Dracula series.   Satan
transforms a woman desiring immortality into a vampiress,
her first victim being Count Dracula (thus giving him yet another origin).

Among the many enterprises of the Warren Publishing
Company were Vampirella shirts, a fan club, posters and a
proposed movie about the character.

Warren Publishing Company established the format of the oversized black and white illustrated horror magazine. There would be numerous imitations of varying quality. Some of the worst of these imitations would also seize upon Count Dracula to sell copies.

THE "ARCHAIC" DRACULA

Dracula cavorted through some of his least respectable adventures in the pages of the Skywald Publishing Corporation's graphic story magazines. In an unsuccessful attempt to maintain the advertised "horror mood," Skywald sacrificed plot for redundant and often misused adjectives and adverbs, emphasized and reemphasized words like "archaic," "lunatic" and "slither-slime," and included stories about insanity with overly written captions packed with morbid text.

Psycho no. 1 (January 1971), Skywald's first horror magazine, featured "The Gruesome Faces of Mr. Cliff!", about a mad actor who learns he is dying and goes on a murderous spree in the guise of Count Dracula, only to rot literally to the bones when someone flashes a stage light on him. A one-page tribute to the 1931 DRACULA film, written by Editor Al Hewetson and drawn by Pablo Marcos, appeared in the ninth issue (October 1972) of Skywald's second magazine, Nightmare. "The Truth Behind the Myth of Dracula," by Hewetson and artist Delafuente, distorted the history of Vlad the Impaler in the first annual edition of Psycho (1972). Vlad Dracula is portrayed as a fanged blood-drinker who cannibalizes living flesh, serves his guests wine mixed with human blood and cuts out his servants' tongues. Dracula dies in bed, a victim of disease resulting from the "debauchery of his own body," alone in his castle. Psycho no. 9 (November 1972) included the story, "A Question of Identity," written by Ed Fedory and drawn by Zesar, in which Von Zorka the Nosferatu is shot with an arrow while his amnesic daughter's vampiric self is later drawn out by two psychiatrists. The story was the progenitor of a Nosferatu series that would later commence at Skywald.

The premiere issue of Skywald's Scream (August 1973) was virtually a Dracula issue. "... Weird Counts, Black Vampire Bats and Lunatic Horror ..." told about Vlad, Stoker and his character, Transylvania, vampirism and Castle Dracula. "... Hickory Dickory Dock ..." was drawn by

Ferran Sostres and featured Anthony Cappeli, one of Skywald's
numerous lunatics. Cappeli, entranced by Dracula on the motion picture screen, enacts the role of the Count until he reclines in a coffin which is burned in a crematorium.   The
issue also officially heralded the Nosferatu series, the format being that Nosferatu would listen to the tragic stories of
his bizarre guests.   Dracula arrives in "Where Lunatics
Live" and introduces himself to Nosferatu as "the one Dracula ... the only Dracula. " Dracula reveals that he was resurrected from his tomb by a group of Greenwich Village
Satanists.   But since Vlad was beheaded (after dying in bed
of natural causes, of course) he emerges from his crypt in
full Lugosi regalia but still lacking a head.   The cultists mistakenly give Dracula the head of an ape, which affords him
supreme agony.   Now Dracula, wearing a mask, is but a
servant of Satan.   The tale ended with a caption aimed at the
other publishers: "... There are many Draculas in this
world ... all unreal ... now you know they are all unreal ...
for the only real Dracula is definately [sic] dead ... He cannot be resurrected ... only mere servants and descendants
and would-be Draculas from macabre foreign other-planets
remain in this Earth-place habitat.... "

   Psycho no. 14 (September 1973), the "Special Psycho
Paranoia Issue, " led off with "The Classic Creeps, " by
Hewetson and artist Cueto.   A lunatic watches the 1931
DRACULA once too often and, again, lives the role in a neck-
biting spree.   "A Man Who Dare Not Sleep!", written by Ed
Fedory and drawn by Dela Rosa, was a take-off on the se-
quence in Stoker's Dracula where the vampire stalks the
Demeter.   The Dracula-type vampire is destroyed by the ce-
lestial Southern Cross.   The concluding tale in the issue was
"I Battle [sic] the Vicious Vampire Bats of Transylvania and
Lived to Tell of It, " written and drawn by Maro Nava.   A
man goes to the alleged Dracula castle where he kills an imposter masquerading as the famous Count and reveals himself
to be the infuriated son of the authentic Dracula.

   Skywald's digs at the other companies' Draculas were
strongest in the fifteenth issue of Nightmare (October 1973).
The cover showed a green-faced Dracula standing before an
orange full moon and boasting, "There is only one Dracula!
... I am he ... I am evil ... only I am DRACULA!" The
story, "Dracula Did Not Die!", by Hewetson and artist Bor-
rell, opened with disparaging remarks aimed at Stoker, Lugosi, a Dracula descendant and "one who claims to serve
chaotic forces and who comes from another planet. " This

"true" Dracula is the same Vlad who died in bed, "riddled by an unmentionable disease." Dracula returns revealing how he feigned death and how his servants buried the body of his horse in his stead. The Count vows to destroy the peasants now storming his castle but the promised sequel, "Hell Is on Earth!" did not appear in the next Nightmare. Baron Meinster (from Hammer's BRIDES OF DRACULA) appeared in "The Old Vampire Lady," by Hewetson and artist Jesus Duran in Psycho no. 16 (January 1974), to make his attacks on an all-girl school. But Count Dracula did return in "Castle of the Vampire Dead," written by Howie Anderson and drawn by Duran, in Nightmare no. 19 (June 1974). Dracula cajoles a group of bored millionaires into becoming vampires to help populate the city of the un-dead he is establishing at the bottom of the sea. Swimming like a merman, Dracula battles a mutant monster spawned by radioactivity until the scaly creature decapitates him and claims his headless body as its mate. "Hell Is on Earth!" by Stuart Williams and artist Emilio was finally published in Psycho no. 19 (July 1974) and ignored the fact that its predecessor depicted Dracula complete with vampire fangs. This was Skywald's origin of Dracula, revealing how vampires had only been old women until an un-dead Gypsy woman gave him her infectious bite, making him the first male of the species in history. This story apparently reinstated Dracula as a more or less regular character, promising a sequel entitled "The God of the Dead." This promised story, written by Hewetson and drawn by Bob Martin, saw print in the 1974 Nightmare Yearbook. Now portrayed with long blond hair, Dracula revives the vampiric bodies of nubile girls to destroy their families until a child hands the Count a small crucifix, which kills him within moments. The story ended with yet another awkward Skywald blast at the competition, including: "So, without being facetious, don't believe all you read, dear reader ... The Dracula's [sic] you read are not merely phonies. They are insignificant phonies--for their 'adventures' are dull-witted, and their 'powers' are limited ... "

With Dracula an inconsistent series character at Skywald, the company continued its ever-changing legend in two magazines dated October 1974. Psycho no. 21's "The Fiend of Changsha," by Hewetson and artist Chull Sanko Kim, brought Dracula to nineteenth century China, looking for the famed mandarin Fu Manchu. He attacks the Chinese Chan 'Hai, who knows nothing of vampirism, and thereby creates an Oriental un-dead and another Skywald series character. (The actual Dracula-Fu Manchu encounter was announced as

future story, "Killer Fu Manchu.") Despite all of Skywald's
previously published Dracula tales, "Let Her Rot in Hell," by
Hewetson and artist Cardona, in Nightmare no. 21, explained
vampirism to be a myth. Spanish prisoners are placed in a
cell where a man claiming to be Dracula drinks their blood.
In the morning, rather than face the sunrise, these victims
commit suicide, having been tricked by the authorities.

Dracula comic strip stories also appeared in a number of monster movie magazines. Major Magazines' For Monsters Only, in the seventh issue (April 1969), presented "Vampire Hunt '69" in The Secret Files of Marc Vangoro, Master
of Horror strip. Illustrated by Jerry Grandenetti, the story
found Count Dragula driven from his castle by Dr. Yon
Yeager and his vampire hunters. Dragula arrives at Haight-
Ashbury in San Francisco where he changes a group of hip-
pies into vampires. They are hunted by Yeager and the police with silver bullets; Dragula himself receives the stake.
A comic strip adaptation of the film NOSFERATU, written by
Dave Izzo and drawn by Berni Wrightson, was presented in
The Monster Times no. 1 (January 26, 1972).

Dracula's appearances in the satire magazines have
been legion. Mad (E. C. Publications), the progenitor of this
type of publication, has used the Count in innumerable stories
such as "Mannie Get Your Ghoul" in the eighty-fifth issue
(1964). The imitators of Mad capitalized on the Count in
stories like "I Was a Teenage Weird-Wolf" in Loco no. 2
(1958), with an ugly adolescent transforming into Count Drag-
gola. Sick no. 41 (December 1965) made Dracula a family
man in "Son of Dracula," by Jim Atkins and artist Jack
Sparling. A more sophisticated satire magazine, National
Lampoon, presented "Dragula" in its twentieth issue (November 1971), by Tony Hendra and drawn by Neal Adams. A gay
vampire is repelled by a woman's naked body, changes into
a French poodle and then "a giant pink flamingo" when a shaft
of sunlight sends him plummeting to the "fabled silver tip of
the world's fifth largest building." Dracula also appeared
frequently in one-panel cartoons like those by Gahan Wilson
in Playboy magazine.

Count Dracula had gone through many forms in the
graphic story. He survived even the bans on vampires and
their King once imposed by the Comics Code Authority. And
as the legend of Dracula survived in the comics, so would it
continue through the many other areas of our popular culture.

Chapter 13

DRACULA ETERNAL

> My friend ... it is time ... I have come for you.
> --Gabriel Dell in "Dracula's Return!" (1963)

The vampire has been established as an immortal being, providing, of course, that he is not beset by such destructive measures as impalement through the heart. Count
Dracula is undeniably the most immortal of all the un-dead.
He has spread his ebony cloak to encompass all manner of
popular media, as though the Earth itself were his victim.

Dracula has contributed to the eerie atmosphere of the
horror chambers in wax museums the world over. Fisher-
man Wharf's House of Wax in San Francisco, Madame Tus-
saud's Hollywood Wax Museum and the Movieland Wax Museum
in Buena Park, California* are but three of the many wax
museums to include the Count in their exhibits. Cortlandt B.
Hull included Dracula in his Witch's Dungeon museum in
Bristol, Connecticut. A dummy of the Count could be rented
from Hollywood's House of Horrors. Dracula has also
haunted the darkened rides at such amusement parks as
Coney Island and came to life as a mechanical doll in the
penny arcade machine, "Dracula and the Spook."

The Count has also placed his mark on the recording
industry. Themes from Horror Movies (Coral, 1960), by
Dick Jacobs, presented new recordings of the music from
films like SON OF DRACULA, HORROR OF DRACULA and
HOUSE OF FRANKENSTEIN. An Evening with Boris Karloff
and His Friends (Decca, 1967) was written by Forrest J
Ackerman and narrated by Karloff. It included soundtrack ex-
erpts from DRACULA (1931) and HOUSE OF FRANKENSTEIN.

---

*An 8mm color film including the Dracula exhibit was made
available with the title MOVIELAND WAX MUSEUM.

There was a Blacula album released by RCA in 1972 with
such music from the film as "Blacula (The Streetwalker),"
"Good to the Last Drop" and "Blacula Strikes!" Apple Records released a soundtrack album, by Harry Nilsson, of Son
of Dracula (1974), based on the Nilsson/Ringo Starr film.
The album included the number "Daybreak."

Christopher Lee enacted a dramatic reading of "Dracula's Guest" in 1964 for a private recording. The next year
he played all the parts, both male and female, on the twin-
record Stamford LP, Dracula, produced by Roy Taylor and
Russ Jones. EMI Records issued an album in 1974 titled
Hammer Presents Dracula with Christopher Lee. The actor
spoke over James Bernard's Hammer Dracula music, reading
a script by Don Houghton simply called "Dracula." The story
is of a young couple whose coach overturns outside Castle
Dracula. The young lady falls prey to Dracula's fangs. Inevitably her husband goes to Dracula's coffin, stakes him,
then sees his fiancée, now a vampire, destroyed by the rising sun. The album also presented music from such films
as THE VAMPIRE LOVERS.

In 1963 Gabriel Dell portrayed the Count and the reporter who finds him in a secret chamber of the British Museum in "Dracula's Return!" for the album Famous Monsters
Speak (A. A. Records), scripted by Cherney Berg. Dracula
shows the reporter his monstrous lair, then attacks a woman
on the street. The Count releases the reporter, promising
to return for him at a later date. First Rush (Eva-Tone,
1973), by Chris Rush, had a BLACULA spoof. And Sounds
to Make You Shiver (Pickwick, 1973) was a sound-effects album with a brief cut entitled "Count Dracula and His Victim."

Dracula music has been presented on records like
"Dinner With Drac" (Cameo, 1957), a two-sided hit song by
John Zacherle (later known on TV as the ghoulish Zacherly).
One side, less gruesome than the other, received more plays
on the radio. Blues for Dracula (Riverside) was an LP by
the Philly Joe Jones Sextet. There were also the Italian
Dracula Cha-Cha-Cha (Pop) and the French Frankenstein et
Dracula and Surboum Chez Dracula. Dracula's Greatest Hits
was an album with such song parodies as "Drac the Knife,"
"I Come from Transylvania," "I Want to Bite Your Hand" and
"Bela Boy." Warner Brothers' Spike Jones in Stereo (also
... in Hi-Fi) featured Paul Frees as Dracula and Luli Jean
Norman as Vampira in parody versions of the songs "I Only

Have Eyes for You," "(All of a Sudden) My Heart Sings,"
"Tammy" and "Spooktacular Finale." The album featured
many of the numbers from the special Halloween "Spooktacular" on the Spike Jones television program.

Bobby "Boris" Pickett imitated the Lugosi Dracula on
such records as "Monster Mash,"* "Bella's Bash," "Transylvania Twist," "Monster Motion," "Monsters' Mash Party,"
"Let's Fly Away," "Rabian, the Fiendage Idol," "Monster
Minuet" and "Blood Bank Blues," all of which were issued on
an album, The Original Monster Mash (Garpax), with music
by the Crypt-Kickers. Pickett also recorded "Monster Swim,"
"Werewolf Watusi" (both RCA), "Monster's Concert" and
"Monsters' Holiday," the latter also being recorded by Lon
Chaney, Jr. at a later date. Zacherly later sang on his own
album entitled Monster Mash, including the title song and
"The Bat." Yet another Monster Mash LP was issued by
Peter Pan Industries with new versions of the title song and
'Dinner with Drac." There was Monster Shindig (Hanna-
Barbera) and Monster Dance Party (Capitol), the latter in-
cluding 'Riboflavin-Flavored, Non-Carbonated, Polyunsaturated
Blood," by Don Hinson and the Rigormorticians in imitation of
Pickett. Dracula invaded country and western music in 1974
with Buck Owens' "(It's A) Monsters' Holiday" (Capitol).

During the early seventies, a New York rock group
with the name The Children of the Night, emerged, with
Geoffrey Black in a Dracula get up. A possible television
show starring the group was announced in 1974.

In advertising, Count Dracula's image has helped to
promote Contac Nasal Mist, Esquire Socks, and S. D. Com-
munications.

To further illustrate the expansive range of Count
Dracula's appeal, there have been Dracula masks, costumes,
plastic model kits, statues, "Create Your Own Monster" fig-
urines, greeting cards, trading cards, buttons, decals, iron-
ons, fan clubs, transfers, posters, colorforms, Horrorscope
Movie Viewer (with Dracula flip books), home movies, wall
placques, wallets, toys that bob their heads, bubble bath,
rings, necklaces, bracelets, dart boards, make-up kits, paint-
by-numbers sets, puzzles, games, kites, patches, stamps,

---

*A comic strip visualization of "The Monster Mash" was pre-
sented in the twenty-first issue of The Monster Times (April
1973).

handkerchiefs, play money, calendars, candy, loose-leaf binders, coloring books, cartoons, T-shirts sweat shirts, banks, drinking mugs, pencil sharpeners, Mon-Stirs swizzle sticks, popcorn boxes, lamps, plastic fangs and other paraphernalia.

Bram Stoker's character, based upon an historical figure whose real life depravities rivaled those of the fictional character into which he would eventually evolve, has indeed proven his immortality. The vampire is immortal, yet that un-dead monster can be destroyed. Yes, Count Dracula has been repeatedly destroyed--by the wooden poniard, by the flesh-eating rays of the sun, by the slash of the great Bowie knife. But his appeal surely has never died. Rather, it continues to grow as he emerges from the dankness of his tomb, over and over again, to merge with the night winds of some fog-swept night and seek the blood of living victims.

Dracula's eternal appeal?

There is nothing attractive about a creature that is technically dead and issues from a grave to suck blood. Or is there? The sexual appeal of the vampire cannot be denied. Perhaps there are in the Dracula character qualities which many of us desire either consciously or unconsciously. Count Dracula is portrayed as living forever, and with vast powers to satisfy his every need and whim. Perhaps there are those of us who crave his ability to dominate others, and others who wish to be so dominated.

Barry Atwater, the actor who portrayed one of television's most successful vampires in THE NIGHT STALKER, told me his theories as to why we often cheer Count Dracula on the screen and hope that he, for once, will triumph over the ubiquitous Van Helsing. "Maybe there are two reasons. Let's assume the first reason is a desire to root for the underdog. We seem to feel that the vampire is getting a bum shake, getting ganged up on by the intellectuals like Van Hensing; whereas the vampire is not an intellectual, he's working on an emotional basis. I have a hunch that maybe we go for someone who is more visceral than intellectual. There seems to be a strong anti-intellectual element in our culture. We don't dig the brain, we dig the body. That can be argued, but let's assume that has a ten per cent chance of being true.

"Maybe there's another reason, though, that the vam-

pire is really an evil person. He lives off other people.
And I think we would like to live off other people. But we
can't because that's considered to be wrong. There are a
lot of people living off us, the tax collectors certainly, and
the merchants and everybody making a big profit off what we
do. And we'd certainly like to have this freedom to go out
into the world and feed on other people. It satisfies our fantasies to do that. And yet we know that this is all going to
be okay because the vampire is going to be destroyed in the
end, good shall prevail and the evil in us is propitiated. Of
course in the back of our heads we know that the vampire is
going to come back in the next picture, so we're not really
too broken up about it. "

   The noted science fiction and fantasy writer Ray Bradbury often stated his own theory as to the appeal of the Dracula character. Count Dracula, said Bradbury, represents
our own symbol of Death, a looming, dark-clad, seemingly
omnipotent force that we all fear. However, when the fatal
stake of wood is pounded through the vampire's chest and
impales his unnaturally beating heart, we can identify with
Van Helsing or some other authorized vampire slayer who
has taken it upon himself to represent us. In effect it is we
who thrust the stake through the heart of Dracula. It is we
who also symbolically defeat that awesome spectre of Death
from which none of us can truly escape in the less romantic
world of reality.

   Death can never be defeated. It is always menacingly
present, awaiting the human victims that will inevitably be
drawn to its dark world. Similarly Count Dracula, though
fastened to his grave by the stake or reduced to ashes beneath a shower of solar rays, always manages to return.
Like the Phoenix, he returns to un-dead life from his own
ashes, revived by the blood of the living. And once he again
prowls the night, Count Dracula continues to stalk his human
game, plunging his fangs into his victims' necks to suck their
crimson blood. Like Death, Count Dracula always overcomes
the human beings and their pitiable and futile efforts to defeat him.

   Professor Van Helsing looks into the coffin of Dracula,
observing the pale corpse into which he has just driven his
stake of wood. There is a cruel, almost victorious smile
upon those dark, blood-flecked lips before the entire body decomposes and crumbles to dust. The doctor would, perhaps,
ignore that smile and assume that the evil Count Dracula has

been finally laid at rest. But we know the truth--as does the Count himself. Dracula is eternal.

AFTERWORD

The bugbear in keeping a book of this nature up-to-date is time. Nearly six months will have elapsed between the final writing and the finished work's appearance. Invariably such a book is dated upon publication. There are new titles, new pieces of information and additions to the "old" text that the author would certainly wish to include. With a character as popular as Count Dracula, there are inevitably last-second additions to supplement the story of his career.

TENDRE DRACULA, OU LES CONFESSIONS D'UN BUBEUR DE SANG is now also known as THE BIG FUNK and as LA GRANDE TROUILLE ("The Big Scare"). The French color film was directed by Pierre Grunstein and starred Peter Cushing as Macgregor, a horror films actor specializing in vampire roles. Macgregor lives in a castle like a real vampire along with a brute servant and weird spouse. Yet despite his eccentricities, the actor wants to make the transition to romantic roles. The crux of the story involves a film producer's sending a team of writers to Macgregor's home to convince him to return to vampire parts. The efforts of the writers (and their girlfriends) create a series of horror and comedy situations.

A unique Dracula film was made in 1974 and released in January of 1975. DEAFULA was produced by Gary Holstrom and directed by Peter Wechsburg. The black and white film was made for a deaf audience, with the characters communicating with each other via sign language. Music and narration were included for those members of the audience able to hear. Deafula (Wechsburg) is Dracula's illegitimate son.

BLOOD, a 1974 film by Andy Milligan, had Dracula's daughter meeting Larry Talbot's son. The same year, BLOOD FOR DRACULA also became known as ANDY WARHOL'S DRACULA and EL GRAN AMORE DEL CONDE DRACULA was given the English title, DRACULA'S GREAT LOVE. The 1972 film TWINS OF EVIL was released in Spain as the more commercial DRACULA Y LAS MELLIZAS ("Dracula and the

Twins") and in Australia as TWINS OF DRACULA. The Count
appeared as a wax museum exhibit in THE MECHANIC (1972)
and as a masquerader at a costume ball in JUGGERNAUT
(1974), both from United Artists. At least four new Dracula
film titles were announced in 1974, including DRACULA IN
THE HOUSE OF HORRORS, ALUCARD, ALUCARD RETURNS
FROM THE GRAVE and Jim Wnoroski's DICK AND THE DE-
MONS, the latter being a pornographic slapstick comedy patterned after the old Abbott and Costello pictures.

A new musical play of DRACULA was presented in
1974 by the Berkeley Repertory Theatre in California. Some
of the numbers were "Welcome to Transylvania," "Boxes of
Clay," "Nosferatu," and "The Bat." Another new DRACULA
opened Halloween night at Theatre 369 in Somerville, Massachusetts. Advertised as "A New Theatrical Concept of Bram
Stoker's classic novel," the play was also based upon Vlad
the Impaler and authentic vampire legends. THE JOLA PUP-
PETS, a show presented by Joe Lasala in 1965, spoofed Dracula with Count Downe, an un-dead real estate salesman trying
to cope with the space age. The rod puppets were designed
and built by Paul and Jackie Blaisdell. (Paul Blaisdell used
the pseudonym of Count Downe while editing the "Tombstone
Times" section of the magazine, Fantastic Monsters of the
Films, in 1962.)

Added to Bela Lugosi's television appearances is a
skit from a 1950 show of NBC's COLGATE COMEDY HOUR.
Lugosi, as Count Dracula, joined Glenn Strange as Frankenstein's Monster and Lon Chaney as the Wolf Man to menace
hosts Abbott and Costello. In 1974, Dracula continued to appear in various forms on such television programs as SHA-
ZAM! and the OUT TO LUNCH special (featuring the SESAME
STREET characters).

Yet another version of Stoker's Dracula was printed in
1974. This newest, adapted by Rosalie Kershaw, was published as a segment of the book, Great Tales of Horror and
Suspense (Galahad Books). The story was told entirely in
third person.

Dracula's Lost World, the last of "The Dracula Horror
Series" books to be published in 1974, was on a par with its
uninspired predecessors. When three people are murdered
for possession of a rare book, Cameron Sanchez is accused of
the killings. The book reveals the location of a hidden South
American village once ruled by Dracula (there known as

"Dracu"). Over a century and a half before, the Count had stored some of his gold in the village and made the native Kabaya its immortal guardian. To exonerate Cameron, (now a fugitive), his boss Damien Harmon--along with a woman named Ktara and the crated-up Dracula--pursues the real killers to the lost village. There Kabaya now awaits "Dracu" with a giant cross made from his own gold. Harmon is captured by the murderers and suspended over a pit of piranhas; Ktara is rendered powerless by a ring of fire; Cam is wounded with a poison-tipped arrow; and Dracula is first staked by savage natives, before the Count is finally permitted to rise. Dracula then commands the rain to extinguish Ktara's flames, and imposes human aging upon the disloyal Kabaya. He then frees Harmon. The only survivor of the real murderers then confesses to the crimes before Dracula fangs her to death in her jail cell.

"Hard Times," a short story by Sonora Morrow in Ellery Queen's Mystery Magazine, vol. 64, no. 6 (December 1974), had Dracula and his werewolf friend sitting on a park bench. While complaining about the jaded and violent world of the 1970s, the pair is accosted by a masked mugger. This gives the Count an opportunity to vent some of his old gusto against the would-be thief. In 1975 Jean-Pierre Bouyxou is due to publish his French book about the Dracula films.

In the graphic story medium, Skywald's Scream magazine presented yet another in their numerous "origins" of Count Dracula. "Creatures of the Night!" was written by Alan Hewetson and illustrated by Cardona for the tenth issue (October 1974). Dracula the child is introduced to his father's torture methods and sense of justice--and also an imprisoned werewolf who escapes and kills both of the boy's parents. Dracula drinks the werewolf's blood, knowing it will change him into a werewolf and begin his sanguinary career.

The Marvel Comics Group satirized the Dracula legend in "Fangs for the Memory!" in the debut issue of Arrgh! The story, by Jack Younger and artist Mike Sekowsky, brought Count Fangula to violent New York City. After his teeth are smashed by muggers, Count Fangula resorts to wearing false fangs. Lilith, Daughter of Dracula was relocated once again in the ever-changing Marvel world. Her latest series "premiered" in Dracula Lives!, no. 10 (January 1975), in "The Blood Book," written by Steve Gerber and drawn by Bob Brown. Lilith single-handedly defeats a gang of narcotics peddlers, then discovers that her host body is pregnant. As for

Count Dracula himself, Marvel began planning an authorized story in which the King of Vampires meets the insidious Dr. Fu Manchu.

With the Count's popularity ever mushrooming, Warren Publishing Company revived its own version of Dracula in Vampirella, no. 39 (January 1975), in the story "The Circus of King Carnival!," by Gerry Boudreau and artist Esteban Maroto. Dracula comes to a carnival in 1906 to give his own brand of eternal life to a woman suffering from a terminal illness. The same issue featured "The Curse of Castle Vlad!" by Doug Moench and artist Auraleon. A motion picture crew rents the Impaler's castle to make the film CURSE OF CASTLE DRACULA. The very real curse changes everyone involved into a vampire, werewolf or other species of monster.

In 1974, Les Publications Aredit in France began a new series of Dracula comic strips, while Pyramid Books published a paperback of Dracula humor, titled Vampire Jokes and Cartoons; "A Comedy of Terrors," edited by Phil Hirsch and Paul Laikin. Writer Mark Evanier created perhaps the final statement in the Dracula/Alucard cliché in his story "Duckula!" in the 92nd issue of Daffy Duck (Gold Key). The vampiric Count Duckula conceals his true identity under the unlikely backwards name of "Alukcud."

Pickwick International issued the record album Sounds of Terror in 1974, which featured not only the perennial "Monster Mash" but also a brief cut entitled "Dracula and the Vampires of Death." In 1975, Power Records released a dramatic performance of "Terror in the Snow!," Marv Wolfman's story for the 19th issue (April 1974) of Tomb of Dracula, wherein the Count and Rachel Van Helsing face the elements of the Transylvanian Alps. In 1974 Christopher Lee was honored on British television's THIS IS YOUR LIFE. And in 1975 the bizarre film title DRACULA'S DOG emerged. There was even more Dracula merchandise in 1975, including key chains, View-Master slides, dolls and a film strip with accompanying soundtrack record.

Now, as the new year commences with its various shortages and scandals and real-life carnage, it is reassuring to know that a more romantic world, the world of Count Dracula, continues to exist alongside our own.

D F G

January 1975